COMPUTER APPLICATIONS IN BUSINESS

[For the Undergraduate Students of Commerce]

Dr. R. PARAMESWARAN
Associate Professor
Department of Commerce
T.S.A.A.S.T. College
(Affiliated to Bharathiar University)
Perur, Coimbatore
Tamil Nadu

S. CHAND
PUBLISHING

S Chand And Company Limited

(ISO 9001 Certified Company)

S Chand And Company Limited

(ISO 9001 Certified Company)

Head Office: D-92, Sector–2, Noida – 201301, U.P. (India), Ph. 91-120-4682700

Registered Office: A-27, 2nd Floor, Mohan Co-operative Industrial Estate, New Delhi – 110 044, Phone: 011-49731800

www.**schandpublishing.com;** e-mail: **info@schandpublishing.com**

S. CHAND
PUBLISHING

Marketing Offices:

Chennai	:	Ph: 23632120; chennai@schandpublishing.com
Guwahati	:	Ph: 2738811, 2735640; guwahati@schandpublishing.com
Hyderabad	:	Ph: 40186018; hyderabad@schandpublishing.com
Jalandhar	:	Ph: 4645630; jalandhar@schandpublishing.com
Kolkata	:	Ph: 23357458, 23353914; kolkata@schandpublishing.com
Lucknow	:	Ph: 4003633; lucknow@schandpublishing.com
Mumbai	:	Ph: 25000297; mumbai@schandpublishing.com
Patna	:	Ph: 4011400; patna@schandpublishing.com

First Edition 1996
Subsequent Editions and Reprints 1997, 98, 99, 2002, 2004, 2006, 2007, 2008, 2010, 2012
Seventh Edition 2013
Reprints 2018, 2019, 2020 (Twice), 2023 (Twice), 2024, 2025

Reprint 2026

ISBN: 978-81-219-1200-6 **Product Code:** H8CAB48COMP10ENAG13R

PRINTED IN INDIA

By Shri Shyamlal Printing Press Private Limited, Plot 20/4, Site-IV, Industrial Area Sahibabad, Ghaziabad – 201 010 and Published by S. Chand And Company Limited, A-27, 2nd Floor, Mohan Co-operative Industrial Estate, New Delhi – 110 044.

FOREWORD

The book on Computer Applications in Business by Dr.R. Parameswaran, will be an excellent guide for the commerce and management students who want to know the Computer Applications in Business.

Chapter 1 deals with the introductory concepts of computer, discussing the characters and important features of the computer, history and types of the computers and the different areas of business where the computers have been applied in modern times.

The basic principles of the operations of the computer have been dealt in detail in chapter 2 and the concepts of computer system including hardware, software, and firmware are given in chapter 3.

Chapter 4 deals with the concept and types of operating systems in an easy way to understand. And the chapter 5 gives the essence of the programming languages with examples and compares the Low Level Languages with High Level Languages.

Basic concepts of system analysis and design are given in chapter 6 and the chapter 7 deals with data processing concepts and types. Chapter 8 deals with the concepts of File Organization and management. Chapter 9 covers the concept of database in detail.

Chapter 10 explains the computer networks and chapter 11 deals with e- commerce and internet in detail.

The computer based information systems and functional information systems are explained in the chapters 12 and 13 respectively. And the final chapter 14 gives the concept of BPO.

Each section has lots of solved examples and the students will be highly benefitted from the book. Apart from being a textbook for commerce and management students, it can also help the beginners to know all about the computers in the area of Hardware and Software and the applications of computer.

I wish the author every success in all his activities.

B.MURALI
Professor & Head
Department of Computer Science
PSG College of Arts & Science
Coimbatore.

PREFACE TO THE SEVENTH EDITION

It is great pleasure in presenting this thoroughly revised edition of the book on **"Computer Application in Business"**. In this revised edition, all chapters have been thoroughly revised with the latest development in computer and information technology.

The applications of computers in different facets of business have been growing at a phenomenal rate in the recent times. Keeping these developments in view the contents of the book have been strengthened to ease the understanding of these developments.

Many concepts are given with new examples, diagrams and charts to enable the readers to capture the essence of the concepts and ideas at a glance.

The practical applicability of the computer concepts in different areas of the business has been highlighted in the book to enhance the interest of the students.

I hope that the present book will be more useful and cater to the needs of Commerce and Management students in understanding the applications of Computer in Business arena.

Model Question Papers have been added which will certainly give a fair idea of the pattern of examination.

We are thankful to the Management Team and the Editorial Department of S. Chand & Company Pvt. Ltd. for all help and support in the publication of this book.

Dr.R. PARMESWARAN

PREFACE TO THE FIRST EDITION

The last phase of this century can be hailed as the Computer Age. As computers have woven their web in all business activities, sea changes have become inevitable. Hence, business people have felt the dire need of computers in business applications. A world without computer presents a serious challenge to business.

The awareness of computer is essential for budding commerce and corporate secretaryship students. The need for such computer course has been felt by then universities, and thus the paper 'Computer Applications in Business' has been introduced in the curriculum.

This book is intended to cater to the needs of commerce students in understanding the applications of computer in business arena in such a way that they may be easily intelligible.

The contents have been strengthened, updated and modified to improve clarity and arouse enthusiastic interest in the subject of computer. Care has been taken to reduce the complex vocabulary to the minimum. Charts and diagrams are liberally used to enable students to capture the essence of the concepts and ideas at a glance.

Dr.R. PARMESWARAN

ACKNOWLEDGEMENTS

The author is greatly thankful to Swamiji, Thavathiru Santhalinga Ramaswamy Adigalar, and and Dr.Maruthasalam Adigal, Perur Mutt, for their grace and blessings. The author is highly grateful to Dr. K. Meenakshi Sundaram, Former Secretary of the College and Ex-Director, Collegiate Education - Tamilnadu, and Dr.M.Manonmani, Former Principal for their constant encouragement.

The author is very much thankful to Prof. B. Murali, Head of the Department of Computer Science, PSG College of Arts and Science, Coimbatore, for his guidance, encouragement and indispensable help in all respects.

The author is deeply indebted to Prof. J.Karunanithi, Head of the Department of Computer Science, Mr. R. Theivarasu, Department of Mathematics, and Prof. Mrs. T.Jeyalakshmi, Department of Computer Science and Mr. Saravana Kumar for their valuable suggestions and encouragement.

Many friends, scholars and students have given their valuable suggestions for the development of this book. The author expresses his sincere thanks to them.

The author is highly indebted to Mr. P.Rajalingam, Asst. Area Manager, Mr. V. Chandrababu, Senior Branch Manager, Mr. A.M. Arunachalam, Former Branch Manager S. Chand & Company Pvt. Ltd., Chennai Branch, and Mr. Sivakumar Sales Manager Coimbatore Branch for their constant encouragement and kindness.

The author is thankful to all those who have contributed even in a small way towards the successful completion of this book.

Suggestions are welcome and will be gratefully acknowledged.

R. PARAMESWARAN

CONTENTS

CHAPTER

1

Computer Introduction

1.1. MEANING AND DEFINITION

The origin of the word computer is taken from Latin, meaning "to reckon or to compute". Computer is an electronic device and it can perform a sequence of operations. With these operations, computer converts raw data into meaningful information. That is the computer is a machine that accepts data as its input, processes it and produces the desired results as output.

Thus the computer can be defined as, "an electronic device with the ability to:

* Accept user-supplied data and instructions
* Store data and instructions
* Perform arithmetic and logical operations and
* Output the results according to user specifications".

Computer is a group of integrated parts that have common purpose of performing the operations required in the program being executed. It is capable of performing calculations and other manipulations of various types of data, under the control of a stored set of instructions. The device itself is the hardware and the instructions are the software. In simple, the term computer is used to describe a collection of devices that function together as a system.

1.2. CHARACTERISTICS OF COMPUTER

Today the computer plays a major role in the modern society and its development, with its inherent qualities. Let us see the characteristics that make the computer possible to play such vital role:

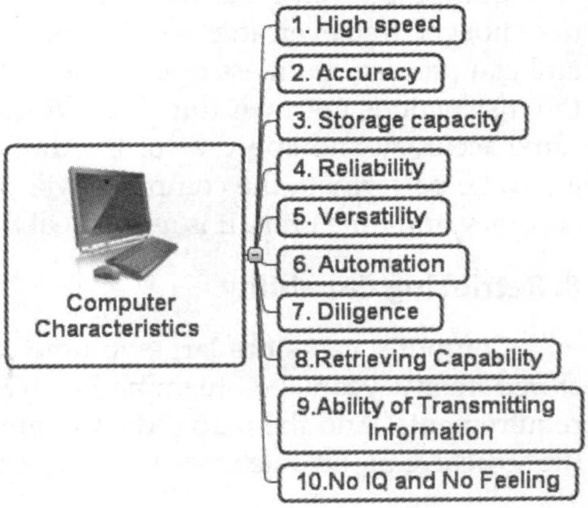

1. High Speed

All operations of the computer are caused by electrical pulses and thus the computers can perform large number of operations in just one second. The processing speed of a computer is generally measured in Nano seconds. [1 Nano second = one billionth of a second = 1/10]. Since computers are electronic devices and work with electrical pulses which travel at incredible speed, their internal speed also virtually instantaneous. The speed of the processing varies with the computer hardware.

2. Accuracy

The accuracy of the computers is consistently very high. Computers do not make mistakes. Errors in computing are generally due to negligence, such as inaccurate data, improper procedures, poor designs etc. The computers follow the simple rule of GIGO.

3. Storage Capacity

Computers have very large storage capacity. The computer can store large amount of data and information, which is expressed in terms of kilobytes of memory. Moreover, the storage capacity of the computers can be increased by using secondary storage devices. The information stored in the main memory and secondary storage devices can be retrieved quickly. The storage capacity of the computers is finite since we built it.

4. Reliability

Computers give very accurate results with predetermined values. They correct and modify the parameters automatically, giving suitable signals. They give formatted results with high degree of precisions.

5. Versatility

Computers are capable of performing different tasks. Thus, they are very versatile machines, with manual and automatic controls. They are capable of solving any problem and can be applied in all sorts of business and other activities.

6. Automation

The special feature of a computer is automation. That is, the computer executes a program continuously without any human intervention until completion. Once a program is given in to the computer, the individual instructions are then transferred, one after the other, to the control unit for execution. The Central Processing Unit of the computer makes it possible. It follows these instructions until it meets a last instruction which says 'terminate program execution'. When Babbage claimed that his Analytical Engine would be automatic, he meant that once the process had begun, it would continue without the need for human intervention until completion.

7. Diligence

Computers being machines do not suffer from fatigue and lack of concentration. It does not get tired even after long hours of work. The computers can work for hours together and can perform limitless calculations. Once the program is stored in the main memory, the instructions are then transferred one by one to the control unit for execution in the same accuracy and speed as of the first computation. That is, if millions of calculations are to be performed, the computer will perform every calculation with the same level of accuracy and time limit. It is more ideal for those who do their tedious and repetitive jobs.

8. Retrieving Capability

Computer can store large volume of data and can retrieve the required data, even stored many years before,immediately. The users can modify the data as per their requirements. And the required data can be retrieved sequentially or at random based on the structure of the data stored.

9. Ability of Transmitting Information

The unique feature of computer is its capability of transmitting information through on line and by soft copy and hard copy.

10. No IQ and No Feeling

Computer cannot do any work without instruction from the user. It performs the instructions at tremendous speed and with accuracy. It is the user to decide what he/she wants to do and in what sequence. So a computer cannot take its own decision as human beings.

And the computer does not have feelings or emotion. It does not distinguish between users.

1.3. IMPORTANCE OF COMPUTERS

The modern computer possesses the following abilities:

1. Computers provide new time dimensions for the working day and for the human concept.
2. They provide effective and efficient controls over human error.
3. They provide large capacities to store information and the capability to rapidly access this information.
4. They can perform complex and repetitive calculations rapidly and accurately.
5. They can hold a program of a model which can be explored in many different areas.
6. They can make decisions on the basis of given conditions. The computer chooses between alternative paths to perform a routine.
7. They can correct and modify certain parameters automatically.
8. They can provide meaningful information to the user and are able to draw and print graphs.
9. Self checking - a computer verifies the accuracy of its work by means of parity check.
10. Performing new and additional tasks - A computer can calculate or summarize quantitative information more effectively than any human clerk because it is not subject to boredom.

1.4. LIMITATIONS OF COMPUTERS

Computers generally subject to the following criticisms:

(*a*) It lacks common sense.
(*b*) Failure to derive meaning from objects
(*c*) Inability to generate information on its own
(*d*) No IQ
(*e*) No feelings

1.5. DEVELOPMENT OF COMPUTERS AND COMPUTER GENERATIONS

1.5.1. History of Computers

The history of the computer dates back to long ago, when man used his fingers for counting. The Stone Age man used stones for counting. Later the stones were replaced by sticks, marks on the earth, scratches and symbols on the stones, knots on the ropes. He found it very difficult to use these computing aids, because they required some physical efforts from him. Moreover, the computing speed was also very slow. This necessitated developing a new technique and as a result the number system was discovered. The number system laid the foundation for the modem computer.

Even though the computer is basically a product of the late 1940's, there were many important developments preceding this. Let us now see some important developments that enrooted to the invention of modern day computers.

3000	B.E	-	Chinese Abacus
1617	A.D	-	Logs and bones by John Napier
1620	-	Slide Rule by William Oughtred	
1642	-	Adding Machine by Blaise Pascal	
1673	-	Mechanical Calculator by Gottfried Von Leibniz	
1801	-	Punched Card Controlled Looms by Joseph Jacquard	
1833	-	Difference Engine by Charles Babbage	
1896	-	Electro-Mechanical Card Tabulators by Herman Hollerith	
1937	-	ABC Computer by Dr. Atanasoff and Berry	
1944	-	Mark I Calculating Machine by Howard Aiken	
1946	-	ENIAC Operational by Eckart and John Mauchly	
1949	-	EDVAC -Began performing basic tasks in 1951	
1949	-	EDSAC - Completed in England.	
1951	-	UNIVAC - I	

ABACUS

It is manual mechanical device developed in China. It consists of a wooden frame with two compartments and beads sliding along the steel wires for counting. Multiplication and divisions are done using repeated additions and subtractions. Even today, it is still in use in many countries like Japan, China, etc. The beads on an abacus may be round or rhombus in shape. Traditionally, there are two beads above the horizontal bar and five below. Simplified modern versions have one bead above and four or five below. The methods of calculation remain unchanged.

NAPIER'S LOGS AND BONES

John Napier, a Scottish mathematician invented logarithms. The use of logarithms enabled him to transform multiplication and division problems into problems of additions and subtractions. In the beginning he called logarithms as artificial numbers. But later he named them logarithms.

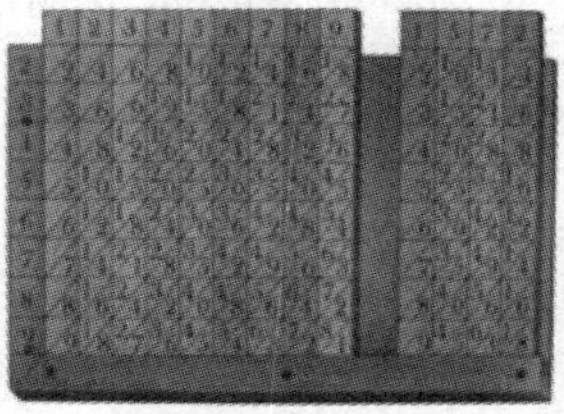

Napier also invented a computing device consisting of sticks with numbers carved on them. These sticks are called bones as they were made of bones. These bones helped a lot in multiplication involving large numbers. Napier's bones was used for calculation of products and quotients of numbers that was based on Arab mathematics and lattice multiplication. Napier published his version of rods in a work printed in Edinburgh, Scotland, at the end of 1617 entitled Rabdologiæ. Using the multiplication tables embedded in the rods, multiplicationsare reduced to addition operations and division to subtractions. More advanced use of the rods can even extract square roots.

SLIDE RULE

Napier's log became the basis for a well-known invention called Slide Rule by William Oughtred. In the slide rule the final value can be straight away read on the scale. It is capable of doing mathematical operations and functions. It is an analog device used the principle of logarithms and could perform simple multiplication and division problems.

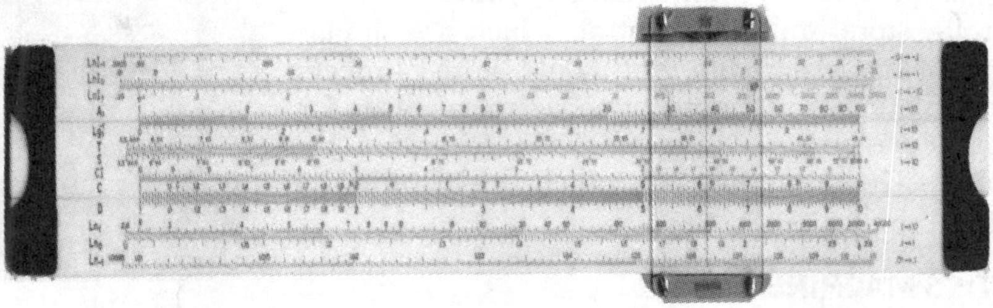

It consists of 2 graduated scales, devised in such a way that suitable alignment of one against othermakes it possible to obtain products, quotients etc.

PASCAL'SADDING MACHINE

The great French mathematician, Blaise Pascal, made the next attempt in the computing history. Pascal invented a machine that used gears, wheels and dials. Pascal's adding machine consisted of a series of gears with 10 teeth each, representing the numbers 0 to 9. As each gear made one turn it would trip the next gear up to make 1/10 of a revolution. This machine displayed numbers by the rotation of wheel. It was used only for addition and subtraction of numbers. This principle remained the foundation of all mechanical adding machines for centuries. The Pascal programming language was named in his honour.

JACQUARD'S LOOM

Joseph Jacquard initiated actual developments in the early 19th century. Jacquard

was a textile manufacturer. He invented automated loom in 1804. He used punched cards to produce complex cloth patterns with automated looms. Jacquard's loom provided the way for the modern storage mechanism on punched cards and binary coding system. In the Jacquard Loom, a specific combination of holes punched in a row through an individual card allowed selected sprung rods or needles to pass through the card and pick up certain threads. The connected cards create a continuous loop allowing for repeated patterns. Charles Babbage later used the punch-card system to create the first computer.

BABBAGE'S ANALYTICAL ENGINE

Charles Babbage, a British Mathematics Professor is known as "Father of Computer". He developed and demonstrated a working model of a mechanical computer called Difference Engine in 1822.

Encouraged by the success of Difference Engine, he developed another device called "Analytical Engine" in 1833. Analytical Engine used the concepts of Automated loom and Difference Engine. This machine had five units. They are input, output, store, mill and control, which are similar to the units of modern computer.It could store numbers and the calculating "mill" used punched metal cards for instructions. It was powered by steam. It was accurate to six decimal places.The inputmaterial in the form of program was developed by Lady Ada Love Lace.

HOLLERITH'S MACHINE

In 1889, Herman Hollerith a census statistician of USA, devised a machine run on electricity for the first time for calculation and recording data. His machine was capable of reading both numbers and letters, programming them and giving out letters and numbers in the desired form. It was called tabulator. The Census Bureau of US put Hollerith's machine to work on the 1890 census. It did the job in just two years, and saved the government resources. In 1896, Hollerith established his own company called "Tabulating Machine Company". Today the same is known as International Business Machines Corporation IBM.

ABC COMPUTER

In 1937, Dr. John Atanasoff with the help of his assistant Bery designed the Atanasoff Berry Computer (ABC). The ABC computer was the first fully electronic digital computing device. It is considered the first electronic digital computer, and was the first machine to use vacuum tubes. The computer was approximately the size of a large desk. It had approximately 270 vacuum tubes. Two hundred and ten tubes controlled the arithmetic unit, 30 tubes controlled the card reader and card punch, and the remaining tubes helped maintain charges in the condensers. It employed rotating drum memory. Each of the two drum memory units could hold about thirty fifty-bit numbers.

The computer operator's console contained a series of buttons, meters, lights and controls, mounted on top of the computer's metal frame.It was designed to solve systems of linear equations. The machine laid the foundation for the development of Electronic Digital Computer

MARK- I COMPUTER

It was an electro-mechanical device, since both mechanical and electronic components were used in its design.This device was developed by Howard H. Aiken and was officially known as the IBM automatic sequence controlled calculator (ASCC), but is more commonly referred to as the Harvard Mark-I. The Mark I was constructed out of switches, relays, rotating shafts, and clutches. The machine contained more than 750,000 components, was 50 feet long, 8 feet tall, and weighed about 5 tons.

The architecture of Mark I was significantly different from that of modern machines. The device consisted of many calculators that worked on parts of the same problem under the guidance of a single control unit. Instructions were read in on paper tape, data was provided separately on punched cards, and the device could perform operations only in the sequence in which they were received. This machine was based on numbers that were 23 digits wide.

ENIAC - ELECTRONIC NUMERICAL INTEGRATOR AND COMPUTER

In 1946, John Mauchly and John Presper Eckert developed the ENIAC I . The American military sponsored their researchsince the army needed a computer for calculating artillery-firing tables, the settings used for different weapons under varied conditions for target accuracy.

TheENIACcontained17,468vacuum tubes, along with 70,000 resistors, 10,000 capacitors, 1,500 relays, 6,000 manual switches and 5 million soldered joints. It covered 1800 square feet of floor space, weighed 30 tons and consumed 160 kilowatts of electrical power.. The use of vacuum tubes instead of switches and relays created the increase in speed, but it was not a quick machine to re-program. It ran on a decimal, rather than a binary, system and took up 1,800 square feet

(167 square meters) of floor space with 42 separate panels. The intense heat generated by ENIAC required it to be run in a climate controlled room, and the vacuum tubes failed rather frequently. Programming changes would take more time, and the machine always required long hours of maintenance. It had to be manually set when a program needed to be run, and it had no stored memory. Input and output were achieved through punch cards.

EDVAC (ELECTRONIC DISCRETE VARIABLE AUTOMATIC COMPUTER)

EDVAC (Electronic Discrete Variable Automatic Computer) was an early electronic computer that embodied several important technological advances, including the stored-program concept. Though construction of EDVAC was completed in 1949, this large and complex computer was not fully operational until 1951. Unlike its predecessor the ENIAC, it was binary rather than decimal, and was a stored program machine. tIn EDVAC there was more improvement upon ENIAC.

Memory was provided through the use of mercury delay lines. The on/off switchability for the memory was required because EDVAC used binary rather than decimal numbers and it simplified the construction of the arithmetic units.

EDSAC-ELECTRONIC DELAY STORAGE AUTOMATIC CALCULATOR

Murice V. Wilkes of Cambridge University completed EDSAC IN 1949. EDSAC was the first computer to operate on the storage program concept. EDSAC was the world's first practical stored program electronic computer. It was one of the first stored program computers and one of the first to use binary digits. Its memory was 51236-bit words of liquid mercury delay lines, and its input and output were provided by paper tape. The EDSAC could do about 700 additions per second and 200 multiplications per second. It was in routine use at the university until 1958.

UNIVAC - I - UNIVERSAL AUTOMATIC COMPUTERS

The Universal Automatic Computer-UNIVAC was developed by Dr. Eckert and Dr. John Mauchly, who invented the ENIAC computer. In 1947, after ENIAC became operational Mauchly and Eckart formed their own Company - "TheEckart - Mauchly Computer Corporation".

Immediately after this they started the design of UNIVAC-I. The first UNIVAC- I was delivered to US Census Bureau in June, 1951.

The size of UNIVAC- I was 25x50 feet in length. And it contained 5,600 tubes, 18,000 crystal diodes, and 300 relays. It employed serial circuitry, 2.25 MHz bit rate, and had an internal storage capacity 12,000 characters. It used a Mercury delay line, magnetic tape, and typewriter output. It handled both numbers and alphabetic characters. The UNIVAC was the first computer used buffer memory. It had the processing speed of 0.525 milliseconds for arithmetic functions. It was used for general purpose computing with large amounts of input and output. The UNIVAC was the first General-Purpose Computer for commercial use.

1.6. GENERATIONS OF COMPUTERS

The term "Generation of Computer" refers to the major developments in electronic data processing". The developments in computers are closely associated with the developments in technology. Thus "Generation" is a phase in technology. In simple, the term generation indicates the type of technology used in the computer construction. It provides a base for the growth of the computer industry. As new technology was emerging, it was being used in the making of computer. The new technology improved the speed, accuracy and storage capacity of the computers. Different technologies have been used for computers in different times.

Generations of Computers

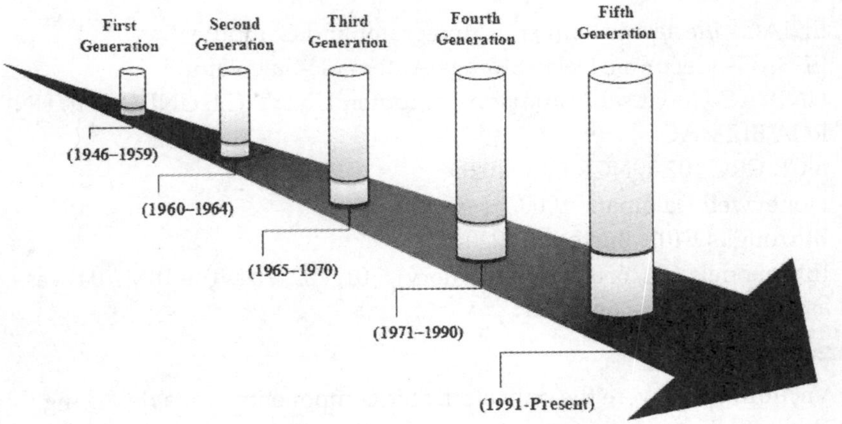

Computers right from ENIAC are classified into different generations and there are five computer generations known till today. The approximate dates shown against each generation are generally accepted.

FIRST GENERATION (1946-1959)-The Age of Vacuum Tube

World War gave rise to numerous developments and started the computer age. First generation computers were made possible by the invention of "Vacuum tube", which was a breakable glass device that could control and amplify electronic signals. Vacuum tube computers are referred to as first generation computers. First Generation computers used magnetic drums for data storage.

In first generation computers, the operating instructions or programs were specifically built for the task for which computer was manufactured. The Machine language was the only way to tell these machines to perform the operations. There was great difficulty to program these computers and it was very difficult to set right when there were some malfunctions.

Characteristics:

1. These computers were based on Vacuum Tube technology
2. First Generation computers used magnetic drums for data storage.
3. Punched tape input or output were used
4. Many number of circuits were required per cubic foot

Examples:

(*a*) ENIAC - Electronic Numerical Integrator and Computer
(*b*) EDSAC - Electronic Delay Storage Automatic Calculator
(*c*) UNIVAC-Universal Automatic Computer: UNIVAC I, UNIVAC II, UNIVAC 1101
(*d*) RCA BIZMAC
(*e*) NCR CRC 102A, NCR CRC 102D
(*f*) Honeywell Datamatic 1000
(*g*) Burroughs E101, Burroughs 220
(*h*) IBM models 604, 650 (drum memory), 701, 702, 704. The IBM 704 was considered as the first super-computer.

Advantages:

1. Vacuum tubes were the only electronic components available during those days.
2. Vacuum tube technology made possible the advent of electronic digital computers.
3. These computers were the fastest calculating devices of their time. They could perform computations in milliseconds.

Limitations:

1. The first generation computers were too bulky (large) in size and required a lot of space for installation.
2. These computers were non-portable because of their huge size.
3. Their results were mostly unreliable.
4. Thousands of vacuum tubes were required for a single computer and they produced large amount of heat and burnt out frequently. For this heavy air conditioning was required.
5. They were subject to frequent hardware failures

6. Constant maintenance was required to these computers
7. They lack in versatility and speed.
8. Commercial production was difficult and costly

SECOND GENERATION (1960-1964)-The Age of Transistor

The second generation brought several important developments at all levels of computer system design, the technology used to build the basic circuits and the programing languages used to write scientific applications. In the second-generation computers, the transistors were used in the place of vacuum tubes. The transistor was invented in 1947 and it is a small device made up of semiconductor material like silicon. Even though the Transistor were developed in 1947 but was not widely used until the end of 1950s. The transistors functioned like a vacuum tube and used to relay and switch electronic signals.

There are some important differences between the transistor and the vacuum tube. The transistor was faster, more reliable, smaller, and much cheaper to build than a vacuum tube. One transistor replaced about 50 vacuum tubes. These transistors were made of solid material, such as silicon. Therefore they were very cheap to produce. Transistors conduct electricity faster and better than vacuum tubes and produce less heat. Their use marked a new beginning for the computer. In second-generation computers, transistors were used as the brain of the computer and magnetic core was used as primary storage. This generation computers were also the first computers that stored their instructions in their memory, which moved from a magnetic drum to magnetic core technology.

Regarding software, in second-generation computers, the low level programming languages, symbolic or assembly languages were used in the place of binary machine language. It helped programmers to specify the instructions in words. For this, the translating programs such as assemblers and interpreters were developed. High-level programming languages were also being developed at this time, such as early versions of COBOL and FORTRAN.

Characteristics:

1. In Second generation computers transistors were used in place of vacuum tubes.
2. Second generation computers were smaller comparing to the first generation computers.
3. They are faster to first generation computers. That is, the computational time of the computers was reduced to microseconds from milliseconds.
4. This generation computers were more reliable
5. Second generation computers were less prone to hardware failure. Hence, they required less frequent maintenance.
6. Second generation computers were more portable and generated less amount of heat.
7. Second generation computers also required air conditioning.
8. Like in first generation, the manual assembly of individual components into a functional unit was required in second generation computers also.

9. The second generation computers moved from cryptic binary machine language to symbolic, or assembly, languages. Hence, programming became more time-efficient and easier.

Examples:

(*a*) UNIVAC III
(*b*) Mark III
(*c*) ATLAS
(*d*) RCA 501
(*e*) NCR 304
(*f*) IBM 7070, 7080, 7090, 1400 series, 1600 series
(*g*) Honeywell 800, 400 series
(*h*) General Electric GE 635, 645, GE 200
(*i*) Control Data Corp. CDC 1604, 3600, 160A
(*j*) Burroughs B5000, 200 series

Advantages:

(*a*) The second generation computers are smaller in size and are portable
(*b*) They are more reliable when comparing with first generation computers
(*c*) These computers generate less heat and thus avoided frequent hardware failure
(*d*) The second generation computers increased the processing efficiency – that is, the processing was done in microseconds.
(*e*) Programming became more time-efficient and easier.
(*f*) They are used for commercial use

Disadvantages:

(*a*) The second generation computers require air-conditioning
(*b*) For the second generation computers also frequent maintenance required
(*c*) For these computers also, manual assembly of individual components into a functioning was required
(*d*) Commercial production of these computers was difficult and costly

THIRD GENERATION (1965-1970) - The Age of Integrated Circuits

Advances in electronics technology made it possible to integrate large number of circuit elements into very small surface of silicon known as "Chips". The new technology was named "integrated circuits" (ICs).

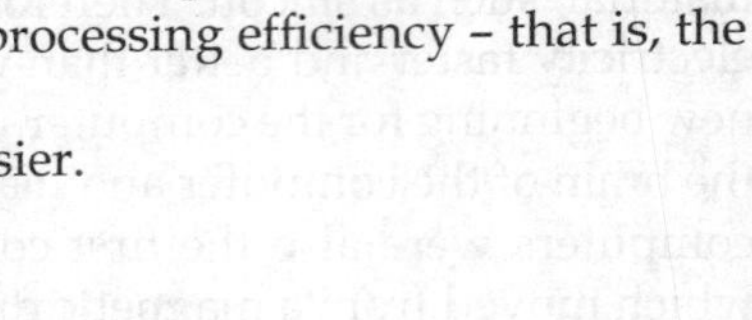

That is, thousands of transistors (now millions) were compacted in such a small space called integrated circuit (semiconductor chip-a single wafer of silicon). Placing such large numbers of transistors on a single chip increased the power of the individual computers and lowered their cost considerably.

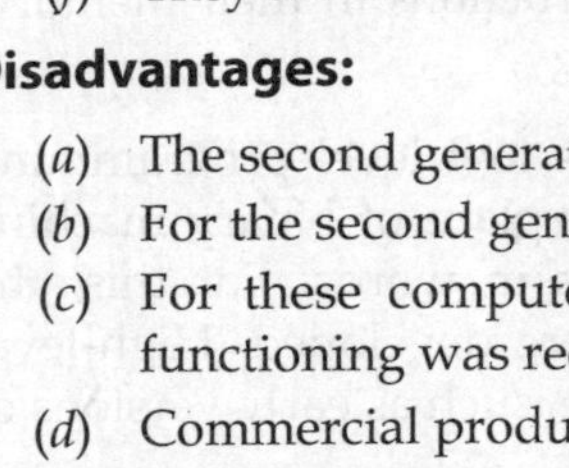

The invention of integrated circuits reduced both the size and cost of computers even further and enhancing their power. These third generation computers could carry out instructions in nano seconds. Today the integrated circuits are placed on printed circuit boards (thin pieces of bakelite or fiberglass that have electrical connections) called motherboard. The third generation was based on IC technology and the computers that were designed with the use of integrated circuits were called third generation computers. Many high level programming languages were used for writing the programs.

Characteristics:

1. IC technology was used instead of transistors in the third generation computers.
2. Third generation computers were smaller in size and cheaper as compare to the second generation computers.
3. They reduced the processing time from microseconds to nanoseconds
4. These computers consumed less power and generated less heat. Air conditioning was still required.
5. Hardware failure is rare in third generation computers. Thus, the maintenance cost was less.
6. In this generation computers high-level languages are used.
7. Manual assembling of individual components and rewiring of the circuits are not required for these computers. Thus, it reduced the large requirement of labor and cost.
8. In this generation computers magnetic core and solid states were used as main storage.
9. In third generation computers, the operating systems allowed the machines to run many different applications.
10. Input/output devices became more sophisticated. Instead of punched cards and printouts, users interacted with third generation computers through keyboards and monitors.
11. In third generation computer technology, the production of computers on commercial basis was made easy and cheap. So, computers for the first time became accessible to a mass audience.

Examples:

(*a*) Burroughs 6700
(*b*) Honeywell 200
(*c*) IBM System/360, System 3, System 7
(*d*) NCR Century Series
(*e*) RCA Spectra 70 series

Advantages:

1. Third generation computers were smaller in size and easily portable.
2. They are more reliable than second generation computers
3. Processing speed of these computers was very high as compared to previous generations
4. They consume lesser power and the overall maintenance cost of these computers was low
5. Since, writing programs in high level programming languages was possible, programming became easy.
6. The computer was monitored by a central operating system.
7. They are general purpose computers and used for various commercial applications all over the world
8. Commercial production of these computers became easy and cheaper

Disadvantages:

1. For the smooth functioning and reduce the hardware failure, air-conditioning was still required in many cases
2. Manufacture of IC chips required high level of technology.

FOURTH GENERATION (1971-1990) - The Age of Microprocessor

This period was a period of active research and development in many areas of computer technology. This generation can be characterized by both the large-scale integrated circuits and the invention of the microprocessor. In this generation ICs were replaced with microprocessor. A microprocessor is a very large scale integrated circuit (VLSI) chip, ie., very advanced integrated circuit and it contains millions of transistors within a single package. A single chip could do all the processing of a full-scale computer. Invention of microprocessor reduced the size of the computer. This development leads to higher processing speed.

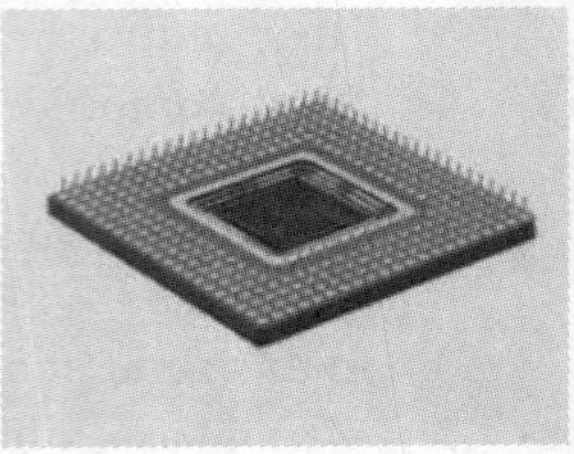

Microprocessor paved the way for the development of personal computers. During this period, there were greater developments in software including very high level languages such as functional programming and Prolog (programming logic).

Characteristics:

1. Fourth generation computers are microprocessor – based systems.
2. The computers are very small and are easily portable.
3. Fourth generation computers are highly reliable and totally accuracy.
4. These computers generate lesser amount of heat and do not require air conditioning.
5. Hardware failure is highly reduced and because of this, the maintenance is very minimal. The production cost of the fourth generation computers is very low and they are very cheap among all other computer generations.
6. The processing efficiency of the fourth generation computers is very high than previous generations. The operating speed increased to MIPS (Millions of Instruction per Second).
7. In fourth generation computers multi-processing, and multi-tasking are made possible.
8. Various high level programming languages were developed for these computers.
9. This generation computers support of GUI and pointing devices.
10. Interconnections of computers are made possible in fourth generation technology.
11. In fourth generation computers magnetic disks and optical devices are normally used.
12. In fourth generation computers the audio respond terminals are made possible and word processing and e-mail system are also introduced.
13. May operating systems including DOS, Windows etc are developed to cope up with this generation technology.
14. In fourth generation, Microcomputers/desktop, Laptop and Palmtop are introduced.

Examples:

(*a*) IBM System 3090, IBM RISC 6000, IBM RT

(*b*) ILLIAC IV
(*c*) Cray 2 XMP
(*d*) HCL
(*e*) DCM
(*f*) HP 9000

Advantages:

1. Fourth generation computers were very small in size and are easily portable.
2. They are highly reliable
3. These computers generated less heat and generally no air conditioning was required.
4. They are faster in processing to the previous generations
5. In this generation computers, hardware failure is minor and the cost of maintenance was greatly reduced.
6. They are mostly used for general purpose applications.
7. GUI and pointing devices enables users to learn to use the computer quickly.
8. They lead to better communication and resource sharing.
9. The memory capacity of this generation computers was abnormally high.
10. In fourth generation computers the cost involved at all stages of production is minimum and thus, they are cheap and reached mass audience.

Disadvantages:

1. Advanced technology was required in manufacturing of microprocessors
2. Most of the countries did not have the technology of ICs.
3. For manufacturing of these computers highly skilled people are required.

FIFTH GENERATION (1991-Present) – Age of AI-Mimic Human Brain

The fifth generation of computer systems is characterized mainly by the ability of parallel processing. The fifth generation makes it possible that hundreds of processors working on different parts of a single program. The scale of integration in semiconductors continued at an incredible pace, that is very large scale integrated circuits are used to build chips with a million components - and semiconductor memories became standard on all computers.

In fifth generation, computer networks and single-user workstations were developed. In computer networking, both local area network (LAN) and wide area network (WAN) technology was developed at a rapid pace. This provides the way for distributed computing environment in which each user has his own workstation for relatively simple tasks (compiling and editing programs, reading mail etc) and sharing large, expensive resources such as file servers and supercomputers.

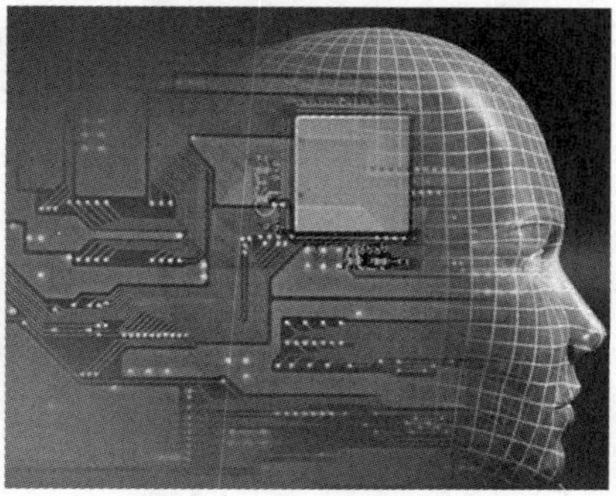

The main requirements of the fifth generation computers are incorporating the features of Artificial Intelligence, Expert Systems, and Natural Language. A lot of research is going on the fifth generation computers. Fifth generation computing devices, based on artificial intelligence, are still in development, even though there are some applications like voice recognition are being used today. Artificial intelligence includes: Games Playing: programming computers to play games. Expert Systems: programming computers to make decisions in real-life situations, Natural Language: programming computers to understand natural human languages, Neural Networks: Systems that simulate intelligence by attempting to reproduce the types of physical connections that occur in animal brains, Robotics: programming computers to see and hear and react to other sensory stimuli. The major shortcoming in the earlier generation was lack of thinking power. The fifth generation computer combines both hardware and software to produce human intelligence.

Special Characteristics:

1. Extremely large scale integration
2. Capability of Parallel Processing
3. High speed logic and memory chips- Use of Super Conductor Technology Bio-Chip.
4. High performance, micro-miniaturization
5. Voice/data integration- knowledge-based platforms
6. Artificial intelligence, expert systems
7. Virtual reality generation
8. Satellite links They will be Intelligent and mimic human brain
9. Improved flow of information
10. Large Subset of Natural Language like English- more user friendly.

1.7. CLASSIFICATIONS OF COMPUTERS

Computer can be classified according to the basic principles of operation as Digital,

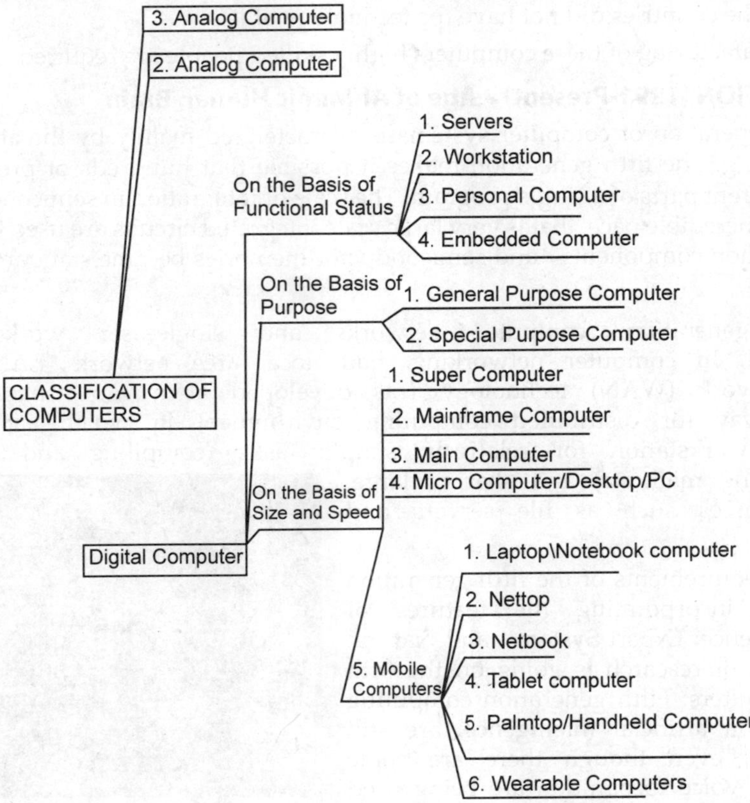

Analog and Hybrid computers. Further the digital computers can be classified on different ways including their functional status, purpose and their size and speed. The common types of digital computers are based on their size and speed and include Super Computers, Mainframe Computers, Mini Computers, Micro Computer/Desktop/PC and Mobile computers. The classifications of computers can easily be identified from the following chart:

Computer Classification Based Operating Principles

Analog
Operates on continuous data by measuring physical quantities like temperature, voltage. Eg., Fuel Station, Chemical Industry Equipment

Digital
Operates on digital Data performing arithmetic and logical operations on the data. Eg., Business, R&D

Hybrid
Operates on both analog anddigital data representation. Eg., Hospitals, Research Institutions

Let us see the meaning of different types of computers here in below:

1. Digital Computers

As the name suggests, these computers work with quantities represented as digits. In digital computers, both numeric and non-numeric information are represented as strings of digits. The information is given to the computer in the form of discrete electrical signals. They operate on discrete quantities. The discrete quantities are represented with binary numbers. Binary digit means two digits. That is, binary system is a system of numbering in which only 2 digits 0s and 1s are used. The meaning of 0 is either OFF/ NO/FALSE and the meaning of 1 is ON/YES/ TRUE. So the basic principle of these computers is either present or absence of electrical pulses in the signals. For the examples of analog concept we can mention -thermometer, analog clock, vehicle speedometer etc.

The digital signal is represented as follows:

Digital Signal Diagram

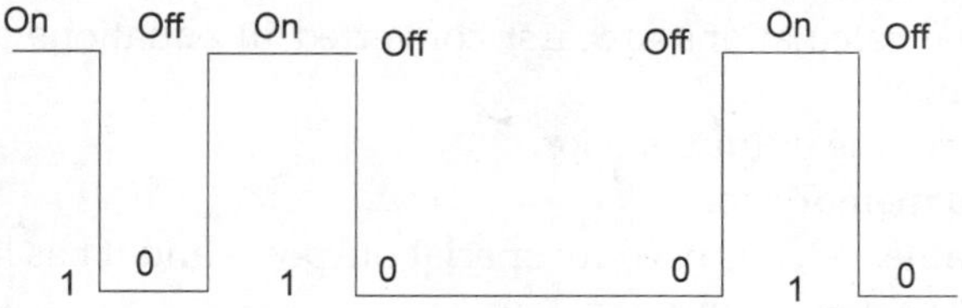

Characteristics of Digital Computer

The digital computer has the following characteristics;

1. It operates by counting.
2. It functions on discrete numbers.
3. The calculations are converted into binary numbers i.e., 1s and 0s.
4. The output is represented in the form of discrete values.
5. Its accuracy is good.
6. It has large memory space.
7. It is versatile in nature and is used for general purpose. It is suitable for a number of applications
8. In digital computers, the numbers, words and symbols can be used.

9. Its processing speed is high.
10. It is highly suitable for business applications.

Digital computers are useful for evaluating arithmetic expressions and manipulation of data such as payroll preparation, billing, solving simultaneous equations, etc.

2. Analog Computers

Analog is the Greek word, which means similar. So, in analog computers, the similarities between any two quantities are measured by electrical voltages or current. The analog computers operate by measuring instead of counting. The analog computer works on the supply of continuous electrical signals. The display is also continuous. Its output is in the form of graphs. It generally deals with physical variables such as voltage, pressure, temperature, speed, etc.

The analog signal is represented as follows:

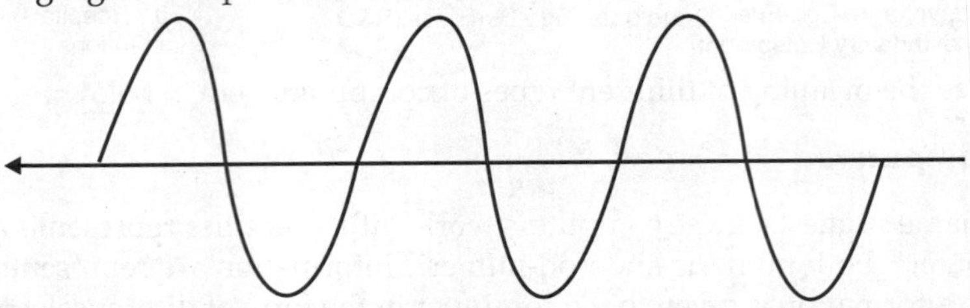

Analog Signal: An analog signal is a continuous variable electromagnetic wave. It can consume an infinite number of voltage or current values.

Characteristics of Analog Computer

The analog computer has the following important characteristics:

1. It operates by measuring.
2. It requires physical analog.
3. It functions on continuously varying quantities.
4. The output is usually represented in the form of graph.
5. In analog, the calculations are first converted in equations and later converted electrical signals
6. The accuracy of the output is poor.
7. It has limited memory space.
8. It is not versatile, i.e., it is used for special purposes and it has limited applications.
9. The speed of analog computer is low.
10. Not suitable for business and industry.

Analog Vs Digital Computer

Sl.No.	Analog Computer	Digital Computer
1.	It operates by measuring	It operates by counting
2.	It requires physical analog	It functions on discrete numbers
3.	The output is in the form of graph	The output is in the form of discrete values
4.	In analog computers the operations of the components are parallel.	In digital computers the operations of the components are sequential.

5.	Analog computers have no state like on and off.	Digital computers have two states- on and off,
6.	Limited memory is available	More memory is available
7.	Lacks flexibility	Highly flexible
8.	Limited applications	More number of applications
9.	It is difficult to use	It is easy to use
10.	Its operation speed is high- analog computer does not have to encode and decode from binary. They use the physical properties of electricity directly and thus, the functions are performed very faster comparing to digital computers.	Its operation speed is comparatively low since it has to encode and decode from binary.
11.	Not suitable for business applications	Highly suitable for business applications

3. Hybrid Computer:

The computer which possesses the features of both analog and digital computers called hybrid computers. That is, the hybrid computer has the good qualities of both analog and digital computers. With the hybrid computer the user can process both continuous and discrete data. This computer accepts either digital or analog or both types of input and gives the results as per requirement through special devices. In the hybrid computer a converter is fixed to convert the analog data into digital data and vice versa. The idea behind the hybrid computer model is to create a working unit that offers the best of both types of computers. With most designs, the analog components of the equipment provide efficient processing of differential equations, while the digital aspects of the computer address the logical operations associated with the system.

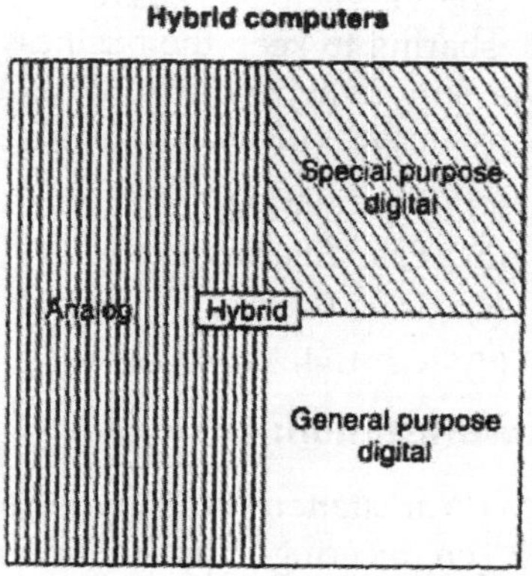

Thus, we can define the hybrid computer as "a digital computer that accepts analog signals, converts them to digital and processes them in digital form". The integrationanalog and digital is obtained by digital to analog and analog to digital converter. The hybrid computer accepts a continuously varying input, which is then converted into a set of discrete values for digital processing. It offers a cost-effective method of performing complex simulations. The hybrid computer capable of real-time solution has been less expensive than any equivalent digital computer. Hybrid computers have been necessary for successful system development. For example,in hospitalsanalog devices are used to measure the patient's blood pressure, temperature, heart rate etc. These measurements which are in analog might then be converted into numbers and supplied to digital components in the system. These components are used to monitor the patients and send signals if any abnormal readings are detected. Hybrid computers are mainly used for specialized tasks.

1.7.1. CLASSIFICATIONS ON THE BASIS OF FUNCTIONAL STATUS

1. Servers:

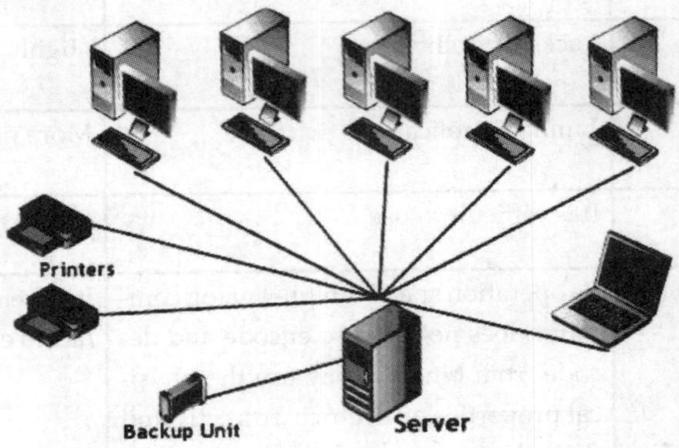

A server is "a computer designed to provide services to other computers over a network". Thus, server is not an ordinary computer and its hardware is designed in such a way to fulfilthe physical demands placed on it. Servers usually have powerful processors, lots of memory and large hard drives.

Types of Servers: There are many types of servers used for different purposes. They include application servers, database server, file server, ftp servers, game server, mail server, network server, print server, proxy server, real-time communication servers, standalone server, virtual servers (cloud), web server etc.

Operating System: The common operating systems used for servers are Solaris UNIX, Linux and Windows server.

Benefits of server:

Servers help business enterprises by increasing the data availability and by organising file sharing to keep the business operations running smooth. They offer various benefits over simple networking. With a centralized server, administrators and users can enjoy many services including the following:

(*a*) File Sharing
(*b*) Print Sharing
(*c*) Data Backup
(*d*) Centralized Security

2. Workstation:

Workstation is a type of computer used for engineering applications including CAD/ CAM, desktop publishing,graphic design, video editing, software development and other types of applications that require a moderate amount of computing power and relatively high quality graphics capabilities. Workstations generally come with higher end fast processor, large and high-resolution graphics screen, higher RAM memory, built-in network support, and graphical user interface. Workstations are targeted to professional users.

In terms of computing power, workstations lie between personal computers and minicomputers. Like personal computers, most workstations are single-user computers. However, workstations are typically linked together to form a local-area network, although they can also be used as stand-alone systems.

Operating System: The common operating systems used for workstations are UNIX, Linux, and Windows workstation.

3. Personal computers(PC)

Personal computers are designed for use in home or office productivity. In general, personal computer is a microcomputer designed for an individual user. And the price of the PC is an important consideration. These computers are based on the microprocessor technology and an entire CPU is put on one chip.

Business firms commonly use personal computers for word processing, spreadsheet applications, accounting, desktop publishing, and for database management applications. At home, the most common use for personal computers is for multimedia applications, playing games etc.

4. Embedded computers

Embedded computers are incorporated into other devices, rather than being standalone computers. It is a system built to perform its function independent of human intervention. It is designed to perform some specific tasks in the most efficient way. In embedded computer systems, the software typically resides in a flash memory or in a ROM chip. The embedded software makes the system dedicated for an application.

Embedded OS is designed to work in much less memory than desktop operating systems. They also typically work in real time. Small embedded systems may run an application that contains its own input/output routines and not require a separate operating system. Embedded computer systems typically have limited storage.

Examples of embedded computer systems include, digital timer on air conditioner, digital cameras,automatic washing machine and other digital consumer electronics, office appliances, video games, mobile phones, PDAs, GPS navigation, multitasking toysetc

Operating System: The embedded versions of the operating systems available in Linux, Windows and Macintosh (Mac). Other commercial and proprietary operating systems specialized for embedded systems are also available.

1.7.2. CLASSIFICATIONS OF COMPUTERS BASED ON PURPOSE

The digital Computers can also be classified in accordance with their overall versatility levels viz., general purpose computers and special purpose computers.

1. General Purpose Computers

These are designed and constructed to cater almost all the needs of the society. They can perform various operations in the fields of engineering, science, commerce and industry. They are able to perform according to the programs created to meet different needs. The general-purpose computer can be used to prepare stores reports, sales reports, payroll, etc. A general purpose computer can solve a much broader class of problems and it is remarkably versatile.

2. Special Purpose Computers

These computers are designed to solve a particular problem or a specific function for a company, department or for a government. For example of a special purpose computer can be a custom system designed and configured for use in defense department. This special purposes computer will have the capabilities related to following defense strategy, supply and services and human resources.

Software is created specifically for use on the special purpose computer system. Making special purpose computers is very expensive, and it can be time-consuming. Sometimes, a company or person will outsource the task of creating a special purposes computer.

Embedded computers are also in a way special purpose computers. These computes are provided with limited memory and speed necessary for a particular job. The instructions needed to perform the particular task are incorporated into the internal memory of the computer. It does not possess unnecessary options, hence embedded computers are economical.

1.7.3. CLASSIFICATION BASED ON SIZE AND SPEED

The computers can also be classified on the basis of their size and Speed. Such classification can be explained with the help of the following diagram.

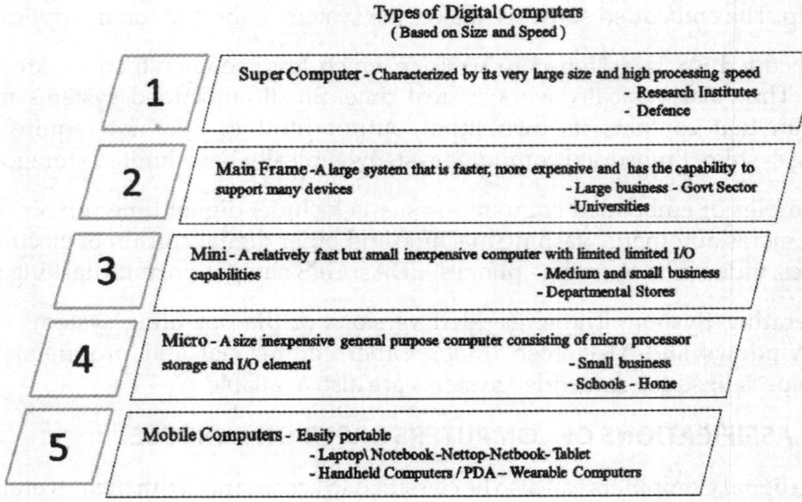

1. Super Computers:

Super computers are the most sophisticated, complex and advanced computer. It has a very large storage capacity. It can process trillions of instructions in one second. Super Computer is the fastest and most powerful computer comparing to other types. Super computers were designed primarily by computer scientist - Seymour Cray at Control Data Corporation.

Today super computers are used for highly calculation-intensive tasks such as problems involving quantum physics, weather forecasting, climate research, molecular modeling and physical simulations such as simulation of airplanes in wind tunnels, simulation of the detonation of nuclear weapons, animated graphics, fluid dynamic calculations,nuclear energy research,space science, petroleum exploration etc.

They have operations done in parallel, rather than sequential. The chief difference between a super computer and a main frame computer is that a super computer channels all its power into executing a few programs as fast aspossible. But main frame uses its power to execute many programs concurrently.

Operating Systems: Generally Linux and UNIX operating systems are used. Some other proprietary operating systems are also used for these types of computers.

The LINPACK Benchmark was introduced by Jack Dongarra. This Benchmark is used to rank the most powerful computers in the world. The LINPACK Benchmarks are a measure of a system's floating point computing power. They measure how fast a computer solves linear equations, which is a common task in engineering. LINPACK Benchmark is widely used

The Japanese "K Computer" - a joint project between RIKEN and Fujitsu - was officially named the world's fastest super computer by the International Super computing Conference. The official benchmark for the world's super computers is determined by LINKPACK, which rates the speed at which the computers solve a system of linear equations using matrix computation. In June 2010, with 68,544 CPUs, the K Computer was rated 8.162 petaflops – which is 8.162 quadrillion floating-point operations per second. (A petaflop is a measure of a computer's processing speed).

Now, the K Computer has met one of its major goals, as RIKEN announced today that using the LINKMARK benchmark, the K Computer has crossed the 10 petaflop barrier, being rated at 10.51 petaflops. That's an incredible speed, and it was achieved by continuing the process of adding CPUs to the computer. According to RIKEN, the K Computer now has 88,128 CPUs.K is expected to help the government predict earthquakes and other natural disasters, analyze climate change, develop new drugs, explore outer space, etc. Fujitsu and Riken plan to put it to practical use in November 2012.

Other popular super computers include Tianhe-1A, Jaguar, Blue Gene Watson and Baku.

2. Mainframe Computers:

Mainframe computers also called as 'Big Iron'. These computers are huge and dynamic with action. The name mainframe originated after minicomputers to distinguish the larger systems from the smaller minicomputers. They were introduced in 1975.

A mainframe computer is a very large computer in size. It is more powerful comparing to minicomputer. It consists of multiple processors. It is designed to perform multiple tasks for multiple users at the same time.

Mainframe computers are used in processing and information storage in a centralized location. Mainframes are also used as high-capacity server computers for networks with many client workstations or for serving files over the Internet.The mainframe computer is powerful and can handle the multiple processing simultaneously up to several hundred users. Users connect to the mainframe using terminals and submit their tasks for processing by the mainframe. The processing power of the mainframe is time-shared between all of the users. Mainframes are expensive and its cost is very high when comparing with mini computers.

These computers used mainly in large business and governmental organizations for bulk data processing operations and other critical applications. The organizations used these types of computers in census (to maintain the information of population), industry and consumer statistics, enterprise resource planning (ERP), airline ticket reservation systems and the like transaction processing operations.

Features:

(*a*) They are capable of handling a large number of tasks.

(*b*) The storage capacity of mainframe computers is large. Hence they can handle much number of operations simultaneously and support many terminals.

(*c*) Mainframes have the ability to run (or host) multiple operating systems

(*d*) Mainframe computers can handle a wider variety of tasks

(*e*) The transfer rate of mainframe computers is very high

(*f*) They are able to accept any high level language.

(*g*) Mainframe computers replace many smaller servers and thereby reducing management and administrative costs while providing greatly improved scalability and reliability.

(*h*) They require large room space.

(*i*) They are very expensive.

(*j*) They consumemore electricity and the maintenance cost of mainframe computers is also very high.

3. Mini Computers:

Minicomputer is the smallest computer designed specifically for the multi-user environment. The size of the mini-computer is in between the size of workstations and mainframe computers. In other words, minicomputer is a smaller version of the mainframe computer. It is more powerful than a microcomputer. Initially, the minicomputer was used as a standalone device by small and mid-sized businesses to fulfill their data processing and management and storage requirements. But now the minicomputer is being used as server

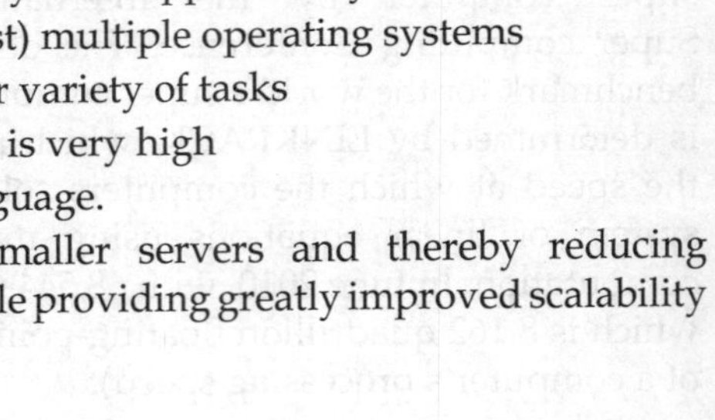

of a larger network. All applications run on the centralized computer system and all data are stored on the minicomputer. Users interact with the minicomputer through terminals which are connected to the minicomputer with cables. Today, mini-computers are the popular data processing systems in the fields of business and industry. These computers accept all high level languages.

4. Micro Computers:

Micro computers are also called as desktop computers and personal computers. Because of its small size and the use of micro-processor, this computer is called microcomputer. All the computers have three units namely Input, Output and Central Processing Unit (CPU). The entire CPU is contained in a single or a few microchips. When equipped with memory and input/ output control circuitry, it is called microcomputer. Its storage capacity is low when compared to mini and main frame computers. It is able to accept most of the high level languages. However, it uses an interpreter or compiler for running high level languages. Microchips contain microelectronic circuitries which are very tiny. Large numbers of these can be packed tightly on to a single tiny piece of silicon. The microchip is made by building up a series of very thin layers of silicon and of the tiny components which are held in it.

The Micro computers are small and portable. They are relatively inexpensive. The micro computers have excellent graphic capabilities. They are mainly used in home, small business, educational institutions and government offices for their routine data processing and reporting and communication requirements.

5. Mobile Computers:

There is wide variety of mobile computers available for the users according to their requirements and convenience. Most popular and common types of such computers are discussed below:

1. Laptop\ Notebook:

Laptop computers are portable computers. They are lightweight computers with a thin screen. They are also called as notebook computers because of their small size. They can operate on batteries and hence are very popular with travellers. The screen is connected with keyboard and CPU by hinges and folds down onto the keyboard when not in use.

2. Nettop Computer:

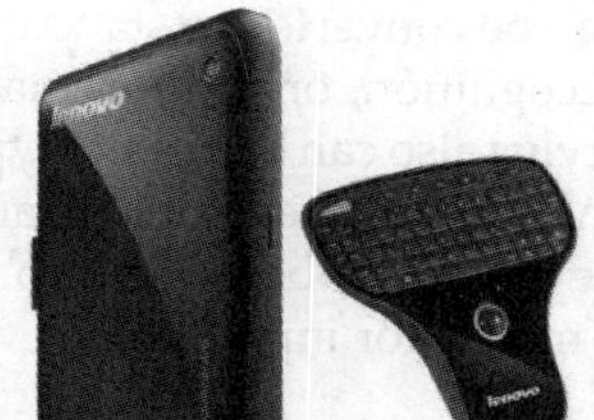

Nettop is the common name for a very small, less expensive, low-power desktop computer. It is designed for some common tasks such as internet browsing, accessing web-based applications, document processing,media playback etc. The word nettop is a designed in the combination of internet and desktop.

The common feature of nettopsis its"all-in-one form factor". That is, all hardware components except the keyboard and mouse are integrated with the monitor. They consume less power. Most current nettops run on the Intel Atom processor. The operating systems used are Windows XP or some version of Linux.

3. Netbook Computer:

Netbooks are a category of small, lightweight, legacy-free, and inexpensive laptop computers. Lightweight and compact, a netbook is the ideal companion to browse the Web and access e-mail. Netbooks may look like laptops, but they do not have the full capabilities of a laptop computers. The common features of netbook computers include the following:

(a) Screen sizes are less than 12" for portability

(b) CD/DVD drive is not included to reduce weight and thickness

(c) Wireless networking is built in to connect on the go.

4. Palmtop/PDA:

A palmtop is a small computer that we can hold in our hand and carry in our pocket. That is why it is also often called a handheld computer or a pocket computer. It is also called as PDA. PDA is the abbreviation of 'Personal Digital Assistant'.

It is a small integrate and fully enclosed unit looks like a mobile phone and serving to perform the number of specific functions. And the palmtop has a full-fledged operating system, where we can work with documents and data, play games and multimedia applications. They possess the capacity of coordinating with PCs.

Now the PDAs have a color liquid-crystal touch-sensitive screen. We can work on it either with a stylus or with our fingers. It also has a QWERTY keyboard and other facilities like Wi-Fi, Bluetooth, GPS etc. Thus, today a typical PDA can serve not only as an organizer for storing and accessing personal information, but also as an e-reader, a translator, a navigator, a portable game device, a video and audio player etc.

5. Tablet PC:

Tablet PC is a type of computer that has a LCD screen on which the user can write using a special-purpose pen, or stylus. The handwriting is digitized and can be converted to standard text through handwriting recognition, or it can remain as handwritten text. The stylus also can be used to type on a pen-based key layout where the lettered keys are arranged differently than a QWERTY keyboard. Tablet PCs also typically have a keyboard and/or a mouse for input.

A tablet PC is a device that has all of its hardware components housed inside a flat touchscreen. All user input is done via stylus or fingertip. Tablet PCs are popular for their portable size and functionality. Many have the ability to connect to a cellular or wireless network, allowing you to browse the web or check your email. Tablets are also designed for handling different types of media, such as photos, music, videos and books.

When comparing with PDA, the PDAs are more convenient for the people always in travel because they offer pocket-sized convenience and connectivity. However, tablet PCs offer almost all the same functionality as a PDA as well as better media consumption experience, but they are less portable comparing to PDAs.

6. Wearable Computers:

A wearable computer is a device that is attached to the user. The user wears it around and has the power to enter and execute commands while performing other tasks. The wearable computer is always accessible and allows the user to multi task. They are also called as 'body-borne computers'. It is a computing device small and light enough to be worn on one's body without causing discomfort. Wearable computer is constantly turned on and interacts with the real-world task.

The wearable computer normally consists of a battery powered computing unit. The display would be with a head mounted unit. The input is either voice driven or with wireless wrist mounted devices and the data storage is local. The wearable computers came with different models including Wrist Wearable PC, Glass Wearable PC, Attachable on Cloths, iBangle etc.

1.8. COMPUTER APPLICATIONS IN MODERN BUSINESS

In modern days computer has various applications viz., scientific and business applications. Let us discuss some examples of business applications in detail.

1. Payroll preparation

To prepare the payroll of the employees the following details are required Employees name, Employees number, Basic pay, Allowances, Deductions (Income-Tax, Provident Fund and the like).

Employees are relatively permanent and do not change very often. But such particulars are being used every month. So they are stored in the master file. On the basis of which the data base is developed.

All the details stored in the data base, few items need to be changed such as change in the employee a pay or increment etc and such items are updated using the master update module of the payroll system. The computer reads details from master file and calculates net pay. The program also prints out pay slip for each employee to hand over to him. A pay slip shows the employees number, name, basic pay, various allowances, various deductions and net pay.

The payroll system also generates a number of statements. It prints out the statement stating employee's number, name, bank account number and new pay. This statement is sent to the bank, which transfers the net pay from the company's account to the individual employee's account in the bank. The payroll system also generates a provident fund deduction statement. This statement shows the employee numbers, name and amount deducted. Another statement stating the name, number and amount of tax deducted is also prepared. It is sent to income Tax Office. In this way, various statements can be prepared from the data so created.

2. Inventory Control

In each and every business organisation inventory management and control is the main determining factor of the profitability of the concern. If the inventory is not properly administered and controlled, the firm cannot achieve its target profit, Inventories include raw materials, spare parts, components etc. The set of programs used to keep track of the purchase and issue of those inventories constitute the inventory control system.

In the business concerns, various items of raw materials are needed in different quantities. They are to be stocked optimally i.e., neither more nor less. Too less a stock would result in non-availability of these items, when the firm wants to exploit the new orders. If they are over stocked, more money is invested in buying the excess stock which results into more interest on loan, etc., which is a loss to the business.

Hence, the firm has to maintain the optimum level of materials. The inventory control system maintains a file with party number, name, quantity on stock, a level of stock at which the company orders for fresh quantities and supplier's address. This file is the inventory master.

When an item is issued, the inventory update program updates the inventory Master reducing the stock by the quantity issued. If the resultant stock falls below the reorder level, the inventory control program prints out an order to the supplier. When the supplier supplies the item, the inventory control program updates the stock on hand. The Inventory Control System keeps track of the Purchases and issues, so that, the firm can easily know the usage of these items over a period of time.

3.. Sales Order Processing

Real-time systems offer the possibility of a greatly prompt service to the customer. His order can be processed within virtually no time. The finished goods inventory file may have data terminals throughout the sales territory. So that the monitors can be made to display the invoice on a terminal for the salesman who is in the customer's plant and can input the particulars then and there, The customer would get to know of the availabilities instantaneously. All appropriate journal entries would be made immediately in the general ledger. The invoice can also be posted to the accounts receivable file instantaneously. The selection of warehouse that is closest to the customer can also be made and a copy of the invoice could be displayed at the warehouse terminals. Besides, the following functions can be performed rapidly:

(i) The inquiries about the customer's accounts status can be answered by the salesman.

(ii) Credit appraisal can be carried out on-tine.

(iii) Sales analysis master file can be updated online. This file provides a ready information to the sales manager regarding sales trends, etc.

(iv) Inventory replenishment orders can be determined as a part of the sales order processing.

4. Banking

Banks are the major users of computers. Much of their work centers on paper, an area where data processing finds its greatest utility. When the customer presents a cheque for withdrawal, the clerk verifies the signature of the customer with the specimen signature in the records. Then he checks the balance of amount at his credit. if the customer has sufficient balance then the clerk passes the cheque for payment and updates the balance. Likewise, the bank has to carry out various operations with utmost care.

In personal banking system, when one wants to open a bank account he has to fill up the application form with necessary details along with the specimen signature. Such details are stored in a computer on which banking software runs. The customer's signature is scanned by a suitable device called the scanner, and incorporated in the computer file. When the customer presents a cheque in the bank, the signature is checked manually. In this operation, the accounting is automatic but the payment is manual.

In some advanced branches, the accounting and payments are made automatically by the computer using "Automated Teller Machine" system. The ATM is installed at selected places of the city. It is connected to the bank's main computer When one opens an account, the bank gives him a special type of card. The name, account number and address of the customer are suitably recorded. His specimen signature is magnetically recorded in that card All these details are recorded in the computer suitably Thereafter

when the customer needs cash, he inserts his card in the slot provided in the machine. The machine reads his account number and signature from the card. It sends them to the host computer which checks his account number and stored information. If such particulars tally, the computer sends a relevant message to the ATM. The ATM asks the customer to enter the amount he wants to withdraw. Such information is given by pressing the relevant buttons of the machine. Again the computer checks if he has sufficient balance If he has sufficient balance, it instructs the machine to pay the amount. The ATM then delivers the cash on the tray fixed an it and the computers of different banks are connected together, it facilitates "Electronic Fund Transfer".

5. Insurance

The insurance industry uses computers to simplify the handling of administrative paper work. The volume and repetition of the work like calculation of premiums, billing of policy holders etc, require the use of computers. In addition to this, the computers produce a variety of external reports and handle statistical jobs such as calculating insurance reserves. The modern applications of computer in insurance industry include, Policy Administration, Claims Processing, Agency Reporting, Actuarial Analysis, etc.

6. Transportation

Transportation includes airlines, railroads and motor trucks. Computers are used in the transport system for cost analysis, accounting, calculation of tariff rates, vehicle maintenance, complex reservation systems etc. In addition to this, computers are being used to analyse, update and maintain tariff tables, and to calculate bills automatically on the basis of individual loads and routes.

The railway and air reservation systems are based on on-line applications. There is a lot of flexibility in reservation.: Due to computers, one can reserve for his journey for different destinations, from his principal place, itself. For example, he can reserve from Coimbatore for his journey from Bangalore to Chennai.

7. Computer Applications in Accounting:

Today the number of transactions in modern business has increased substantially and computers are used to process accounting data instantly. With computer accounting maintaining accounting records become more convenient. The computerized accounting uses the concept of databases. For this purpose, accounting software is used to implement a computerized accounting system. Accounting software includes Tally, Cash Manager, etc.

8. Computer Applications in Marketing:

In today's extremely competitive business environment business firms are searching for ways to improve profitability and to maintain their position in the marketplace. As competition becomes more intense the formula for success becomes more difficult. Two particular things have greatly aided companies in accomplishing these goals. They are the innovative software products of CAD/CAM and World Wide Web. In CAD, engineers and designers use specialized computer software to create models that represent characteristics of objects. These models are analyzed by computer and redesigned as necessary. This allows companies needed flexibility in studying different designs without the high costs of building and testing actual models. This way they can bring new models and designs to attract the customers and sustain in the business.

Above all, computers are widely used in market survey and analysis which is the rock bottom for the success of business enterprises.

9. Computer Aided Manufacturing:

Manufacturing businesses are integrating computers and software such as CAD/CAM with other aspects of production, including inventory tracking and scheduling. It is called as computer-integrated manufacturing. It speeds up processing of orders, adds to effective materials management, and creates considerable cost savings.

10. Office Automation:

Office automation is the integration of office information functions, including word processing, data processing, graphics, desktop publishing and e-mail. The backbone of office automation is the company's local area network (LAN). All office functions are replaced with the automated computer resources:

Office automation brings the following benefits:

(*a*) Improvement in quality of final results
(*b*) Improved efficiency
(*c*) Improved productivity
(*d*) Optimal utilization of resources
(*e*) Reduction in time taken in execution of activities
(*f*) Better Information sharing
(*g*) Transparency
(*h*) Better way of delivery of information to users at a place convenient to them
(*i*) Reduction in the dependency on human beings
(*j*) Simplified procedures
(*k*) Better customer support

The general applications of computer in various fields are given below :

Let us have a look on the general applications of a modern computer:

Area	*Application*
1. General Business	Payroll Accounts Receivables & Payables General Ledger Inventory Management & Control Human Resource Tax Preparation Office Automation Customer records Time sharing Database
2. Discrete Manufacturing	Accounting Order Entry and Processing Purchasing Inventory control Forecasting Numeric Control Design automation Production Scheduling Market Analysis Project Management and control Standard Costing Production Planning CAD/CAM [Computer Aided Design/ Computer Aided Manufacturing]
3. Process Manufacturing	Accounting Order Processing Purchasing Inventory control Mix Formulation Process Control Simulation Revenue Models
4. Retail Sales	Customer Billing Sales Analysis Accounting Inventory Reporting Point of sale automation Sales forecasting Merchandising Cash flow Analysis
5. Banking	Demand deposit accounting Proof and Transit operations Cost Control Online Savings Centralised File System Counting Machine

	Automatic Teller Machine System
	Profile System
	Electronic Fund Transfer
	Cash flow Analysis
6. Insurance	Policy Administration
	Premium Accounting
	Customer Billing
	External Reports
	Reserve Calculating
	Actuarial Analysis
	Investment Analysis
	Cash flow Analysis
	Claims Processing
	Commissions and Agency Reporting
7. Transportation	Rate Calculating
	Reservation System
	Vehicle Maintenance
	Cost Analysis
	Accounting
	Traffic Analysis (of Pattern)
	Automatic rating
	Tariff analysis
8. Government	Budgeting
	Tax Collection, Reporting and Accounting
	Census Analysis and Urban Planning
	Elections
	License and Permit
	Administration and Accounting
	Welfare-Pollution control etc.
	Central Data Bank
	Intelligence
	Lottery
	Command and Control
	Utility billing
9. Education	Administration
	Attendance Accounting
	Grading and Scoring
	Alumni Records
	CAI, CBT [Computer Assisted Instruction Computer Based Training]
	Library Cataloguing
10. Public Utilities	Customer billing
	Accounting
	Meter Reading
	Inventory Control
	Rate Analysis
	Operational Simulation
	Financial Models

11.	Distribution	Order Processing Inventory Control Purchasing Warehouse Control Vehicle Scheduling Forecasting
12.	Health Care	Patient Accounting Drug interaction Diagnosis Health Care Statistics Patient History Intensive Care Lab/operation Scheduling
13.	Printing and Publishing	Circulation Accounting Classified advertisements Automatic type setting Home finder Media Analysis Word Processing Computer - aided Graphics and Design Page Formatting
14.	Entertainment	Video Games Synthesized Music Movies.

REVIEW QUESTIONS

Short Answer Questions

1. Explain the importance of computer
2. Explain the following
   (*a*) Slide rule
   (*b*) Napier's logs and bones
   (*c*) Pascal adding machine
3. Write a short note on vacuum tubes with advantages and disadvantages
4. Give any 5 points about the Characteristics of ICs
5. Give any 5 points on Characteristics of forth generation computers
6. Write a note on fifth generation of computers
7. Give a brief note on digital computer
8. Distinguish between analog and digital computer
9. Explain about hybrid computer
10. Give a short note on mainframe computer

Essay Type Questions

1. Explain the characteristics of computer
2. Explain about the history of computers
3. Explain about

(*a*) ENIAC
(*b*) EDVAC,
(*c*) EDSAC
(*d*) UNIVAC

4. Brief note on Generations of computers
5. Explain about the classifications of computer
6. Explain the following
   (*a*) Embedded computers
   (*b*) Personal computers
   (*c*) Servers
7. Explain about the super computer and mainframe computer with its features
8. Explain about the mini computer and micro computers in detail
9. Brief note on mobile computer.
10. Distinguish between analog computer and digital computer

CHAPTER

2

Basic Principles of Operation of Digital Computer

2.1. INTRODUCTION

Today, the most commonly used computers in business are digital computers. Even though they may differ in constructional details, the basic principles of operation are almost the same. A computer is basically a device used for processing of data. It performs the following three operations in sequence:

Receives the data and instructions

Processes the data as per the instructions

Output the result- information

This cycle of operation of a computer is known as the IPO cycle (Input- Process - Output Cycle).This can be seen as in the following figure.

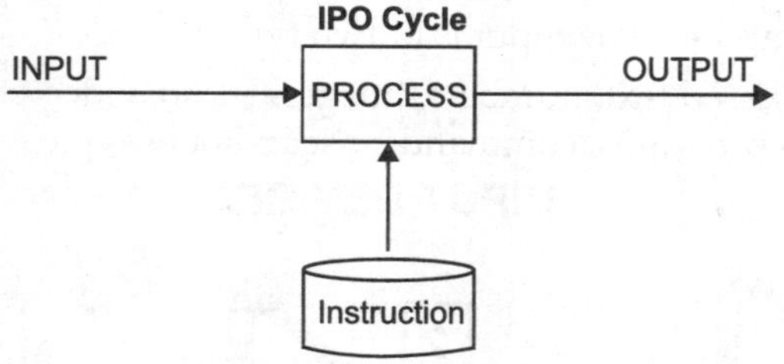

The data are provided to the computer through the input devices. They are encoded in such a way, which the computer can understand. The computer then processes the data with the help of instructions provided to it. Then it produces a meaningful and desired output known as information.

The above functions are collectively known as the basic principles of operation of a digital computer. These can be expanded as follows:

1. Accepting inputs
2. Memory manipulation
3. Arithmetic operations
4. Decision making and
5. Giving Output

These operations can be seen in detail from the following Block Diagram of the digital computer:

BLOCK DIAGRAM OF DIGITAL COMPUTER

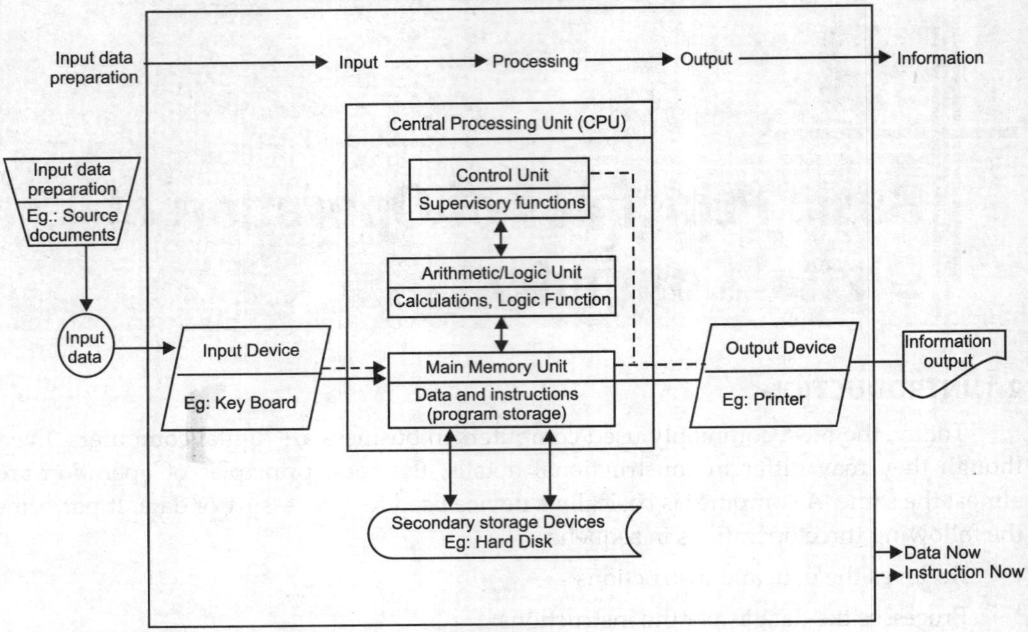

Let us discuss the above in detail below:

2.2. INPUT UNIT

Input Unit consists of hardware devices that are used to enter data and instructions/programs in to the computer. The input is of two types:

1. **Data** – unprocessed text, numbers, images, audio, video etc.
2. **Instructions** – programs, commands, user responses etc.

INPUT DEVICES

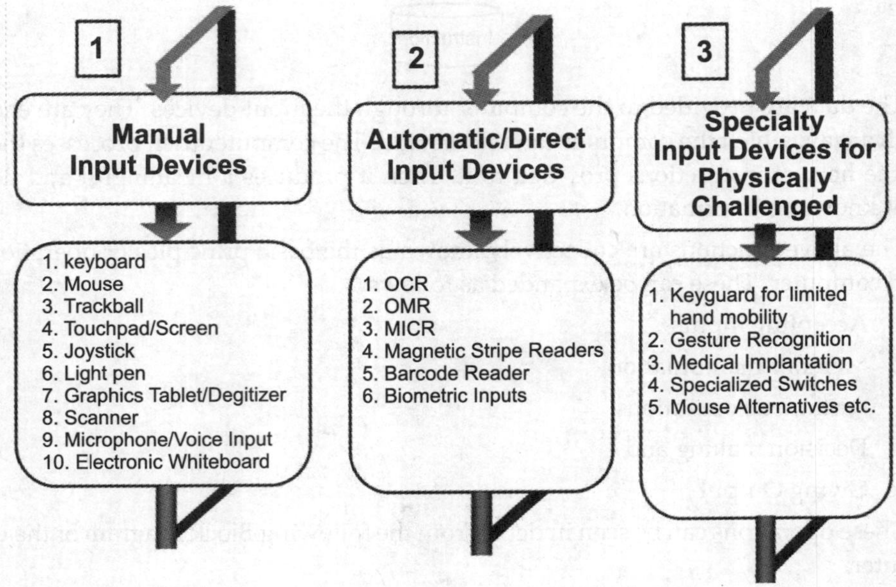

Computer accepts the data to be processed and the instructional details required for the processing. When the data and instructions are entered into the input unit, they are passed to the memory unit of the CPU. Various input devices are available in this regard. Thus, an input device is a device that accepts the data or the information from the user and translates the information into a form, which the computer can interpret. The commonly used input devices are as follows:

2.2.1. Manual Input Devices

1. Keyboard:

The keyboard is the most commonly used and most versatile of all input devices. The data is entered by manually keying in or typing certain keys. The keyboard layout is similar to that of a typewriter's (QWERTY keyboard), with some additional keys. Whenever a key is pressed the electrical contacts and circuits just below the keys translate the message from the key into equivalent binary codes.

The keyboard is divided into three parts - the main keyboard (typing area) the function keys and the numeric keypad. Function keys perform some special functions such as loading programs and offering help. These are programmable (i.e., they can be usually made to perform a different function other than the original). Keyboards are available for desktop computers, laptop computers, PDA and smart phones.

Types of Keyboards:

Normal Keyboard:

The normal keyboard is an important peripheral that is used as an input device of a computer and many other devices. Usually, there are around 110 keys on a computer keyboard. The keyboard is used to enter letters, numbers and other special function keys, which are used for some special functions. The standard layout of letters, numbers, and punctuation is known as a QWERTY keyboard because the first six keys on the top row of letters spell QWERTY. The types of keyboards vary according to their connection with the CPU, the application, the layout of the keys and some special function keyboards.

Ergonomic Keyboards

The ergonomic keyboards are designed considering the ergonomic aspect of the keyboards. It is specially designed as per the comfort of the hands and wrist of the keyboard user. The ergonomic keyboards are designed to prevent the carpal tunnel syndrome(Occurs with repetitive motion of hands & wrists-especially with high force levels, compression of nerves and tendons) which causes numbness and tingling sensation in hands and fingers after typing for a long duration. These keyboards also help the keyboard user maintain a comfortable position.

Internet Keyboards

The internet keyboards are designed to increase the comfort level of the internet user. Features with Internet Keyboard includes (*i*) Internet Hot Keys - Get online access with the push of a button, then easily browse the Internet - right from our keyboard (*ii*) E-mail Hot Key - Open our e-mail program to check messages with a single keystroke (*iii*) Custom Hot Keys - My Computer and Calculator Keys gives us quick access to these popular Windows features etc.

Multimedia Keyboards

The multimedia and gaming keyboards are designed for playing audio and has hot-keys for volume control, play, stop and mute operations.

Virtual Keyboards

The virtual keyboard is not actually physical keyboard, but the keyboard is simulated using software. Normally, these used in the PDAs.

Wireless Keyboards - The cable free keyboards.

2. Mouse:

Mouse is a small hand-held device that controls the location of a cursor on the screen when it is slide over the top of a table or other horizontal surface. Its movement tracked by optical means. The mouse communicates with the computer through its electrically conducting tail. Now, cordless mouse is very common among the users. Buttons on the top of the mouse add an extra element of control.

It enables the user to manipulate a pointer or arrow on the screen. The movements of the mouse enable the user to:

(*a*) Point to icons (tiny pictures that identify the processing choices)

(*b*) Click on such icons to run those programs

(*c*) Choose an item from a list (menus)

(*d*) Draw lines or pictures on the screen. But they cannot be used where text has to be entered

3. Trackball:

Trackball is a pointing device like mouse, consisting of a ball held by a socket containing sensors to detect a rotation of the ball. The user rolls the ball to move a cursor. There are buttons next to the ball, which can be used just like mouse buttons.

The benefit of trackball over the mouse is that the trackball is fixed in a box. Hence, it does not require more space to use it. In addition, we can place a trackball on any type of surface. Track ball is popular pointing device among portable computers.

4. Touchpad/Screen:

A is a pointing device featuring a tactile sensor, a specialized surface that can translate the motion and position of a user's figure to a relative position on screen.

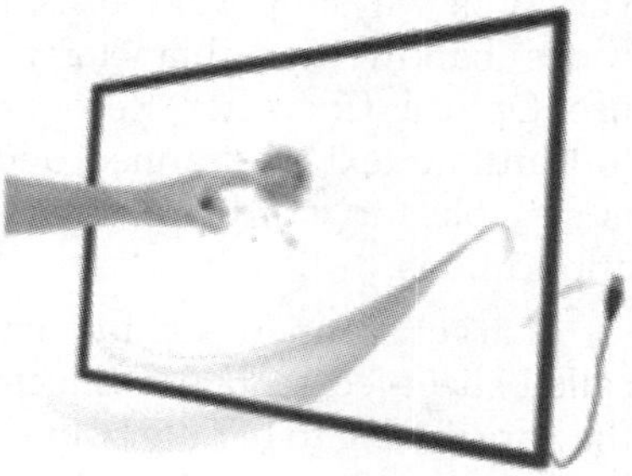

A touch screen is a computer display screen and it is also an input device. The screen is sensitive to pressure. They are favorite user friendly method for feeding data into computer. The user interacts with the computer by touching pictures or words on the screen. Users can command the computer to perform various useful tasks simply by touching specific sectors of the screen with their forefingers. The computer senses the location of the finger in various ways. They include computer touch screen and video walls, touch tables etc

5. Joystick:

A joystick is an input device consisting of a stick that spindles on a base and reports its angle or direction to the device it is controlling. Joysticks are often used to control video games, and usually have one or more push-buttons whose state can also be read by the computer. Using joystick is the easiest way to navigate the characters or objects within a game

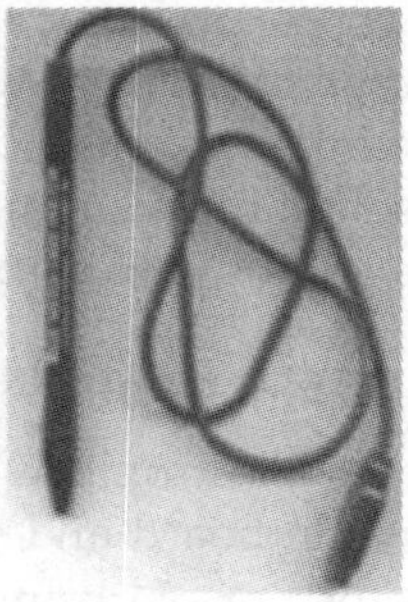

6. Light Pen:

Light pen is an input device shaped like a pen that is connected to a computer's monitor. It is a pointing device and the user points at the screen with the pen and selects items or chooses commands. The tip of the light pen contains a light-sensitive element which, when placed against the screen, detects the light from the screen enabling the computer to identify the location of the pen on the screen. Light pens have the advantage of drawing directly onto the screen, but it functions on a CRT monitor and not on TFT or LCD screen. Hence, they are not common in use.

7. Graphics Tablet/Digitizer:

Digitizer pads are similar to light pen except that a Digitizer pad is mounted horizontally so that it provides a much more comfortable way to enter data into a computer. Its horizontal mounting makes it convenient for tracing, engineering drawings, charts and graphs into a computer.

8. Scanner

An inexpensive way to get entire documents, pictures, and anything into a computer is by using a scanner. Scanners use optical recognition systems that have a light beam to scan input data to convert it into electrical signals, which are sent to the computer for processing. Optical recognition is the most common type of source input, appearing in a variety of ways: optical marks, optical characters, bar codes, handwritten characters, and images. Scanners use Optical Character Recognition (OCR) software to translate text on scanned documents into text that is suitable for word processors and other computer applications.

Larger scanners include machines into which we can feed sheets of paper. These are called sheet-fed scanners. Sheet-fed scanners are excellent for loose sheets of paper, but they are unable to handle bound documents. A second type of large scanner, called a Flat-bed Scanner, is like a photocopy machine. It consists of a board on which we lay books, magazines, and other documents that we want to scan. Another type of scanner is Over-head Scanner or Copy Board scanner. It looks somewhat like overhead projectors. We place documents face-up on a scanning bed, and a small overhead tower moves across the page.

9. Voice Input/ Microphone:

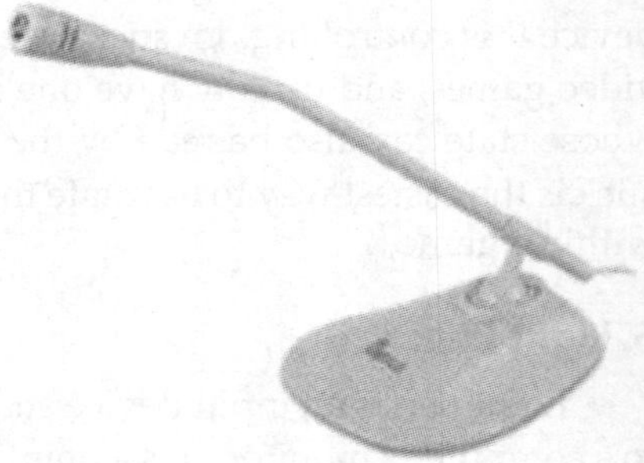

The voice input/speech recognition system used to give input in to the computer through speech. Voice input systems can allow a person to operate a computer without using a keyboard or mouse. It learns how a particular user pronounces words and uses information and find what words are being spoken. Speech recognition is a type of input in which the computer recognizes words spoken into a microphone. For this special software and a microphone are required. The primary function of a microphone is to send a good sound signal to the computer.

10. Electronic Whiteboard:

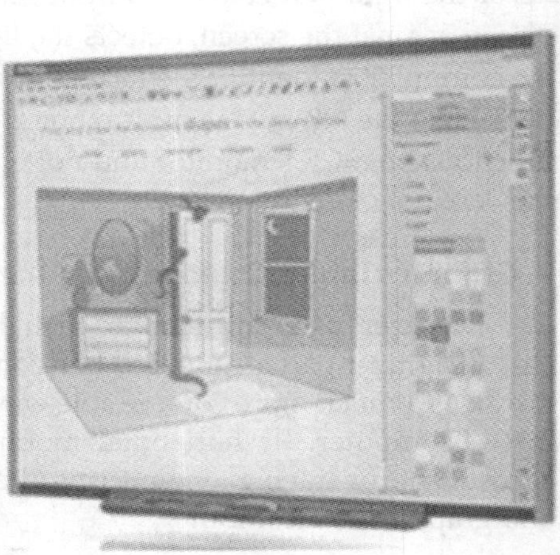

Electronic whiteboard is also called as white board and smart board. There are two types of electronic whiteboards. The first is a projection screen that looks very similar to the boards used with erasable markers, but it works electronically without the use of ink. The board displays digital images and is capable of tracking drawings and writings in different colors. Electronic whiteboard use computer and projector to display information to people in the same physical location. They are becoming common both in business environments, and in the classroom. A projector displays the computer program on the screen. The operator then uses a pen to control the computer. In this way, it is very similar to the touchscreens available with some personal computers. The second type of electronic whiteboard is a computer program that allows users in a teleconferencing environment to work on the same document in real time.

2.2.2. Automatic/Direct Input Devices

Direct Data Entry refers to entry of data directly into the computers through machine readable source documents or through use of on-line terminals. Direct Data Entry does not require manual transcription of data from original paper documents. These devices can scan source documents magnetically or optically to capture data for direct entry into the computer. Magnetic ink character readers and optical character readers are examples of such devices.

Let us now describe the commonly used devices under this category.

1. OCR- Optical Character Recognition

OCR readers are the most versatile data entry tools. The Optical Character Reader recognises or interprets printed or handwritten data directly from documents. The essence of OCR is pattern recognition. That is, the ability to identify a recorded symbols as familiar form. The machine reading is done by light scanning techniques in which each character is illuminated by a light source and the reflected image of the character is analysed in term of the light-dark pattern produced. Optical Character readers can read upper and lower case letters, numerics and certain special characters from handwritten, typed and printed paper documents. OCR devices are used when the volume of data to be fed into the computer is large.

Turn-Around Documents: Large volume billing applications (e.g., the bills of utility companies, credit - card organisations, and magazine subscription outfits) increasingly are being adapted to OCR methods. The customer paying the bill returns the bill, which has OCR data (e.g., customer number and amount of the bill) recorded on it, along with payment. Thus, the organisation's bill (or the part returned by the customer) becomes input for recording cash payments received from the customer. This procedure, sometimes, referred to as the used of "turn-around documents" and it has the advantage of minimizing or eliminating the keying process when cash receipts are received from customers.

The main benefit of OCR is the elimination of human effort of transcription and the paper work explosion can be handled effeciently because OCR is economical for a high rate of input.

2. OMR -Optical Mark Reader

Optical mark readers are commonly used for scoring tests and standard quiz. Optical Mark Reading is recognised as an efficient and cost effective data entry method for the large scale processing of category data. From its origins in examinations, it is now widely used in other large-scale exercises. OMR can relieve much of the effort and difficulty in keyboard entry.

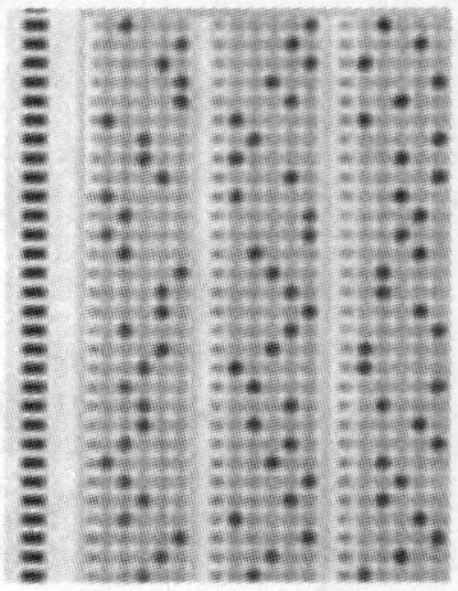

An Optical Mark Reader reads marks made on purpose designed forms and transfers the data straight to a computer system. It is a technology that is reliable, simple to operate, complementary to other data capture techniques and easily integrated with other elements of a computer based solution.

For example, the persons taking a test or quiz marked in a pre-designed OMR sheet.And the sheets are read by the optical mark page reader. The results are instantaneous. Most of the recruitment tests conducted in large scale like bank recritment etc, it is highly useful and reliable.

3. MICR - Magnetic Ink Character Recognition

MICR is a technology used to verify the legitimacy or originality of paper documents, especially checques issued by banks. Special ink, which is sensitive to magnetic fields, is used in the printing of certain characters on the original documents. Information can be encoded in the magnetic characters.

An MICR can identify and decode characters printed with special ink that contains particles of magnetic material. The reading process is called Magnetic Ink Character Recognition. The major advantage of these characters is that they are machine-readable. Since MICR systems can recognize only certain styles, the characters have to be accurately formed. The use of MICR can enhance security and minimize the losses caused by some types of crime. If a document has been forged - for example, a counterfeit cheque produced using a color photocopying machine, the magnetic-ink line will either not respond to magnetic fields, or will produce an incorrect code when scanned using a device designed to recover the information in the magnetic characters.

In computing, a technique that enables special characters printed in magnetic ink to be read and input rapidly to a computer is MICR. The device used to read MICR documents is called MICR-reader. MICR is used extensively in banking because magnetic-ink characters can be machine-read with much greater accuracy than human reading or other optical character recognition (OCR) systems, and are therefore ideal for marking and identifying the account and sort code numbers on cheques. MICR employs a system of printed characters, which are easily readable by human beings as well as a rnachine reader. Special printing font is used to represent characters. In this font, each character is basically composed of vertical bars. The characters are printed in special ink.

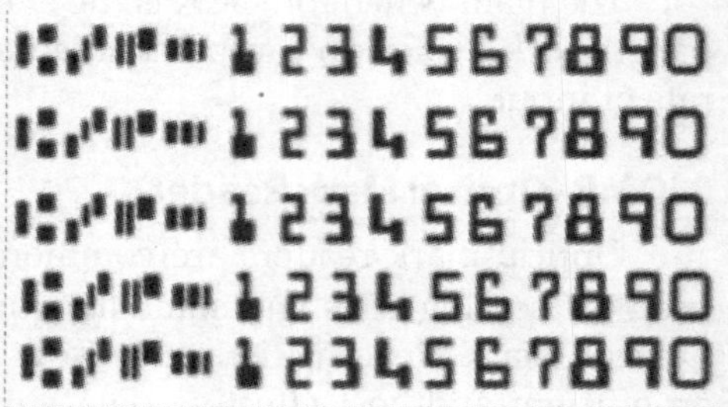

4. Magnetic Stripe Readers

Magnetic Stripe Readers are another divice used to input data directly in to the computers. Strips are found attached to a plastic card and used for recording data. Magnetic strips are used on credit cards, bank ATM cards etc. When the cards are entered in to the device, the data are read and transfered in to the computer instantly for further processing.

5. Barcode Reader:

These devices are another important input device. Certain data like the product codes of groceries or books etc., can be recorded on small strips called "bar-codes". A bar code is a set of parallel printed lines of varying thickness and separation/spaces which represent data in binary form. These lines are normally alternate lines of black and white. They represent a number, which is sometimes written at the bottom or above the bar code for the convenience of the human reader. The typical example of the bar code can be seen on the back cover of this book.

Normally a bar code has on it the number of that particular product. The bar codes are useful because of the names of products do not have repeatedly written down. They are very much useful in places like supermarkets, at the point of sale, hospitals, warehouses etc. However, the bar codes having the limitation of being read only by a machine.

6. Biometric Inputs:

Biometric inputs authenticate the persons' identity by verifying personal characteristics. With the increased use of computers, it is necessary to restrict access to sensitive/ personal data. To give authorization on the basis of standard basis as biometric elements, such biometric data have to be fed in to the computer. Biometric elements such as fingerprint, retina or face recognition access control systems can function as biometric controller for inputting data in to the computer. These systems decide if the input data is authorized or not by comparing with the saved biometric data in the device.

For example, fingerprint reader captures curves and identifies the fingerprint. Likewise hand geometry system measures shape and size of the users' hands. Signature verification system recognizes the pattern and size of the signature. Likewise eye retina is also used in biometric systems. Modern laptops with webcam can recognize the face of the user (biometric data) saved inside to authorize to use the computer. Now- a- days, biometric data is stored in smart cards as well.

7. Video Input:

Video input is the process of entering a full-motion recording into a computer. Video input device includes web cam etc. Webcam captures a video image of the scene in front of it. It is either built in to the computer (e g laptop) or it is connected through an USB cable.

2.2.3. Specialty Input Devices For Physically Challenged

Now-a-days many types of special input devices are available for the physically challenged people to give input and interacting with the computers. Such devices include Keyguard for limited hand mobility, Gesture Recognition devices, Medical implantation equipment, Specialized Switches, Mouse alternatives etc.

2.3. OUTPUT UNIT

In computer system, it is the output unit that determines the efficacy and importance of computers. Anything that comes out of a computer is called output. That is, after the data are given by the input units, they are processed and converted into meaningful information and this output is presented to the user with the help of output devices. Output unit consists of one or more output devices to respond to user requirements. It is not mandatory that the output unit should have all devices to make available the results to users. Users determine the way or the form of output based on the demands of their work. Hence, output unit can be defined as "an integral part of computer system which provides the data processing results in the manner based on user demands and requirements". The output unit is used to present both soft and hardcopy of information.

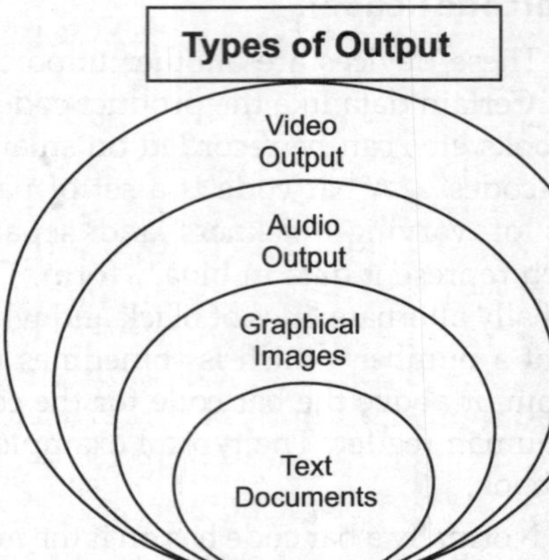

2.3.1. Types of Output

The processed results are given in different forms or ways and means. They are commonly called as output whether it is a printout or is seen on the monitor or is copied in in a CD or other media. The various types of output can be seen in the following figure:

These types of outputs are obtained through various output devices. Let us see the different types of output devices in the following chart:

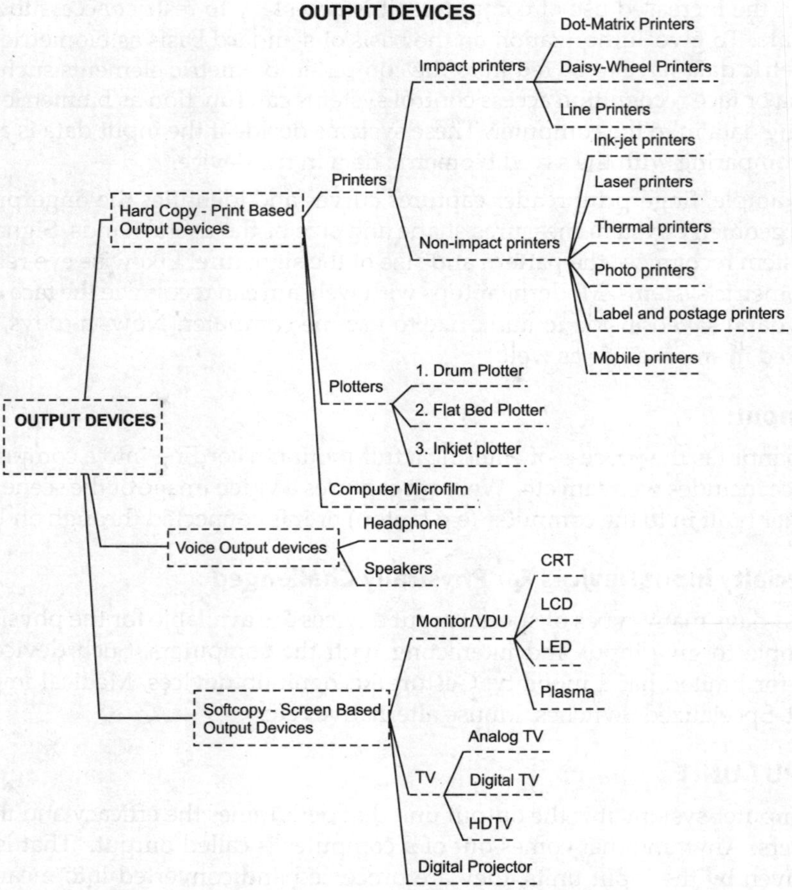

Let us see the details of these devices one by one in turn:

2.3.2. Hard Copy – Print Based Output Devices

1. Printers:

Printer is one of the most commonly used output devices. It is an electromechanical device capable of converting the text and graphical documents from electronic form to the physical form. Generally they are the external peripheral devices and are connected with the computers or laptops through a cable or wirelessly to receive input data and print them on the papers. A wide range of printers are available with a variety of features ranging from printing black and white text documents to high quality colored graphic images. Generally the printers are classified as impact printers and non-impact printers.

A. Impact-Printers

The impact printer is one which prints character hitting on ink-coated ribbon against paper just as an ordinary typewriter. That is, impact printer uses pins to strike against an inked ribbon, making dots on the paper and forming the desired characters. This is the oldest printing technology, but it is still used because of the cost per page is very low. And, printing of large forms or copy with carbon paper can be done only with impact printers.

Impact printers include the following:

(*a*) **Dot-Matrix Printers:** In the early 1970sa new print system called dot-matrix printing was developed for use with data processing systems. They became the standard printers for many minicomputers and nearly all microcomputers and consequently, were also used for word processing requirements. Dot-Matrix printers utilize wire needles or pins which strike the ribbon against the paper in the pattern necessary to produce each character ribbon against the paper in the pattern necessary to produce each character image.

The printing head is a matrix block which consists of rows and columns of holes through which pins appear. The characters being printed are formed by activating the printing head so that certain pins appear through the holes to form a pattern, which resembles each character. The pins are formed into the shape of the character to be printed, then pressed against an inked ribbon and the pattern printed on the paper. The characters, whether they are letters, numbers or graphical symbols are printed as a series of dots which merge together to form the character. The paper is pressed against a drum/cylinder and the paper is moved forward as printing progresses. The electromagnetically-driven printhead moves across the paper and strikes the printer ribbon situated between the paper and printhead pin. The impact of the printhead against the printer ribbon imprints ink dots on the paper which form human-readable characters. Thus, the name impact printers.

(*b*) **Daisy-Wheel Printers:** Daisy Wheel' printers work in a similar manner to an electronic typewriter. The major difference is that they use a new type of printing element called a 'daisy wheel'. This is a molded metal or plastic disc-shaped printing element which looks very much like a daisy flower hence the same.

The main element in the Daisy wheel printer consists of a circular fan of metal or plastic petals radiating from a central hub. A single character (a letter-capital and lower-case, number, or punctuation mark) is embossed on each petal. An electromechanical hammer slams the proper daisy wheel into contact with the ribbon, which transfers its inked impression on to the surface of the paper. Daisy-wheel printers create noise and also it is slow in printing speed. They cannot print graphics, and cannot change fonts unless the print wheel is physically replaced. With the introduction of laser printers, daisy-wheel printers are generally not used in business environments today.

(*c*) **Line Printers:** Line printers have a mechanism that allows multiple characters to be simultaneously printed on the same line. Large spinning print drum or a looped print chain is used in this type of printers. When the drum or chain is rotated over the surface of the paper, the electromechanical hammers behind the paper push the paper (along with a ribbon) onto the surface of the drum or chain, marking the paper with the shape of the character on the drum or chain. These printers are much faster than dot-matrix or daisy-wheel printers. But they also create noise and have limited multi-font capability. They quality of print output is poor when comparing with impact printing technologies.

Thus, the impact printers are ideal for printing multipart forms because they can easily print through many layers of paper. And, as a special feature, they can normally withstand dusty environment, vibrations, and extreme temperature. But they are noisy because of the striking activity.

B. Non-Impact Printers

All the impact printers print slow due to the slow mechanical movement of the print head. Efforts were made to eliminate the mechanical motion of the print head to increase the speed of the printers and as a result non-impact high speed printers were developed. Non-impact printers print characters and graphics without striking on the paper. That is, non-impact printers do not hit the ribbon against the paper while printing. Ribbons are not used in this type of printers. Some of these printers use spray ink while others use heat and pressure to create images. These printers are faster than impact printers. Ink-jet printers, Laser printers, Thermal printers, Photo printers, Label and postage printers fall under this category of printers.

(*a*) **Ink-jet Printers:** Inkjet printer spits out tiny drops of ink along parallel paths, and then uses electrical forces to control. Ink drops are pumped through a tiny nozzle. Each tiny ink drop is ejected from its nozzle at very speed and as it emerges, it is either charged with (millions of) electrons or it left unchanged. All the drops pass between two charged metal plates. Those without charges move straight ahead to impact the paper at a predictable location. Those with charged are deflected into a tiny gutter that collects them for latter reuse. Ink jet printers are ideal for providing drawings, graphs etc.

(*b*) **Laser Printers:** Laser printers are page printers and they resemble photocopiers in size and appearance and use similar technology. They are very fast and silent in operation. The print quality is good and the resolution of current models is 600 dots per inch (dpi), though some of the latest versions offer 1400 dpi. Laser printers can handle graphics as well as text. In laser printer the image to be printed is not formed in one brief photographic exposure. Instead, it is painted on selenium sheet, one line at a time by a laser beam controlled by computer. Selenium sheet is a non-metallic element with a peculiar property. It loses its charge in a small, local region when it is exposed to low intensity laser illuminations. The beam from the laser systematically sweeps across the selenium surface from left to right, top to bottom, using a scanning pattern. In other words, the laser beam prints the desired image on the selenium sheet, one thin horizontal strip at a time. When the entire image has been formed the sheet of selenium is routed across a container filled with toner particles-tiny dry granules of jet-black ink of the type used in conventional xerographic copying machine. This charged toner particles adhere to any region of selenium sheet that has not been illuminated by the laser beam. The charged toner particles are then transferred the selenium sheet into the paper - which is also changed with electricity. Finally the paper is subjected to sheet and pressure to back and compress the toner particles permanently into its surface. Laser printers are common in business community for their high quality and high volume output and low cost-per-page.

(*c*) **Thermal Printers:** This type of printer employs the non- impact technique but uses the thermal effect to produce a particular character. The printed character will be in the form of Dot matrix. For printing, the ordinary paper as we used for the above printers is not useful and hence we have to use special thermal sensitive paper, which is generally more costly than the ordinary paper. The appropriate temperature is produced by the printer head, which changes the sensitized paper into black as per the shape of the character without using an inked ribbon. The speed of these printers is very slow which ranges from 25cps to 100 cps. These printers are used mostly for business presentation transparencies and for color proofing.

(*d*) **Other Type of Non-impact Printers:** Impact printers include other type of printers such as, Label and Postage Printers and Mobile printers.

Label and Postage Printers: Label and postage printers are used to print labels and postage stamps, envelops etc.

Mobile Printers: For many busy professionals, printing can become a challenge, especially if traveling and meeting with clients often on the road. Mobile printers are very much useful for these types of requirements and demands. These printers come in a variety of styles and functionalities. Some work wirelessly, while some connect using wires.

In brief the non-impact printers are generally much quieter than impact printers because there is no striking mechanism and they can produce high quality output. But they cannot print multipart forms.

When we talk about printers we refer to two basic qualities associated with printers:

(*a*) Resolution and

(*b*) Speed

Print resolution is measured in terms of number of dots per inch (dpi). Print speed is measured in terms of number of characters printed in a unit of time and is represented as characters-per-second (cps), lines-per-minute (lpm), or pages-per-minute (ppm).

2. Plotters

In some cases we need the results of some problems in the form of figures to come to immediate conclusions and to take decisions. In such cases we need graphical plotters. The familiar plotters used in the computer systems include Drum Plotter, Flatbed Plotter and Inkjet Plotter.

Flatbed Plotter: It consists of a flat paper retainer on which the plain paper or a graphic paper is firmly held by the principle of, "Electro-Static Field Attraction". Above this paper a pen is moved for drawing on the paper using different colour pens. The pen is inserted in the penholder or carriage, which is fixed to a cross bar which moves up and down the beam. The beam slides between the rib of the bend, through, "V" slot from left to right and vice-versa. The plotter provided with pen nest in which at least four different colour pens will be kept ready for use. It is also provided with a control panel by which the movement of the pen can be controlled. When it is connected with the computer, control for the pen movement is provided by the computer signals. A flat bed plotter is widely used for all types of computers.

Drum Plotter: It consists of plastic drum on which the paper is held or with appropriate attachment; a continuous paper can also be fed. The drum is held horizontally and is rotated. The pen is held by means of a cross bar which moves in the X-axis direction. In this case also single or multi-colored pens may be used.

2.3.3. Voice Output Devices

Those devices which produce voice after input are called voice output devices. Audio output is the ability of the computer to output sound. To get high quality audio output, sound card as well as good speakers are required. There are many types of voice output devices. Speakers and headphones do the same work i.e., giving audio output. When we play a song or a video on the computer without speakers we cannot hear the sound. Speakers and headphones come in different sizes and qualities. Audio recording studio requires high quality speakers and headphones for better quality recording.

2.3.4. Softcopy-Screen Based Output Devices

1. TVs as Output Devices:

TVs are also used as output devices these days. All TVs - Analog TV, Digital TV, HDTV (High-Definition Television) are connected to computers and are used. For analog TV converters are required. Modern TVs are designed in such a way to get connected to computers.

2. Monitors/VDU:

Monitor is an output device that resembles the television screen which displays viewable text and images generated by a computer without producing a permanent record. In monitor, the images consist of small dots known as pixels (picture elements). A number of horizontal and vertical pixels in monitors give the resolution and is responsible for sharpness and clarity of image. More pixels give clear image and better resolution. Monitors look more or less similar to a television with a screen of 15, 17, 21 or more inches. When we give the command to the CPU through any input devices such as the keyboard, mouse, we get the desired result on the screen in the monitor. The number of times per second the screen image is redrawn is known as refreshing rate of monitor. Higher the refreshing rate better the quality.

Types of Computer Monitors:

Cathode Ray Tube- CRT:

CRT is a type of VDU/monitor. Keyboard is used to enter data into the computer, and a cathode ray tube (CRT) like a T.V.Screen is used to display the input data as well as the messages and processed output from the computer.

The CRT produces a beam of electrons that makes the picture on the screen. Within CRT, the Raster Scan is done. The Raster Scan helps to convert the beam produced by the CRT into a picture. Scanning the screen back and forth, from the top left hand comer to the bottom right corner within the monitor is the Raster Scan. The Raster Scan helps to convert the beam produced by the CRT into a picture.

CRT monitors are most popular before the development of LCD monitors. But now most of the computers come with LCD or LED monitors.

Liquid Crystal Display- LCD

LCD means Liquid Crystal Display. It is also known as Liquid Crystal Diode. It is one of the most popular display technologies today. Liquid Crystal Display consists of two sheets of polarizing material with a liquid crystal solution between them. When an electric current passed through the liquid crystal solution, crystals align so that light cannot pass through them.

LCD monitors are lightweight, compact, occupy less space and consume lesser power. There are two types of LCD technology. They are:

1. Active matrix LCD technology
2. Passive matrix TFT technology.

The TFT (Thin-Film Transistor) technology is more reliable with better image quality but the passive matrix technology has a slower response and hence it is not common in use.

LCD is primarily used for laptops and other portable devices. LCD monitors do not have high radiation emission and they cause less eye fatigue to the user comparing to CRT.

Light Emitting Diode –LED

LED displays are one of the latest developments in the field of display technology. In LED monitors light emitting diodes are used. Such diodes boost the display performance of the monitors. LED monitor comes with a LCD panel and a LED backlight is used to power up the LCD panel. LEDs are placed behind or around the LCD panel to enhance the brightness and video performance of the monitor screen. Electric current stimulates diodes to glow in the form of images, texts, numbers and symbols.

Plasma Monitors:

Plasma monitors are display devices that use gas plasma technology and offer wider screen sizes. Plasma technology is used to illuminate tiny colored fluorescent lights to create image pixels. Each pixel is made of three such fluorescent lights – red, green and blue lights. To create a wide range of colors, intensity of these lights is varied accordingly.

3. Digital Projector:

Digital projector is also called as digital projection display system. It is a specialized computer output device and projects an enlarged image of the computer output on the projector screen. Whether a business or classroom presentation, it gets motivation when backed with projections. For the images, graphs and figures are made easier to explain and understand for both the presenter and observer. Today it is one of the most commonly used output device around the globe.

There are two main types of digital projection display systems.

1. **LCD Projection-** Advantages of LCD technology includes efficiency, ease of brightness and contrast adjustment, and high image resolution.
2. **DLP Projection (Digital Light Processing)** – Advantages of DLP technology include light weight, high contrast, and lack of pixelation

2.4. CENTRAL PROCESSING UNIT - CPU

CPU will process the data, which is delivered by the input unit. It has three components:

1. Control Unit
2. Arithmetic Logic Unit
3. Memory Unit

It is arranged as in the following diagram:

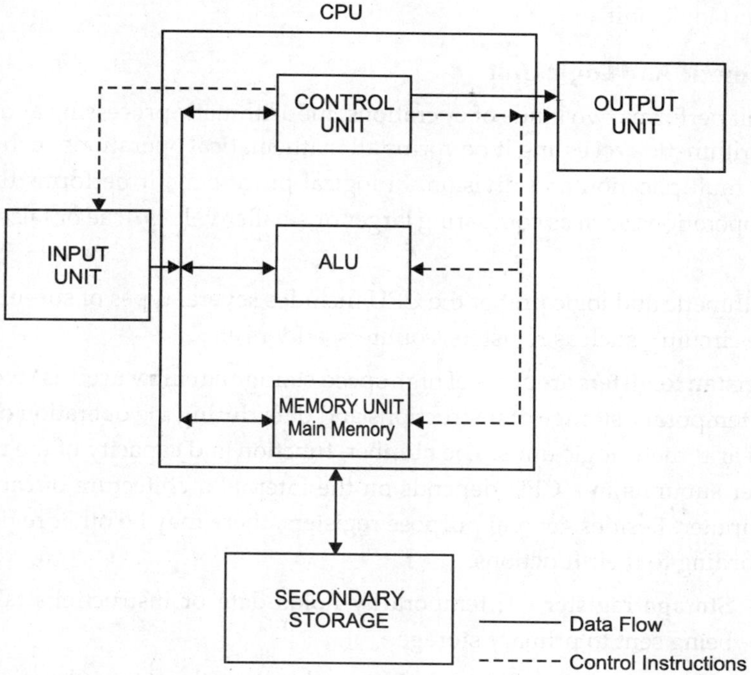

2.4.1. Control Unit

It controls the overall operation of the computer system. It is considered as the heart of the computer system. It controls all the other units, directs them to operate in a proper way and co-ordinates various operations performed. It instructs the input device to transfer the data and instructions to the main memory and then to the arithmetic and logic unit (ALU). Then, it sends the processed result from ALU to the memory unit for storage and transfers it to the visual display unit or to the printer.

The control unit coordinates the various parts of the computer system - the arithmetic logic unit, the memory unit and the peripheral units. Besides, it controls the flow of data into, from and within the main storage as per the program instructions.

To perform its control operations effectively and quickly, the control unit has four basic components. They are:

1. Instruction Register
2. Decoder
3. Address Register and
4. Instruction Counter

The instruction register receives one by one the instructions to be executed in the required sequence. Then, the operation code of the instructions is transferred to decoder, which decodes the operation code. And it activates the appropriate circuits of the arithmetic and logic unit to perform the operation. The address register enables the data in the location specified in the instruction to be transferred to a specified accumulator for the arithmetic and logic unit.

2.4.2. Arithmetic And Logic Unit

This unit performs two kinds of operations, the arithmetic processing and logical processing. In arithmetic processing it performs all mathematical operations such as addition, subtraction, multiplication and division. In logical processing, it performs the relational and logical operations such as comparing larger or smaller values, true or false statements, etc.

The arithmetic and logic unit of the CPU includes several types of sub-units and special purpose circuitry such as registers, counters, adders etc.

(*a*) **Register:** Registers are areas of high speed storage circuitry used as "work area" for the temporary storage of instructions and data during the operation of the control and arithmetic logic units. The number, function and capacity of the registers and other subunits in a CPU depends on the internal architecture of each particular computer. Besides general purpose registers, there may be other registers named according to their functions.

(*i*) **Storage register** - It temporarily holds data or instructions taken from or being sent to primary storage.

(*ii*) **Address register** - It may hold the address of the storage location of data, or the address of an input/output device, or a control function.

(*iii*) **Instruction register** -It contains the instructions being executed by the CPU.

(*iv*) **Accumulator** - It is a register which accumulates the result or arithmetic or logic operations.

(*v*) **The multiplier** - quotient register - It holds either a multiplier or a quotient.

(*vi*) **Floating point register** - It is used for floating point arithmetic operations.

(*b*) **Buses:** Buses carry data from registers to the ALU and results back to the register unit.

(*c*) **Counter:** The counter is closely related to the register. It is a device whose contents can be increased or decreased by a specific amount. The instruction counter is also called the instruction address register and contains the storage location address of the computer instruction being executed. The index register is a counter specifically set aside for modifying the portion of an instruction that indicates the address of data to be manipulated. This results in an operation known as "indexing" in which the CPU automatically repeats the performance of the same instructions until all of the data covered by instruction is processed.

(*d*) **Adders:** Adders are sub-units that perform the arithmetic operations of the arithmetic logic unit. They receive data from two or more sources, perform the specific arithmetic operation desired, and then convey the result to a receiving register such as the accumulator.

2.4.3. Memory Unit

The memory unit is the part of the computer that holds data and instructions for processing. Even though it is closely associated with the CPU, actually it is separate from it. The computer memory is nothing but storage of data in electronic computers. The evolution of the computer memory starts with latches, relays and flip-flops. Core memories, magnetic drum, magnetic disk, optical storage, cache and registers follow it. In memory unit, the data and instructions are stored and are transferred to ALU during processing. Similarly, the processed results are stored again for further calculations or sent to the output unit. The main storage consists of several static and dynamic devices.

The computer need not remember all the data, all the time. Some of the data or instructions can be kept elsewhere for retrieval at a later stage. Only the data that is being processed and the instructions to process it are stored internally, whereas the data and instructions that are required later are stored externally. The internal storage is commonly called as the primary memory or the main memory. This is usually limited. But, the external storage or the secondary memory or auxiliary memory is unlimited.

The different types of computer memory can be seen in the following diagram:

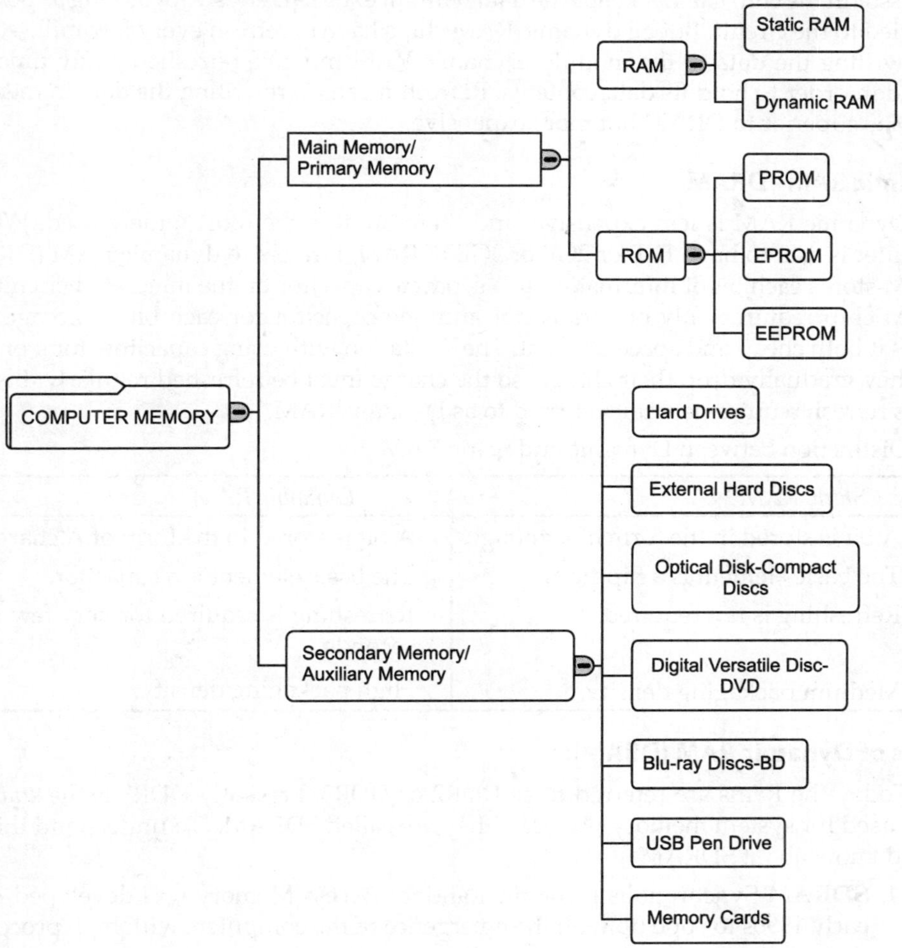

Let us discuss the main memory first. There are two types of main memory, Random Access Memory (RAM) and Read Only Memory (ROM).

2.4.3.1. Random Access Memory - RAM

RAM is the main memory in a computer system. RAM is considered "random access" because any storage location can be accessed directly. That is, we can access any memory cell directly, if we know the row and column that intersect at the particular cell. This is the area where the data and instructions actually get stored during the processing. The operating system, application programs and the data being used are kept temporarily in RAM, so that they can be accessed by the processor at fast. The more RAM a computer has, the more data a computer can process. RAM is also called as Read/Write memory. It is the temporary memory of a computer and is 'volatile'. It holds its data as long as the computer is switched on and all contents of RAM are deleted once the computer is turned off. The RAM can be either static or dynamic. Although both types require constant electrical current to function, they have some important differences.

Static RAM -SRAM

Static RAM is the main RAM in the memory hierarchy. It is placed next to the processor in the chip itself. It keeps the data without external refresh, for as long as power is supplied to the circuit. But all dynamic RAM chips have to refresh every few milliseconds by rewriting the data to the module. Dynamic RAM must be refreshed many times per second in order to hold its data contents. Refresh means is rewriting the data in memory. SRAM is superior to DRAM but more expensive.

Dynamic RAM - DRAM

Dynamic RAM is less expensive, and therefore it is the most widely used. When a computer is said to have 1GB or 2GB or 3GB of RAM, it refers to dynamic RAM (DRAM). DRAM stores each bit of information in a separate capacitor on the integrated circuit. The DRAM chip requires only one transistor and one capacitor for each bit of storage. This makes it both cheap and space efficient. The limitation with using capacitors for storage is that they gradually drop their charge, so the charge must be refreshed regularly. Because of this refresh requirement it is referred to as Dynamic RAM.

Distinction between Dynamic and Static RAM

Static RAM	*Dynamic RAM*
1. A bit is stored in the form of a voltage.	A bit is stored in the form of A charge.
2. The basic element is a flip-flop.	The basic element is a capacitor.
3. Refreshing is not required.	Refreshing is required for very few milli seconds.
4. Medium packaging density.	High packaging density.

Types of Dynamic RAM (DRAM):

Today the Rams are referred to as DDR2 or DDR3. Presently DDR3 is the standard RAM used for system memory. Actually they are called SDRAM. To understand this, we should know about SDRAM.

1. **SDRAM-**Synchronous Dynamic Random Access Memory was developed in the early 1990s to cope up with the emergence of the computers with high processing

capabilities. Traditional DRAM used an asynchronous interface, which means it operated independently of the processor. And, DRAM was not suitable when the memory could not keep up all of the requests to the processor. So to cope up with the requirements SDRAM was developed. SDRAM streamlined this process by synchronizing the memory's responses to control inputs with the system bus, allowing it to queue up one process while waiting for another. It made the computers to execute tasks much more quickly than with DRAM technology.

But, SDRAM had certain limitations. Initially, SDRAM operated via a single data rate (SDR) interface and could accept one command per clock cycle. Due to development of information technology, more complex requests were demanded by the users and the memory could not keep phase with such requests and this reduced the final performance of the system.

2. **Double Data Rate (DDR):** In the beginning of 21st century, a new interface method called Double Data Rate (DDR) was developed. It enables the memory to transfer data on both the rising and falling edges of the clock signal and thus, giving it the capability to move information nearly twice as quickly as with regular SDR SDRAM. Another advantage of this development is that the memory could run at a lower clock rate (100-200MHz), using less energy (2.5 volts), and achieve faster speeds (transfer rates of up to 400 MTps).

   DDR2: As technology progressed and processors became still more powerful and demanding, DDR alone became insufficient. As a result, in 2003, DDR2 was introduced with an internal clock running at half the speed of the data bus. It increased the speed at 200-533MHz. And around 2006, the DDR2 memory was gradually improved to 667MHz and 800MHz to match processor bus speed.

   DDR3: In 2007, DDR2 memory was made available at higher speed and DDR3 was designed with 1,066MHz speed and the power usage was also reduced to 1.5 volts. And finally, the DDR4 is in development, and will be introduced soon.

2.4.3.2. Read Only Memory-ROM

Another type of computer memory is the read-only memory (ROM). It is used for micro programs not available to normal programmers. The term read-only means the storage cannot be altered by regular program instructions. The information is stored permanently in such memory during manufacture. The information from the memory may be read out but fresh information cannot be written onto it. It is also known as firmware, is an integrated circuit programmed with specific data when it is manufactured. ROM chips are used not only in computers but also in most of the electronic items.

The special feature of ROM is, its stability. That is, the values stored in ROM are always there, whether the power is on or not. Thus, it is called non-volatile storage. And it has the feature of security in the sense that ROM cannot easily be modified and it provides a measure of security against accidental or malicious changes to its contents. It is most commonly used to store system-level programs needed for the PC all times. For example, the system BIOS program is stored in ROM.

Different Forms of ROM:

The different forms of ROMs are given below:

1. **Programmable Read-Only-Memory (PROM):**

   Producing the ROM chips totally in small quantities is expensive and time-consuming. For this reason, mainly, developers created a type of ROM known as programmable read-only memory (PROM). These are supplied in blank form and the users can program their own requirements by applying high voltage pulses to the data output pins of the device.

   Once programmed, these devices cannot be reprogrammed so that they become Read Only Memory and are useful in development systems in which the program has been well proven.

2. **Erasable Programmable Read-Only-Memory (EPROM):**

   Even though PROMs are inexpensive per chip, the cost can add up over time. To solve this problem, the erasable programmable read-only memory (EPROM) chip was developed. These chips can be rewritten many times. Erasing an EPROM chip requires a special tool that emits a certain frequency of ultraviolet light. EPROMs are configured using a tool called EPROM programmer that provides voltage at specified levels depending on the type of EPROM used. We cannot erase the contents of the EPROM selectively. Because the EPROM eraser is not selective, it will erase the entire EPROM. To a strong Ultra-Violet Light for about 20 to 50 seconds it can be then reprogrammed in a similar way like a PROM.

3. **Electrically Erasable PROM (EE-PROM):**

   The EPROMs are reusable. But they require special equipment and involves large amount of labour-intensive process to remove and reinstall them each time when a change is necessary. Moreover, the changes cannot be made incrementally to an EPROM. For this, the whole chip must be erased. These problems are greatly solved with the development of Electrically Erasable Programmable Read-Only Memory (EEPROM).

In this type, the information can be changed by electrical signals. They can be reprogrammed electrically without removing from circuit board. And for this, one does not need ultra-violet light to erase the program. It needs electricity and the knowledge of erasing the programmable ROM, in using electricity.

The main features of this chip are as follows:

(*a*) No need of ultra-violet light to erase the program.

(*b*) The information can be changed by electrical signals.

(*c*) The chip does not have to be removed for rewritten.

(*d*) The entire chip need not be completely erased to change a specific portion of it.

Now we can understand the concepts discussed above with the following diagram of memory hierarchy in a computer system.

2.4.3.3. Virtual Memory:

It is a common part of most operating systems of microcomputers. It has become so common because it provides a major benefit at lesser price for users. Most of the computers today have lesser capacity of RAM available for the CPU to use. But this lesser capacity of RAM may not be enough to run all of the programs that most users expect to run at once. For example, if we load our computer RAM with operating system, a Web browser, word processor and many other applications simultaneously, the memory capacity may not be enough to hold all the items that we have loaded in to. Hence the system will not respond to our requirements. This problem is now solved with virtual memory. With virtual memory, the computer can look at RAM, for areas that have not been used recently and copy them onto the hard disk. This frees up space in RAM to load the new application. The new memory location created temporarily is called virtual memory. It exchanges programs and data between the hard-disk and RAM as the CPU requires them for processing. If more virtual memory is created, the speed of the system will slow down and times it gets struck and hang for some time. The CPU can access RAM in nanoseconds but hard-disk in milliseconds and thus, virtual memory is much slower than RAM. If we close some applications, then it will come to normal state. To solve this problem, the capacity of the RAM should be increased.

2.5. SECONDARY STORAGE DEVICES

Secondary storage is also called as auxiliary storage. It is separate from the computer itself, that is, from CPU. We can store all types of data and other audio and video files in these devices. It is necessary because primary memory is volatile in nature. In large organizations both Government and private sectors, it is necessary to take regular backups and are stored outside the computer systems. Besides, for data transfer and reporting also these devices are very much useful. There are many such devices available today with varying size, technology and storage capacity. Let us see some of those devices herein below:

Most of the storage devices we are acquainted with come under this category. They are not a part of the processor. People make use of these devices, so that the storage capacity of the computer can be increased. Like the ROM, the secondary computer storage is also nonvolatile. The information stored on these devices is retained, even if the computer has been switched off.

1. Hard Disc/Drive

It is a form of secondary storage that stores data on platters divided into concentric tracks and sectors, which can be read by a read/write head that pivots across the rotating disks. The information stored in a disc can be read many times without affecting the stored data. Hard disc is an important part of secondary storage and is fixed in the computer and is non-removable. It is also called as internal hard drive. It stores and provides relatively quick access to large amounts of data on an electromagnetically charged surface or set of surfaces. Today's computers typically come with a hard disk with large capacity of storage up to 1TB. Now- a- days, external hard discs are also common in use in addition to internal hard disc to store large volume of data and is portable.

2. Optical Storage Devices:

It is a form of secondary storage in which a laser reads the surface of a reflective plastic platter. This category includes Compact disk, DVD and Blu-ray discs.

Compact Disc-CD: It is an optical disc and is a flat, circular, plastic disc coated with material on which bits may be stored in the form of highly reflective areas and significantly less reflective areas, from which the stored data may be read when illuminated with a narrow-beam source, such as a laser diode. These discs are capable of storing enormously high amount of data in a limited amount of space. The optical disc storage system consists of a rotating disk coated with a thin layer of metal that acts as a reflective surface and a laser beam, which is used as a read/write head for recording the data onto the disc. There are different types of CDs including write once read many CDs, rewritable CDs etc. Their normal capacity is up to 700MB.

Digital Versatile Disc-DVD: They are also optical discs. The format of storing data in the digital versatile discs (DVD) is similar to that of a compact disc. The difference lies in the storage capacity. DVDs are also used as backup device. The most common DVD type is DVD-5 (1 side, 1 layer) having 4.7GB of storage. DVDs are available in the following specifications:

Single sided, Single layer -4.70GB

Single sided, Dual layer -8.50GB

Double sided, Single layers- 9.40GB

Double sided, One side single layer, one side dual layer-13.20 GB

Double sided, Dual layer- 17GB

Blu-ray Disc-BD: Blu-ray discs are 120 mm in diameter and 1.2 mm thick and are similar to the CDs and DVDs in their looks. Blu-ray is the name of a new optical disc format jointly developed by the Blu-ray Disc Association (BDA), a group of the world's leading consumer electronics, personal computer and media manufacturers (including Apple, Dell, Hitachi, HP, JVC, LG, Mitsubishi, Panasonic, Pioneer, Philips, Samsung, Sharp, Sony, TDK and Thomson). The format was developed to enable recording, rewriting and playback of high-definition video (HD), as well as storing large amounts of data. The format offers more than five times the storage capacity of traditional DVDs and can hold up to 25GB on a single-layer disc and 50GB on a dual-layer disc. It requires a special drive to read and write.

3. USB Pen Drive

They are also known as Thumb Drives, Static Drives and Flash Drives. The USB pen drives consist of a NAND type flash memory. It has an integrated Universal Serial Bus (USB) interface. They are non-volatile and data can be rewritten on them. They are very small in size, but have very large memory space. They are extremely portable because there are no moving parts and they are very reliable.

4. Memory Cards

Memory card is a small storage medium used to store data such as text, pictures, audio, and video, for use on small, portable or remote computing devices. Most of the current products use flash memory. There are different types of including the SD card (secure digital card), the CF card (CompactFlash card), the SmartMedia card and the MultiMedia Card. Data is stored in digital format on the memory cards. They can be used in various electronic devices from hand held computers, mobile phones, cameras, etc. They are also rewritable. Although they are small in size, they can store a high amount of data.

There are many other devices like flash drives etc are available and the use of secondary storage devices are enormous and are inevitable in the modern day world in all fields.

2.6. UNDERSTANDING MEMORY OPERATION IN COMPUTER

CPU is processing unit and all processing is done in it. For the processing operation requests are sent to the CPU. The CPU does not have a memory of its own to hold data and instructions for performing the process request. Hence, the data and instructions are stored in the RAM.

Ram is connected to CPU through bus lines and it takes time to access the stored information in RAM. This cause delay in processing and there is a small time lag between receiving information to be processed. Hence, the demand for speedier reference is raised and as a result the cache memory is designed. Now the architecture of the CPU can store required data and instructions in the CPU cache. This will theoretically reduce the delay. This cache memory amount is really small and has levels L1, L2, L3. They are arranged in the order as shown in the following conceptual diagram:

CONCEPTUAL ORGANISATION OF MULTILEVEL MEMORIES IN COMPUTER

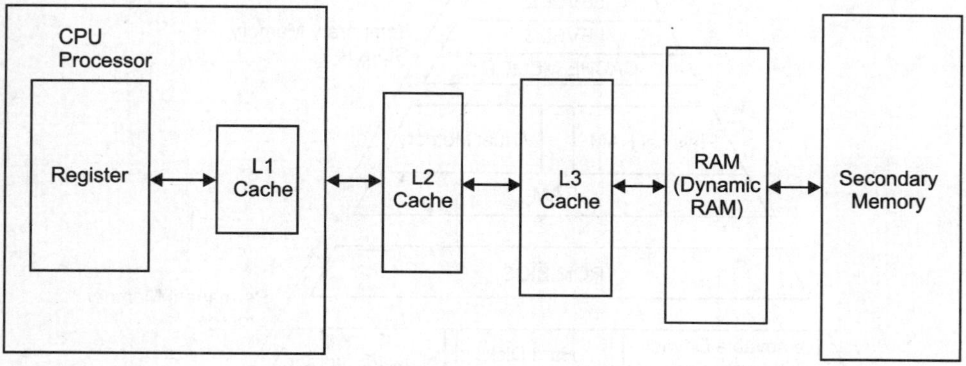

The L1, L2, L3 cache memory is Static RAM and is small but very expensive.

Level 1 cache- a memory cache built into the microprocessor. In the processor, there may be more than one core. The L1 Cache is the fastest Cache and each core has its own L1 cache. It the fastest memory and the core processor first accesses L1 for the data.

Level 2 cache- cache memory that is external to the microprocessor. Now-a-days it is also built into the processor and becomes internal. The L2 Cache is slower than L1 cache memory. And L2 cache is the 2nd cache that the core processor searches for its data. It is bigger than L1.

Level 3 cache- is the name for the extra cache built into motherboards between the microprocessor and the main memory. The L3 Cache is shared between all of the cores in the CPU. For example, in the Core i7, L3 is shared between all 4 cores, and bigger than both L1 and L2.

In simple terms, CPU first searches L1 cache, if data is not found, then it goes to the next bigger cache L2, if it does not find the required data in L2, then it goes to the next bigger Cache L3 which is Shared between all cores in the CPU.

Working of Memory:

In computer, the term memory denotes any form of electronic storage. Generally it is considered as fast and temporary forms of storage. For example, if the CPU of our computer were to constantly access the hard drive to retrieve every piece of data it needs, it would operate very slowly. When the information is kept in memory, the CPU can access it much more quickly than before. Most forms of memory are intended to store data temporarily. The structure and design of the computer memory can be seen in the following diagram.

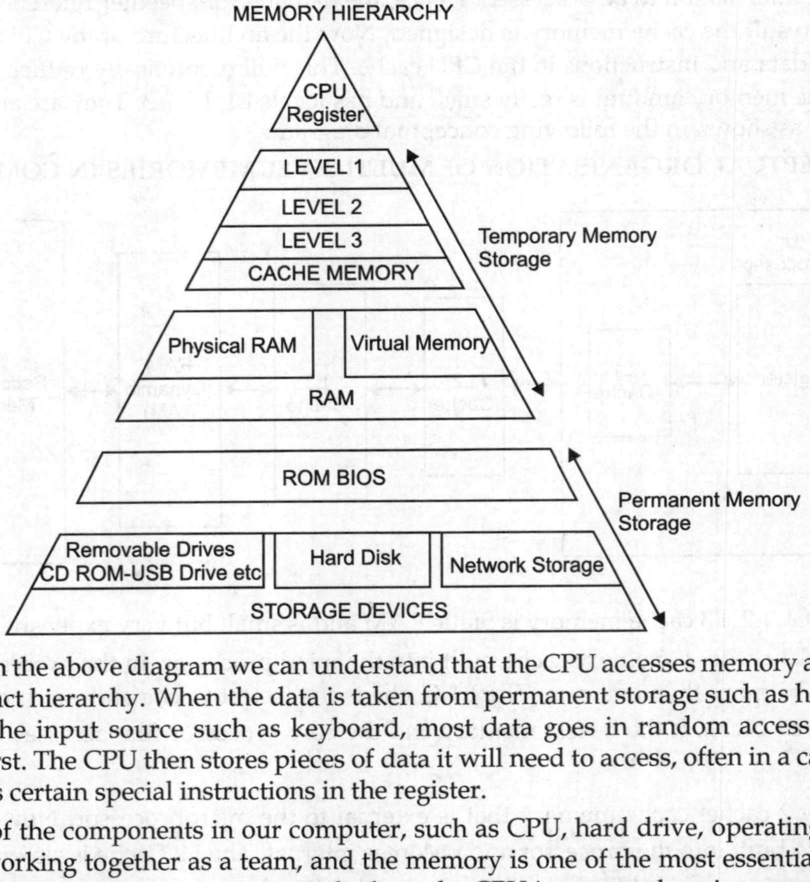

From the above diagram we can understand that the CPU accesses memory according to a distinct hierarchy. When the data is taken from permanent storage such as hard drive or from the input source such as keyboard, most data goes in random access memory (RAM) first. The CPU then stores pieces of data it will need to access, often in a cache, and maintains certain special instructions in the register.

All of the components in our computer, such as CPU, hard drive, operating system, etc, are working together as a team, and the memory is one of the most essential parts of this team. When the computer is switched on, the CPU is constantly using memory till it is shut down.

Let us see typical working of the computer memory.

1. When the computer is switched on, it loads data from ROM and performs a Power-On Self-Test (POST) to make sure all the major components are functioning properly. As part of this test, the memory controller checks all of the memory addresses with a quick read/write operation to ensure that there are no errors in the memory chips. Read/write means that data is written to a bit and then read from that bit.
2. The computer loads the basic input/ output system (BIOS) from ROM. The BIOS provides the most basic information about storage devices, boot sequence, security, Plug and Play (auto device recognition) capability etc.
3. The computer loads the operating system from the hard drive into the system's RAM. Generally, the critical parts of the operating system are maintained in RAM as long as the computer is on. This allows the CPU to have immediate access to the operating system, which enhances the performance and functionality of the overall system.
4. When we open an application, it is loaded into RAM. To conserve RAM usage, many applications load only the essential parts of the program initially and then load other pieces as needed.
5. After an application is loaded, any files that are opened for use in that application are loaded ir.to RAM.
6. After the completion of the work, when we save a file and close the application, the file is written to the specified storage device, and then the file and the application are removed from RAM.

In brief, every time some information is loaded or opened, it is placed into RAM. This simply means that it has been put in the computer's main memory area so that the CPU can access that information more easily. The CPU requests the data it needs from RAM, processes it and writes new data back to RAM in a continuous cycle. In most computers, this shuffling of data between the CPU and RAM happens millions of times every second. When an application is closed, the processed file and other accompanying files if any are usually deleted from RAM to make space for new data. If the changed files are not saved to a permanent storage device before being removed, they will be lost.

Measurement of Theory

Term Abbreviation	Number of bits	Number of bytes	Number of Kilobytes KB	Number of Megabytes-MB	Number of Gigabytes GB
Bit	1	-	-	-	-
Byte	8	1	-	-	-
Kilobit	1024	128	-	-	-
Kilobyte KB	8192	1024	1	-	-
Megabit	1048576	13072	128	-	-
Megabyte MB	8388608	1048576	1024	1	-
Gigabit	1073741824	134217728	131072	128	-
Gigabyte GB	8589934592	1073741824	1048576	1024	1
Terabyte TB	87960930222208	1099511627776	1073741824	1048576	1024
Exabyte EB	9007199254740992	1125899906842624	10999511627776	1073741824	1048576

2.7. NEED OF MANY MEMORY SYSTEMS

Generally, a typical computer has cache memory, random access memory, virtual memory and a hard disk. These different types of memory systems are needed because fast and powerful CPUs need quick and easy access to large amounts of data in order to maximise their performance. If the CPU cannot get the required data it needs for processing immediately, it eventually stops and waits for it. Modern CPUs running at speeds of about 1 Gigahertz can consume massive amounts of data normally billions of bytes per second. The problem that computer designers face is that memory that can keep up with 1-Gigahertz. CPU is extremely expensive and cannot be afford by all. Hence, they have solved the cost problem by mixing up of different types of memory. That is, by using expensive memory in small quantities and then backing it up with larger quantities of less expensive memory.

REVIEW QUESTIONS

Short Answer Questions

1. Explain about IPO cycle
2. Explain the types of keyboards
3. Explain the following
   (*a*) Light pen
   (*b*) Mouse
   (*c*) Joystick
   (*d*) Scanner
   (*e*) Track ball
4. Write short note on OCR ,MICR
5. Explain the non-impact printers
6. Differentiate between impact and non-impact printers
7. What are the differences between LCD and LED monitors
8. Explain the block diagram of digital computer
9. Explain about the ALU
10. Write a short note on memory unit

Essay Type Questions

1. Explain the input devices
2. Explain the printers and its types
3. Explain about the output devices
4. Explain the types of monitors
5. Give a brief note on the operations in CPU with diagram
6. Explain in detail on memory unit
7. Explain about the RAM
8. Difference between RAM and ROM
9. Explain about the Memory operation in computer
10. Why do we need many types of memory systems? Justify your answer.

CHAPTER 3

Computer System

3.1. INTRODUCTION

COMPUTER SYSTEM

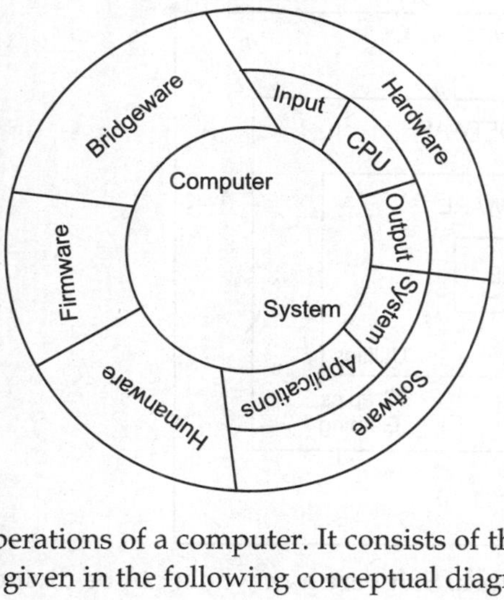

A computer system is a combination of various components. It includes both hardware and software. In addition to this, other components such as firmware, bridgeware etc. are also required for the smooth and effective functioning of the system. These concepts can be seen in the alongside diagram.

3.2. HARDWARE

The physical components of the computer, such as electrical, electronic and mechanical units are known as the hardware of the computer. That is, the input unit, output unit and CPU are called hardware. Thus hardware is all equipment involved in the processing operations of a computer. It consists of the components that can be physically handled. It is given in the following conceptual diagram of hardware:

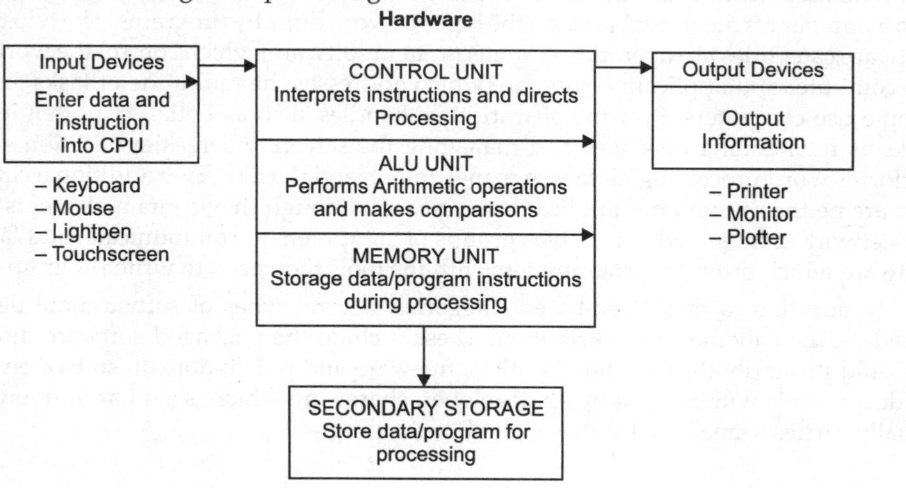

These items have been discussed elaborately in the previous chapter. Please refer to the second chapter for further details.

3.3. SOFTWARE

As we know computer is of mere hardware and cannot perform any task by its own. The user has to instruct the computer to perform an operation in a specified manner. The instructions given by the user is the software. That is, the set of instructions to manage, regulate and integrate the sequence of operations in a computer is a program and the programs are collectively called as known as software. The software is developed in the form of programs written in different computer languages. Without software the computer cannot do anything. Software is a set of instructions (programs) written in the prescribed form to get proper result. It acts as an interface between the user and the computer. Thus software can be defined as "the complete set of instructions written to solve a problem or to get the results in a desired way with a computer".

Hardware and Software Relations

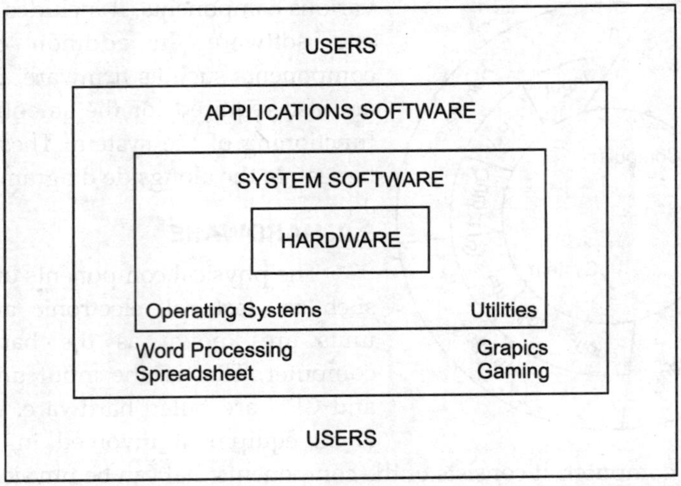

Thus software causes the hardware to do work. Software as a whole can be divided into a number of categories based on the types of work done by programs. The two primary software categories are operating systems (system software) which control the workings of the computer and application software which addresses the multitude of tasks for which people use computers. System software thus handles such essential, but often invisible, tasks as maintaining disk files and managing the screen, whereas application software performs word processing, database management, and the like. Two additional categories that are neither system nor application software, although they contain elements of both are network software which enables groups of computers to communicate, and language software which provides programmers with the tools they need to write programs.

In addition to these task-based categories, several types of software are described based on their method of distribution. These include the packaged software developed and sold primarily through retail outlets, freeware and public-domain software which is made available without cost by its developer, shareware which is similar to freeware but usually carries a small fee for those who like the program.

3.3.1. Types of Software

The software can be broadly classified into the following two categories. They are:

1. System Software and
2. Application Software

These software can be categorized as given in the following chart:

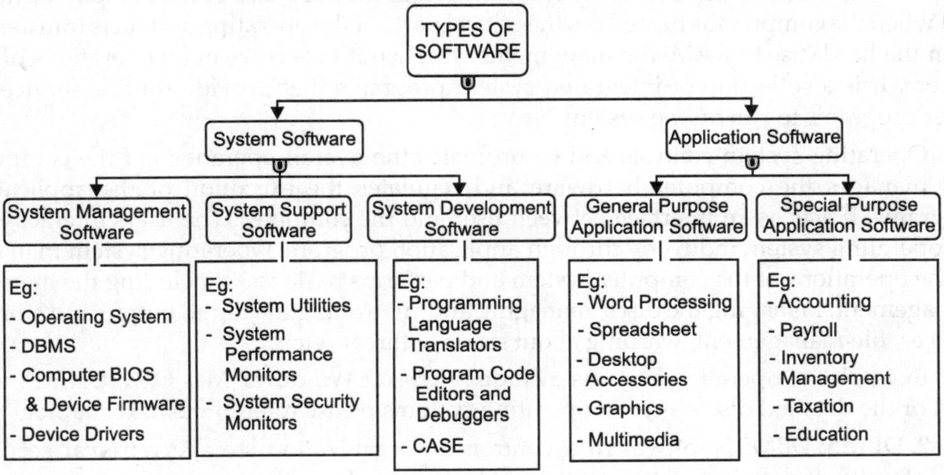

3.3.1.1. System Software

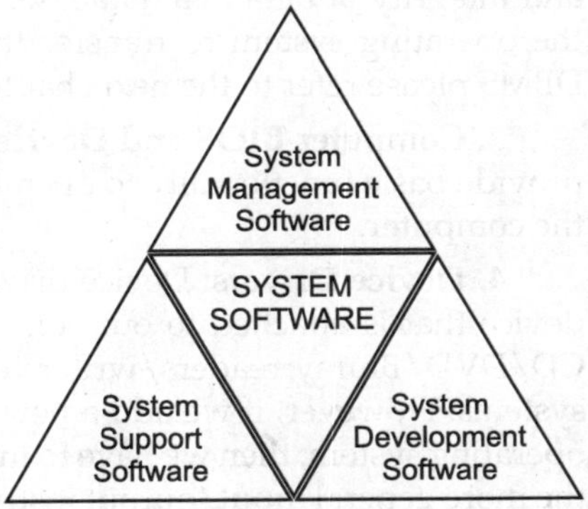

System software is a set of programs that control the operations of a computer and devices attached with the computer. It creates links between hardware components of the computer, application programs and users. It controls the execution of application programs. It is essential for the computer to perform operations because it keeps ready all devices of the computer for use. The user can concentrate on application programs without bothering to know about the details of internal working of the computer.

There are many types of system software and can be grouped as follows:

(*a*) **System Management Software:**

System management software are the programs that control and manage the hardware resources of the computer and facilitate the execution of other programs. The basic software programs included in this category are Operating Systems, DBMS and Communication Monitoring Software etc.

(*b*) **System Support Software:**

This category of software provides support services to hardware and other system programs run efficiently. Examples for system support software include System Utilities, System Performance Monitors, and System Security Monitors etc.

(*c*) **System Development Programs:**

System development programs assist in the creation of information processing programs and in developing user application programs. Examples for system development software include the Programming Language Translators, Editors and debuggers, CASE (Computer-Aided Software Engineering) packages etc.

Let us see some of the important system software herein below:

1. Operating Systems: Operating system is system software that is stored in the secondary storage device. Normally it is installed in the hard disc of the computer system and when the computer is turned on, the critical parts of the operating system is transferred from the hard disc to RAM–the main memory. Then it takes care of all operations of the system. It is a collection of integrated system programs that provide routine services to other programs to run on the system.

Operating system controls and co-ordinates the overall operations of the computer and manages the computer hardware and regulates the execution of the application programs. It acts as an interface between user and the computer. The users interact with the operating system indirectly through application program. Operating system manages all the operations of the computer system and performs basic tasks including the memory management, managing the discs, managing and controlling the input, output and storage devices, file management, warning about security threats etc.

Examples of operating systems include Microsoft Windows, Mac OSX, UNIX, Linux etc. For the detailed discussion on operating systems please refer to the next chapter.

2. DBMS: DBMS is software that controls the organization, storage, retrieval, security and integrity of data in a database. It accepts requests from the application and instructs the operating system to transfer the appropriate data. For the detailed discussion on DBMS please refer to the next chapter.

3. Computer BIOS and Device Firmware: The computer BIOS and device firmware provide basic functionality to operate and control the hardware connected to or built into the computer.

4. Device Drivers: Device drivers are the programs that control a particular type of device that is attached to our computer. There are device drivers for printers, displays, CD/DVD/Bluray readers/writers etc. Many device drivers are built into the Operating systems. However, if we add a new device and the required driver is not included in the operating system, then we have to install the new device driver. The device drivers convert the more general input/output instructions of the operating system to messages which the devices can understand.

5. System Utilities: System Utilities are utility programs that assist in maintenance or correcting the problems in a computer system. The commonly used utility programs include file correction and recovery software, virus detection and internet security software, file-compression software, Spam filters, pop-up blockers, uninstaller, disc scanner, disc defragmenter etc.

6. Programming Language Translators: Translator is a software program. It converts statements of a program written in one language to statements in machine language. Examples for translators are Assemblers, Compilers and Interpreters.

7. Editors and Debuggers: They are essential software in programming activities and are used for editing the codes and debugging.

8. CASE : Computer-Aided Software Engineering is the use of a computer-assisted method to organize and control the development of software. It is mostly used in large, complex projects involving many software components and people. In simple it is the use of computer-based support in the software development process.

3.3.1.2. Application Software

Application software is a computer program designed to help people perform a certain type of work. An application thus differs from an operating system (which runs a computer), a utility (which performs maintenance or general-purpose chores), and a language (with which computer programs are created). Depending on the work for which it was designed, applications can manipulate text, numbers, graphics, or a combination of these elements.

Application software utilizes the abilities of the computer directly for a dedicated task. It can be the software focused on a certain single specific task like word processing, spreadsheet or tax calculator or insurance premium calculator or playing of audio and video files etc. They can also be in the form of application packages. Application package consists of a group of applications combined to perform related functions. For example Microsoft Office comes with many office applications such as word processing, spreadsheet applications, database application, presentation software, publisher, outlook, etc.

Application software may be of either proprietary application software or off-the-shelf application software. Proprietary application software is the software specifically made to address a specific need of a company. It may be developed by the company itself with in its IT resources or it may be hired out and designed with the external third party software firms. Off-the-shelf application software is the software that is readily available in the market which can be used immediately. Normally they have the option that they can be customizable, i.e., the software can be adjusted to the user-specific requirements/ environments.

3.3.2. STRUCTURE OF SOFTWARE SYSTEM

The System software and Application software are structured in a manner as given in the following diagram.

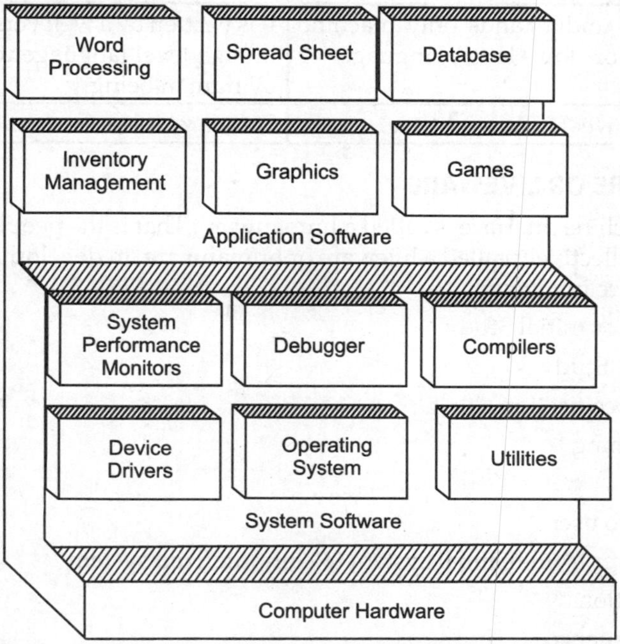

System software is required for the controlling and management related tasks in the computer. And the application software is designed to help the users to get done the real-world tasks.

3.4. DIFFERENCES BETWEEN HARDWARE AND SOFTWARE

The differences between hardware and software can be seen as follows:

Differences between Hardware and Software

SI. No.	HARDWARE	SOFTWARE
1.	Hardware is all the physical devices of the computer required to store and execute the software.	Software is collection of programs to bring the Hardware system into operation and enable the user to interact with the computer.
2.	Hardware is physical in nature.	Software is logical in nature.
3.	It consists of electronic components, like transistors, ICs, Diodes, Crystals, Resistors, insulators, etc. They are grouped under Input, storage, processing, control, and output devices.	It consists of numeral, alphabets, special symbols, signs, control key-words, etc. They are used in System software and Application software.
4.	The hardware consists of input unit, output unit, ALU and control unit of the CPU, main memory and auxiliary memory etc.	The software in categorized as System software and Application software and include operating systems, utility programs, language process, word processors, spreadsheet etc.
5.	It is almost constant for all types of computers except some additional built-in functions.	It will vary as per computer and its built-in functions and programming languages.
6.	Hardware understands only machine language or low level language or binary.	It is written by a well versed programmer in high level language which is readable by human being.
7.	Hardware wears out over time.	Software does not wear out over time.

3.5. HUMANWARE OR LIVEWARE

The man-machine interface is called a humanware. That is the people, who work with the computer is collectively called a liveware or humanware. In developing any system the following stages are involved:

1. Inception or Initial Study
2. Feasibility Study
3. Design Specification
4. Programming
5. Testing
6. Training to user
7. Changeover from manual system to computerized system
   (*a*) Operations
   (*b*) Maintenance
8. Enhancements if any

For a large commercial organization, the following computer personnel are needed for carrying out various operations involved in the above mentioned stages.

1. Systems Manager
2. Systems Analysts
3. Programmers
4. Data Base Administrators
5. Data Entry Operators
6. Network Administrators and many others

The Systems Manager is concerned with planning, monitoring and controlling all activities related to computerization. The systems analyst studies the problems to be solved in detail and prepares solution and program specifications. The programmer prepares computer programs based on the specifications given by the systems analyst. The data entry operator operates the computer system for entering data. And all people involving in the usage of computer system are collectively called as Humanware or Liveware.

3.6. FIRMWARE

The computer programs permanently stored in ROM/BIOS are called firmware. These programs are provided by the hardware manufacturer along with the computers. Generally, these are booting programs, which help in starting the computer. Such programs cannot be erased or overwritten.

3.7. BRIDGEWARE

The computer components and programs used to translate instructions and information written for one type of computer into a format that another type of computer can understand is called bridgeware. This is necessary because different computers are being made by different manufacturers.

REVIEW QUESTIONS

Short Answer Questions

1. Give the meaning of software.
2. Explain briefly the system software
3. What do you know about application software? Give examples.
4. What do you mean by hardware?
5. Write a short note on system development programs.
6. Give the meaning of the following:
   (*a*) Firmware
   (*b*) Bridgeware
   (*c*) Humanware

Essay Type Questions

1. Explain about the classifications of software in detail.
2. Explain the software structure.
3. Differentiate between the hardware and software.

CHAPTER 4

Operating Systems

4.1. INTRODUCTION

The operating system is a software program that acts as an interface between the users and the computer. It is a software package that allows the computer to function and control all of its activities. It manages all hardware components such as keyboard, monitor, printer, scanner etc. Every computer system requires some type of operating system that tells the computer how to operate and how to utilize other software and/or hardware that is installed onto the computer. It is the first piece of software loaded into memory when a computer starts.

The operating system controls and manages the functioning of hardware resources. Application program cannot get access to input/output devices and executing the instructions of the program modules by itself. For this it requires an interface and it is the operating system that performs these tasks through CPU on behalf of the application program. Operating system functioning as a platform for the application programs being executed. The user requests the application program to perform a particular task and the application program refers these requests to operating system. And the operating system gets it done with the system's resources as per the requests made by the users.

BLOCK DIAGRAM OF OPERATING SYSTEM

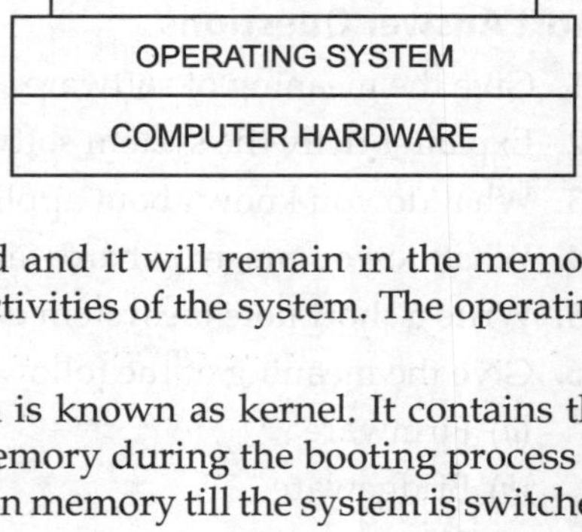

The following diagram explains the state of operating system in the computer system.

On system starts the operating system is loaded and it will remain in the memory until the system turns off. It will take care of all the activities of the system. The operating system consists of two parts:

1. **Resident Part:** This part of operating system is known as kernel. It contains the critical modules. It is loaded into the main memory during the booting process of computer and these modules reside in the main memory till the system is switched off.
2. **Non-resident Part:** This part of operating system consists of other supporting modules and is loaded into main memory when required.

4.2. CLASSIFICATIONS OF OPERATING SYSTEMS

Modern operating systems are developed in such a way as to be used in all types of computer configurations. And thus, they are machine independence. The different types of operating systems can be classified into two categories as shown in the chart below:

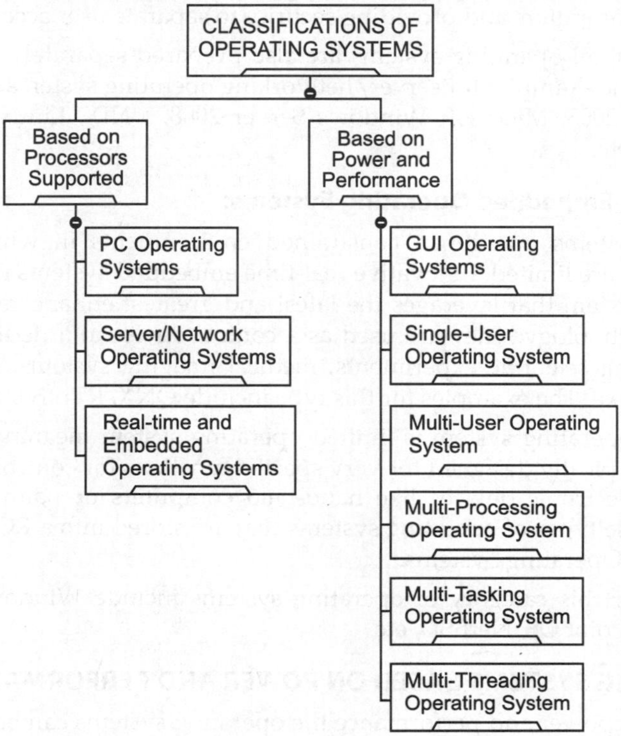

4.2.1. OPERATING SYSTEMS BASED ON PROCESSORS SUPPORTED

Based on processors supported the operating systems can be grouped into three types as follows:

1. PC Operating Systems:

PC operating systems are the personal computer operating systems. They are also called as 'Stand-alone' operating systems or single user operating systems. They are used in the micro/desktop/personal computers. In laptop computers also these operating systems are used. The most commonly used software under this category includes Microsoft Windows, Apple Mac OS X, and Linux. Windows 8 is the Microsoft's new operating system. The Microsoft using its 25 years' experience introduces Windows 8 with new touch interface. Windows 8 is an operating system can be used for both the computer and tablet.

2. Server/Networking Operating Systems:

Server operating systems are also called as network operating systems. A Network Operating System is a computer operating system designed to manage and support workstations, personal computers and servers normally connected to a local area network. Such operating systems typically reside on a server and control the devices or computers connected to the network.

They network operating systems have the features of maintaining the network connection to the server, dealing with users logging on, facilitating the file system to view folders on other computers and providing security to separate user accounts.

Today almost all operating systems are also prepared separately for servers called server editions. The examples for server/networking operating systems include Microsoft Windows Server 2003, Microsoft Windows Server 2008, UNIX, Linux, Mac OS X, and Novell NetWare etc.

3. Real-time and Embedded Operating Systems:

Real-time systems operate in constrained environments in which memory and processing power are limited. Innovative real-time embedded systems need a strong real-time operating system that leverages the latest and greatest enhancements in processor and hardware technology. They are used as a control device in a dedicated application such as controlling scientific experiments, medical imaging systems, industrial control systems and the like. The examples for this type include QNX, RTLINUX, VxWorks etc.

Embedded operating system is limited operating system meaning limited number of features. It is typically designed for very specific functions for controlling an electronic device. Special electronic devices like hand-held computers or palmtops etc. are also controlled by these types of operating systems that are stored into a ROM chip. Thus the name Embedded Operating Systems.

Examples for this category of operating systems include Windows CE, Palm OS, Symbian OS, PenPoint OS, NetBSD, etc.

4.2.2. OPERATING SYSTEMS BASED ON POWER AND PERFORMANCE:

Based on the power and performance the operating systems can be grouped into six types as follows:

1. Graphical User Interface Operating Systems (GUI):

The Graphical User Interface operating systems are the operating systems having the capability of using graphical elements. For the user interface a mouse is also attached to. GUI Operating Systems are much easier for end-users to learn and use because commands do not need to be known or memorized. Because of their ease of use, GUI Operating Systems have become the dominant operating system used by end-users today. Examples for the GUI Operating Systems include Microsoft Windows, Mac OS X etc.

2. Single-User Operating System:

Single-user operating system provides access to the computer system by a single user at a time. If another user needs access to the computer system, they must wait till the current user finishes what they are doing and leaves. Microsoft Windows, Apple Mac OS X are the common examples for this category.

3. Multi-User Operating Systems:

The Multi-User operating systems allow multiple users to utilize the system resources simultaneously and run programs at the same time. That is, it allows concurrent access by multiple users and work at the same time. Access to the computer system is normally provided via a network, so that users access the computer using a terminal.

Examples of multi-user operating systems are UNIX, Linux and in Windows early versions where single user and later, i.e., after Windows NT, Microsoft Windows 2000,

Windows Server 2003, Windows Server 2008, Windows HPC Server 2008, Windows Server 2008 R2, Windows Server 2012 are multi-user operating systems.

4. Multiprocessing Operating Systems:

Multiprocessing is the use of two or more processing units within a single computer system. The Multiprocessing operating systems provide for the use of multiple processors. These operating systems enable several programs to run concurrently. These are much more complicated than single-process systems because the operating system must allocate resources to completing process in a reasonable manner. UNIX, Windows 2000, Windows XP Professional, and Windows Server 2003 are examples of operating systems that can use multiple processors.

5. Multitasking Operating Systems:

Multitasking is the ability of a computer to execute more than one task/program at the same time. It is different from single-tasking where one process must entirely finish before another can begin. The multitasking operating systems allow multiple software processes to be run at the same time. Multitasking operating systems quickly switch between each computing task to give the impression that the different applications are executing multiple actions simultaneously. Multi-tasking operating system allows the user to run more than one task at once, so this leads to increased productivity. Most modern operating systems, like UNIX, Linux, and Windows, support multitasking.

6. Multithreading Operating Systems:

Multithreading means subdividing the specific operations within a single program/ application into individual threads. The parts or divisions of the program/application are called threads. Multithreading operating systems allow different parts of a software program to run parallel. The operating system allocates the processing time not only among different applications, but also among each thread within an application. The operating systems like Windows XP/2000, Solaris, Linux, Tru64 UNIX, Mac OSX support multithreading.

4.3. FUNCTIONS OF OPERATING SYSTEM

The operating system is the core software component of the computers which controls overall operations of the computer. It acts as an interface between the computer and the users. On boot up it is loaded into the main memory of the computer so that computer becomes in live and is able to respond the commands issued by the users. An Operating System is thus most important program that runs on a computer. It manages and coordinates computer resources and provides the following functions:

1. Provides User Interface:

Operating systems provide an interface between the user and the computer and manage large number of applications. User interface means the communication between users and the computer systems. The user interface services are provided in two ways:

(*a*) Services directly available for end users through all kinds of I/O devices, such as mouse, keyboard, monitor, printer etc.

(*b*) Services for application programs, which in turn provides services for end users.

Users interact with application programs and computer hardware through the operating system– the interface. Today generally all operating systems provide windows-bases Graphical User Interface to the users, in which graphical objects called icons are used to represent commonly used features or commands.

2. Controlling and Communicating with Peripheral Devices:

The main function of the operating system is communicating and controlling peripheral devices. The modern operating systems have a feature called plug and play/use. That is, just attaching a new peripheral to the computer and start using it is possible now.

3. Memory Management

The most important component of the computer system is memory. It is used to store all the instructions given by the user. It is very difficult to manage the entire memory area effectively. To manage the whole memory efficiently the operating system divides the memory into four different types. They can be categorised as under:

(*a*) Paged memory allocation

(*b*) Segment memory allocation

(*c*) Contiguous memory allocation

(*d*) Partitioned memory allocation

The instruction stored in the memory can be modified or deleted by the user. The memory area allocated for each file can be reused or modified by the operating system.

4. Processor Management

The program given by the user is converted into machine readable form and is called as process. The devices used to execute the process are called processors. The processors may be hardware or software. The process may be the operating system programs or application programs. The main objective of the processor is to allocate the process to the processors and manage the processors. A process can work in three states:

(*a*) **Running State:** A processor executes the process is called running state.

(*b*) **Blocked State:** During the processing of operation the second task is not processed until the first one is completed. So it will wait for the processor to complete the first process. This state is called blocked state or wait state. In multi-processing environment it is handled in a different way more effectively.

(*c*) **Ready State:** A processor ready to execute the next process is called ready state.

All the processes done by the computer are controlled and managed by the processor management.

5. File Management

The main work of an operating system is to manage the data and information that is stored in the system. In general, we can call the computers as Information Processing Systems. Operating System is called as information resource because all the operations performed by the operating system are based on the information and data. Each module in the operating system will manage the data.

In simple terms, the operating systems create file structure on the computer hard drive where user data can be stored and retrieved. When a file is saved, the operating system saves it, attaches a name to it, and remembers the address of the file where it is kept. The way the operating system organizes information into files is called the file system. Generally the operating systems use hierarchical file system and the files are organized into directories/folders.

File system plays an important role in managing the information. They assist in creating new documents with various applications and allow the retrieval of files already created by some application.

6. Program Execution

To execute a program a number of tasks are to be performed. Instructions and data must be loaded to the main memory. I/O Devices and files must be made available and so on. These are handled by the operating systems.

7. Controlled Access of Files

In the case of files, control is based on the nature of the I/O device and the file format on the storage medium. The operating system handles them and provides protection mechanisms for the controlled access to the files. In the case of shared or public system environment, the operating system controls the system and the system resources. For instance, data is protected from the unauthorized users by facilitating control execution.

8. Facilitates Running Multiple Applications

Operating systems facilitate load and run many applications such as word processors, PowerPoint, spreadsheets and audio applications simultaneously. Modern operating systems support multitasking, i.e., the ability to run more than one application at a time. When a user requests a program, the operating system locates the application and loads it into the primary memory of the computer. When more applications programs are loaded, the operating system allocates the resources of the computer more effectively to get the work done smoothly in a hassle-free way.

9. Offers Built-in Utility Programs:

Operating system includes utility programs that give the user control over various features of the computer system. It uses utility programs for maintenance and repairs. Utility programs help identify problems, locate lost files, repair damaged files, and backup data. Such utilities are given in the system tools menu of the programs under Accessories. The utilities included are Disk Clean up, Disk Defragmentation etc.

10. Error Detection:

The operating system ensures correct computing by detecting errors in the CPU and memory hardware, in I/O devices, or in user programs.

11. Resource Allocation and Accounting:

The operating system facilitates allocating resources to multiple users. That is, it keeps track of the usage and records which users use how much and what kinds of computer resources for account billing or for accumulating usage statistics.

12. Facilitates Computer Network:

The computers connected on a network need to be able to share files and communicate with other computers. The operating system facilitates linking all the terminal nodes into the server and sharing of common resources.

4.4. FEATURES OF OPERATING SYSTEMS

Let us see the special features of selected operating systems right from the earlier operating system DOS.

4.4.1. DOS (Disk Operating System)

DOS stands for Disk Operating System. It is a single user operating system used in microcomputers. It is a command line interface operating system. Microsoft Corporation developed it for IBM 8086 microprocessor computers. It was the most popular operating system in microcomputers before the Windows.

The DOS is a set of computer programs. The main functions of DOS are to manage disk files, allocate system resources according to the requirement. It provides essential features to control hardware devices such as keyboard, screen, disk drives, printers, modems etc. Thus, DOS is a medium through which the user and external devices attached to the system communicate the command with the system. DOS translates communication issued by the user in the format that is understandable by the computer and instruct computer to work accordingly. It is also translates the result and any error message in the format for the user to understand. Today it is rarely used.

Features of DOS

1. Single user system
2. Machine independence
3. Program control
4. Peripheral management
5. Operating with Directories
6. Managing files
7. Processing commands
8. Managing input and output
9. Data securing
10. Using Batch files
11. Managing memory
12. Setting up environment
13. Command processing - DOS shell (a set of commands which is used to create the programs)
14. Operating with Assembler.

Advantages of DOS

The DOS provides the following advantages:

1. Machine independence
2. More security
3. User-friendly environment
4. More useful in commercial applications.
5. Error finding and recovery is more efficient
6. Facilities more graphical user interfaces.
7. Easy debugging

4.4.2. UNIX Operating System

The UNIX operating system was developed at AT&T Bell Laboratories in 1969. It provides a convenient environment for text processing and program development. It is a multi-user operating system and it can be used in all types of computer systems. It is based on multi-user, time-sharing and multi-programming concepts.

Features of UNIX

1. Written with the high-level programming language C
2. Initially designed for medium-sized minicomputers, and then moved to mainframe computers and personal computers.
3. For different hardware platforms, there are many different UNIX versions including AIX, Digital UNIX, Hp UNIX, Sco UNIX, which is a PC-based UNIX operating system
4. Mature and stable operating system
5. Graphical User Interface operating system
6. Simple and easy to understand
7. Machine independence
8. UNIX Shell - mechanism for interfacing between users and system (provides service to users).
9. Multiuser capability–allowing multiple users to utilize the computer and run programs at the same time
10. Multiprogramming
11. Multiprocessing
12. Multitasking capability
13. Time sharing
14. Contain Kernel–provides services to application programs
15. Hierarchical file system
16. Inter-process communication
17. Availability of utility programs
18. Possibility of background processing
19. Availability of software development tools
20. Pipes and filters–used to interface with the hardware devices
21. Memory management

Advantages of UNIX

1. Less cost
2. Simple to understand
3. Supports many languages
4. Helps in the development of software
5. Highly flexible
6. Runs on different hardware configurations
7. Machine independent.
8. Useful in scientific and other applications.
9. Sharing the database can easily be made.
10. File handling is easy

4.4.3. WINDOWS Operating System

Windows Operating System is an advanced operating system, developed by Microsoft Corporation, U.S.A. It is an improved version replacement of DOS. MS-DOS was the earliest consumer operating system that gained Microsoft worldwide attention. In the beginning, Windows was regarded primarily as a graphical user interface (GUI) that did little more than provide an easier and more visually pleasing way to use MS-DOS. The strength of the Windows operating system is its ability to do what its name implies. That is, it allows a computer user to have more than one program or process operating simultaneously in various windows on the computer screen.

Features of Windows

1. Graphical User Interface

Windows is a graphical user interface program. It provides user-friendlier interface to work on. Its improved graphical user interface makes learning and using windows more natural and easier for all types of users. It is more powerful, customizable and efficient. It provides the flexibility of using graphical icons and work interactively with the computer. User need not remember all operating system commands. He/she just has to move the mouse arrow key, known as mouse pointer, around the screen and select the required command by processing the click button. Each window, which represents programs, can be resized and moved around the screen. Multiple windows can appear on the screen at the same time giving user the flexibility of operating more than one. The entire screen is termed as windows desktop, on which all windows are displayed.

2. Type of icons (Small Pictures)

There are three types of icons:

(*a*) **Applications icons** – the minimized version of the currently running application programs. It appears at the bottom of the desktop and can be maximized.

(*b*) **Document icons** – the reduced document windows.

(*c*) **Program icons** – appear within program manager and clicking on these icons activate the associated applications and also load the related documents or files.

3. Enhanced User Experience:

Microsoft added advances to make the user experience more enjoyable and the development of software for the operating system easier. Windows 2.0 was the first to feature Control Panel, a tool that allowed the user to navigate a graphical interface to adjust settings on the computer.

4. Networking Support:

Subsequent advancements included peer-to-peer networking support, Internet support and dial-up networking capabilities. Software became "plug and play," which allowed users to insert diskettes/CD-ROM into their computer and install software more easily.

5. Compatibility:

Windows operating system offers increased compatibility with different types of networks and with a wide array of hardware and software. It also provides:

(*a*) Improved driver support

(*b*) Increased support for new-generation hardware and multimedia technologies

(*c*) Integration of the new Euro currency symbol

6. Reliability and Security:

The basic feature of Windows operating systems is its reliability and security. With its effective and powerful performance, they provide industrial standard reliability and the highest level of security.

7. Windows XP and Vista

The Windows XP and Vista operating systems can run in a more stable environment and use preemptive multitasking and multithreading to perform several actions at the same time. They offer enhanced multimedia, more powerful mobile features and integrated and seamless networking.

Microsoft Windows xp Professional   Windows Vista

8. Windows 7- 64-Bit Support and Touchscreen Functionality

Windows 7, released in 2009, is Microsoft's most recent version of the Windows operating systems. On the surface, it features full 64-bit support, remote media streaming, and touchscreen functionality (when paired with a touchscreen monitor).

Jump Lists - Windows 7 features a new tool call Jump Lists, which makes accessing your most used media and programs easier. The desktop features Snap, a new way to organize, order and size the windows on your desktop so that they are easier to read and compare

9. Microsoft Windows 8

Microsoft released the version of Windows 8 'Consumer Preview'. It is a prerelease version of Windows 8 to be launched this year. The Win 8 view has a series of square tiles that show the status of applications in real time. This revision of the interface is a revolutionary change in the standard user interface and may be integrated with the touch interface too.

10. Versatility:

The special feature of the forthcoming new Windows 8 operating system is its versatility. The new Windows 8 operating system will run on PCs, smart phones and tablets and the idea of a common interface for all electronic gadgets may now finally be realized. Microsoft assures that the OS is exceptionally friendly with a mouse and keyboard as it is with the touch interface. Windows 8 can run on Intel, AMD, and the smart phone ARM CPUs.

REVIEW QUESTIONS

Short Answer Questions

1. What is operating system?
2. Write a note on the operating systems based on Processors
3. Explain the following functions of operating system:
   (*a*) File management
   (*b*) Memory management
   (*c*) Processor management
4. Write a short note on windows operating system
5. Explain the features of UNIX Operating system

Essay Type Questions

1. Give the meaning of operating system with concept diagram
2. Explain the different classifications of operating system
3. What are the features of operating systems? Explain.
4. Explain the various functions of operating system.

CHAPTER

5

Computer Programming and Languages

5.1. PROBLEM SOLVING AND PROGRAMMING

As in the case of all branches of knowledge, computer also concerned with solving problems. The peculiar feature in solving problem with computer is its versatility in exploration. Here, the term problem refers to the requirements of the user for his/her routine business or mundane demands. It also includes the exceptional situations arise in all fields. Finding solution for exceptional or critical probletms requires exceptional skills, expertise with diversified thinking and logical reasoning in finding the best solution. Sometimes it is found that a computer alone cannot yield the solution that we are aiming for. But an acceptable solution can be arrived at by allowing interaction between the power of a computer and the application of human judgment. The issues with problem solving can be avoided, if all steps of programming are fully identified, clearly defined and followed. Let us discuss the various steps involved in problem solving herein below:

5.1.1. Steps in Problem Solving

The problem solving involves the following steps.

STEPS IN PROBLEM SOLVING

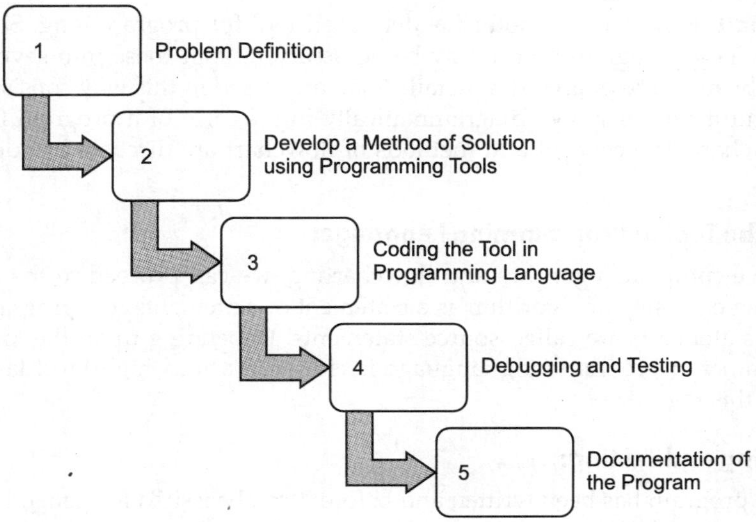

PROGRAMING

1. Problem Definition:

The first step in applying a computer to problem solving is to define the problem. Problems in commercial data processing are usually quite difficult to define because of the immense amount of details involved. With such problems, a great deal of fact finding must go on before the definition and this is a part of Systems Analysis. Even after a solution has been proposed, it is common for new facts to come to light to show that the definition of the problem was not entirely correct in the first instance. Problem definition begins with the concerned user/expert in the field where the problem arose, and not with the computer scientist. Since only the concerned person can explain what is involved, the process of defining problem starts therefrom.

This step involves defining the problem in all its aspects, i.e., input, output and processing requirements. In this stage, the following should be clearly identified:

(*a*) **Input available:** In what forms the inputs are available

(*b*) **Output needed:** On what forms the outputs are needed

(*c*) **Processing steps requested**: to convert the available input into the required output

Generally the programs are used by the people of all departments, viz., purchase, sales, stores, finance etc. Thus the end users decide the form of output involved and this is essential in defining the problem. This ensures that the programs developed will meet all the requirements of the users.

2. Develop a Method of Solution using Programming Tools:

The next step is to develop a solution for the problem defined above. Such a solution can be obtained by using the programming tools. The usual programming tools are as follows:

(*a*) Algorithm

(*b*) Flowchart

Algorithm: It is a step-by-step problem solving procedure that can be carried out by the computer. The concept of algorithm is dealt in detail later in this chapter.

Flowchart: Flowchart is another widely used tool for programming. Some jobs require a very large program and it may be necessary to split these into several parts so that the problem can be analysed in detail. A job organised in this way consists of several segments and it can be shown diagrammatically in the form of a program flowchart or system flowchart. The concept and methods of flowchart are discussed in detail later in this chapter.

3. Coding the Tool in Programming Language:

Once we complete algorithm and flowcharting, we can proceed to the next step of writing down each step of algorithm as a statement or statements in a programming language. The statements are called source statements. Depending upon the knowledge of the programmer, a programming language is chosen. Various high level languages are available in this regard.

4. Debugging and Testing:

After a program has been written and before it can be issued for general use, it must be thoroughly tested. When a program is incorrect, it will do one of three things. It may produce an incorrect result or it may halt in some error condition or it may fail to halt at all.

Generally, the most computing systems permit programs to run only for a limited time. If a program attempts to overrun than the time limit set, it will be halted by the system and an error report will be generated.

Thus the compiler is loaded into the system for compiling the program. The compiler checks the program for syntax errors, errors due to the programmer not following the rules of the programming languages etc. If there are no syntax errors, the compiler generates an object module.

If the compiler points out a syntax error, the statements are to be corrected and then compiled with the compiler. This process is called debugging and it is repeated till all syntax errors are corrected.

When the executable file is finally achieved, it is run with test data. The results obtained are compared with already available results, which were probably prepared manually. If they agree, we may release the program for use. If not, the error should be corrected and compiled and program will be run again for testing. This process is called testing.

5. Documentation of the Program:

As and when the program is developed, the steps carried out are recorded in suitable medium for future reference. This record forms the basis for documentation. Documentation contains details about:

(*a*) Input
(*b*) Output
(*c*) Processing steps
(*d*) Operating instructions to load and run the program
(*e*) Files that the program uses
(*f*) Name of the source program files
(*g*) Source listing
(*h*) Flowcharts

It also contains any abnormal conditions that may arise during program execution and steps to deal with such conditions.

Documentation is important for end users who are not aware of the program logic and operating steps. Often the programmers who develop the program have to modify the program in course of time. Documentation helps them do this. If others have to modify the programs, documentation helps them to study the programs and modify them.

Need for Proper Documentation: The proper documentation of programs is essential for several reasons:

1. Anyone using a program must know what it will and will not do, how to prepare data for it, and how to interpret the output.
2. Because programs have to be maintained, their structure and mode of operation must be meticulously recorded to make things as easy as possible for the maintenance programmer.
3. A program may require to be modified in the future– to make it more useful or to provide it with additional facilities. So whoever updates it must have access to full information including ideas that occurred to the original writer but which the writer did not have time to incorporate.

4. When two or more programmers cooperate to produce a large program or suite of programs, it is essential that proper documentation be provided from the outset in order to resolve disputes and ensure that everyone knows just what is expected of them.
5. Good documentation is invaluable in helping to solve problems caused by holidays, sickness, or staff turnover, as well as making it easier for a group leader to monitor and assess the work of the staff.
6. Proper documentation can make it easier to remember details that were worked out some time ago, or to get down to work again after a short holiday or a period of attention to other affairs.

Documentation layout

The following is a standard layout which could be adopted for the documentation of programs. For each program or group of programs, a documentation file should be maintained containing some or all of the elements listed below:

Sl.No	Base Division	Particulars
1	Identification	(a) Title Page (b) Contents (c) Program outline (d) Amendment record
2	Program Specification	(a) Basic concept of the problem (b) Narrative program description (c) Restrictions and limitations
3	User Information	(a) Specification of input (b) Description of output (c) Operating information
4	Programming Information	(a) Detailed program flowchart (b) Specimen test data (c) Program listing (d) Specimen of output from the test data (e) Record of program development (f) perating instructions

5.2. CONCEPT OF PROGRAMMING

Before going to know about programming languages, one should understand the meaning of the terms program and programming.

Program (Small)

"The sequence of instructions used to tell the computer what to do is called a program". It is simply a list of instructions that direct the computer to perform operations in a specified manner. The computer always does what the program tells it. But at the same time it does exactly what the program tells it without any reasoning. For example, supposing a program has been written to count l, 2, 3 and so on. The computer would start to count and will go on counting ... and on ...and on. It will still be counting even if the user went out after office hours and till it is stopped. Thus, what the user has to do in the program is tell it when to stop counting.

Programming

Working out the correct sequences of instructions is called Programming.

5.3. MEANING AND NEED FOR PROGRAMMING LANGUAGES

The computer being an electronic machine understands only the electric circuitry. It does not understand any of the languages that are used in our daily life. However, if we send an instruction to computer by the specified words, which it could understand, it will prove the power of computers. The specified words are the electronic signals that have only zeros and ones called binary and the machine code/program is written on it. In simple words, computers must be communicated by machine code to make them perform any type of operation. Thus, programming language is a means for communicating with the computers. Thus, we can define Programming Language as "an artificial language which is designed to communicate instructions to a computer and can be used to create programs that control the behaviour of a computer more precisely".

Programming languages are part of the software or programming aids provided by the manufacturer. It is a language used in writing programs to direct processing steps to be carried out by a computer. The operations of the computer are controlled by instructions. Instead of setting switches as with conventional instruments, the user can select a sequence of computer operations and processes by entering instructions through the same input device through which data is entered. Such instructions developed for accomplishing a particular task constitute a program. The languages are not flexible and free style but they follow very limited vocabularies and rigid rules of syntax and construction. The user has to learn the programming languages to communicate with the computer. Programming languages are generally divided into two components of syntax and semantics. Here the sense of syntax is form and of semantics is meaning.

5.4. CLASSIFICATIONS OF PROGRAMMING LANGUAGES

Programming languages are the ways of communication between users and the computer. The instructions are given to the computer to perform a particular task. These instructions are given to the computer according to the syntax/rules of programming language. Computer programming languages are used to develop programs or software.

Different types of programming languages are used in the common parlance. They are invariably used for various applications. They can be classified on the basis of the following bases:

1. Intended application areas such as business, numerical computing, simulation etc.
2. Whether the language is to be compiled or interpreted.
3. Operations such as pattern matching, list manipulation, unification etc.
4. Whether the processing required is sequential or parallel.
5. Syntax of the language such as ALGOL, APL and the like.
6. Whether the language is deterministic or not.
7. Nature of programming language such as procedural, functional, declarative, object-oriented.
8. Data structures such as lists, arrays, records, graphs, strings etc.

In brief, Programming languages are generally considered into two categories:

1. Low-level languages
2. High-level languages

Low-Level Languages:

The programming languages that are very close to machine code/binary (0s and 1s) are called low-level programming languages. Machine language and Assembly language are called low-level languages because they are machine dependent. The programs have to be written according to the circuitry configurations of the machines concerned and cannot be used for other configurations. That is why they are considered as low-level languages. These languages are discussed in detail under First and Second Generation Languages below.

High-Level Languages:

The languages which are user friendly, machine independent and are not binary are called as high-level languages. These languages are discussed in detail under Third, Fourth and Fifth Generation Languages below.

5.4.1. Classifications Based on Generations of Languages

Like computer generations, the programming languages can also be divided into five generations as follows:

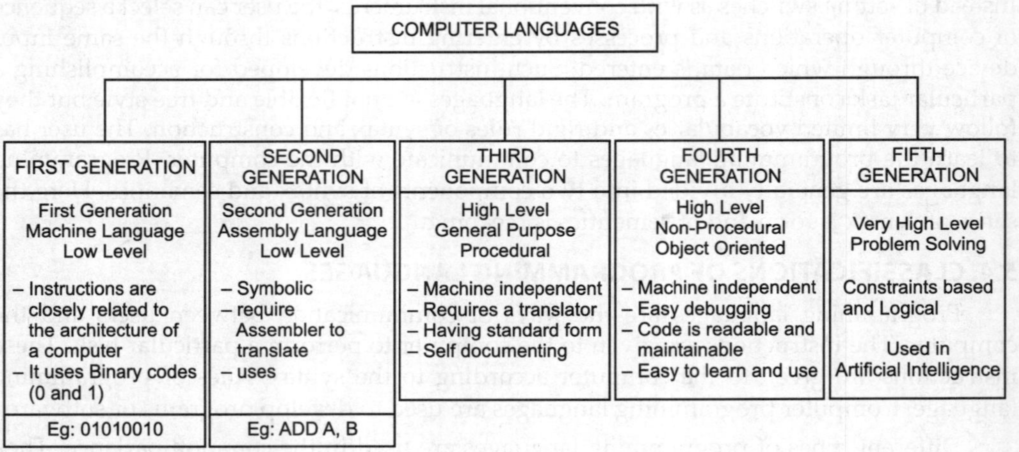

5.4.1.1. First Generation - Machine Language- 1940s:

Machine language is known as first generation of programming language. It is also called as machine code. The computer understands machine language-binary language directly. The instructions prepared in the machine language have two parts, the operation and the operand. The general format is:

Operation (Code)	Address (Location) (Operand)
Add in	A
Subtract 5 in	C

The first part tells the type of operations to be performed and the second part tells at which location such operations are to be performed. However, the computer works only with numeric codes. This language uses only two elements, either 0 or 1. Therefore it is called as Binary language. There is an instruction for every machine operation, and thus machine language is a one-for-one language. In machine language, every operation is specified in terms of the actual numeric code (binary), and each operand in terms of its absolute address in machine memory or in terms of a register number (or some combination of these). The basic architecture of most machines includes the following:

(*a*) Memory locations - contain data or instructions, organized, into bytes or words

(*b*) Registers - large enough to hold one work of information

(*c*) Instruction set - numerically encoded commands

Writing a Program in machine language is a very difficult process. Programming in machine language requires deep knowledge of the machine architecture. For each instruction different codes are used. The rules of machine language differ from one computer to another. Thus it is very difficult to modify the machine language programs.

Characteristics of Machine Language

The following are the characteristics of the machine language.

1. Programming in binary.
2. Direct control of each operation.
3. Each machine-language instruction does only one very low-level task
4. Each type of processor has its own set of specific machine instructions
5. A large number of instructions are required for even simple tasks.

Advantages of Machine Language

(*a*) Efficiency at run time.

(*b*) Simplicity of instruction - One-for-one language.

(*c*) The computer understands the language without translation.

Limitations of Machine Language

(*a*) Difficult to learn

(*b*) Time-consuming and tedious to write

(*c*) Subject to errors

(*d*) One machine language program written for one type of computer cannot be run on another type of computer without significant alterations

(*e*) Difficult to debug

5.4.1.2. Second Generation - Assembly Language -1950s:

Assembly language is another low-level programming language because the program instructions written in this language are close to machine language. It is also known as second generation of programming languages. To reduce the burden of the programmers, assembly/symbolic languages were developed. It uses symbolic notations to represent the instructions of the machine language. They employ symbols for both arithmetic and logical operations and even for location of addresses. These languages specify each operation and operand with a symbolic name. Assembly languages are machine dependent because their features depend on the hardware for which they are intended. A mnemonic is assigned to each set of ones and zeros that corresponded to a machine instruction. The programmer could then write his/her program using these easier-to-read mnemonics.

As the computer cannot understand any language other than machine language, the program written in assembly cannot be executed directly and the assembly language has to be translated into the form that the computer can understand. It is done with a translator program called Assembler. That is, the Assembler would take those mnemonics/symbolic instructions and translate them into ones and zeros. This is a special program usefully supplied by the computer manufacturer. The Assembler turns assembly code into machine code. This can be seen with the following diagram:

The Assembler simply translates each instruction in symbolic language to its machine language equivalent. They are machine dependent and used mainly for system software.

Characteristics of Assembly Languages:

The following are the characteristics of the Assembly languages:

1. It uses mnemonic codes to represent machine-language instructions
2. A translating program–Assembler is needed to translate it to machine language
3. Machine dependent
4. Low level language

Advantages of Assembly Language:

(*a*) Simple to understand and use.

(*b*) Easy to write and modify the programs.

(*c*) Since it is machine dependent the programmer can write the programs that suit

(*d*) The capabilities of the computer at hand.

(*e*) Time saving.

(*f*) Easy debugging.

(*g*) Manipulation of individual data is possible.

Limitations of Assembly Language:

(*a*) Machine dependent

(*b*) Knowledge of hardware is required.

(*c*) More number of statements are required to write even a simple program.

(*d*) There is little compatibility between the assembler languages used with various computers. The program coded in assembler language for one computer will not run on a computer of a different manufacturer unless the internal design is exactly the same.

5.4.1.3. Third Generation–High Level Languages–(Procedural Languages) - Late 1950s:

To write the program in low-level languages, the programmer should have a sound knowledge of hardware and should remember many operation codes. So, programming is a slow and time-consuming process when low-level languages are used. To overcome these difficulties several high level languages were developed. The introduction of the compiler in 1952 encouraged the development of third–generation computer languages. These languages enable a programmer to create program files using commands that are similar to English. Third-level computer languages have become the major means of communication between the digital computer and its user.

The high level language does not require the programmer to have a detailed knowledge of hardware of the computer. The high level languages contain statements that are much like English and Maths. So, the programmer can concentrate more on the logic of the problem than on the hardware details.

These Languages are procedure oriented. The development of mnemonic techniques and macroinstructions paved the way for the development of procedure-oriented languages. In a procedural language, a program is designed using procedures. A procedure is a sequence of instructions having a unique name. The instructions of the procedure are executed with the reference of its name. In procedural programming languages, the program instructions are written in a sequence or in a specific order in which they must be executed to solve a specific problem. It means that the order of program instructions is very important.

Macroinstructions allow the programmer to write a single instruction that is equivalent to a specified sequence of machine instructions. Several languages have been designed to process the problems of scientific or mathematical nature and others lay emphasis on file processing. In procedure-oriented languages, English–like and mathematical expressions are used. This improves overall efficiency and simplifies the communications process between the programmer and the computer.

High Level languages are closer to the natural languages used in a particular application. Therefore, the programmer can concentrate on the problem being programmed, rather than the features of the machine on which the program is to be implemented and with the details of computer operation. These languages are detached from the machine design and thus they are machine independent. The instructions of these languages may be equivalent to more than one instruction in a machine language. An instruction in these languages is usually called a statement.

The examples for the procedure-oriented languages are BASIC and FORTRAN for scientific or mathematical problems, COBOL for file processing and PASCAL and Ada, ALGOL, LISP, C, C++etc. for enhanced programming ability and general purpose programming.

Characteristics of High Level Language

The following are the important characteristics of high level languages:

(*a*) Machine independent

(*b*) English-like Commands and Keywords.

(*c*) Fewer Instructions

(*d*) Detailed knowledge of internal working is not required

(*e*) Standardised and portable.

(*f*) Better self-documentation is possible because they are easier to read and trace.

(*g*) Many development aids are available.

(*h*) Designed for particular tasks, (COBOL, FORTRAN, etc.)

Here compilers are used to convert the instructions from high-level languages to machine-readable form. The computer is a translating program used to translate the instructions of high level language into machine language. This can be seen with the following diagram:

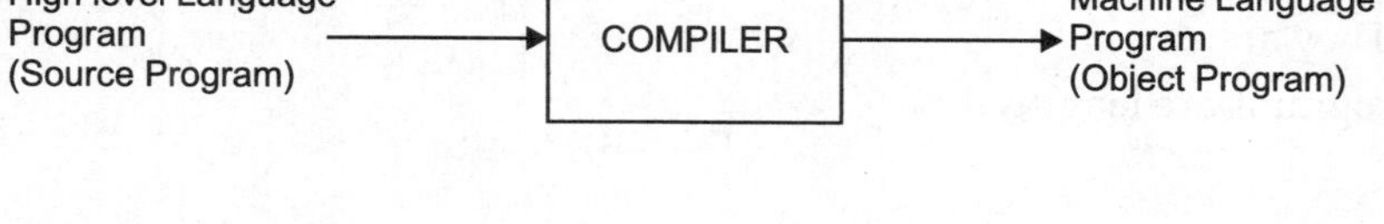

Instead of compilers, the interpreters may also be used for translating the high level languages into machine language. The main difference between the compiler and interpreter is that the compiler merely translates the programs in high level language into machine language and is not involved in their execution whereas the interpreter translates the instructions and involves in their execution also.

There are many high level languages available today, most of which have been standardised under American National Standards Code. Examples of high level languages are given below.

HIGH LEVEL LANGUAGES

Scientific Languages	Commercial Languages	Special Purpose Languages
1. BASIC	1. PL/[Programming Language]	1. IQL [Interactive Query Language]
2. PASCAL	2. COBOL	2. LOGO
3. FORTRAN	3. ADA	3. PILOG
4. COMAL [Common Machine Algorithmic Language]		4. CAL [Computer Assisted Learning]
5. ALGOL		5. SNOBOL [Sring Oriented Language]

Advantages of High Level Languages:

The high level language has the following advantages:

(*a*) Simple and easy to understand and use. They are easier to learn than symbolic languages.

(*b*) Machine independent.

(*c*) Higher efficiency.

(*d*) They require less time to write.

(*e*) Improved debugging capability. That is, high level languages provide for the possibility of syntax checking and more thorough type checking to detect errors.

(*f*) They provide better documentation.

(*g*) Relatively error-free programs can be written.

(*h*) Programs written in them are highly compact.

(*i*) Availability of program libraries.

(*j*) The source program language is not linked to the machine language of a particular computer. Therefore a degree of compatibility can be realized among the numerous types of computers.

(*k*) The programmer can use very sophisticated subroutines in his object program logic, which could be written only by a very advanced programmer in symbolic.

(*l*) The high level language can be designed to blend with the terminology with which the programmer is familiar.

(*m*) It reaches towards the ultimate objective of a system concept rather than the present programming concept.

Limitations of High Level Languages:

Though the high level languages have the above merits, they have certain shortcomings also. They are:

(*a*) Programs are lengthy.

(*b*) Storage constraint, that is, they require more space in memory.

(*c*) They process data at a slower rate than symbolic languages.

5.4.1.4. Fourth Generation Languages–Non-Procedural/Declarative –1980s:

Fourth generation languages are also high level languages but they are non-procedural or declarative languages in nature. In non-procedural/declarative programming languages, the order of program instructions is not important. The importance is given only to "what is to be done"rather than "how to do it". With a non-procedural language, the programmer writes English-like instructions to retrieve data from databases. These languages are easier to use than procedural languages. Thus the non-technical users can access data from databases using non-procedural languages. These languages provide the user-friendly program development tools to write instructions. The programmers need not spend much time for coding the program. Examples include report-generating languages, database processing languages.

These languages are highly productive with lesser number of instructions required to generate an application than in Third Generation languages. The data and instructions may be fed in through a variety of techniques such as sequential statements with branches and loops, form-filling, menu selection, direct screen interaction and computer-aided graphics.

Fourth Generation Languages exist greatly varied in power and capabilities. They range from simple query languages to report generators and graphic package, which the users can directly handle. Many of these languages are designed only for a specific class or range of applications.

Characteristics of Fourth Generation Languages:

The following are the basic characteristics of fourth generation languages:

1. Machine independent.
2. User-friendly.
3. Easy to learn and use.
4. Built-in library functions
5. A non-professional programmer can obtain results with it.
6. A database management system is employed.
7. Non-procedural code is used to handle routine tasks; that is, every step in the procedure need not be detailed.
8. Intelligent default assumptions are for example, in formats.
9. An online interactive mode of operation is used.
10. Structured code, if any, is employed.
11. Code is readable and maintainable.
12. Debugging is easy. .
13. Application prototypes can be created and modified quickly.

Fourth generation languages include the languages for specification, query, report generation, systems engineering etc. For example, Maple, Mathematica, Postscript, SPSS, SQL etc. are considered under this category.

5.4.1.5. Fifth Generation Languages–Very High-Level and Problem Solving Languages: 1990s:

The fifth generation languages are considered as very high-level languages because of their problem solving/logical thinking abilities. They are centred on solving problems using constraints entered by the programmer which the computer uses to solve the given problem. That is, to solve the problems these languages use constraints given to the program and they do not use the algorithm written by a programmer. They are mostly used in artificial intelligence. The special feature of fifth generation language is that it makes the computer to solve the problem by itself and computer draws inferences based on codes. So, the programmer can concentrate on the problem needs to be solved and the conditions have to be met without bothering about how to implement a routine or algorithm to solve the problems. Example for fifth generation languages include Prolog (Programing Logic), Mercury (logical and functional programming language), OPS5 (Production rule programming language for AI research and building expert systems) etc.

5.5. LANGUAGE PROCESSORS

Computer understands only the instructions in machine code. That is, in the form of 0s and 1s. But, for writing programs in machine language, it needs expertise in binary and machine configuration. Hence, it is very difficult for the other users to write the programs in machine code. Today, almost all types of programs are written in high level languages which the machine cannot understand and follow. Every language has its own language processor/translator. Thus, language processor can be defined as "the translator system software that is used to translate the program written in high-level language /Assembly language into machine language".

5.5.1. Source Program and Object Program

Writing programs in high level languages necessitates the translation of the program written in Assembly and High level languages into machine language to run on the computer. The programs written in high level languages are called as Source Programs and the programs translated into machine language are called as Object Programs.

5.5.2. Types of Language Processors

The language processors can be classified into three types as follows:

1. Assemblers
2. Interpreters
3. Compilers

5.5.2.1. Assembler

In assembly languages, memory is used to represent operation codes and strings characters to represent address. In order to execute an assembly languages program on a computer, it should be translated into its equivalent machine language program, because computer can recognize only machine codes. This would be done manually, but it would involve too much clerical effort. Since the translation is essentially a clerical task, it was logical that the computer itself would be expected to perform this conversion.

This is accomplished by the use of processor/translator which is a program in machine language that will convert a symbolic program into a machine language program.

A processor/translator is something like a person who acts as an interpreter between two persons who speak different languages. The program is called as Assembler.

The programmer instructs the computer to read the symbolic codes and then instructs it to translate these codes and prepare another program in machine language. As seen above, the symbolic language program that must be translated into machine language is called as source program. After the source program has been translated in the computer according to instructions supplied by the processor/translator, a machine language program results and is called as object program. That is, the input to an assembler in the assembly language program is known as source program while output in machine language is called as object program.

5.5.2.2. Interpreter

Instead of compilers, the interpreters may also be used for translating the high level languages into machine language. An interpreter takes a source statement, checks for syntax, executes it, checks the next statement, and executes it and so on. That is, the interpreter converts each statement of source program into machine code and executes it immediately before translating the next statement. Suppose, if there is an error in the statement, the interpreter terminates its translating process at that statement and displays an error message.

5.5.2.3. Compiler

Usually the programs are written in high level languages. The computer can understand only machine instruction. The process of translating a program from high level language (source program) to a machine understandable (object) language is known as compilation. The programmer that performs this translation is known as a compiler. It resides on a disk, when needed it is called by the computer and loaded into RAM.

The process of compilation consists of the following steps:

1. The user enters the source program on the terminal and stores it in the RAM.
2. The compiler is called and asked to perform the translation. This is repeated till all the errors in the source program are identified and rectified.
3. The object program is executed in order to derive the desired result.

5.6. DIFFERENCES BETWEEN ASSEMBLER AND COMPILER

The differences between the two basic types of the translating programs are given below:

SI. No.	Assembler	Compiler
1.	Assembler translates the source code written in the assembly language to machine language and it is a translator that generates one machine language instructions for each symbolic instruction.	Compiler translates the source code written in the high-level language to machine language and the resulting output is the pure executable machine code.
2.	One-to-One translator.	One-to-many tranlator, one statement of input generates many machine instructions.

3.	It requires more amount of programmer's time.	It requires lesser amount of programmer's rime.
4.	Less sophisticated program.	More sophisticated program.
5.	The assembler system requires that instructions be written in mnemonic codes.	Compiler system allows statements to be written in the form of statements in English-like high level programming languages.
6.	Assemblers produce an object code which might have to be linked using linker programs in order to run on a machine.	Compilers usually produce the machine executable code directly from high level languages.

5.7. DIFFERENCES BETWEEN COMPILER AND INTERPRETER

The differences between compiler and interpreter are as follows:

SI. No.	Compiler	Interpreter
1.	Compiler merely translates the program in high level language into machine language and is not involved in their execution.	Interpreter translates the instruction and involves in their execution.
2.	Compiler stores the high level language program, scans it and translates the whole program into an equivalent machine language program.	It takes one statement of a high level language at a time and translates it into a machine instruction which is immediately executed. That is, it translates the statements of the source code one by one and executes immediately.
3.	A compiled machine language program runs much faster than interpreter program. That is, the program execution under compiler is very fast.	The running execution speed of interpreter program is slow.
4.	In compiler, it is not easy to correct the errors in the source code.	In interpreter, it is easy to correct the errors in the source code.
5.	The compiler requires large memory space and is not easy to write.	The interpreters are easy to write and they do not require large memory space.
6.	Compiler is suitable for large programs	Interpreter is suitable for small programs
7.	In compiler the translator program is not required to translate the programe each time user wants to run the program.	In interpreter, the translator program is required to translate the program each time the user wants to run the program

5.8. PROGRAMMING TOOLS

To write the some tools may be used. They are used to develop logical sequence for the solution of the problem. They help to communicate the steps for solving problem. The following are the most commonly used tools in programming.

A. Algorithm

B. Flowchart

C. Pseudocode

D. Decision Table

E. Decision Tree

F. Data Dictionary

A. Algorithm

The origin of the word algorithm comes from the name of a famous Arab mathematician, Abu Jafar Mohammad Ibn Musa Al-Khowrizmi and was coined as "Algorithm". He wrote a famous book, "Rules of Restoration and Reduction". In this book he explained the concept of algorithm.

An algorithm can be defined as "a step by step problem solving procedure that can be carried out by a computer". It has the following characteristics:

(*i*) An algorithm starts with input instructions. These inputs are processed by the subsequent instructions in the algorithm.

(*ii*) Each and every instruction should be precise.

(*iii*) It should be universal and unambiguous.

(*iv*) The total time to carry out all steps in the algorithm must be finite.

(*v*) It should produce results.

(*vi*) Each algorithm must have an end statement.

e.g., (1) Obtain the sum of 3 numbers.

Let the number be *A*, *B* and *C* and assume the value of the numbers are given

Step 1 : Read the values of A, B and C

Step 2 : Add A, B and C and call it D

Step 3 : Write the value of D

Step 4 : End

e.g.,(2) Find the largest of three numbers.

Step 1 : Read the first number (A)

Step 2 : Read the second number (B)

Step 3 : Read the third number (C)

Step 4 : Compare if A> B and A>C, Print A is largest else.

Step 5 : Compare if BC and B>A Print B is largest else.

Step 6 : Print C is Largest

Step 7 : End.

B. Flowchart

A Flowchart is " a pictorial or diagrammatic representation of the steps involved in solving a problem". It also shows the logical sequence in which these steps are to be performed. The first formal flowchart was made by John von Neumann in 1945. A Flowchart consists of blocks called symbols and arrows called flow lines. The block tells us what to do and flow lines show us the next step to be followed.

Types of Flowchart

There are two types of flowchart.

(*i*) System flowchart, and

(*ii*) Program flowchart,

This can be explained with the help of the following diagram:

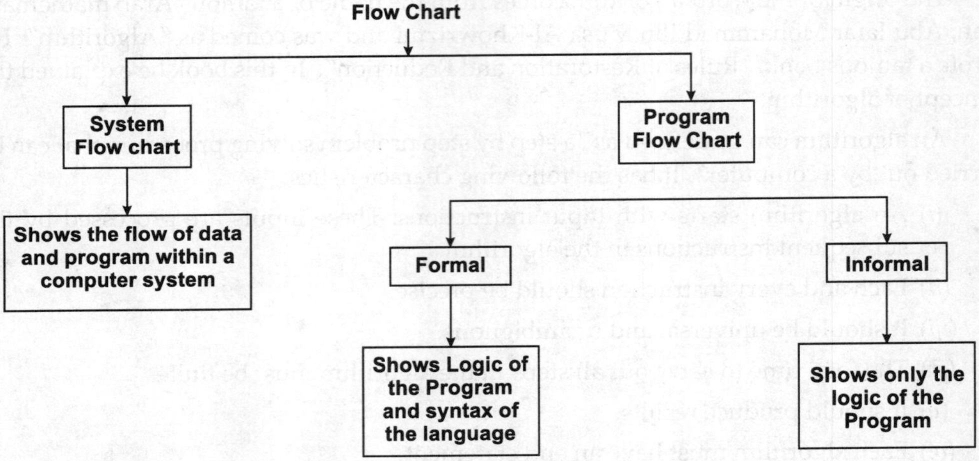

System Flowchart

A system shows the path through which the data is passed from one processing unit to another within a company. That is, the system flowchart depicts the flow of data flow and sequence of operation in a system. It is used by System Analyst to design and evaluate a new system.

A system flowchart depicts the entire data flow throughout a data processing system. That is, the system flowchart shows the path through which the data is passed from one processing unit to another within the Company. It illustrates which data is used or produced at various points in a sequence of operations, along with input media, operations performed; output media, and the nature of output. It is a visual representative of the interaction among data, hardware, and personnel. Symbols representing input, processing, and output are frequently used in system flowcharting - as well as specialized symbols to emphasize a particular operation or device. System flowcharting illustrates the components of the system.

SYMBOLS OF SYSTEM FLOWCHART

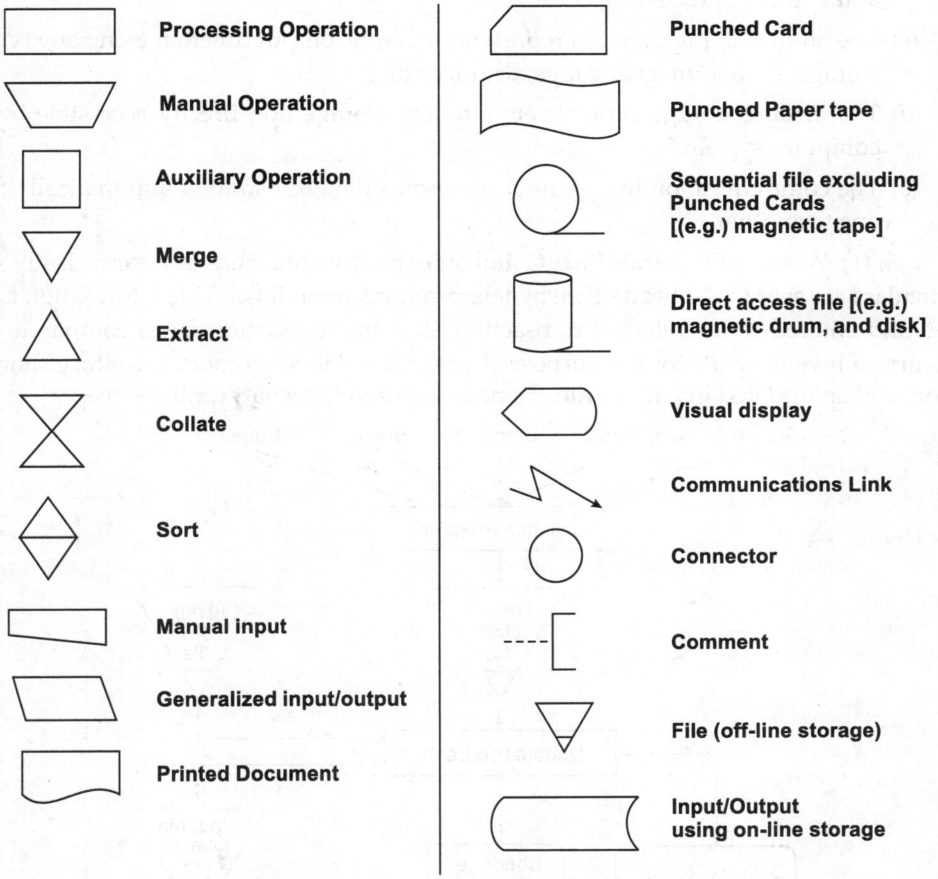

The basic symbols used in system flowchart are input-output symbol, processing symbols, annotation symbols annotation symbol and flow line symbol. These symbols are used in program flowcharts also.

The other common symbols used in system flowchart are explained hereunder:

1. Input-Output symbols for Media

Several specialized symbols have been developed representing the input-output functions in system flowcharting. They are:

(*a*) The punched card symbol represents an input-output function using a punched card, mark-sense card, stub card, deck of cards and the like.

(*b*) The punched tape symbol represents a punched tape routine.

(*c*) The punched magnetic tape symbol represent a magnetic tape routine.

(*d*) The document symbol represents a printed document format.

2. Symbols for equipment and process

(*a*) The display symbol represents an input-output function in which the information is displayed for human use at the time of processing by means of video devices, console printers, plotters or the like.

(*b*) The manual input symbol represents entering input manually through a keyboard at the time of processing.

(*c*) The on-line storage symbol represents an input-output function using any type of storage, such as magnetic tape, drum, or disc.

(*d*) The off-line storage symbol refers to any storage not directly accessible by the computer system.

(*e*) The communication link symbol represents data transmitted automatically from one to another.

e.g., (1): Western Electricals Ltd., Coimbatore has five branches in the city. Daily sales particulars are sent to the head office by telecommunication links. This information is collated and entered in the relevant transaction file. This transaction file is compared with the current inventory file for the purpose of preparing delivery report, inventory shortage report and an updated inventory file. Prepare a system flowchart for the same.

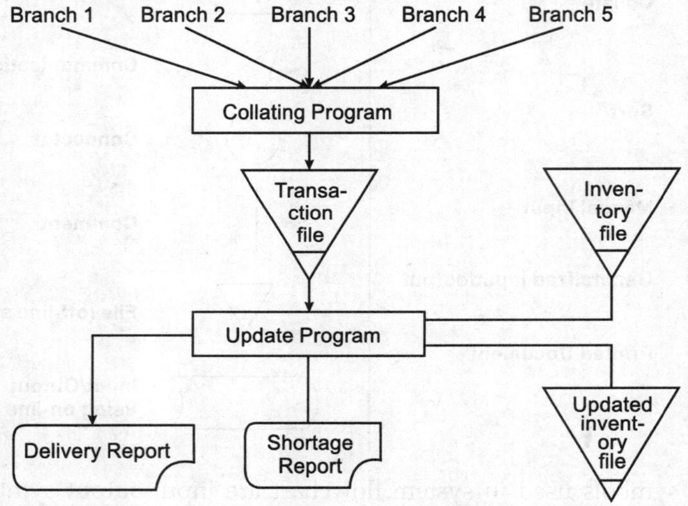

e.g., (2) The Perur Tamil College requires the new students to fill up a printed bio-data form. The data are first punched on cards, sorted, and then incorporated in the student's master file. Prepare a system flowchart.

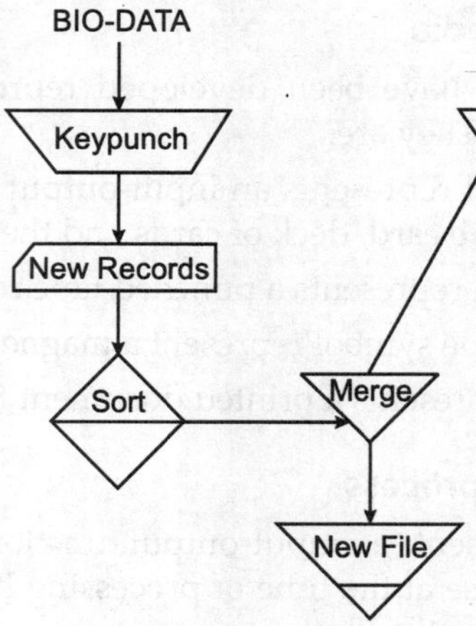

Draw a system flowchart for an inventory control system:

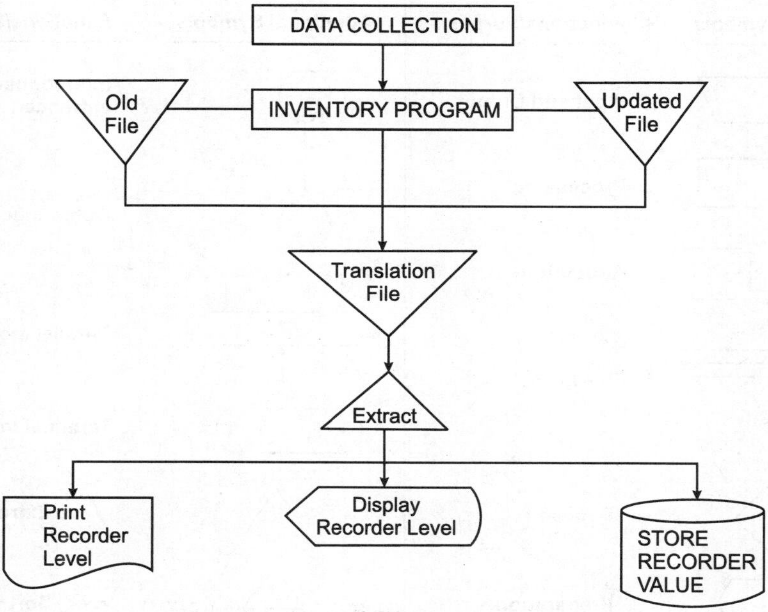

e.g., (3) Draw a system flowchart for the payroll Program.

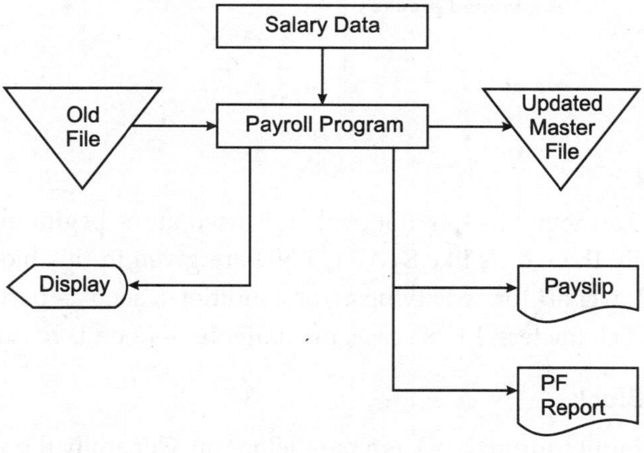

Program Flowchart

It is often useful to draw a diagram showing how a program of instruction to work. Diagrams of this kind are called a program flowchart. It is used to describe the logic of a program. That is, how the different instructions fit together. This is a commonly used flowchart in solving the problems. It represents the sequences of instructions for solving a particular problem. Thus, it is a graphic means of describing the operations and decision logic done on data. It details the flow of the computer's sequential steps necessary for the transformation of data. It is "graphic" because it uses a two-dimensional pictorial format, incorporating to identify the data and operations.

PROGRAM FLOWCHARTING SYMBOLS

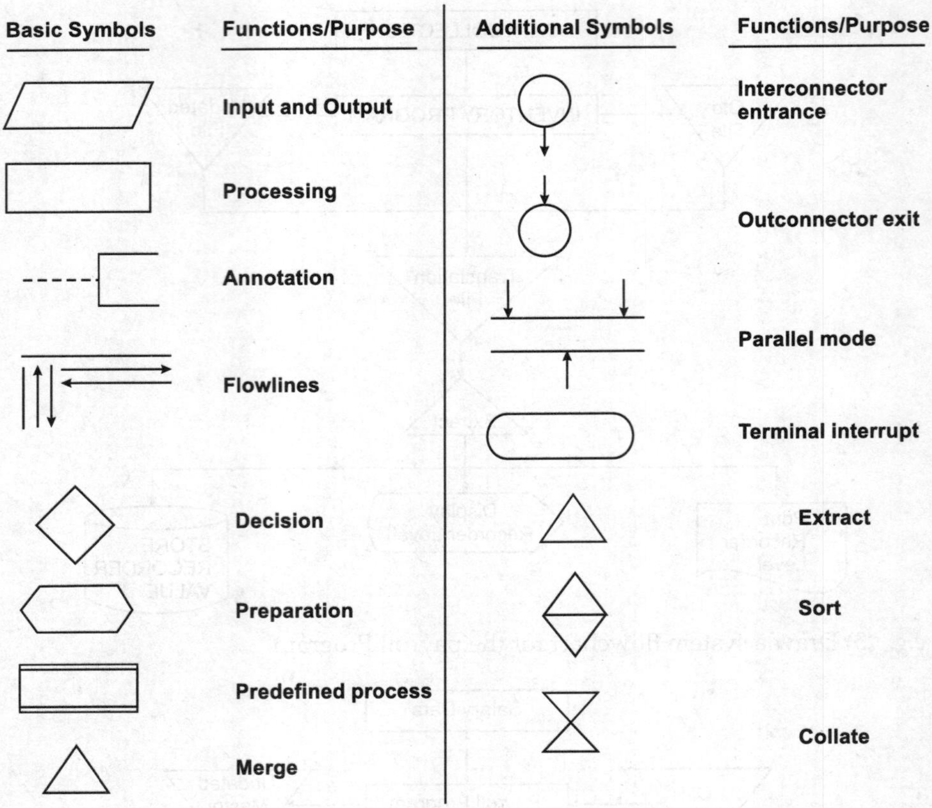

1. Terminal Block

The shape of Terminal Block is 'flat oval'. It is used at the beginning and end of each flowchart. Generally the words like START, END are given in this block. It can be used elsewhere in the flowchart for specifying error conditions, such as parity error checks or detection of invalid characters. In this case, manual intervention is required.

2. Input/Output Block

The shape of input/output block is a parallelogram. Generally the words like INPUT, READ, PRINT are given in this block. This symbol represents an instruction to an input or output device.

3. Processing Block

The shape of the processing block is a rectangle. It is used to show an action. All of the processing functions such as addition, subtraction, multiplication, division etc., are represented in this block.

The words LET, FOR GO TO are used here. It denotes action to be taken by the CPU in the actual processing of data.

4. Comment or annotation symbol

The shape of this symbol is an open rectangle with a broken line connecting the symbol to another flowchart symbol. It does not signify any action in the program but it is used to give descriptive comments or explanatory notes for clarification.

5. Flow-Line symbol

The shape of this symbol is a straight line. It is used to link symbols and to indicate the sequence of operations. Flow-lines may cross, form junctions, or connect any two symbols so that the symbols follow a logical, meaningful flow. Occasionally broken arrows are used to specify a possible flow change in the computer during the program run, depending on the conditions dictated in the process.

6. Parallel mode symbol

It consists of two parallel lines or any equal length. It represents the beginning or the end of two or more simultaneous operations.

7. Connector Symbol

The shape of the connector symbol is a circle. It is used when a diagram has to be continued on another page, or when drawing a line between two points on the same page whould unnecessarily complicate the drawing.

8. Decision Block

The shape of a decision block is diamond. It is used to show a decision being taken between two paths of action. There is one line going into a decision block and two going out. This is because the block always asks a question and gives two possible paths to take, depending on whether the answer to the question is yes or no.

9. Predefined symbol

The preparation symbol is used to specify operations such as control, initiation, an index register, and anything that will alter the program's course of execution. In addition, some programmers used this symbol for various preparatory routines.

Construction of program flowchart

The following points to be considered while drawing flowcharts:

(*i*) The flowchart should be legible, clean, and simple. Use a standardized template with clearly recognizable symbols. The flowchart will look neat and more presentable than a hand-drawn flowchart.

(*ii*) Each page should be designed sequentially, and enough space should be allowed for the title of the application, the name of the programmer, and the data on which the flowchart was constructed. The title should be short and clear.

(*iii*) The language used in describing each stop in the flowchart should be English or common notations, not coded language. The use of English contributes to a better understanding or the instructions by people other than the programmer who may not be familiar with the system used.

(*iv*) In each instruction, the wording should be clearly written within the symbol and consistent with the level of detail in the flowchart.

(*v*) The flowchart should maintain a consistent, general flow direction–from top to bottom and from left to right. When this is done, arrowheads are not needed.

(*vi*) Where possible, only one entrance and exit flow-line should be drawn for each symbol. Also, the flow-line should be drawn so that it enters or exits at the visual midpoint of the symbol. Symbols that may require more than one exit flow-line are decision and input-output symbols.

Advantages of Program Flowcharts

Program flowcharts are the most widely used graphic method for describing computer operations. Their major uses are in documentation and in programming. As a documentation tool, a flowchart helps a person communicate the nature of the operation, regardless of the programming language or the computer in use. Because of the considerable mobility of computer programmers, a company often finds itself modifying programs that were written by programmers who are no longer with the computer center. In such cases, a program flowchart is an invaluable aid to understanding the original programmer's logic flow.

The following are the advantages of Program Flowcharts:

(*i*) They are language-independent. Flowchart can be learned and applied without formal knowledge of a programming language.

(*ii*) By their very nature, flowcharts force the user to give attention to significant matters over the less significant ones.

(*iii*) As a visual representation, flowcharts provide an alternative to the usual narrative description of a system or a program. The graphic format enables the user to grasp a lot at a glance.

(*iv*) The wide range of detailed options available to the one who prepares the flowchart enhances the communication value of the flowchart.

Limitations of Flowcharts

(*i*) Some programmers complain that flowcharts are a waste of time. Since thinking in graphic terms is not normal, they cannot be viewed as a natural means of communication.

(*ii*) They are often unwieldy and costly to produce. Certain details that require only few lines in descriptive form often take more than a page of space to present in flowchart form.

(*iii*) Sometimes, they do not highlight what is important. Each step receives as much attention in a flowchart as any other.

(*iv*) Flowcharts do not represent a programming language. They are actually more a person-to-person than a person-to-computer means of communication. A computer cannot accept a program described in flowcharting form.

(*v*) Condensing details is subjective. Summarizing the wrong details can render the flowchart useless.

(*vi*) A flowchart generally tells how but rarely why a given set of operations is made.

Despite the limitations, a program flowchart can be translated into any one of a large number of programming languages. Since it graphically represents the logic of a computer program, it provides a convenient reference for locating logic errors. For complex problems, some installations use a special computer program designed to write program flowcharts. Once it is fed the data for each symbol and the squares into which the data goes, the program utilizes the printer to draw flowchart symbols on paper market with numbered squares and to connect them to one another. This technique is quite efficient, convenient for the programmer to look over the results and make changes where necessary.

e.g., (1) Draw a flowchart to find out the total of 3 subjects:

Step (1) Read marks in 3 subjects and call them A, B and C.

Step (2) Add A, B and C and call it Total

Step (3) Write TOTAL

Step (4) Stop

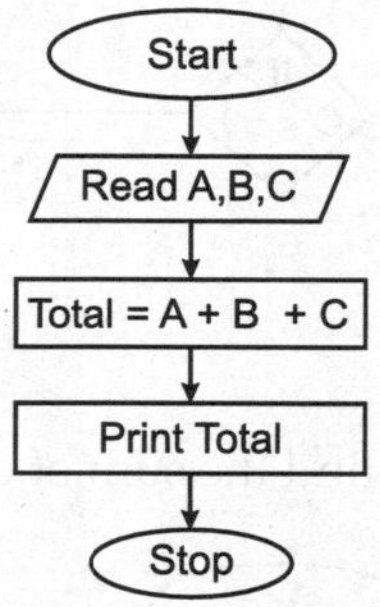

e.g., (2) Draw a flowchart to find the avarage of 20 numbers.

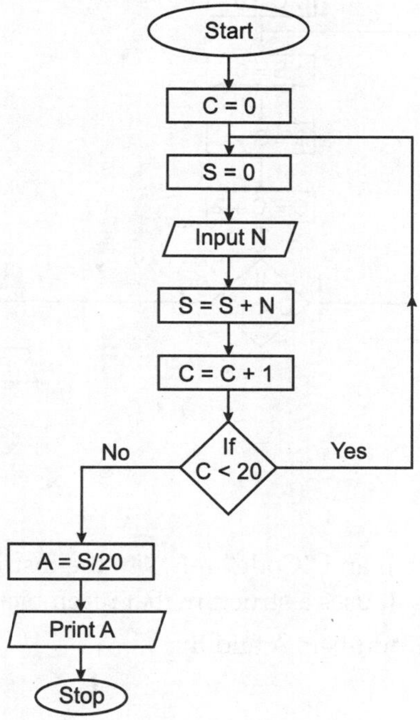

e.g., (3) Draw a flowchart to find the sum of even numbers up to 50.

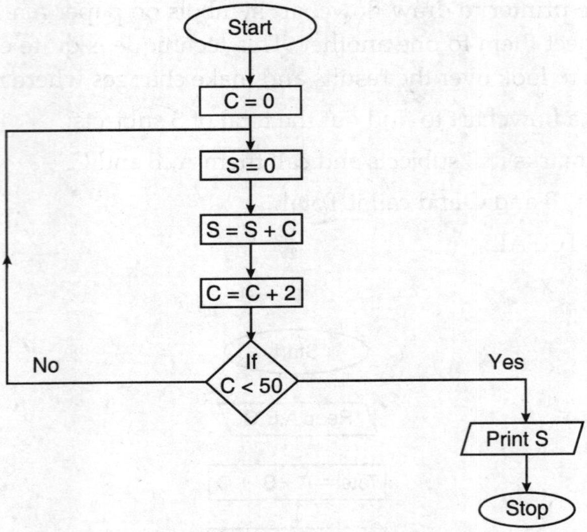

e.g., (4) Draw a flowchart to find the sum of odd numbers between 1 and 40.

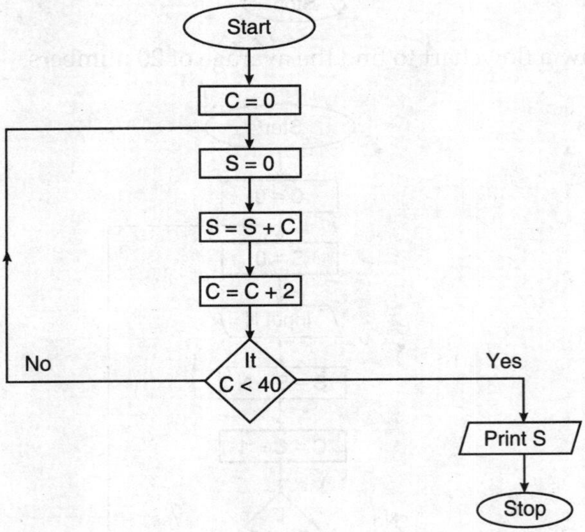

C. Pseudocode

"Pseudo" means imitation and "Code" refers to the instructions. It is an imitation of actual computer instructions. It uses a structure that resembles computer instructions.

e.g., Finding largest of 2 numbers A and B

```
Being
        Read A
        Read B
        If A is larger than B then
                Write A is largest
        Else
        Write B is largest
        Endif
  End
```

D. Decision Tables

It is a table used for representing the program logic. It reveals what decisions or actions the computer is to take as a result of the input data.

e.g., Draw a decision table to satisfy the following conditions:

(1) If order value > 5000 and if he is creditworthy a discount of 9% should be given.

(2) If order value = 5000 and if he is not creditworthy refer to the supervisor.

(3) If he is creditworthy a discount of 5% should be given.

(4) Otherwise refer to the supervisor.

	Rules			
Conditions	1	2	3	4
Order > = 50,000	Y	Y	N	N
Is Creditworthy?	Y	N	Y	N
Action				
Discount 5%			X	
Discount 9%	X			
Refer to Supervisor		X		X

E. Decision Trees

Decision Tree is a pictorial representation of the alternatives in any situation. It is a graphical representation of decision tables.

Example:

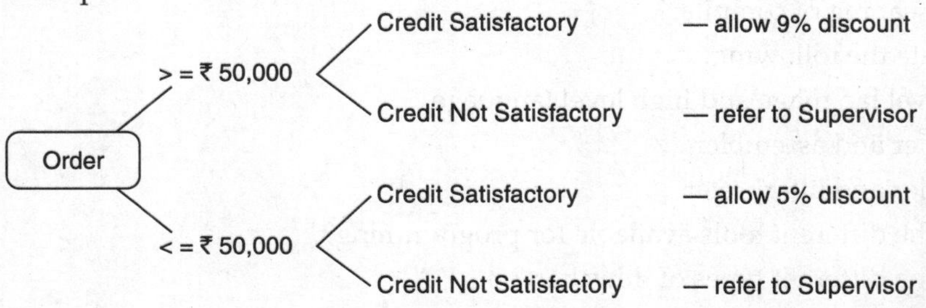

F. Data Dictionary

Data Dictionary is used to define a record structure. It lists the name, type and length of each field in a record. It holds a glossary of approved names, error messages and validation rules. It is a centralized collection of definitions, characteristics and inter-relationships which describe all the data stored within the system.

e.g., **Delivery Note**

< Order Number, Vendor Name, Vendor Address, Item Name, Delivery Challan Number, Quality supplied, Units >.

Invoice

< Invoice Number, Invoice Data, Party Name, Party Address, Item Name, Item quantity, Units, Rate per unit, Total Amount>.

REVIEW QUESTIONS

Short Answer Questions

1. What is the meaning of problem solving in the computer programming?
2. What is the meaning of algorithm?
3. What do you know about flowchart?
4. What are the classifications of flowchart?
5. What does debugging in computer programming mean?
6. What do you know about the documentation of the program?
7. What is a computer program?
8. What do you know about the meaning of programming languages?
9. What are the classifications of programming languages?
10. Give a brief note on documentation in programming.
11. Explain the concept of programming.
12. Explain the characteristics, advantages and disadvantages of machine language.
13. Difference between procedural and non-procedural languages
14. What do low-level languages mean?
15. Give the meaning of assembly language..
16. What do you know about high-level language?
17. What are the different generations of programming languages?
18. What is an assembler?
19. Give the meaning of compiler?
20. Differentiate the following:
    (*a*) Low level language and high level language
    (*b*) Compiler and assembler
    (*c*) Compiler and interpreter
21. What are the different tools available for programming?
22. What are the different types of flowchart?
23. Give any six symbols used in program flowchart.
24. Give any five symbols used in system flowchart.
25. What are the advantages of program flowchart?

Essay Type Questions

1. What are the steps involved in problem solving with computer programming?
2. Explain the generations of computer languages
3. Explain the different kinds of programming languages.
4. Write a detailed note on the characteristics and merits of high-level languages.
5. Explain the meaning and need of programming languages in detail.
6. Explain about the language processor and its types.
7. Give a brief note on different types of flowcharts with examples.
8. Give the various symbols used in system flowchart.
9. What are the merits and demerits of program flowchart?
10. Explain about various programming tools.

CHAPTER

6

System Analysis and Design

6.1. INTRODUCTION

The world system has a number of meanings. A system is an assembly of parts or The world system has a number of meanings. A system is an assembly of parts or components connected together in an organized way. The particular assembly has been identified by a human as being of social interest. In general the parts are affected by being in the system and are changed if they leave it. The particular assembly of parts performs some function. On this basis, the following concepts can be derived.

1. The parts perform some function: there must be input and output flows to and from the system.
2. The performance of these functions must be measurable, which implies monitoring.
3. The parts are organized, which implies control of actions and a decision-taking process.
4. The organization of parts also means that if a part has no interaction or connection with other parts, it is not in the system. The system must therefore have boundaries.
5. The environment beyond the boundaries can affect and be affected by the system.
6. Different resources are available for the system.
7. A number of sub-systems exist which interact with each other. There are four categories in particular.
   (*a*) The information sub-system deals with the flow of information between parts of the system, and between the system and its environment.
   (*b*) The control sub-system experts control on the components of the system.
   (*c*) The logistic sub-system collects resources, and feeds the system with resources.
   (*d*) The process sub-system provides the functional output from the system.

Thus, a system is essentially a group of interdependent components function together to achieve a specific and common objective. A collection of components that work together to realize some objective forms a system. Basically there are three major components in every system, namely input, processing and output.

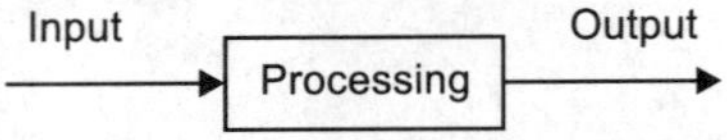

In a system the different components are connected with each other and they are interdependent. For example, human body represents a complete natural system. We are also bound by many national systems such as political system, economic system, educational system and so forth. The objective of the system demands that some output is produced as a result of processing the suitable inputs.

The organisation as a system

Organisation is considered as a system. For example the 'input' and 'output' reveal the differences: a factory has an input of raw materials and an output of finished goods; a library has an input of money and books and an output of information; a shipping company has an input of goods and delivers an output of the same goods elsewhere. There is no one methodology which can be applied to the study of all the organisations as systems. There are a number of different formal methodologies which are useful in different circumstances as an aid to understanding the interactions of the components in the system.

6.2. SYSTEM LIFE CYCLE

System life cycle is an organisational process of developing and maintaining systems. It helps in establishing a system project plan, because it gives overall list of processes and sub-processes required developing a system.

System development life cycle means combination of various activities. In other words we can say that various activities put together are referred as system development life cycle.

6.3. PHASES OF SYSTEM ANALYSIS AND DESIGN

The system analysis and design includes the following phases:

1. Problem definition
2. System Analysis
3. System Design
4. Coding
5. Testing and communicating the solution
6. System specification
7. Document control and charge control
8. Implementation and
9. Maintenance

1. Problem Definition

This phase is triggered by a competitor, a problem or an opportunity. Certain important issues are clarified at this stage like:

1. The problem perceived - a clear understanding of the problem.
2. The goals to be achieved - identifying the goals to be achieved after the problem is solved.
3. The benefits from the solution - estimating benefits in the new system over the current system.
4. The scope of the project - identifying what other areas are affected by the problem solution.

Some external influence has drawn attention to a problem area and the management requests an investigation of it. Before proceeding with investigation, the analyst must establish the terms of reference, to include the following.

(*a*) The scope and boundaries of the investigation area.

(*b*) The environment affecting it.

(*c*) Any expected changes in the environment.

(*d*) The time scale required and the resources available for the investigation.

(*e*) The aims of the investigation, *e.g.*, to improve cash flow, to assess the use of bluetooth technology etc..

(*f*) The stages of reporting required; often these will be a feasibility study, a statement or requirements and a detailed system design.

Thus, this stage can also be described as the phase of system study. This gives a clear picture of what actually the physical system is? In practice, the system study is done in two phases. In the first phase, the preliminary survey of the system is done which helps in identifying the scope of the system. The second phase of the system study is more detailed and in-depth study in which the identification of user's requirement and the limitations and problems of the present system are studied. After completing the system study, a system proposal is prepared. The proposed system contains the findings of the present system and recommendations to overcome the limitations and problems of the present system in the light of the user's requirements.

Once the problem has been defined and terms of reference established, a feasibility study is undertaken. On the basis of result of the problem definition etc., feasibility study takes place. The feasibility study is basically the test of the proposed system in the light of its workability, meeting user's requirements, effective use of resources and .of course, the cost effectiveness. The main goal of feasibility study is not to solve the problem but to achieve the scope. In the process of feasibility study, the cost and benefits are estimated with greater accuracy.

2. System Analysis

Analysis involved a detailed study of the current system, leading to specifications of a new system. Analysis is a detailed study of various operations performed by a system and their relationships within and outside the system. During analysis, data are collected on the available files, decision points and transactions handled by the present system. Interviews, on-site observation and questionnaire are the tools used for system analysis. Using the following steps it becomes easy to draw the exact boundary of the new system under consideration:

- Keeping in view the problems and new requirements
- Workout the pros and cons including new areas of the system

All procedures, requirements must be analysed and documented in the form of detailed data flow diagrams, data dictionary, logical data structures and miniature specifications. System Analysis also includes sub-dividing of complex process involving the entire system, identification of data store and manual processes.

The main points to be discussed in system analysis are :

1. Specification of what the new system is to accomplish based on the user requirements.
2. Functional hierarchy showing the functions to be performed by the new system and their relationship with each other.
3. Function network which are similar to function hierarchy but they highlight the those functions which are common to more than one procedure.
4. List of attributes of the entities - these are the data items which need to be held about each entity (record).

In this stage the present system and the requirements of the new system are analysed in detail. Solutions are discussed and chosen. The system analysis phase includes the following.

(*a*) **Fact Finding:** This involves establishing the detail of what work is done, what decisions are taken, by whom, when and where. It must include not only the routine flow of work but the treatment of exceptions, errors and enquiries. The system being investigated will be one of the information processing, the facts to be found are the details of input, processing, storage and output.

There are four main techniques of fact finding and are listed below:

(*i*) The formal record of present procedure is inspected. The record may consist of external documents such as statutory requirements and standards, or it may be documentation prepared within the concern, setting out the way procedures are intended to operate. It provides the essential skeleton for fact finding.

(*ii*) Interviews and record collection are the most frequently used and most effective method of acquiring information on what is actually done, as opposed to what is supposed to be done. Each interview should be prepared in advance, with a list of information to be obtained but the interview must be allowed to diverge from the plan to discuss other relevant aspects of which the analyst was unaware. Copies of documents and records with information entered must be obtained, both by obtaining examples at interviews and by sampling past records at random. Legible notes of the interview, points can be clarified in telephone conversations. Information obtained in interviews can be confirmed by sending a copy of the notes.

(*iii*) Questionnaires are valuable where a large number of branches or outside contacts are involved, but their use needs careful consideration as recipients find them a nuisance to answer. They may, of course be sent to a sample of contacts.

(*iv*) Observation is most likely to be an adjunct to interviewing. It may be necessary in establishing information such as the rate of arrival of customers and the length of time taken to serve them, using techniques of work study etc.

(*b*) **Analysis:** This uses the concepts of boundary, environment, input, output and process. Logically, analysis follows fact-finding. In practice, the two must overlap since it is only by analysing facts that gaps can be found in the information collected. There are a number of systematic methods of analysis, some of then linked to the design and programming methods to form a coherent whole. A particular data processing department may choose to use one of these methods as its standard.

Systematic methods include the following:

(*i*) **Top-down structured analysis:** The system under investigation is broken down by stages into smaller sub-systems, overall functions being established and documented before details of procedure are analysed.

(*ii*) **Information flow diagrams:** A chart is drawn showing every person and department involved in the system, and all the formal information flows between them. The flows are analysed to ascertain whether they are needed, before proceeding to the design stage.

(*iii*) **Precedent:** The documentation or experience of a system previously is used as a standard starting point and the analysis establishes the equivalents to the components of the system under investigation.

(*iv*) **Performance analysis:** This is particularly useful in examining an existing computer system with a view to updating it. Several aspects need to be investigated; a critical examination of the good and bad points of the facilities provided to the users; the computer resources used by the system; and the costs and benefits achieved by the system.

(*v*) **Cost/Benefit analysis:** Once the solution along with the alternatives is decided upon, the costs and benefits of each alternative guide the selection of the best system of the job. Costs and benefits may be tangible or intangible, direct or indirect, fixed or variable. Cost estimates also take into consideration hardware, personnel, and facility and supply costs for final evaluation. Cost/benefits analysis then identifies the costs and benefits of a given system and categorises them for analysis. Then a method of evaluation is selected and the results are interpreted for action.

3. System Design

Based on the user requirements and the detailed analysis of a new system, the new system must be designed. This is the problem solution and system designing phase. The design of a new system extends to clerical procedures and all ancillary operations as well as the design of the computer system itself. Facts have been collected and analysed. It is now necessary to construct the logic of a set of procedures to perform the operations needed, and also to decide on what computer those procedures will run, what methods of input will be used, and what information must be held in files.

Normally, the design proceeds in two stages :

(*a*) Preliminary or general design and

(*b*) Structure or detailed design

Preliminary or general design: In the preliminary or general design, the features of the new system are specified. The costs of implementing these features and the benefits to be derived are estimated. If the project is still considered to be feasible, we move to the detailed design stage.

Structure or Detailed design: In the detailed design stage, computer oriented work begins in earnest. At this stage, the design of the system becomes more structured. Structure design is a blue print of a computer system solution to a given problem having the same components and inter-relationship among the same components as the original problem. Input, output and processing specifications are drawn up in detail. In the design stage, the programming language and the platform in which the new system will run are also decided.

System design includes the following:

(*i*) Aims of the enterprise.

(*ii*) Needs of the user.

(*iii*) Statutory, audit, other external requirements.

(*iv*) Data processing strategy of the enterprise.

(*v*) Cost benefit analysis .

(*vi*) Interfaces to other existing or planned systems.

(*vii*) Requirements of the particular system as revealed by fact-finding and analysis, including reliability and time constrains.

(*viii*) Predecessor system minimizing change and making use of existing procedure where appropriate.

(*ix*) New technology; consider options of hardware, systems software, applications packages, communications, special purpose computers which have become available since the data processing strategy was set.

(*x*) Good data processing practice. This includes the flowing

(*a*) Adequate control procedures.

(*b*) Validation of input.

(*c*) Use of exception reports and enquiry systems to minimize output.

(*d*) Turn-round documents to minimize errors and effort in input.

(*e*) Adoption of standards.

There are several tools and techniques used for designing. These tools and techniques include: flowchart, data flow diagram, data dictionary, decision table, decision tree etc.

4. Coding

After designing the new system, the whole system is required to be converted into computer understanding language. Coding the new system into computer programming language does this. It is an important stage where the defined procedure is transformed into control specifications by the help of a computer language. This is also called the programming phase in which the programmer converts the program specifications into computer instructions, which we refer as programs. The programs coordinate the data movements and control the entire process in a system.

5. Testing and communicating the solution

These are logically two steps, but in practice a great deal of the testing of the solution comes from constructing documentation, communication it back to those involved in the system and considering their comments. Prior to this the systems design team should return to the analysis and ensure that every feature identified has been catered for in the design, by inclusion in the new system, or by exclusion with a note of the way it will be handled.

Before actually implementing the new system into operations, a test run of the system is done removing all the bugs, if any. It is an important phase of a successful system. After codifying the whole programs of the system, a test plan should be developed and run on a given set of test data. The output of the test run should match the expected results.

Using the test data following test run are carried out:

(*a*) Unit test

(*b*) System test

Unit test: When the programs have been coded and compiled and brought to working conditions, they must be individually tested with the prepared test data. Any undesirable happening must be noted and debugged (error corrections).

System Test: After carrying out the unit test for each of the programs of the system and when errors are removed, then system test is done. At this stage the test is done on actual data. The complete system is executed on the actual data. At each stage of the execution, the results or output of the system is analysed. During the result analysis, it may be found that the outputs are not matching the expected out of the system. In such case, the errors in the particular programs are identified and are fixed and further tested for the expected output.

The communication of the solution will include a prime document, termed system definition or statement of requirements. There may be an accompanying document with confidential material, for example the cost benefit analysis and effects on staffing. The solution is likely to be presented verbally at meetings, and amended as a result of discussion. Within the prime documents, flowcharts, decision tables and diagram of information flow will be used to show the proposed procedures.

6. System specification

From the previous stage, details of equipment, software, procedures and people involved will have been decided. The next stage is to turn this into a form, which can be handed over to a programming team. The document produced as a result will be the systems specification. This involves:

1. Detailed file design, with organization and content of records or data base design.
2. Design of forms for input
3. Design of all printed reports
4. Display formats for terminals and details of dialogue between computer and terminal user.
5. Function of each program with input, output and performance constraints.
6. Schedule for the project through to live running.

7. Document control and change control

In the above stages documents are produced and distributed then amended as a result of comment of changing requirements. A change control procedure is required for the proposal, consideration and authorization of changes. A document control procedure is needed to ensure that authorized changes to document states its issue number or date of issue, so that it can readily be ascertained whether it is to date.

8. Implementation

Implementation means converting a new system design into operation. Implementation is the stage of a project during which theory is turned into practice. This involves creating computer compatible files, training the operating staff, installing hardware and telecommunications network before system is up and running.

A system may run at a bureau, within the data processing department or on a computer within the user department. The following two strategies are followed for running the system:

Parallel run: In parallel running, the old and new systems are run side by side for a period and their output are compared; if it is the same, the old system is discontinued. This method may be impossible, for example if the old and new system has different ways of serving customers. In this case direct change is necessary, which is more risky and therefore needs more thorough system testing.. This strategy is helpful due to the following reasons:

(*a*) Manual results can be compared with the results of the computerised system.

(*b*) Failure of the computerised system at the early stage, does not affect the working of the organisation, because the manual system continues to work, as it used to do.

Pilot run: In this type of run, the new system is installed in parts. Some part of the new system is installed first and executed successfully for considerable time period. When the results are found satisfactory then only other parts are implemented. This strategy builds the confidence and the errors are traced easily.

The implementation phase, however, will contain the following:

(*a*) Construction of test data and test files. These will include a typical period or batch of input and batches with extreme and incorrect values.

(*b*) Staff negotiation

1. User documentation
2. Ordering of forms and media
3. Installation of computer equipment terminals and communications lines.
4. Training
5. Acceptance test
6. Parameter setting, tailoring
7. Data input or conversion for files.
8. Setting up error reporting and correcting procedures for hardware software system and communication.
9. Changeover, pilot run, parallel run or direct change.
10. Review.

9. Maintenance

Maintenance is necessary to eliminate errors in the system during its working life and to tune the system to any variations in its working environment. It has been seen that there are always some errors found in the system that must be noted and corrected. It also means the review of the system from time to time. The review of the system is done for:

(*a*) knowing the full capabilities of the system

(*b*) knowing the required changes or the additional requirements

(*c*) studying the performance

If a major change to a system is needed, a new system or project may have to be set up to carry out the change. The new system or project will then proceed through all the above phases.

REVIEW QUESTIONS

Short answer Questions:

1. What is meant by system in system analysis ?
2. Give a note on system life cycle ?

Essay type questions:

1. Give a detailed account on various activities involved in system analysis and design.

CHAPTER 7

Data Processing

7.1. DATA PROCESSING CONCEPTS

Data

The word data is the plural of the word datum, which means fact. Therefore, data means collection of facts. Data can be considered as the raw material of information. The data may be numerical such as sales report, inventory figures, etc. or non-numerical like customer names, addresses, etc.

Data Processing

Mere data cannot solve any problem. The solution can be arrived at by organising and manipulating the data. Data processing is the conversion of data into a more useful form. That is, transmission of data into meaningful information is called data processing.

Information

The result obtained by data processing is called information. That is, the processed data is known as information. However, information produced in one data processing step may be used as data in the next data processing step.

DATA Vs INFORMATION	
Data	*Information*
Raw facts or figures	Finished One.
Unstructured	Structured
Unprocessed Data	Processed Data
What exists	What is required

7.2. DATA PROCESSING CYCLE

Data Processing is viewed as a system that accepts data as input, processes it into information as output. Once data is collected, it is processed to convert it into useful information. The data is processed again and again until the accurate result is achieved. This is called data processing cycle. This can be explained with the help of the following diagram.

Simplified Version

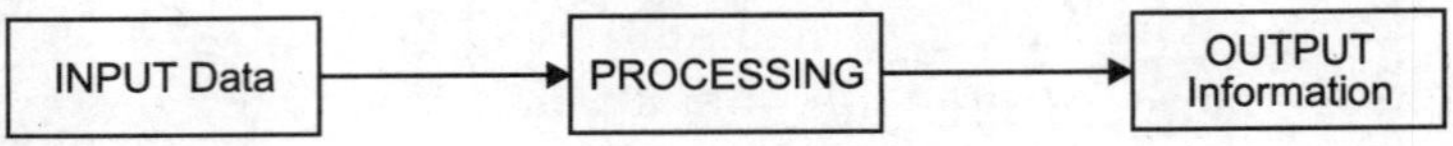

In data processing technique, data are frequently collected and recorded on document for input. These documents are called source documents. For example, Employee's basic pay, loan amount, allowance, etc., when put together, is treated as a source document and from which data can be taken and processed to deliver a pay slip.

Detailed Version

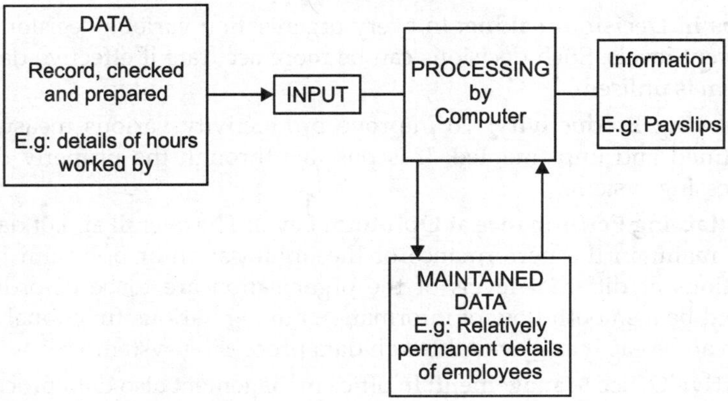

Then collecting such types of data and arranging them in more meaningful and manageable way to process is called Data coding. Data coding is particularly useful with Qualitative data.

7.3. DATA TYPES

The data types may be as follows:

1. **Qualitative data:** It indicates the classification characteristics nature of things such as good, blue etc.
2. **Quantitative data:** It is expressed in terms of measurable quantities such as 100 tons, 98.4 degres F etc.
3. **Numeric Type:** The data types may also be an integer (+, –) without any fractional part or real number which includes integers and fractions.
4. **Floating Point Representation:** These data type consist of 3 components namely: (1) Mantissa (2) Radix or Base (3) Exponent

   Besides the above, the data types include alphabetic data and alphanumeric data.

7.4. OBJECTIVES OF DATA PROCESSING

After the industrial revolution, the needs of the making increased. Man had to deal with large volume of data. He had to cope up with more and more information. The information collected is to be sorted out, stored and retrieved at short intervals. This necessitated the concept of data processing.

As the complexities of business increases, the number of functions to be performed also increased. The data processing system must be responsible to supply the information when it is needed so as to make the performance of the organisation optimum.

Let us have a look at the general objectives of Data Processing.

Handle Voluminous Data: The basic objective of data processing is to handle voluminous data in order to enable the organisation to function smoothly.

Qualitative and quantitative information: The next important aim of data processing is to provide qualitative and quantitative information.

Appropriate and Timely Information: Different kinds of information are needed in almost all organisations. Provision of appropriate and timely information is made possible through data processing system.

Storage and Retrieval of Data: Through data processing, information can be stored and retrieved as and when necessary.

Helps in Decision-making: In every organisation various decisions are taken at different levels. Such decisions can be more accurate if effective data processing system is utilised.

Improving Productivity: To improve productivity various measures are to be identified and implemented. It is possible through the properly designed data processing system.

Maintaining Performance at Optimum Level: The overall aim of data processing is to maintain the performance of the organisation at optimum level. Various functions at different levels of the organisation are to be co-ordinated. There should be a smooth flow of information among various functional departments. This can be easily achieved through data processing system.

Effective Office Management: In office management also data processing plays a vital, role, through which office automation can be done.

Automation of Workflow: To automate work-flows and make them more flexible and to improve throughput times.

7.5. KINDS OF DATA PROCESSING

The important kinds of data processing are as follows:

1. **Manual Data Processing:** In Manual Data Processing, human being converts the data into information. Here the data is processed using manual operations such as abacus, slide rule, Napier bones etc.
2. **Mechanical Data Processing:** In Mechanical Data Processing, a person uses and controls various machines to get the work done. It consists of various electromechanical devices such as calculators, tabulators, etc.
3. **Electronic Data Processing:** In Electronic Data Processing, the data is processed by either analog or digital computer. Hereafter, the term 'Data Processing' in this book denotes Electronic Data Processing.

7.6. STEPS IN DATA PROCESSING

Data processing includes any operation or set of operations performed upon data, whether or not by automatic means, such as collection, recording, organization, storage, adaptation or alteration to convert it into useful information. Processing of data on a computer has become a part and parcel of everyday life. Especially in commerce and industry it becomes inevitable. Data processing involves the following basic steps:

Steps in Data Processing

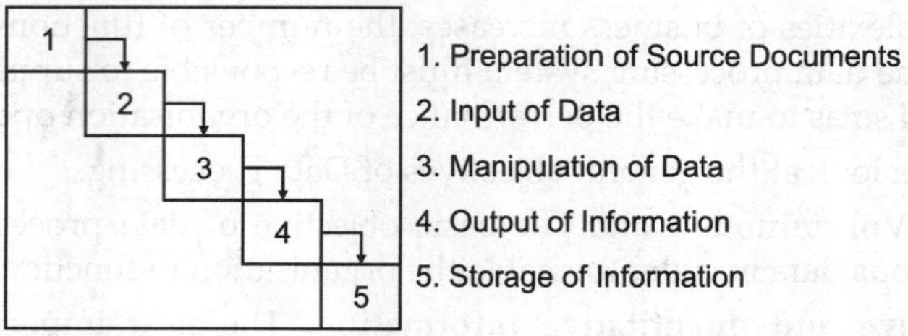

1. Preparation of Source Documents:

This step refers to the collection of necessary facts and figures. Such data are set out on source documents, i.e., to determine what types of data are required for obtaining the desired output.

2. Input of Data:

After extracting the necessary data from the source documents, they must be transposed into a suitable form that is acceptable to the computer. Great care should be taken not to make wrong entries in the forms. Sometimes it may be necessary to develop suitable codes to refer to the facts and only such codes are entered into the designed forms.

3. Manipulation of Data:

This refers to the action taken. It involves the process of shifting, sorting and rearranging the given input. Before processing, a program called Edit program may be used to check the correctness of the data entered. This ensures the validity of the data.

4. Output of Information:

The main purpose of data processing is to provide meaningful information to the decision-maker. The output result must be easy for the user to comprehend. Hence, in data processing the person involved must be very clear what information is needed and in what form he likes to have it.

5. Storage of Information:

The data processes need to be kept for future use. All the processed data will need some form of secondary storage. When storing the data, it is always important to maintain a backup. It should be noted that at each and every step the storage might be done.

7.7. PRACTICAL DATA PROCESSING APPLICATIONS IN BUSINESS

The following are some data processing information undertaken by commercial organisations:

1. Process Control:

In the production process, a computer is directly connected to some plant to control and monitor it. Here, the computer receives the data directly from the plant. It analyses the input data and initiates action to control the ongoing process.

2. Accounting:

The data processing system can be used to maintain the accounting records and in preparation of final accounts. The general ledger, accounts payable, accounts receivable, etc., are the examples for the computerised accounting systems followed in most business organisations.

3. Payroll Preparation:

In the personnel department the data processing system is used to record the operations of the number of employees of different departments in each shift, leave taken, deductions such as ESI, PF and finally in the preparation of payslips.

4. Sales Analysis:

The Data Processing system is highly useful in sales analysis. The sales manager can prepare the sales forecast on the basis of per month's sales reports and subsequent future actions can be taken.

5. Inventory Management:

Actually the data processing system is a boon to every organisation in respect of inventory management. Data processing is used to maintain up-to-date information about stock, their costs and to initiate orders when the times are about to be exhausted.

6. Office Automation:

The modern offices and business organisations are dependent upon computer–based office automation for their competitiveness and better management.

7. Banking Application:

Data processing systems are highly needed in banking sector where the customer satisfaction is the main criteria. To provide quick and perfect service, data processing system is used. Automatic Teller Machine is placed in many places of cities and linked to central computers. Hence, the delay in processing is completely avoided.

8. Insurance and Stock Broking:

Insurance companies and stock broking firms also use the computerised data processing systems. Large volume of data have to be processed for the preparation of policy statement, interest calculations, renewal notices and in dealing with the securities.

9. Managerial Aid:

The Data Processing System is used as a managerial aid in decision-making by solving business problems. It is also very useful in the areas of linear programming, PERT, CPM etc.

Today it appears that the computer is everywhere. Not only the business organisation, the other institutions are also using data processing system for their regular use. We cannot think about a situation without a computer. Robotics and Artificial Intelligence are the two promising areas of applications.

7.8. DATA PROCESSING OPERATIONS

The data after some processing is transformed into information which is organised and meaningful. Data Processing includes the following operations:

1. Data Generation:

It involves the operation of collecting the original data. It implies that the raw data are collected and set out in the form of original document called a source document.

2. Recording:

Here raw data is converted into an acceptable form. That is, the data is transcribed from the source documents on some specified forms and are made readable for the machines. Recording basically means transferring of data onto some form of document. This operation is performed throughout the IPO cycle.

3. Verification and Validation:

After the data have been recorded, their accuracy has to be checked. Since recording is usually done by manual means, it is important that recorded data be carefully checked for any errors or omissions. This can be done with the help of another machine called verifier or by re-reading.

4. Classification:

Classification of information is the next important operation in which the data is separated into various categories.

5. Sorting:

Sorting involves sequencing the data in a predetermined order to facilitate processing. The order may be either alphabetic or numeric.

6. Merging:

It is the operation of combining two or more ordered (stored) sets of data to form another single ordered set.

7. Processing and Calculating:

Here the calculation is carried out and greater magnitude of data is processed. Calculation involves solving equations and manipulation of the source data such as addition, subtraction, etc.

8. Data Storage:

The results of the processing of data are retained in storage for future use of reference. The basic requirement for utilising the computer in all business applications is the ability to store and access data. The data is stored in the location called memory referred by its address. In large organisations, huge volume of data is to be stored and accessed. Hence, some auxiliary storage devices are also needed for the effective data processing.

9. Data Retrieving:

Data retrieving is the process of searching or locating a data item from the storage. In EDP system, the data is retrieved from the storage device in sequential, indexed sequential or random access mode. The on-line data storage and retrieval is very useful for the proper functioning of a modern establishment.

10. Reporting:

Generally in business data processing, the processing operation comes to an end with the reporting of data. In this operation the results of the data processing are made available to others. The processed information may be reported in a number of ways depending on the use of results. The results may be printed out in the form of payslips, bills, etc. or in the form of reports as ESI Reports, PF Reports or Sales Report, etc. At is common in modern organisations to send reports electronically as well.

For effective data processing, all of the above operations are to be performed.

7.9. METHODS OF DATA PROCESSING

A processing method is the way in which transactions are grouped and handled for input to the central processor for computation or generation of reports and outputs. The method of data processing depends upon the following factors:

(*a*) Volume of data to be processed

(*b*) Complexity of data processing operations

(*c*) Computational demands

(*d*) Processing time constraints

(*e*) Economic factors

Based on the above factors many data processing methods have been developed and widely used in all areas of operations especially in business fields. The commonly used methods are given below.

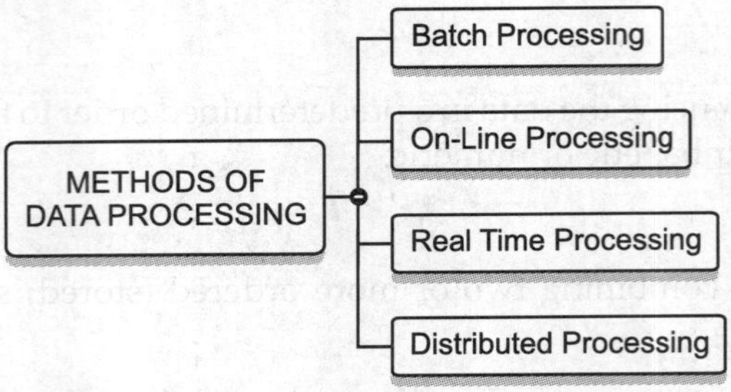

Let us discuss these methods.

7.9.1. Batch Processing

This is an old system but even today it is used for data processing. Batch processing is a method in which a number of similar items or transactions to be processed are grouped/ batched for processing as a single unit at predetermined times. When a batch of transactions is accumulated, the batch total compiled for it and the transactions are transcribed on to some input media such as CD etc. or other media at regular intervals for a predetermined period of time.

The time for the accumulation of transactions into batches may vary depending on the nature of data and on the basis of results demanded and it is done on monthly, weekly or even daily basis. After the accumulation of batches, it is processed to produce the desired output. In batch processing, the batch processing cycle repeats itself at every regular interval. The elements of this cycle are given below:

(*a*) Data capture

(*b*) Data transmission

(*c*) Data transcription, verification and validation.

(*d*) Job processing.

(*e*) Job assembly putting together the batch for processing.

(*f*) Job disassembly (separating out the reports after processing)

(*g*) Reports and distribution

Features of Batch Processing:

The following are the features of batch processing:

(*a*) The data is accumulated into batches and processed periodically.

(*b*) The jobs are processed one after the other without any user interaction.

(*c*) Results are not required immediately.

(*d*) One set of data is processed by the whole series of programs.

(*e*) The set of data is passed through each program in turn.

(*f*) It is normally used when transaction activity is low or periodic.

(*g*) Once the data are submitted for processing, the computer may be left running without human interaction.

The concept of Batch Processing is clearly explained with the help of the following diagram:

CONCEPT OF BATCH PROCESSING

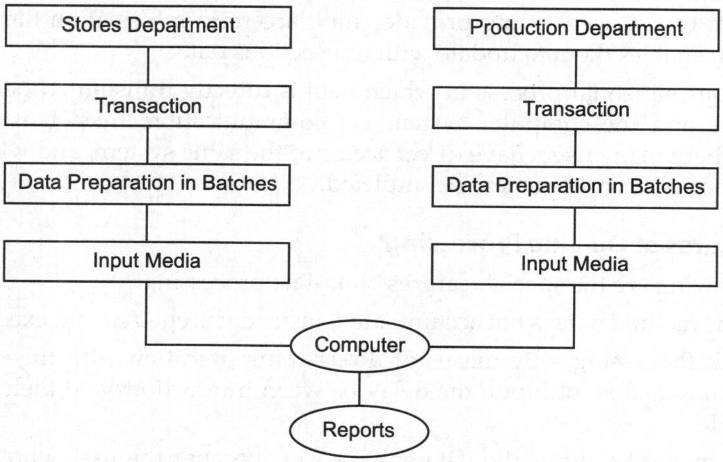

Examples of applications which can use batch processing are:

1. **Payroll Processing**: In payroll processing the data are collected for a stipulated period of time, usually one month, and processed at regular intervals after which payments are distributed to all the employees.
2. **Telephone Billing**: Here the subscriber does not get a bill for every call he makes. Instead, his calls are recorded at a centralised place and are processed on a predetermined period of time to prepare his bills.

   Others: Batch processing can be used in many numbers of business applications including Financial Accounting, Budgeting and Budgetary Control, Production planning and control, Project planning and control, Stock control, Gas and electricity billing etc.

Benefits of Batch Processing:

The benefits of batch processing system include the following:

1. Once the data are submitted for processing, the computer may be left running without human interaction.
2. Processing jobs can be scheduled and done for a time when the computer is not busy.
3. Batch processing leaves a good audit trail.

Limitations of Batch Processing:

The following are the limitations of batch processing:

1. Time gap between capture of data
2. Time consuming to debug
3. Delay in generating reports.

7.9.2. On-Line Processing

On-line processing refers to processing of individual transactions as they occur from their point of origin as opposed to accumulating them into batches. In this method of processing, the system interacts directly with the user. That is, as soon as the user inputs data it is processed immediately. This is made possible by such direct access devices and number of terminals connected to and controlled by a central processor. In this way, various departments in a company can be connected to the process by LAN. If operating companies are a number of miles away from the processor then they are linked by means of WAN. This type of processing provides multiaccess to information files by terminal users and also enables them to update with transactions data.

It is a non-sequential process in which data is directly transmitted between input/ output device and the computer system via communication links. It is a method of processing where many users have direct access to the same system, and where the file is updated as soon as the transaction is completed.

Special Features of On-Line Processing:

The following are the special features of on-line processing:

1. In this method data is not accumulated, instead it is entered and executed directly.
2. Quick Processing – By means of direct communication with the computer and continuous flow of input, the delay between transactions and their processing is avoided.
3. This method reduces the data entry errors, because the user who generates the data is the one who keys it in.
4. This system validates data at various points and ensures that correct data is being entered.
5. Under this method the system performs the whole task in a conversational manner helping the data entry process.
6. In on-line processing, one has the latest update. On-line processing ensures that the records are in updated status at any time.

Concept of On-Line Processing:

Under on-line processing the input data enters the system from the point of origin and output is transmitted directly back to the user. This processing method involves direct communication between the CPU and the user for both input and output. The concept of on-line processing can be seen as follows:

Concept of On-Line Procesing

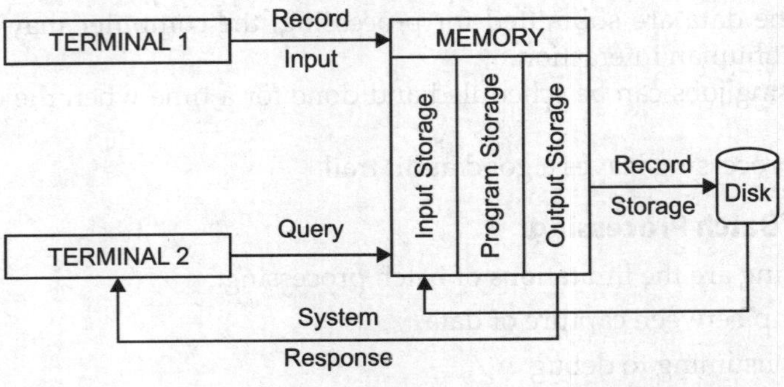

On-line Data Processing Applications:

On-line processing systems are being developed and are already in use for a wide range of application in different types of industries described below:

1. **Showroom:** By means of terminals situated in showroom it is possible to inform prospective customers of the availability of the appliances in response to their inquiries.
2. **Banking:** It is possible to inform bank customers about the status of their accounts in response to an inquiry by accessing relevant file using on on-line terminal.
3. **Financial Institutions:** The credit appraisals can be carried out immediately.
4. **Tour Operators:** Reservation Offices accept telephone inquiries from travel agents regarding the availability of holidays in respect of client's inquiries. By means of terminals, the availability of the required holidays can be checked and booked immediately.
5. **Train and Airline Reservation:** These systems receive requests from the terminals of many numbers of travel agents for booking of seats on a particular train/flight on a particular date.
6. **Stock Exchange:** Terminals located in major stock exchanges throughout the country and the offices of participating brokerage firms enable the speedy processing of share dealings.
7. **Stock Control:** Terminals located in warehouse provide the means for automatic reordering of stocks, updating of stock records, reservations, follow-up of outstanding orders and the printing of picking list etc.

Benefits of On-line Data Processing Systems:

On-line Data Processing systems provide a number of benefits all of which assist in improving administrative efficiency which is essential in today's competitive business environment. The main benefits are outlined below:

1. Integration of Clerical Work with the Computer:

On-line systems assist in joining activities of clerical staff to the computer by the use of terminals. They can have access to information which they require for the efficient performance of their jobs in dealing with customer enquiries and order processing. When systems are integrated, common and updated information is available to all the users. There is less file duplication.

2. Elimination of Tedious Tasks:

Routine clerical tasks are replaced by terminal operations providing a greater degree of job interest, operating efficiency and job satisfaction.

3. Reduction in Paper Work:

Volume of paper work generated by normal clerical system and batch-processing system is relatively high. On-line system reduces the volume of print-out required for management report since the information can be displayed on terminal screen on demand.

4. Improved Accuracy:

As terminal messages are checked for accuracy before being transmitted to the computer by data validation programs, the quality of information in a system increases as the input errors are reduced. Hence, information is more reliable.

5. Improved File Updation:

Master files are more easily updated by terminal keyboard with regard to transaction data, as special runs do not require to be set up, as is the case with batch processing applications.

6. Management Information is More Readily Available:

Management information becomes more readily available by direct access facilities, which enables managers to obtain a greater degree of control to the operations for which they are responsible.

7. Improved Customer Services:

Improvements in the level of customer's service can be expected in the systems concerned with appliances sales, booking systems and accounting enquiries.

8. Reduced Data Preparations Cost:

On-line system dispenses with the need to convert human sensible data into machine sensible data thereby eliminating printing and verifying operations. This saves time and the cost associated with such operations.

9. Communicating the Information:

The messages may be sent from person to person or to individuals or to departments easily.

10. Use of a Remote Computer:

In the system of on-line processing a number of users can have access to computing facilities, which is not possible on a stand-alone basis at remote sites.

7.9.3. Real Time Processing

The term real time refers to the technique of updating files, transactions and data immediately after the occurrence of the relevant events. This is in distinction to batch processing, which processes related data in batches of pre-defined periods of time. It is also called as interactive mode or direct mode.

This system makes the user to have direct contact with the computer through his terminal. It is an alternative approach to an on-line processing system. That is, real time systems are on-line systems with tighter constraints on response time. Here the data is processed in the instant it occurs and results are generated fast enough to influence on-going activity or function. There is no delay between the time data is available and the time it is processed.

Special Features of Real Time Processing:

The following are the special features of real time processing:

1. In real time processing, the program is always under execution.
2. It produces output to control, direct or affect the outcome of an on-going activity or process.
3. In this method, the control is exercised during the actual functioning.
4. It is meant exclusively to perform one task. At any one time only a small volume of data is processed.
5. It is like an on-line system with tight constraints on response time availability.
6. In this method, processing efficiency is subordinate to response need.
7. It is called a real time system because it has to give results based on deadlines which are imposed by the real world outside.
8. In real time processing, the decision is to be made on the basis of the latest information available from files which are getting continuously updated
9. In real time processing error messages are immediate and messages are designed to help in correcting errors.

Thus the response of a real time system is one type of feedback control system. The response time would naturally differ from one activity to another. If, for example, it is the launching of a space vehicle, the response time should be in split of second, whereas in business situation even a few minutes of response time may be all right. Real time systems offer accountants and others in the business a chance to fully utilise the potential of the computer as a tool of management.

Concept of Real Time Processing

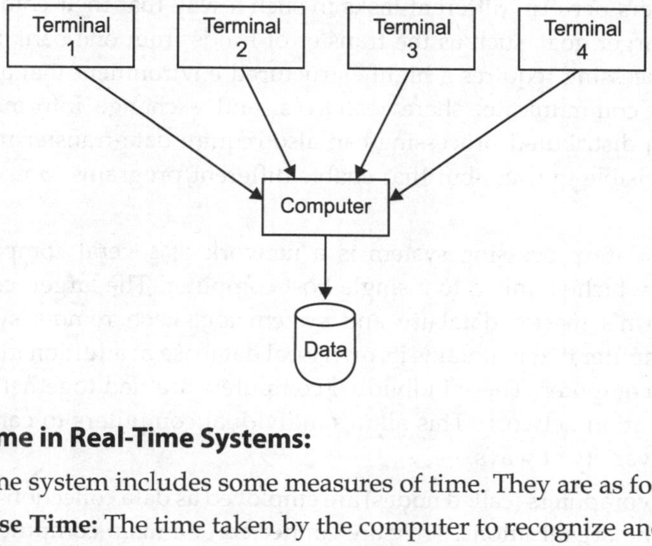

Measures of Time in Real-Time Systems:

The real-time system includes some measures of time. They are as follows:

1. **Response Time:** The time taken by the computer to recognize and response to an external event.
2. **Survival Time:** The time during which data will stick around and waiting to be noticed. In other words, it is the time gap to which the data remains valid, irrespective of the response time.
3. **Throughput:** It is the total number of events which a system can handle in a given amount of time.

Real Time Processing is suitable in the following type of operations:

1. Wholesale supplier and manufacture–Availability of stocks.
2. Airline–Flight seat availability.
3. Manufacturing–Status of production orders.
4. Process Control.
5. Spacecraft Control.
6. Guided Missile System.

Real time systems usually operate in multi-programming and multi-processing: This increases both availability and reliability of the system. CPUs in real time system should possess the capability of what is known as program interrupts. These are temporary storage or halts in the execution of a program so that more urgent messages can be handled on priority. It may be worth noting that some computer systems are dedicated to real time operations and others are designed to operate in both batch and real time modes so that they can also serve as stand-by unit to each other.

7.9.4. Distributed Data Processing

Distributed data processing is a form of information processing in which work is performed by separate computers that are linked through a communications network. Distributed processing is usually categorized as either plain distributed processing or true distributed processing. Plain distributed processing shares the workload among computers that can communicate with one another. True distributed processing has separate computers perform different tasks in such a way that their combined work can contribute to a larger goal, such as the transfer of funds from one bank to another. This latter type of processing requires a highly structured environment that allows hardware and software to communicate, share resources, and exchange information freely. At the highest, such distributed processing can also require data-transfer mechanisms that are relatively invisible to users but that enable different programs to use and share one another's data.

Distributed data processing system is a network of several computers in remote stations, each of which is linked to a single host computer. The larger, central computer maintains the firm's master database and system log. Each remote system is a fully independent computer that maintains its own local database in addition to communication with the master computer. These individual computers are tied together through a high speed communication network. This allows individual computers to communicate with one another in a variety of ways.

Many small computers (called nodes) are employed as data collection points in several departments of the organisations. They are connected to a main computer system (called File Server) in a centralised department, which controls the entire database. The processing involved here is known as distributed processing. The distributed data processing system exists because of the need for large interactive installations with a high degree of reliability and accuracy. Moreover, large number of mini computers can be connected in this system which results in cost reduction.

Concept of Distributed Data Processing:

Distributed data processing is a system in which one or more components run on separate computers and communicate across a network. The concept of distributed data processing can be explained clearly with the help of the following diagram:

Concept of Distributed Data Processing System
Banking System

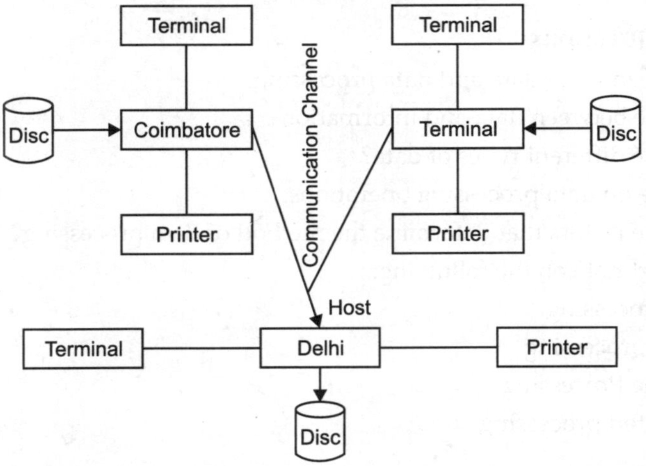

Features of Distributed Data Processing:

The following are the features of the distributed data processing:

1. It is a decentralised computer system.
2. It is interconnected by communication network.
3. More reliable.
4. In this method, computer processing ability is situated at more than one location.
5. Certain common standard of the conduct and regulations of operations must be followed.
6. Since more than one computer is used in the network, it is economical.
7. Real time processing involves the processing of each transaction as it arises and is captured

Advantages of Distributed Data Processing:

Distributed data processing system has many advantages which include the following:

1. Local computers on the network offer immediate response to local needs.
2. System can be expanded in modular fashion as needed because many small computers are used. The system is not dependent on large unit that could shut down the network if it failed.
3. Equipment operating and managing costs are often lower.
4. Minicomputers tend to be less complex than large systems and, therefore, the system is more useful to local areas.

In distributed data processing system a number of computer systems are linked together. So all can share the facilities available in one computer system. Distributed system is different from networking system. In networking system the objective is to transport tasks efficiently to a processing source. This source is not usually situated at the point of user activity. But, the objective of distributed system is to process as many tasks as economically possible at the point of user activity. Networking takes the job to the processing source, but distributed system takes the processing source to the user.

REVIEW QUESTIONS

Short Answer Questions

1. Give the meaning of data and data processing.
2. Differentiate between data and information.
3. What are the different types of data?
4. Write a note on data processing operations.
5. What are the factors that determine the method of data processing?
6. Write a short note on the following:
   (*a*) Batch processing
   (*b*) On-line processing
   (*c*) Real time Processing
   (*d*) Distributed processing

Essay Type Questions

1. Explain the data processing cycle.
2. Explain the objectives of data processing.
3. Write in detail the steps in data processing.
4. Give a detailed note on the applications of data processing in business with examples.
5. Explain the methods of data processing.

CHAPTER

8

Data Structure, File Organisation and Maintenance

8.1. DATA STRUCTURE

The execution of program on a computer requires data that is stored at memory locations. But the elements of data do not exist in isolation, except in the very simplest programs. They are related in some way to one another. It is often useful to arrange these data elements in a convenient manner. Such an arrangement is called data structure. Hence, the data structure can be defined as "away of organising data that considers not only the items stored but also their relationship with each other."

Factors Governing Data Structures:

There are some important factors to be considered for designing the data structures.

They are:

(*a*) Relationship between the data items.

(*b*) Rapid access and retrieval of related data.

(*c*) Ease to modification of data.

(*d*) Cost and other factors.

Data Structure Operations

The basic operations to be performed on data elements are as follows:

(*i*) Searching

(*ii*) Accessing

(*iii*) Sorting

(*iv*) Inserting

(*v*) Deleting

(*vi*) Combining

(*vii*) Separating

The desired data structure can be obtained by performing these operations.

Kinds of Data Structure

The following are the important kinds of data structures:

1. Tables
2. Arrays
3. Queues

4. Stacks
5. Linked lists
6. Trees

Let us discuss these structures one by one.

1. Tables

The data can be presented in the form of a table. It is known as table structure. The tables may be simple with one argument or may be complex with more than one argument. It can be explained with the help of the following examples:

Eg : (1) For simple table (with one argument)

A frequency distribution of the number of letters in a word from a given passage can be tabulated as follows:

Table of Frequency Distribution

Number of letters in a word	*Frequency*
1	9
2	42
3	25
4	36
5	20
6	14
7	8
8	5
9	5
10	1
11	3
12	1

Eg: (2) Table having two arguments. The weight and height of 20 persons can be tabulated as follows:

Weight in lbs / Height in inches (X)	115–125	125–135	135–145	145–155	155–165	165–175
Below 64	2	1				
64-66	2		3			
66-68	1	2	1			
68-70	2		2			
70-72		1	1		1	1

From the above examples it is clear that the tables are the simplest form of data structures.

2. Arrays

An array is a set of data items of the same stored together. The number of elements in the array is fixed when the array is created.

In computer programming an array is a group of related items that can be referenced by one variable name. Individual items within the group are referenced by subscripts. Each value in an array is called an element of the array.

There are two types of arrays, namely:

(*i*) Numeric array and

(*ii*) String array

(*i*) Numeric array: It is a list of values, where each one is a numeric value such as number of an employee.

(*ii*) String array: It is a list of values, where each one is string value such as name of an employee.

Array is the commonly used data structure in programs written for scientific applications. In an array, the memory locations are so arranged that it looks like a matrix. The array can be demonstrated or multi-dimensional.

Single Dimensional Array or Vector

Now we consider a simple array of 12 numbers. (marks of the student in computer science)

54, 75, 45, 40, 37, 63, 84, 96, 62, 61, 78, 80. If the array is named X then each element of X which holds marks would be named as follows:

X(1) = 54, X(2) = 75, X(3) = 45 and so on. This particular array is single and hence referred as one-dimensional array. Hence, the locations of this array are as follows:

One-dimensional array

54	75	45	40	37	63	84	96	62	61	78	80

While studying about arrays one should know the meaning of subscript.

X(1) is a subscripted variable, where (1) the whole number enclosed within parenthesis is called a subscript. The number of subscripts is called the dimensions of the array.

Multi-Dimensional Arrays

The linear array has single dimensions only. Most of the computers can handle arrays with 2 to 3 subscripts. If the same data in the above example is arranged as follows, it is called a multi-dimensional array.

54	75	45
40	37	63
84	96	62
61	78	80

(Here the location areas of the data have been changed to form a multi-dimensional array.)

Dimension	*Column 1*	*Column 2*	*Column 3*
Row 1	54	75	45
Row 2	40	37	63
Row 3	84	96	62
Row 4	61	78	80

We call it as a 4 × 3 (four by three) array. It has 12 elements. Each element is indicated by two items, the first indicating the row number and second indicating the column number.

If we like to address 96, it is coded as (3,2) which means row three and column two.

3. Queues

Another important linear structure is a queue. Queues are used for temporary storage, and hence the characteristics that items can only be added to one end, and can be removed from the opposite end. Thus, a queue follows a First In First Out (FIFO) discipline.

The queue has two pointers, front pointer and rear pointer.

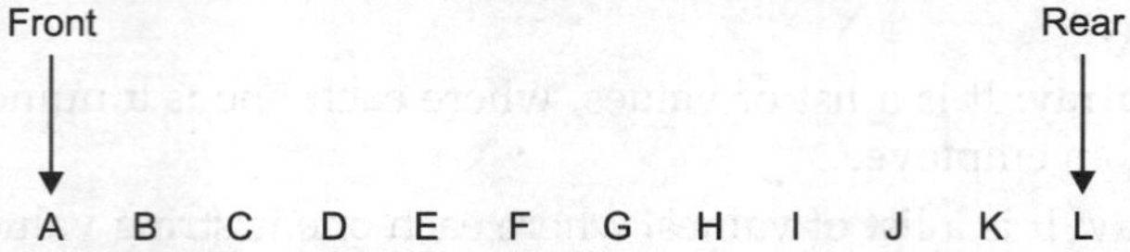

When an element is added at the back of the queue, the rear pointer is adjusted to point to the new elements. Similarly when an element is removed from the front of the queue, the front pointer is adjusted to point to the new front element. Thus the length of the queue is increased or decreased depending upon the added or removed element. It is useful in the development of operating system for maintaining job queues, queuing files to be processed, etc.

Some applications make use of double-ended queue, or de queue, which is a structure that permits elements to be added or removed at either end.

4. Stacks

A stack is a data structure capable of holding a series of items to be processed on a Last In First Out (LIFO) basis. It is a collection of data items, which may be accessed at one end, usually at the top of the stack.

The name stack is derived from the fact that the data items to be arranged in stack in memory, which resembles a stack of plates in a hotel. Here the data items are stacked one on the other, thus, only the last item placed on the top of the stack is immediately available.

"A stack is a list of items which can be removed or added only at one end, called top". We can explain the concept of the stack with the adjacent example.

We can remove or add the items to the stack at top. Adding items to the stack is called pushing in, while removing the items is called popping out. We push and remove the items from the top. Thus, we pop out the item, which was pushed in last. Hence the stack follows LIFO discipline.

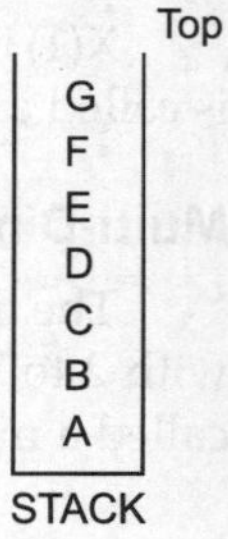

5. Linked Lists

So far we have discussed arrays, which are static in sense that items cannot be added to or taken away from them. The stacks, the queues are dynamic in a restricted sense, since items can only be added or taken away at their ends. If we want to add new items and remove items somewhere in the middle of the structure, it can be done by moving things around. That is, opening a gap in the appropriate place when we want to add something, and closing the gap when something is removed. But time is wasted while moving the thing (data) around. Hence to avoid this drawback a better way is developed in which addresses are used as links.

A structure involved in many data processing activities is the ordered list of data items. In the structure each record has an extra field, called pointer or link. It gives the address of the logically following record. A list makes use of a pointer which starts from one data item and points to the following data item. Such a list is called linked list.

The concept of linked list can be explained as follows:

Physical representation of Linked List

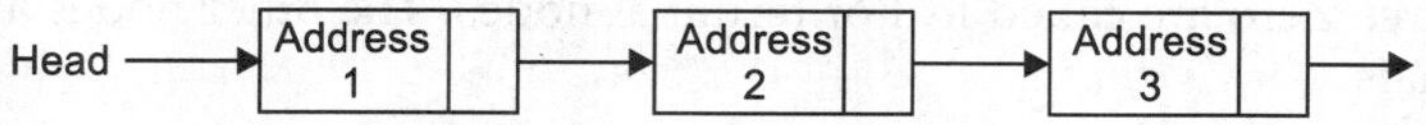

Double Linked List

In this type of list, each element of the record has two pointers. One pointer gives the address of the following record and the other pointer gives the address of the proceeding record. It can be diagrammatically represented as follows:

Concept of double linked list

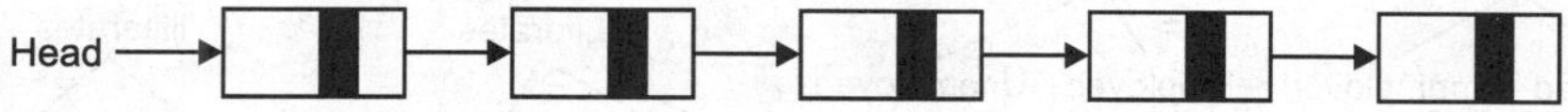

Circular or Ring-Linked List

In this type of list, the pointer of the last record gives the address of the first record. Thus it forms a circle or a ring and hence called as circular list. It can be shown as follows:

Concept of Circular list

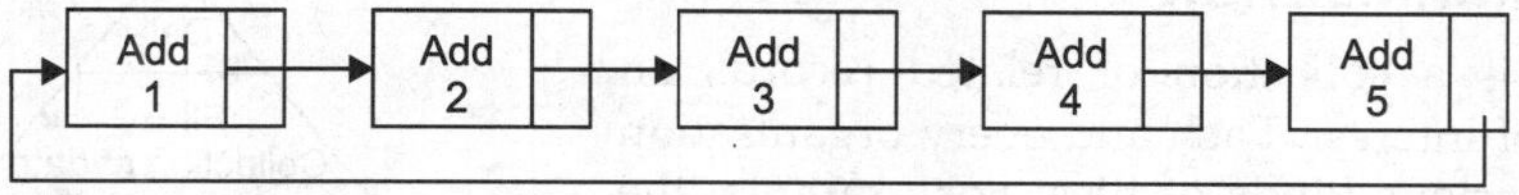

One important application of linked lists in the management of unused space is memory. Alphabetical list of names, a master payroll file containing information about employees in ascending order of employees number are the suitable examples for this structure of data.

6. Tree Structure

The other popular data structure is trees. It can be explained with the help of the following example.

Each junction in a tree is called a node, and each node is connected to one parent node and one or more descendant or child nodes. The lines joining the nodes are thus directed. Every tree has one node without a parent. This node is known as the root, even though it is placed in the topmost position or level. If we remove the root from a tree we are left with one or more sub-trees, the descendants of the original root becoming the roots of the new sub-trees.

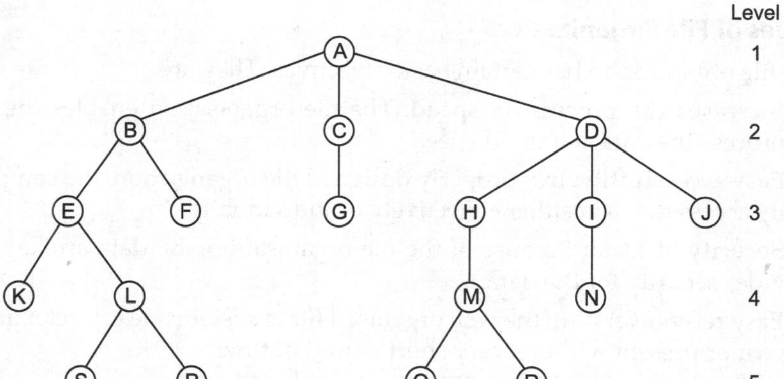

In the above example, the tree has 18 nodes. The root of the tree is A. The number of sub-trees of a node is its degree. The degree of A is 3, of C is 1, and of R is Zero. Nodes that have degree Zero are called leaf or terminal nodes. The other nodes are referred to as non-terminals.

The most popular example for the tree structure is given below:

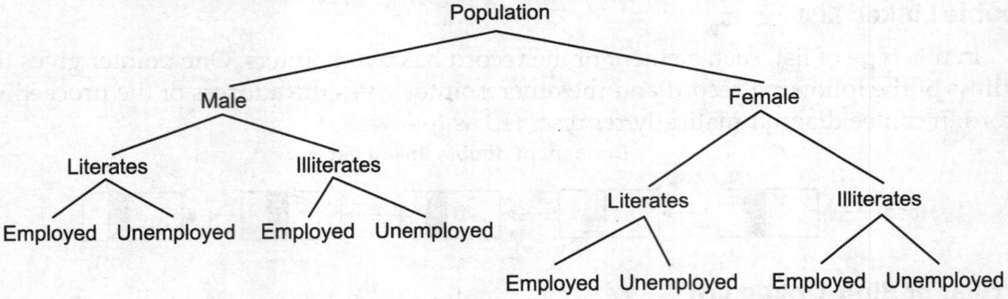

In this example each node has two degrees or descendants, hence it is called as a binary tree.

8.2. FILE ORGANISATION

A file is a collection of related records on some item of interest. Each and every organisation maintains various kinds of files. For example, the name of the employees, their basic pay etc., are collected and kept in a payroll file.

Before going to know about the file organisation, one should have thorough understanding on the basic concepts of file.

The Basic Concept of a File

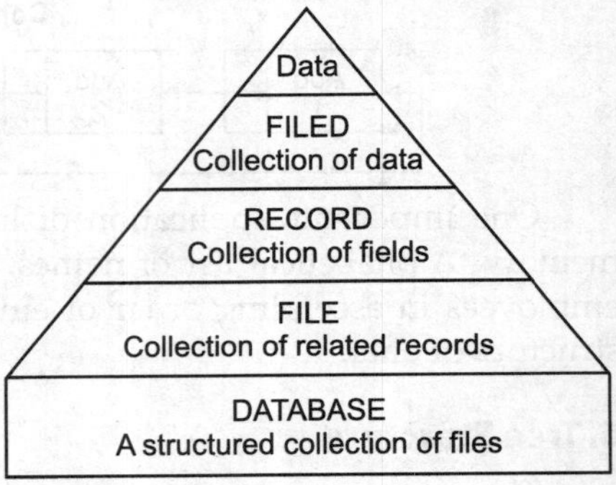

Elements of a file

Field: The collection of data items is called a field. For example, customer's name, address etc., are known as fields.

Record: The collection of related field is called a record.. For example, the customer name, address, balance due etc., may make a customer record.

File: The collection of related records is called a file. That is, a number of records make a file and the name given to this collection is called as file name.

Objectives of File Organization

The file organization has certain basic objectives. They are:

(*i*) **Increases the processing speed:** The file organisation enables the computer to process the data at a rapid speed.

(*ii*) **Easy accessibility:** In a properly designed file organisation, the computer can easily access the data either collectively or individually.

(*iii*) **Security of Data:** Because of the file organisation, the data are kept safe. It provides security for the data.

(*iv*) **Easy reference:** With the well organised filing system one can refer any item of the past or present within a very short period of time.

Classification of Files

The various kinds of files can be classified into the following categories:

1. Master file
2. Transaction file or input file.
3. Transfer file.
4. Work file
5. Output file.
6. Library file.
7. Archival file.
8. Report file.
9. Backup file.

Let us have a look at them.

1. Master file

In every business establishment this file is important because it contains all the current and relatively permanent data. It is a collection of records about the important aspects of the activities of the organisation. For example, the payroll master file contains the employee's name, employee number, basic pay and other particulars of the employees of the organisation. Since it contains permanent records, it should be properly maintained and updated.

2. Transaction file or Input file

The term transaction refers to any business event that affects the organisation. The data is captured on such transactions. Purchases, sales, payments, receipts, etc., are the examples of such transactions. The file containing such event is called as transactions file.

It has two basic purposes:

(*i*) Accumulates the data about the events as they occur and

(*ii*) Updating the master files to reflect the results of current transactions.

e.g.: Hours worked, advance received by an employee etc., (to update payroll file)

Customers order for products (to update order file)

Details of price changes for products (to update product file)

3. Transfer file

As the name suggests, transfer file carries data from one processing stage to another particularly to update the master system.

4. Work file

Work files are intermediate temporary files. They contain data selected from one or more files on which some form of process is required before the contents of the work file can be defined as a proper file.

5. Output file

It carries the output from the computer. It is the final form of the processed data.

6. Library file

The files used for storing application programs, utility programs, etc., required by the computer system are called library files.

7. Archival file

In this file, copies are made for long-term storage of data that may be needed after a long time. It may be used to refer the past events for decision-making etc..

8. Report file

Backup file is a copy of master file and other files. It is created to ensure that a copy is available if anything happens to the original. It is maintained for safety purposes.

File Organisation

The computer system deals with the following kinds of file organisation.

1. Sequential file organisation.
2. Direct or Random file organisation
3. Indexed sequential file organisation

Let us discuss these items one by one

1. Sequential file organisation

In this file organisation the records are arranged serially in a sequence one after another. These records can be accessed in the same manner in which they are stored. Therefore, sequential file organizations will not be helpful for an application that requires immediate access to individual records. But this type of file organization will be useful for a payroll system that is run on a batch basis once a week with almost every record on the master file being accessed. The sequential filing system can be explained with the help of the following examples.

You might have seen the "channel selector knob", in the ordinary portable B/W TV sets. In such a system, one can reach the desired channel, say 7, after passing the first 6 channels. He cannot reach the 7th channel, say 7, after passing the first 6 channels. He cannot reach the 7th channel directly.

Now we can see another example. There are fifteen records in a file. They are arranged sequentially as follows:

Sequential Organisation

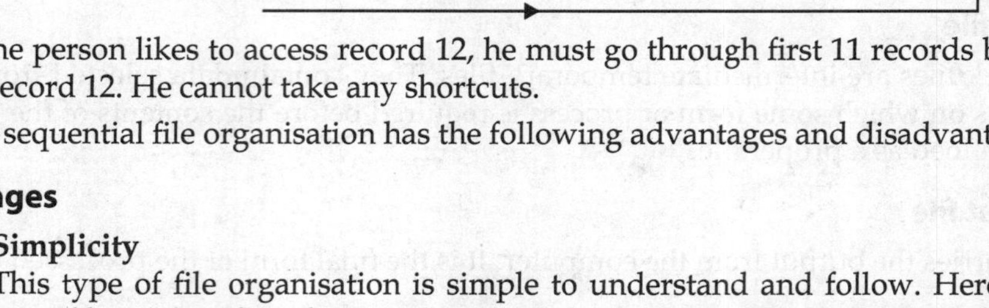

If one person likes to access record 12, he must go through first 11 records before he reaches record 12. He cannot take any shortcuts.

The sequential file organisation has the following advantages and disadvantages.

Advantages

(*a*) **Simplicity**

This type of file organisation is simple to understand and follow. Here, only a record key (identifier of a record) is needed to locate a record. Moreover the record keys need not be unique. It is easy to check whether a record is stored in its proper location by checking the record keys.

(*b*) **Relatively inexpensive**

This system is effected and economical. The input, output media and devices used in this type of organisation are inexpensive.

(*c*) **No gap between records:**

Since each record is stored in the next available space there are no gaps between the records.

(*d*) **Built-in back up facility**

The file can be easily reconstructed since a good measure of built-in backup facility is available.

(*e*) **Simple to create**

The sequential file can be created on any device with ease.

(*f*) **Speed**

The average processing speed of this file organisation is high.

Disadvantages

(*a*) **Inefficient**

The entire file must be processed to read one record.

(*b*) **Mandatory sorting**

Inputs must be sorted and placed in sequence before updating. The input for updating must be in the same sequence as master file.

(*c*) **Deterioration of quality**

The quality of data (regarding time and freshness) deteriorates while batches are being accumulated

(*d*) **Linking of records not possible**

In this file organisation linking of the records of two files is not possible.

(*e*) **Data redundancy**

In this file system, the data redundancy is usually high.

2. Direct or Random file organization

In the sequential file organisation the user finds difficulty in updating a file or accessing a particular record from the file. These difficulties can be overcome by the random file organisation.

The meaning of the term 'random', is 'without any specific order or sequence'. As the name suggests, the user can access any record which is situated anywhere in the file, without reading or passing through other records in the file. Thus, files can be updated without any difficulty.

The random file organisation can be compared with the channel system of the modern TV set, where the desired channel can be reached directly. If a person wants the 7th channel he need not pass through all the first 6 channels to reach the 7th one. He can directly go to channel 7 with his remote control system. Likewise in the random file system, the user can directly access the desired record, and he need not go through all the records in the file.

The random file organisation has the following advantages and disadvantages.

Advantages

(*a*) **Easy accessibility**

Here it is not necessary to read the entire file for one record. Immediate access of record is possible.

(*b*) **Easy and quick updating**

Since the records can be accessed directly, the file updating becomes very easy. Addition or deletion can be done without any difficulty. Moreover, in this file organisation it is possible to update many files.

(*c*) **Sorting is not mandatory**

In random file organisation there is no need to sort the input before updating.

(*d*) **Immediate processing**

Here the data is processed immediately and they need not be accumulated.

(*e*) **Suitable for on-line application**

The main advantage of modern files is that they can be used on-line by direct access.

Disadvantages

(*a*) **Expensive**

In random file organisation, the expensive resources are used. Hence it is relatively expensive when compared with the sequential file organisation.

(*b*) **Not suitable for all storage media**

Random files can be opened only on direct access devices. Thus, it is not suitable for all storage media.

(*c*) **Low speed**

The processing speed of random file system ranges between the sequential and indexed sequential file systems. This speed is not appreciable.

(*d*) **Requirement of special security measures**

In direct file organisation some special efforts such as backup and reconstruction procedures are to be taken as security measures.

3. Indexed sequential file organisation

A common form of the organisation is indexed sequential, in which both sequential and random processing can be used. Such a file is commonly updated sequentially, while the index is available for random interrogation. The indexed sequential file organization is a hybrid between sequential and direct file organization. The records within the file are stored sequentially but direct access to individual is possible through an index.

In this method, part of the file space is devoted to an index of the file. The index an lists each logical key in sequence, and gives the physical address when it may be found. To access a record, it is first necessary to read the index to find the physical address. It is like searching the index of a book to find the page number (physical address) of a keyboard. For a larger file there may be several levels of index. In this file organisation, the index indicates that a specific record is placed in a particular area of the disk.

Hence the user need not search the entire file to access a particular record. The indexed sequential file has the following advantages and disadvantages.

Advantages

(*a*) **Immediate Access**

In this file organisation, the desired record can be immediately accessed and it is not necessary to read the entire file. Moreover the record can be accessed by one or more keys. This enhances the accessing speed and ability.

(*b*) **No need to sort the input**

In this system there is no need to sort the transactions before updating.

(*c*) **Flexibility**

This file organisation is flexible in report of sequential and of random processing.

(*d*) **Easy updation**

Comparing with other file organisation, here it is easy to update the files.

(*e*) **Possibility of immediate processing**

Since this system involves the direct access mode, the transactions can be processed immediately as and when they take place.

(*f*) **Linking facility**

In this file organisation it is possible to line the records of two files.

Disadvantages

(*a*) **Requirement of additional storage**

Since additional space is to be provided for indexes, this file organisation requires more space than sequential file.

(*b*) **No backup facility**

Here the built-in backup facility is not available.

(*c*) **Expensive**

These files must be stored on a direct access storage device, hence, it is expensive.

8.3. FILE MAINTENANCE

1. File operations

As we have seen, the file is the collection of logically related records. In each and every organisation various operations are to be performed in organising and maintaining the files. The important operations to be performed on files are discussed below:

2. File Creation

The major work in creating transactions and master files involves data collection and validation.

In some cases, the space is first allotted to the file, and then the data is loaded into it. In many cases the data are loaded into a transaction or master file in batch mode. The loading of master file is time-consuming and labour-intensive when large volume of data is involved.

(*a*) **Creation of Sequential Files**

The basic operation of creating a sequential file is to input records into main memory and then write them into a storage medium like magnetic tape, etc. The sequence of records entered into the storage medium is the same as the sequence of inputting them. To make the data processing easier, the inputs may be sorted to have the records in some predetermined order. Most of the programming languages provide facilities for creation of sequential files.

(*b*) **Creation of Random or Direct Access Files**

The records within a direct access file are stored in a random order. While the record is being created, it has to be stored temporarily somewhere. This temporary storage space is called a buffer. The processes involved in creating a random file are as follows:

(*i*) The file has to be opened.

(*ii*) A decision has to be made for buffer portion to accept each item of the record.

(*iii*) The items of the record have to be sent to the buffer.

(*iv*) The record has to be sent from the buffer to the file.

(*v*) The file has to be closed.

(*c*) **Creation of Indexed Sequential Files**

For creating this file, the data file must be sorted according to the key value. And, an index must be created and sorted and stored along with the key values in the disk. The programming languages like COBOL, etc. provide facilities for the creation of indexed file.

3. File Sorting

If any set of objects is arranged in an order, it is called sorting of objects. The objects may be numbers or string characters. The numbers can be sorted in numerical order, i.e., either ascending or descending order. The strings of characters can be sorted in alphabetical order.

The various kinds of sorting are as follows:

(*a*) **The Bubble Sort**

The word bubble means interchange. The aim of this sorting is to push the highest key record to the end of the block by successive pair comparison and interchange position if a higher key record precedes the lower one. This can be explained with the help of the following example.

63, 45, 36 is a set of numbers that has to be arranged in ascending order.

The following steps will be taken:

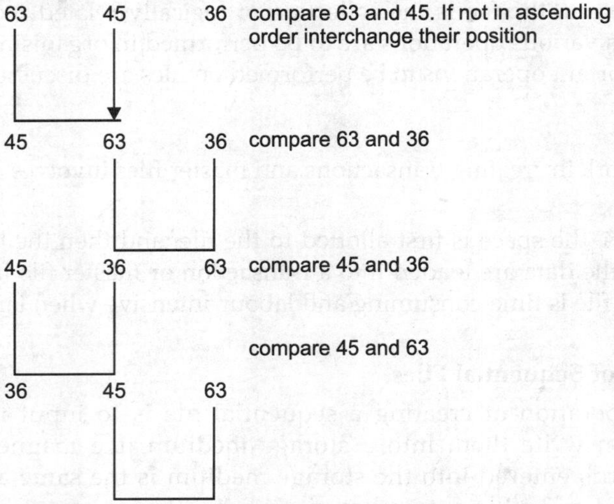

Now the set of numbers is in the sorted order

(*b*) **Insertion Sorting**

Here, the input items are read one by one and inserted into their proper place in memory. This will involve shifting items that have been read in earlier. This can be explained with the help of the following example:

The following inputs are to be sorted in the ascending order:

5, 2, 9, – 3, 6

Insertion Sort

Next input item	Memory contents	Operation
5	– – – – – –	
	5 – – – – – –	insert
2	5 – – – – – –	compare
2	5 5 – – – – –	shift
	2 5 – – – – –	insert
9	2 5 – – – – –	compare (2)
9	2 5 – – – – –	compare (5)
9	2 5 9 – – – –	insert
– 3	2 5 9 – – – –	compare (2)
– 3	2 5 9 9 – – –	shift (9)
– 3	2 5 5 9 – – –	shift (5)
– 3	2 2 5 9 – – –	shift (2)
	– 3 2 5 9 – – –	insert
	– 3 2 5 9 – – –	compare (– 3)
6	– 3 2 5 9 – – –	compare (2)
6	– 3 2 5 9 – – –	compare (5)
6	– 3 2 5 9 – – –	compare (9)
6	– 3 2 5 9 9 – –	shift
6	– 3 2 5 6 9 – –	Insert

Insertion sort completed

(*c*) Scan Sorting

A simple scan of the input block for the lowest key record is deleted from the input block and placed in proper position in an output area. This is repeated till the input block is exhausted.

The other available methods of sorting are, merge sort, shell sort, selection sort, heap sort, shuffle sort etc. Thus, the file sorting involves sequencing information in a predetermined order either alphabetic or numeric facilitate processing.

4. File Merging

Merging of files is the method of combining two or more sorted of data to form another sort set. Even though the records must be the same. The output file will also be in the same order as the input files. This can be explained with the help of the following example:

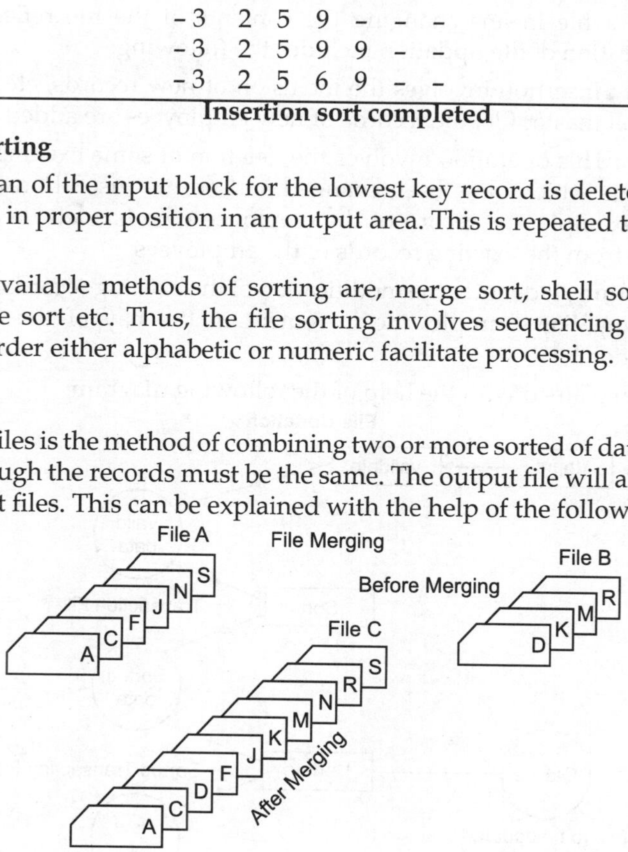

The files A and B are merged to form another file C. Here it may be noted that the records to the input and the output files are in the same order, i.e., in the alphabetical order.

5. File Maintenance

The changes made in the files to improve the performances of the relevant programs are known as file maintenance operations.

The maintenance operations can be classified as under:

(*i*) Restructuring of files, and

(*ii*) Reorganisation of files.

(*i*) **Restructuring of files :** It reveals that some structural changes are made to the files within the context of the same file organisation technique. For example, the width of the fields may be changed or new fields may be added to records or the records of the files may be represented etc. But the file organisation method will be the same.

(*ii*) **Reorganisation of files :** It means a change from one file organisation to another. The various file organisations differ in their maintenance requirements.

Thus, file maintenance is considered as the basic file operation. In general the master files and program files are created, updated and maintained.

6. File Updation

Updation of a file means changing the contents of the file reflecting the current position. The operation of file updation includes the following:

(*i*) **Insertion :** Insertion involves the inclusion of new records, etc., For example, in the payroll master file; the records of new employees are added.

(*ii*) **Deletion :** This operation involves the deletion of some existing records. That is, the records which have been changed and are not useful are deleted from the set. For example, the record of the employee who has left the company can be removed from the existing records of the employees.

(*iii*) **Modification :** It denotes the modification of the existing records without insertion or deletion. For example, the increment in the pay of the employees needs modification.

This can be explained with the help of the following diagram:

File Updation

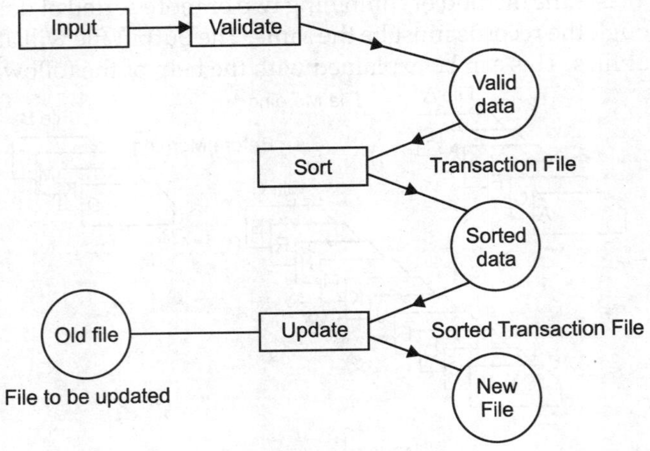

After validation, the details of the changes are put in the transation file. The next stage is to sort the transaction file so that the records are in the same order as in the file which is to be changed. Then the updation is made on the old file by reading with the transaction file. Now the old file is changed and a new file is produced which represents a more current picture of reality.

7. Reporting

A report may be considered as the preparation of facts and figures about certain tasks like production and sales. The report may be routine report or an exception report. The routine reports are meant for the use of everybody.

A report which contains only the important points is called an exception report. It is meant for the use of a few important persons.

Contents and Design of Reports

These have to be decided by the System Analyst after consulting the person who is to use the report. In an organisation, different reports are prepared, some of them are for supervisors, divisional manager and for the general manager. Thus, the contents of the reports are designed according to the needs of the user.

Media of the Report

The various reporting techniques and reporting media are associated with costs and benefits. Some of them are:

(*i*) Preprinted paper forms

(*ii*) Computer generated paper forms.

(*iii*) Optically readable forms

(*iv*) Computer output microfilm (com)

(*v*) Hard copy terminal output

(*vi*) Soft copy (visual display) terminal output etc.

Design of Report

Here, design mainly refers to the way the data is arranged on the medium. Some printers point 80 columns, and some may have 132 columns. Depending upon the number of columns that the printer can print and the number of columns one wants to print, the suitable stationery is selected.

The reports may be prepared on some storage media like magnetic disk, magnetic tape etc.

REVIEW QUESTIONS

Short Answer Questions

1. What is meant by data structure?
2. What is meant by the following data structures?

   (*a*) Tables (*b*) Arrays (*c*) Queues

   (*d*) Stacks (*e*) Lists (*f*) Trees
3. Give is the meaning of file organization.

4. Give the elements of a file.
5. What do you know about the following?

(*a*) Master file	(*b*) Transfer file	(*c*) Transaction file
(*d*) Word file	(*e*) Output file	(*f*) Library file
(*g*) Archival file	(*h*) Report file	(*i*) Backup file

6. What is meant by sequential file organization?
7. What do you know about the random file organization?
8. What is an indexed sequential file organization?
9. Give the meaning of file creation.
10. What does file sorting mean?
11. Give the meaning of file merging.
12. What do you know about file updating?

Essay Type Questions

1. Explain the different types of data structure.
2. Explain the different types of files used in file organization.
3. Explain the sequential file organization in detail.
4. Explain the random file organization along with its merits and demerits.
5. What do you know about indexed sequential file organization? Explain in detail.
6. What are the various operations involved in file maintenance? Explain in detail.

CHAPTER

9

Database

9.1. ISSUES WITH TRADITIONAL FILING SYSTEM

Traditional Filing System means keeping the files in the computer as we create. They are just stored in the computer for the use when required. And it is not kept in any systematic manner. Maintaining the files on traditional basis creates various problems at each and every stage of data processing. It reduces the effectiveness and efficiency of data processing. For example, in companies there are thousands of shareholders. Every day the companies receive many requisitions regarding change of address, name transfer or complaints etc. Besides, the companies have to send regular notice for shareholder's meetings, payment of dividends, right issue if any, and for other details. This poses a severe challenge to the officials to cope up with this volume of data. To perform all these operations manually will result into many errors such as wrong calculation of dividend amount, mailing the letters to wrong addresses etc.

Likewise, in the personnel department, preparation of pay roll for large number of employees is difficult. For example, the salary generally includes the basic pay, allowances such as H.R.A, D.A, C.C.A, M.A, E.A and perquisites such as rent-free house, car facility etc. And the deductions include deductions for provident fund, loan recovery, income tax, insurance, rent etc. When the number of employees increases preparation of pay roll becomes a difficult task and there are possibilities of errors.

Thus traditional filing system may cause overall inefficiency which will in turn result into the reduction of profitability of the organisation. Because, as in the above mentioned examples, the operations are repetitive in nature and require no special skill. The skill used for these routine activities can be better utilised in the jobs which require special skills and intelligence.

In brief, the problems with traditional filing system can be summarised as follows:

1. **Data redundancy** – With traditional filing system, data are stored throughout the company in various departments. There is a tremendous duplication of data in such files.
2. **Inconsistency** – Data may be inconsistent. It is the consequence of updating one file correctly and another erroneously or of processing transactions or making error corrections on different schedules.
3. **Labour-intensive** – Another major problem associated with traditional filing system is that it requires a large amount of labour-intensive data processing activity. Hence, manpower and skill is used in unproductive or repetitive operations.

4. **Time-consuming**—If various files are to be considered for a job (multiple processing activities) it causes additional complexity and it requires time-consuming labour that delays period and reports.
5. **Difficulty in corrections**—Error corrections can also be a major problem with traditional filing system. Data processing schedules must be carefully adhered to, with the consequence that batches and transactions may be accumulated for several days or even weeks before being processed.
6. **Integrity problems**—Preparation of special-purpose reports is difficult with the traditional filing system. Because data from several different data files are to be integrated and such report may require reformatting. The reformatting is laborious as it involves changing record formats and redefining variable names of identical data elements etc.
7. **Difficulty in accessing** the data quickly and is hard to search the files.
8. **Lack of flexibility**—It is hard to add new constraints.
9. **Problems in concurrent access**—When multiple users access to the same data at a time, it creates problems if the data are maintained under traditional filing system.
10. **Data isolation**—Multiple files and formats creates issues in processing
11. No relationship among each file
12. More resources are devoted to file maintenance when they are administered under traditional filing system.

The effects of all these problems increase the costs of data processing, decrease the ability to meet data processing schedules, greater incidence of incorrect information and delayed reports.

Thus the basic solution or remedy for these issues is maintaining data in database.

9.2. FILE PROCESSING SYSTEM VS. DATABASE SYSTEM

Database processing has removed the conventional file processing systems at a considerable level. The differences between file processing and database processing can be explained hereunder.

File Processing System Vs Database Processing System

File Processing System	Database Processing System
1. Nature of Data	
Data are separated and isolated	Integrated data
2. Problem of Data Duplication	
Data duplication - (waste of file space and data integration problem)	Reduced data duplication - (duplication of data is minimal).
3. Dependency of Program	
Applications programs depend on the file formats. (If the format changes, applications programs must also be changed).	Program/Data Independence. (Unlike file processing programs database applications programs need not include the format of all the files and records they process).

4. File Compatibility	
Incompatible files. (because file formats depend on the programming language, files cannot be readily combined or compared.)	More compatible files. (Ex. Access).
5. Data Representation	
Difficult to represent data in the user's perspective.	Easier representation of the user's perpective. (because the relationships among the records of the data are stored as part of the database).

9.3. DATABASE

As already discussed in the previous chapter, data is nothing but raw facts. A perception of the world can be regarded as a series of distinct although sometimes related phenomena. From the dawn of time human beings have shown a natural inclination towards it and try to describe these phenomena in some fashion whether they understand them completely or not. This description of phenomena will be called data. Data correspond to discrete, recorded facts about phenomena from which we gain information about the world.

Webster's dictionary defines data as things known or assumed, facts or figures from which conclusion can be interred.

ANSI (American National Standards Institute) offers a dual definition of data as:

1. Representation of facts, concepts or instructions in a formalised manner suitable for communication, interpretation or processing.
2. Any representation such as characters or analogue quantities to which meaning is or might be assigned.

Data are important resources of the organisation that need to be managed like the important business assets. The organisations could not survive and succeed without quality data about their internal operations and external environment.

Today's management can be defined as a combination of activities which include forecasting, planning, organising and controlling. The combination is symbiotic and overlooking one activity renders the other ineffective. For the effective accomplishment of these activities appropriate information is required. And it is said that information is the life blood of each and every organisation. It must be well organised to maximise firm's value.

Regardless of the quantity and complexity of information, there are three key attributes it must have to be useful to the organisation.

They are:

1. The information must be accessible to the persons who need to use it.,(i.e.)., it must be readily available and in a form useful to the people working with it.
2. The information must be organised.
3. There should be a well-defined relationship between two or more pieces of information. Such a relationship plays a vital role in the management of information.

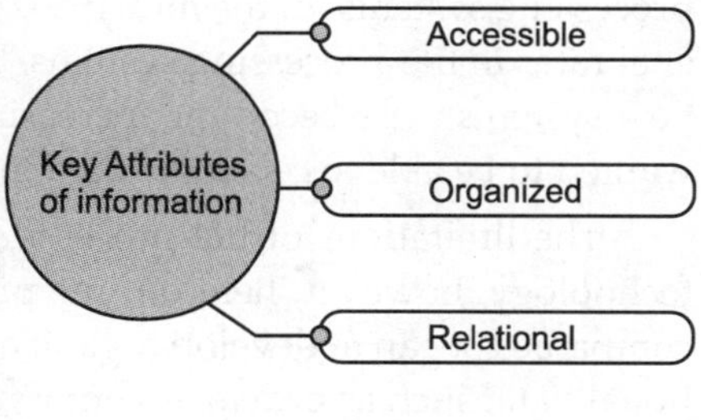

9.3.1. Database: Meaning and Definition

According to dictionary meanings, the word 'Datum' is a fact or proposition from which inferences can be drawn and "Base" is the bottom or supporting part of anything. A database is an integrated collection of data records, files, and other objects. That is, a database is a collection of information. The database can be defined as "A large integrated, share pool of information in a form suitable for handling by a computer which is a basis upon which the computer users within an organisation can draw inferences in conducting their business".

For the efficient conduct of business it is required to find information quickly and easily based on a chosen reference point. Such a task can easily be accomplished by maintaining database. The information is generated as a result of data processing. Firms gather and store data for conversion into information at appropriate times. The integrated collection of basically organised data of an organisation is called a database. It is a very valuable resource to any type of organisation.

Records - the basic data items do not exist in isolation. They have relationships of other records; moreover, they tend to be used in different ways by different units of organisation. An aggregation of data that is structured in a natural manner without bias to any particular mode of storage or usage is known as a database. In a database data are arranged and files are organised in such a way that duplication and redundancy are avoided. Data concerning ongoing activities is captured once, validated and entered into the proper location in the database.

A common and controlled approach is used in adding new data, deleting, modifying and retrieving the existing data within the database. In database, the data is structured so as to make it possible for future application development. The common examples of a database are dictionary and telephone directory, where words and names are arranged alphabetically.

9.4. THE HISTORY AND EVOLUTION OF DATABASE

Database processing was originally used in major corporations and large organizations as the basis of large transaction-processing systems. Later, as microcomputers gained popularity, database technology migrated to micros and was used for single-user, personal database applications. Next, as micros were connected together in work groups, database technology moved to the workgroup setting. Finally, databases are being used today for internet and intranet applications.

9.4.1. First Phase-1960: The Organizational Context

The initial application of database technology was to resolve problems with the file processing systems. In the mid-1960s, large corporations were producing data at phenomenal rates in file-processing systems, but the data were becoming difficult to manage, and new systems were becoming increasingly difficult to develop. Furthermore, management wanted to be able to relate the data in one file system to those in another.

The limitations of file processing prevented the easy integration of data. Database technology, however, held out the promise of a solution to these problems, and so large companies began to develop organizational databases, Companies centralized their operational data, such as orders, inventory, and accounting data, in these databases. The applications were primarily organization-wide, transaction-processing systems.

At first, when the technology was new, database applications were difficult to develop, and there were many failures. Even those applications that were successful were slow and unreliable: The computer hardware could not handle the volume of transactions quickly; the developers had not yet discovered more efficient ways to store and retrieve data; and the programmers were still new at accessing databases, and sometimes their programs did not work correctly.

Companies found another disadvantage of database processing: vulnerability. If a file processing system fails, only that particular application will be out of commission. But if the database fails, all of its dependent applications will be out of commission. Gradually, the situation improved. Hardware and software engineers learned how to build systems powerful enough to support many concurrent users and fast enough to keep up with the daily workload of transactions. New ways of controlling, protecting, and backing up the database were devised. Standard procedures for database processing evolved, and programmers learned how to write more efficient and more maintainable code. By the mid-1970s, databases could efficiently and reliably process organizational applications.

9.4.2. Second Phase-1970: The Relational Model

In 1970, E.F.Codd published a landmark paper in which he applied concepts from a branch of mathematics called relational algebra to the problem of storing large amounts of data. Codd's paper started a movement in the database community that in a few years led to the definition of the relational database model. This model is a particular way of structuring and processing a database.

Benefits of the relational model: The advantage of the relational model includes the following:

(*a*) Data are stored in a way that minimizes duplicated data and eliminates certain types of processing errors that can occur when data are stored in other ways. Data are stored as tables, with rows and columns.

(*b*) According to the relational model, not all tables are equally desirable. Using a process called normalization a table that is not desirable can be changed into two or more that are.

(*c*) Another key advantage of the relational model is that columns contain data that relate one row to another. This makes the relationships among rows visible to the user.

Limitations of Relational Model: Relational database systems require more computer resources, and so at first they were much slower than the systems based on earlier database models. Although they were easier to use, the slow response time was often unacceptable. To some extent, relational DBMS products were impractical until the 1980s, when faster computer hardware was developed and the price-performance ratio of computers fell dramatically.

Because of these problems, even though the relational model had many advantages, it did not gain true popularity until computers became more powerful. In particular, as microcomputers entered the scene, more and more CPU cycles could be devoted to a single user. Such power was a boon to relational DBMS products and set the stage for the nest major database development.

9.4.3. Third Phase-1980: Object-Oriented DBMS and Microcomputer DBMS Products

In 1979, a small company called Ashton-Tate introduced a microcomputer product, dBase II and called it a relational DBMS. Thereafter, microcomputer applications using dBase were invented and the number of dBase applications grew quickly. As a result, Ashton-Tate became one of the first major corporations in the microcomputer industry. The problem found according to the definition prevalent in the late 1970s was that dBase II was neither a DBMS nor relational. In fact, it was a programming language with generalized file processing (not database-processing) capabilities.

Today, the situation has changed as the microcomputer marketplace has become more mature and sophisticated. dBase 5 and the dBase products that followed it are truly relational DBMS products. Although dBase did pioneer the application of database technology on microcomputers, at the same time other vendors began to move their products from the mainframe to the microcomputer. Oracle, Focus, and Ingress are three examples of DBMS products that were ported down to microcomputers. They are truly DBMS programs, and most would agree that they are truly relational as well. The combination of microcomputers, the relational model, and vastly improved user interfaces enabled database technology to move from an organizational context to a personal computing context.

In the late 1980s, a new style of programming called object-oriented programming (OOP) began to be used, which has a substantially different orientation from that of traditional programming. In brief, the data structures processed with OOP are considerably more complex than those processed with traditional languages. These data structures also are difficult to store in existing relational DBMS products. As a consequence, a new category of DBMS products called object-oriented database systems is evolving to store and process OOP data structures.

Limitations of Object-Oriented DBMS: For a variety of reasons, OOP has not yet been widely used for business information systems.

(*a*) It is difficult to use, and it is very expensive to develop OOP applications.

(*b*) Second, most organizations have millions or billions of bytes of data already organized in relational databases, and they are unwilling to bear the cost and risk required to convert those databases to an ODBMS format.

(*c*) Finally, most ODBMs have been developed to support engineering applications, and they do not have features and functions that are appropriate or readily adaptable to business information applications. Consequently, ODBMs are likely to occupy a position in commercial information systems applications.

9.4.4. Fourth Phase-I990: Client-Server Database Applications

In the middle to late 1980s, end users began to connect their separated microcomputers using local area networks (LANs). These networks enabled computers to send data to one 'another at previously unimaginable rates. The first applications of this technology shared peripherals, such as large-capacity fast disks, expensive printers and plotters, and facilitated inter-computer communication via electronic mail. In time, however, end users wanted to share their databases as well, which led to the development of multi-user database applications on LANs. It led to a new style of multi-user database processing called the client-server database architecture. Not all database processing on a LAN is client-server processing. A simple mode of processing is called file-sharing architecture. Larger workgroups, however, would require client-server processing.

9.4.5. Fifth Phase-2000: Databases Using Internet Technology

This category stands on the leading edge of database technology today. Here database technology is being used in conjunction with Internet technology to publish database on the WWW.This same technology is used to publish applications over corporate and organizational intranets. Database applications are delivered using HTTP, XML, and related technologies.

Characteristics of Database:

A database is a huge reservoir of data. It is an organised collection of files of information that has been systematically recorded, and may form the basis of a data processing system. Database is any collection of data organized for storage in a computer memory and designed for easy access by authorized users. The data may be in the form of text, numbers, or encoded graphics.

The following are the common characteristics of database:

1. It is pertaining to data and its manipulation. It has different interfaces through which user can manipulate the data
2. Controlled redundancy: It is a collection of interrelated data. In database the data are stored together without unnecessary redundancy or duplication.
3. It has central dictionary to store information.
4. Real-time Accessibility: It may be designed for all sorts of data processing activities viz., batch processing, real-time processing etc.
5. Easy restructuring: The data can be modified and updated without much difficulties i.e., restructuring is easy.
6. Data Independence: That is, the data and the application programmes are independent. So, each of them may be changed without charging the offer.
7. Interconnectedness: It is concerned with the representation of relationships between data item 1S and records.
8. Compactness -where there is no need for the old paper files that has a big size.
9. Stability–Prevention of unnecessary loss of data
10. Ensures data sharing - Several different users share individual pieces of data in the database. Each of the users may have access to the same piece of data and may use it for different purposes. Data is available for all the sub-systems of the organisation.
11. Represents complex relationship between data
12. Enforces user defined rules.
13. Content reference- Reference by value
14. It has automatic and intelligent backup and recovery procedures.
15. Security Protection: Adequate security measures are needed as it is available for all users in the organisation. It enforces data access authorization and protection against unauthorized access to data is ensured.

9.5. DATABASE STRUCTURE

The database is an integrated collection of automated data files related to one another in the support of a common purpose. Each file in a database is made of data elements. These data elements are to be organised, stored, and retrieved from the database easily. To design such a database one must understand files, records, their data elements and how they are used.

Character

The most basic logical data element is the character. It consists of a single numeric alphabetic or other Symbol.

Field

The next level of data is the field. A field consists of a grouping of characters. For example, the grouping of numbers in a purchases amount forms a purchases amount field. It is an attribute of some entity.

Record

Record is a group of related fields. It represents a collection of attributes that describe an entity. For example, the payroll record of an employee consists of data fields such as name, employee number, basic pay, allowances, deductions etc.

File

File is a collection or group of related records. For example, the personnel file of an organisation would contain the records of the employees of the firm.

Databases

A database is an integrated col1ection of logically related records or objects. A database consolidates records previously stored in separate files into a common pool of data records that provides for many applications. The data stored in a database are independent of the application programs using them and of the type of secondary storage devices on which they are stored. For example, a personnel database consolidates data formerly segregated in separate files such as payroll file, employee training and promotion file, employee service file etc.

Data Aggregates–Common Terms Used in Database:

Data consists of the value of the attributes of the entities.

(*a*) Attribute is the characteristic of interest about an entity.

(*b*) An entity is any quantity or abstract object in the organisation or the user environment.

(*c*) Relationship is some sort of connection between the entities.

(*d*) Data Value is the actual data or information contained in each data element.

(*e*) The values are nothing but symbols assigned to attributes of specific entities in the real world.

(*f*) Data Item is the smallest unit of named data. It may consist of bits or bytes.

(*g*) A data item is also called as field of data element.

(*h*) A record is nothing but collection of fields.

(*i*) A file is a collection of records.

(*j*) A data file is a collection of data records.

(*k*) Data Aggregate is a collection of data items within a record.

9.6. TYPES OF DATABASES

The developments in information technology and its business applications have resulted in the evolution of several major types of databases. They can be classified on the basis of functions and on how the databases model the data. Such classifications can be seen as given in the following chart:

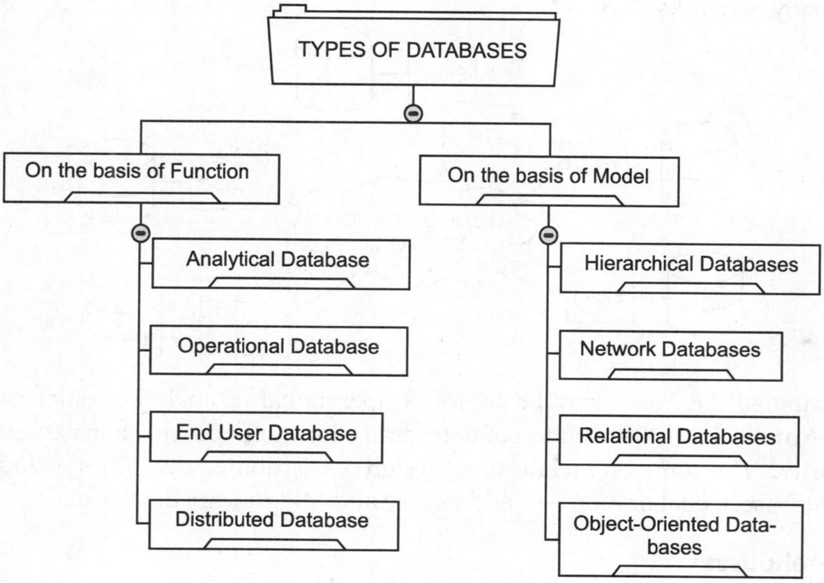

9.6.1. Function-based databases

Based on the functional structure the databases can be categorised as follows:

1. **Analytical Databases**

   Analytical databases are primarily static, read-only databases which store archived, historical data for analysis. The information stored in analytical databases is mostly extracted from operation databases. Analytical databases are also called a management database or information databases because they are generally used by the management of the organizations. They frequently use a multi-dimensional database structure to organize data.

2. **Operational Databases**

   These databases store detailed data needed to support the operations of the entire organization. They are used to manage more dynamic data and modification of dataie, i.e., addition, change or deletion of data is allowed. These types of databases are generally used to track real-time information. They include customer database, personnel database, inventory database, and other databases containing data generated by business operations.

3. **End User Databases**

   These databases consist of a variety of data files developed by end users at their workstations. For example, users may have their own electronic copies of documents they download from the World Wide Web, generate with word processing packages, or received by electronic mail.

4. **Distributed Databases**

   Many organisations distribute copies or parts of databases to network servers at a variety of sites. That is, the databases of an organization are distributed at various geographic locations. These distributed databases can reside on network servers on the World Wide Web, or on corporate intranets or extranets, or on other company networks.

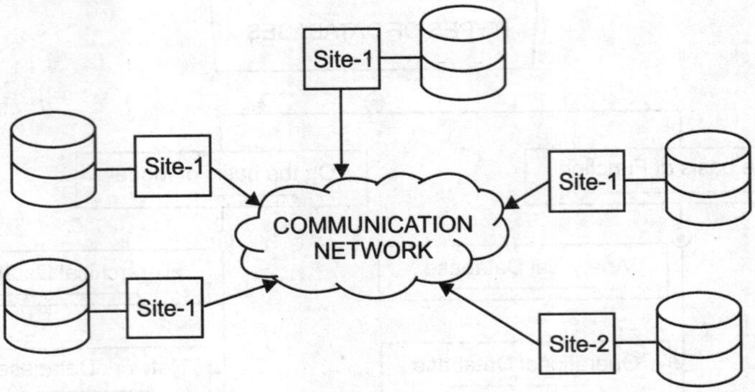

Distributed databases may be copies of operational or analytical databases or any other type of database. Distribution of database is done to improve database performance and security. The common architecture/design of distributed databases includes Client Server database, Collaboration Server database and Middleware database.

Data Warehouses

A data warehouse stores data from current and previous years that has been extracted from the various operational databases of an organisation. It is a central source of data that has been screened, edited, standardized and integrated so it of an be used by managers and other end user professionals for a variety of forms of business analysis, market research, and decision support. Data warehouses may be subdivided into data marts, which hold specific subsets of data from the warehouse. A major use of data warehouse databases is data mining. In data mining, the data in a data warehouse are processed to identify key factors and trends in historical patterns of business activity. This can be used to help managers make decisions about strategic changes in business operations to gain competitive advantages in the marketplace.

9.6.2. MODEL-BASED DATABASES

Data stored in a database can be organised for quick access and viewed in a number of ways. A data model is a collection of concepts for describing data. Depending on the model of data organisation, we can classify the databases into the following four important categories:

1. Hierarchical Database Model
2. Network Database Model
3. Relational Database Model
4. Object-Oriented Database Model

1. **Hierarchical Database:** This system has its contents organised in a hierarchical tree model. It is designed to handle large transaction-based applications. In addition to identifying the date elements in the database, the hierarchical model defines the re-

lationship among data elements. Many types of such models are available. The simplest model is one that organises all the data elements in the database in one-to-one relationships. Other models view the relationships among the data elements as one-to-many. The hierarchical model is highly structured and requires a controlled, finite, rule based approach. In this model, there is a high level of control, backup and security built onto the system. The model can be explained with the following diagram:

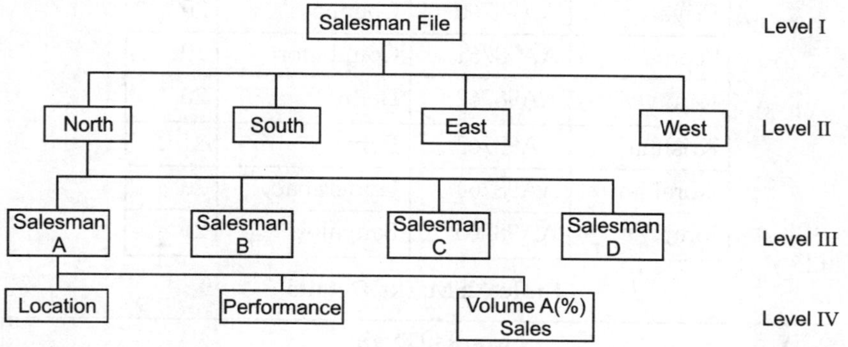

2. **Network Database Model:** It is the oldest model of database. This model organises all the data elements in the database in many-to-many relationships. For example, a salesman record may also include sales by specific product category. The management may like to compile sales under the major heading of product rather than under sales region. Data in the same field can be captured both by region and product. The relationships among many-to-many appear in the form of a network. Thus the structure of a network database is extremely complicated because of these many-to-many relationships in which one record can be used as a key of the entire database.

   This can be explained with the help of the following diagram:

Network Database

3. **Relational Database Model:** The relational database system differs from the hierarchical and network systems. It is a collection of data items organized in a set of formally-described tables and the data can be accessed in many different ways without having to reorganize the database tables. The data is stored in two-dimensional tables, i.e., rows and columns. Each table is identified by a unique table name and each column within a table also has a unique name and rows represent one record in the table. The data is manipulated based on the relational theory of mathematics. This is the most commonly used model today.

This can be explained with the following Tables:

Table –1: Personal Details

Personal Details			
Name	**ID**	**Address**	**Age**
Priya	AA98760	Chennai	20
Seetha	AA98761	Coimbatore	19
Ramu	AA98762	Delhi	20
Krishna	AA98763	Pune	21
Abraham	AA98764	Hyderabad	20
John	AA98765	Bangalore	20

Table –2: Marks Details

Marks Details					
ID	**Maths**	**HRM**	**Accounts**	**Economics**	**Marketing**
AA98760	45	56	45	78	89
AA98761	42	53	60	55	71
AA98762	35	23	59	65	30
AA98763	70	71	73	76	70
AA98764	50	60	70	75	80
AA98765	40	55	65	35	70

In this model a key represents one attribute whose value can uniquely identify a record in a table. And, a key common to two tables can establish connection between corresponding records in the tables. Here in the above Tables, it can be seen that ID number serves as primary key which is used to establish relationship between the Tables as given alongside:

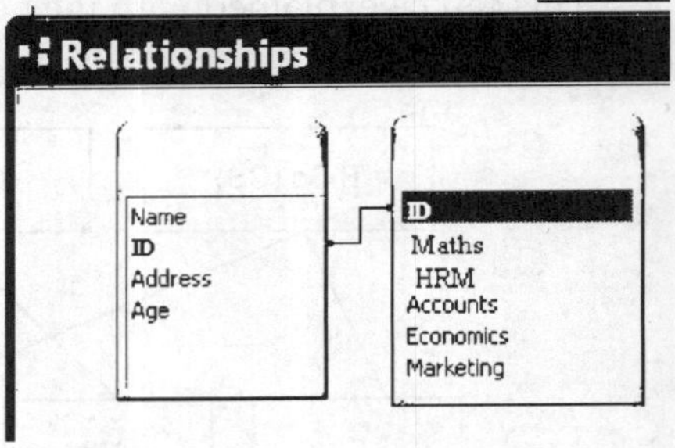

Characteristics of a Relational Database Model

1. The file is in the table form.
2. It has rows and columns. The rows represent individual records and the columns represent attributes of each record. The user deals with the logical view of the file, i.e., the familiar two-dimensional table.
3. Associations between records are made on the basis of the values in a field or records rather than on the basis of addresses (pointers) within records.
4. There is no predefined data retrieved pathway.
5. Records in relational systems may be in any order.
6. In relational system the result of every processing operation is a new table of records. The new files are easily corrected for new purposes.

7. The relational databases seem simple, complete and they are based on strict mathematical constructs.

Advantages of relational database system

1. Relationships between records do not have to be established when the database is created. Users can dynamically establish associates between records to suit their own purposes by selecting fields from files and building new files.
2. Data can be added to files without affecting existing data.
3. Easy to learn. Non-programmers can become familiar with relational systems more easily.

4. **Object-Oriented Database Model:** Object-oriented databases based on objects and classes rather than data such as integers, strings or real numbers. In this model querying is very easy. Objects basically consist of the following:

Object: Object is a collection of data elements and operations that together are considered as single entity.

Attributes: Attributes are data which define the characteristics of an object. This data may be simple such as integers, strings, and real numbers or it may be a reference to a complex object.

Methods: Methods define the behaviour of objects. They are called as procedures or functions.

The concept of Object-Oriented Database can be seen from the following diagram:

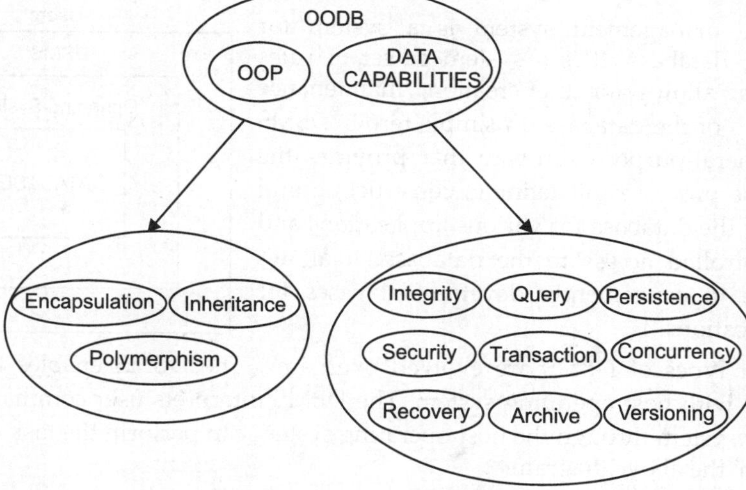

Encapsulation: Wrapping up of data into single unit.
Inheritance: the process of creating new class from the existing class.
Polymorphism: Acquiring the properties of more than one class.

Characteristics of Object-Oriented Databases:

The characteristics of Object-Oriented Databases include the following:

1. They support complex objects
2. They are extensible
3. They support encapsulation

4. They exhibit inheritance
5. They support object identity

Benefits of Object-Oriented Modelling:

The main benefits of Object-Oriented Databases are as follows:

1. These data-bases are able to tackle challenging problems
2. Improved communication between users, analysts, designers, and programmers
3. Increased consistency in analysis, design, and programming
4. Explicit representation of commonality among system components
5. System robustness
6. Reusability of analysis, design, and programming results

Other Types of Modern Databases

The following are the other types of modern databases:

1. Personal (single-user) database.
2. Workgroup (multi-user) database.
3. Intranet (large organizational) database,
4. Internet databases.

9.7. DATABASE MANAGEMENT SYSTEM -DBMS

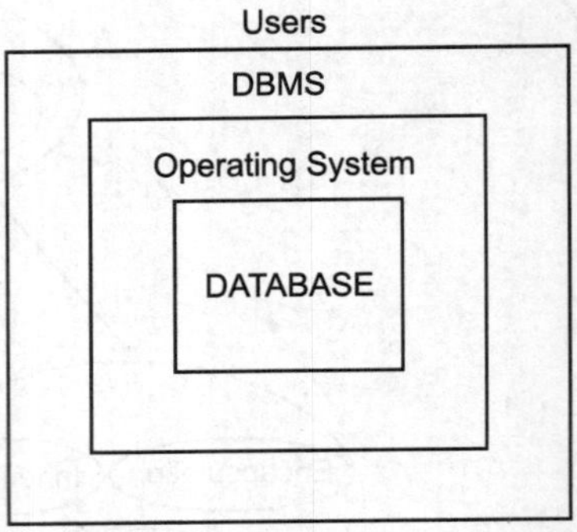

Database management system is a system for operating the database. It is a system or set of rules and methods, allows for the creation, maintenance and protection of the database. In simple terms, DBMS is a It is general-purpose software that provides the users with the processes of defining, constructing and manipulating the database for various applications and provides controlled access to the database. It allows organizations to conveniently develop databases for various applications.

Different types of DBMS are evolved over time. The DBMS enables the user to communicate with host operating system. The DBMS interprets user commands so that the computer system through the host operating system can perform the task required. It can be seen in the above diagram:

Thus, Database management system is software:

(*a*) To Define - data organization capability to support multiple users
(*b*) To Manipulate - access capability for systematic processing to read, insert, modify, or delete
(*c*) To Control - maintaining capability for data integrity, security and concurrency control, backup and recover.
(*d*) To create data structure
(*e*) To generate queries and produce reports through database application
(*f*) Incorporated Structured Query Language (SQL) for processing a database

The basic role of DBMS can be seen as given in the following diagram:

ROLE OF DBMS

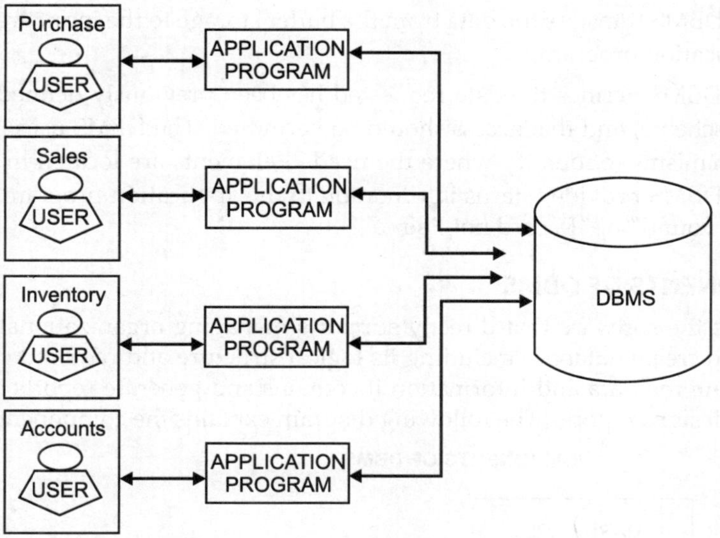

Examples:

Enterprise DBMS: IBM (DB2), Microsoft (SQL Server), Oracle Corporation (Oracle), and Open-source (MySQL)

Personnel DBMS: Microsoft Access

9.8. OBJECTIVES OF DBMS

The DBMS has the following objectives;

1. Provide for mass storage of relevant data.
2. Data independence and efficient access -Make access to the data easy for the user.
3. Support for multiple different views
4. Abstraction into a simple model
5. Provide prompt response to user's request for data.
6. Data integrity and security- Protect the data from physical harm and unauthorized access.
7. Eliminate redundant data.
8. Allow for growth in the database system.
9. Separation of the Data definition and the Program
10. Uniform data administration
11. Concurrent access- Allow multiple users to be active at one time.
12. Reduced application development time – ad hoc queries
13. Immediate modifications to keep the database latest
14. Recovery from crashes

A DBMS can perform various tasks. Some typical tasks are given below:

(*a*) The DBMS requests the operating system to execute an input operation.

(*b*) The operating system causes the data to be accessed, read and transmitted to a buffer storage area in primary storage. This is a special buffer storage used by the DBMS.

(*c*) The DBMS transfers the data from the buffer storage to the input area used by the application program.

(*d*) The DBMS verifies the data requested has been previously defined in the user's sub-schema, and that access should be permitted. The DBMS uses its access path mechanisms to identify where the needed elements are located in the database. The DBMS provides status information to the application program such as, "Record Found" or "Record not Found".

9.9. COMPONENTS OF DBMS

DBMS is the software that directly supports managing organizational data. With a DBMS we can create database including its logical structure and required constraint. We can manipulate the data and information it contains and generate reports in the desired structure or designs reports. The following diagram explains the components of a DBMS.

COMPONENTS OF DBMS

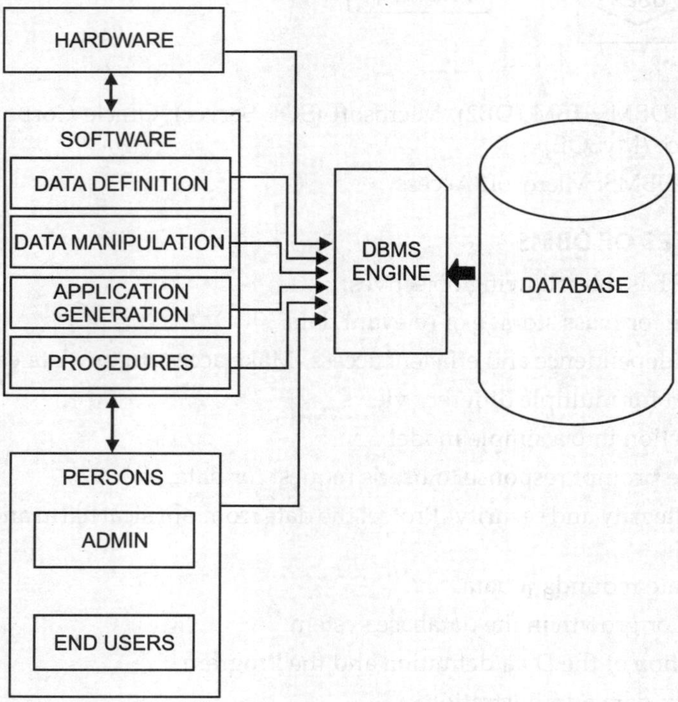

1. **DBMS Component- Hardware:**

The first component of DBMS is hardware and it includes all physical devices of the computers, basically the input, CPU, output and the storage devices. The capacity of the hardware varies based on the size and volume of databases and the expected speed with which the data is to be processed and storage requirements. The hardware ranges from personal computers to mainframe and may also include database server or client-server architecture.

2. DBMS Component- Software:

The next component of a DBMS is software required to create, manipulate and manage database and to control the overall database system. It includes the following:

(*a*) DBMS software itself written in high-level language

(*b*) Operating system

(*c*) Network software

(*d*) Data Definition Programs—They are formal language programmers use to specify structure of database. That is, this software is used to create and maintain the data dictionary and to define the logical structure of the files in a database.

(*e*) Data Manipulation Programs—to add, change, and delete information in a database and query it for valuable information, e.g. SQL.

(*f*) Application Generators/Programs –they help the users to develop applications to database for transactions and it provides easy-to-use data entry screens etc for easy interface with database.

(*g*) Form Generators/Programs

(*h*) Report Generators/Programs

3. DBMS Component—Data

Data is the basic component of the DBMS. In DBMS, databases are defined, constructed and then data is stored, updated and retrieved to and from the databases. The database contains the operational data and the metadata - metadata being the data about data or description about data, for example, the tables containing the details of tables in the database. It also includes schema, entities etc.

4. DBMS Component -Procedures

Procedures refer to the rules and instructions that help to design and use of the database. Users operating and managing the DBMS require the standard procedures to run the DBMS. The procedures in this regard include:

1. Procedures for logging on to the DBMS
2. Procedures for using DBMS functions
3. Procedures for maintaining files and databases
4. Procedures for backing up the files
5. Procedures for handling hardware and software failures
6. Procedures for modifying the structure of the databases
7. Procedures for generating reports

5. DBMS Component - DBMS Engine:

The Database Engine is the core service part in DBMS. It provides controlled access and rapid transaction processing to meet the requirements of the data consuming applications from other subsystems. The Database Engine also provides support for sustaining high availability.

6. DBMS Component - Administrators and Users:

The people who are involved in the administration of DBMS and the users are also an important part of DBMS. Because without the human elements–the livewire, the DBMS cannot exist and is not possible at all. They include:

1. Application Developers/Programmers
2. Database Administrators
3. Database Designers
4. End Users

9.10. TYPES OF DBMS

The Data Base Management Systems developed/designed for the types of databases discussed earlier are the types of DBMS. For example, if a management system is developed for Network database, it is called Network DBMS and so on. In addition to these types, some modern database management systems are developed in combination of the features of the existing types. The classifications of the types of DBMS can be seen in the following chart:

CLASSIFICATIONS OF DBMS

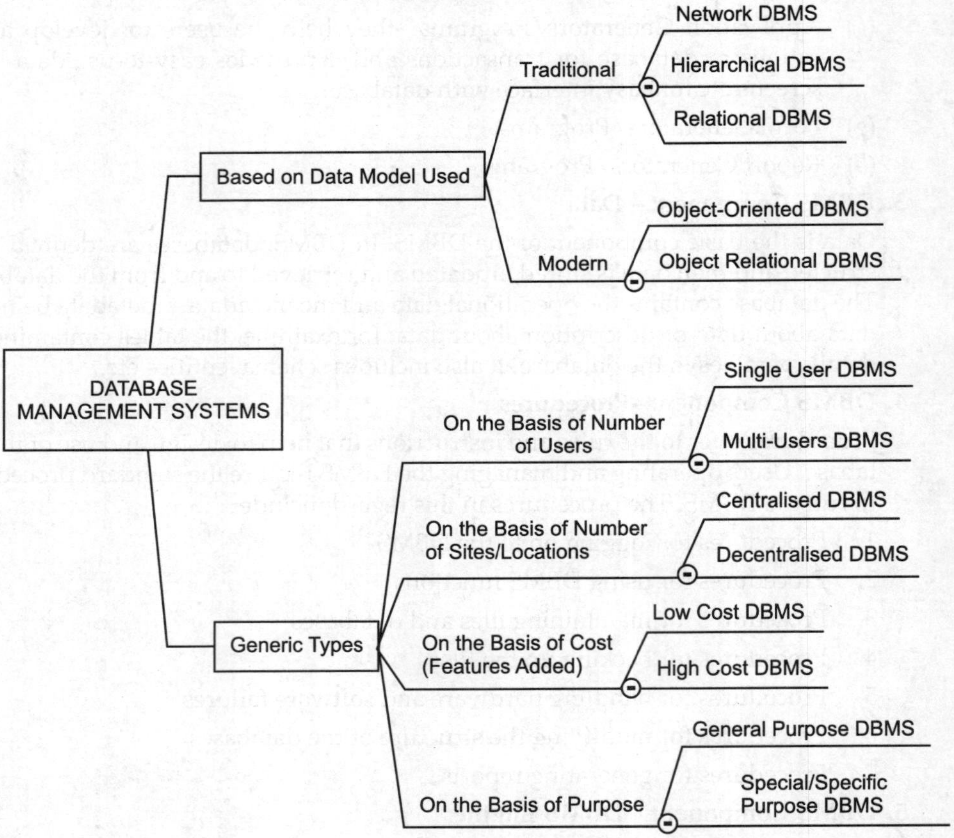

Please refer to the sub-heading 9.6. of this chapter for the details on types of databases.

9.11. BENEFITS OF DBMS

The DBMS provides the following benefits to the management:

1. Helps in Decision-making - More data can be considered when producing information for management decision making.

2. Quick information - Information can be made available more quickly.
3. Effective business transaction - Business can be transacted more efficiently, because the data are available instantly.
4. Information from outside - Databases from sources outside the company are available to assist management in decision-making.
5. Duplication of inputting the data is eliminated. That is, redundant data is eliminated as elements of data are stored in only one location. Access is attained as necessary for specific application requirements.
6. Confidentiality of information is attained by the use of passwords which restrict access to the whole or part of a database to authorized personnel.
7. Data can be stored at a high speed and searched in accordance with defined parameters.
8. Special report layouts can be generated according to specific needs.
9. The cost of storing and using data is considerably reduced and the cost of making changes is also minimised.
10. It avoids having multiple versions of the same data item available to users in different stages of updating. Thus, it ensures accuracy and consistency.
11. A good DBMS prevents the unauthorised access to the data from the database. The same data can be restricted in different ways from different users.
12. It helps in achieving data integrity which enhances the efficiency of the data processing operations.
13. It facilitates fast automatic recovery from failures.
14. In the properly designed DBMS, data migration can be made to improve performance.
15. It helps to achieve distributed processing and computer network operations.

9.12. APPLICATION OF DBMS IN BUSINESS

DBMS is used in all kinds of businesses for all types of operations. And it is not necessary that the firms should have separate DBMS for each and every specific function. The same DBMS may be used to manage all such tasks in the same organization. The following are the common applications of DBMS in business arena.

Manufacturing Industries:

The application of DBMS in Manufacturing Industries can be seen as follows:

1. Accounting - to keep track of accounts payables and receivables
2. Marketing - to track records of advertisers and prospective advertising outlets and for market research
3. Sales - to compile information about clients and potential clients and to keep track of client correspondence
4. Purchasing- to choose suppliers and goods and to place orders
5. Manufacturing - to keep track of supplies of components or raw materials and keep track of orders and shipments

6. Human Resource Management- to maintain records of employees and match resumes of applicants to job openings etc.

Service Industries

For service industries the customer databases are very much important for maintaining ongoing customer relations. The application of DBMS in Service Industries can be seen as follows:

1. Financial institutions- banks, stock brokerages, and insurance companies rely on DBMS to keep track of customers' financial accounts.
2. Utilities- telephone and electric companies also keep databases of customers, tracking usage of utility service, varied rates, and billing information.
3. Maintenance and repair services- those repairing office equipment or appliances keep service and repair records for each customer. Specialized, and often very simple, DBMS are popular for keeping track of clients or contacts.
4. Stock Broking - To keep track of the demands of the clients and matching the placements.

REVIEW QUESTIONS

Short Answer Questions

1. Differentiate between file processing and data processing systems.
2. Give the meaning of database.
3. Write a note on database structure.
4. Write a short note on the following:
   (*a*) Hierarchical database
   (*b*) Relational database
   (*c*) Object-oriented database
   (*d*) Distributed database
5. What is data warehouse
6. What is DBMS and what are its objectives?

Essay Type Questions

1. Explain the issues in the traditional filing systems.
2. Write briefly the history and evolution of database.
3. Explain the types of database on the basis of functions.
4. Explain the types of database on the basis of models.
5. What are the components of DBMS? Explain in detail.
6. What are the benefits of DBMS?
7. Explain the application of DBMS in business.

CHAPTER

10

Computer Networks

10.1. INTRODUCTION

A computer network is an interconnection of computer systems located at different places. It is a set of devices known as nodes, terminals or work stations interconnected by communication links. Computers are linked together for the purpose of communicating data and sharing resources. The computer that provides resources to other computers on a network is known as server. In the network the individual computers, which access shared network resources, are known as nodes.

Network can be defined as "an interconnected group of independent computing nodes which have the characteristics of:

(*a*) Well-defined, mutually-agreed set of rules and conventions called protocols or set of rules

(*b*) Interaction with one-another by authorization

(*c*) Facilitating resource-sharing in controllable manner".

10.2. NEED FOR COMPUTER NETWORKS

Computer networks are used in almost all types of organizations. The main resons for the networking can be seen below:

1. File Sharing: Computer networks help users on the network to share the resources and in communication. When all data files and other resources electronically are centralized in one place of the organization, then, it is much easier for the concerned people to share documents and other data.

2. Hardware Sharing: In networking environment, the users can share hardware devices such as printers, scanners, CD drives, hard drives etc.

3. Application sharing: Applications can be shared over the network, and this allows implementing client/server applications

4. User communication: Networks allow users to communicate using e-mail, news, groups, and video conferencing etc.

5. Cost Reduction: Networking results in cost reduction by sharing hard- and software resources in the organisations.

6. Reliability and Flexibility: Networking is highly reliable and flexible.

7.Communication and Collaboration: Networking allows employees to share files, and share comments on work done by others in the network and suggest measures in case of errors etc. leads to collaborative work environment and enhances the team spirit in the organization.

10.3. COMPONENTS OF A NETWORK

Network is nothing but techniques, physical connections, and computer programs used to link two or more computers. Network users are able to share files, printers and other resources; send electronic messages; and run programs on other computers.

A network has three layers of components:

1. Application Software
2. Network Software
3. Network Hardware

1. Application Software: Application software consists of computer programs that interface with network users and permit the sharing of information, such as files, graphics, and video, and resources, such as printers and disks. One type of application software is called client-server. Client computers send requests for information or requests to use resources to other computers, called servers that control data and applications. Another type of application software is called peer-to peer. In peer-to-peer network, computers send messages and requests directly to one another without a server intermediary.

2. Network Software: Network software consists of computer programs that establish protocols, or rules, for computers to talk to one another. These protocols are carried out by sending and receiving formatted instructions of data called packets. Protocols make logical connections between network applications, direct the movement of packets through the physical network, and minimise the possibility of collisions between packets sent at the same time.

3. Network Hardware: Network hardware is made up of the physical components that connect computers. Two important components are the transmission media that carry the computers signal, typically on wires or fibre-optic cables, and the network adapter, which accesses the physical media that link computers, receives packets from network software, and transmits instructions and requests to other computers. Transmitted information is in the form of binary digits (1s and 0s),which the computer s electronic circuitry can process.

10.4. NETWORK CONNECTIONS

A network has two types of connections:

1. Physical Connections: Physical Connections let computers directly transmit and receive signals and logical, Physical connections are defined medium by the used to carry the signal, the geometrical arrangement of the computers and the method used to share information.

2. Virtual Connections: Virtual Connections allow computer applications, such as word processors, to change information. Logical connections are created by network protocols and allow data sharing between applications on different types of computers in a network.

Some logical connections use client-server application software and are primarily for file and printer sharing.

10.5. TYPES OF COMPUTER NETWORKS

The types of computer networks include:

The types are discussed here in this chapter. Internet is discussed in detail in the following Chapter 11.

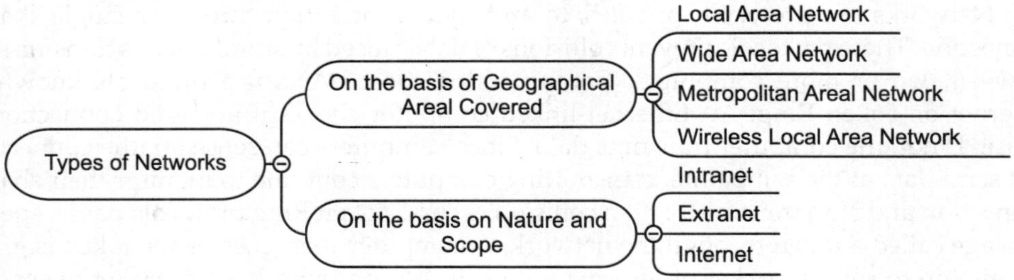

10.5.1. Network Based On Geographical Locations

The networks can be classified on the basis of geographical area covered. Let us see these types of networks below:

I. Local Area Network

A local area network (LAN) is a group of computers and associated devices that share a common communication line and typically share the resources of a single processor or server within a small geographic area (for example, within an office building). Usually, the server has applications and data storage that are shared in common by multiple computer users. A local area network may serve as few as two or three users (for example, in a home network) or may as thousands of users.

A. Features of Local Area Network

- inexpensive transmission media;
- inexpensive devices(modems, repeaters and transceivers) to interface to the media;
- easy physical connection of devices to the media;
- high data transmission rates;
- network data transmission are independent of the rates used by the attached devices, making it easier for devices of one speed information to devices of another speed.
- a high degree of interconnection between devices;
- every attached device has the potentiality to communicate with every other device on the network;
- there is seldom a central controlling processor which polls the attached devices on the network;
- in the majority of cases, each attached device hears (but does not process) messages intended for other devices as well as for itself.

B. Types of LAN connections

1. Internal LAN Connections: A LAN usually consists of a collection of computers, but it also may include printers or data storage devices, such as hard drives. The physical connection LAN devices can be a coaxial cable, pairs of copper wires, or optical fiber. Wireless connections also can be made using infrared or radio-frequency transmissions. A LAN device can send and receive signals from all other devices in the network. Alternatively, each device may be linked to a repeater or hub, specialized equipment that selectively pass information from one device to one or more destinations in the network.

Networks use protocols, or rules, to exchange information through a single shared connection. These protocols prevent collisions of data caused by simultaneous transmission between two or more computers. Computers on most LANs use protocols known as Ethernet or Token Ring. An Ethernet-linked computer checks if a shared connection is in use. If not, the computer transmits data. Since computers can sense an idle connection and send data at the same time, transmitting computers continue to monitor their shared connection and stop transmitting if a collision occurs. Token Ring protocols pass a special message called a token through the network. A computer that receives the token is given permission to send a packet of information or, if the computer has no packet to send, it passes the token to the network computer.

2. External LAN Connections : Connections that link LANs to external resources, such as other LANs or remote databases, are called bridges, routers and gateways. A bridge creates an extended LAN by passing information between two or more LANs. A router is an intermediary device that connects a LAN to a larger LAN or to a WAN by interpreting protocol information and selectively forwarding packets to different LAN or WAN connections through the most efficient route available. A gateway connects and translates between networks that use different communications protocols.

LAN computers use a gateway or router to connect to a WAN such as the Internet, the worldwide consortium of computer networks. Such connections are a security risk because the LAN has no control over users on the Internet. Applications transferred from the Internet to the LAN has no control over users on the Internet. Applications transferred from the Internet to the LAN may contain computer viruses that can harm the components of the LAN, or external and unauthorized users may gain access to sensitive files or erase or alter files. A special type of gateway called a *firewall* keeps external users from accessing resources on the LAN while letting LAN users access the external information.

C. Structures of Local Area Network

The following are the important LAN - structures.

1. Bus Network
2. Star Network
3. Ring Network
4. Token Ring Network, and
5. Hierarchical Network.

1. Bus Network: It is a configuration for a local area network in which all nodes are connected to a main communications line(bus). On a bus network, each node monitors activity on the line. Messages are detected by all nodes but are accepted only by the node(s) to which they are addressed. Because a bus network relies on a common data "highway," a malfunctioning node simply ceases to communicate; it doesn't disrupt operation as it might on a ring network, in which messages are passed from one node to the next.

To avoid collisions that occur when two or more nodes try to use the line at the same time, bus networks commonly rely on collision detection or Token Passing to regulate traffic. Token Passing is a method of controlling access on local area networks through the use of a special signal, called a token, which determines which station is allowed to transmit. The token, which is actually a short message, is passed from station to station around the network. Only the station with the token has the right to transmit information. If a station receives the token and has no information to transmit, it passes the token to the next station in line. Token passing in one means of ensuring that multiple station do not transmit at the same time.

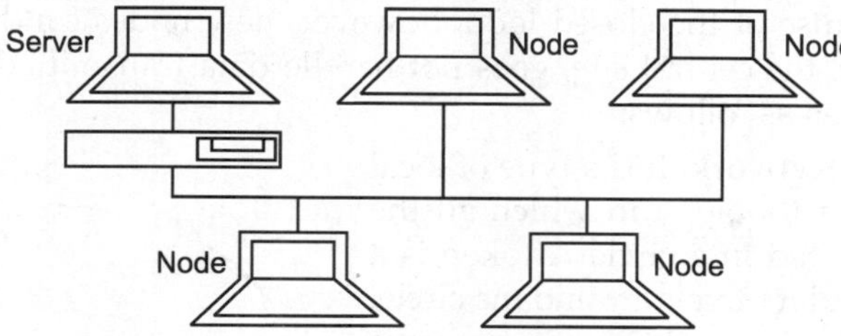

2. Star Network: It is a local area network in which each device (node) is connected to central computer in a star-shaped configuration (topology); commonly, a network consisting of a centre computer (the hub) surrounded by terminals. In star network, messages pass directly from a node to the central computer, which handless any further routing (as to another node) that might be necessary. A star network is reliable in the sense that a node can fail without affecting any other node on the network. Its weakness, however, is that failure of the central computer results in a shutdown of the entire network. And because each node is individually wires to the hub, cabling costs can be high.

When a network is wired as a star, every node has a point-to-point ink with a central post sever. Star Network is just what it sounds like. A star network is particularly appropriate for organization that require a centralized data base or a centralized processing facility. For example, a star network may be used in banking for centralized Record keeping in an on-line branch environment. This can be explained diagrammatically as follows:

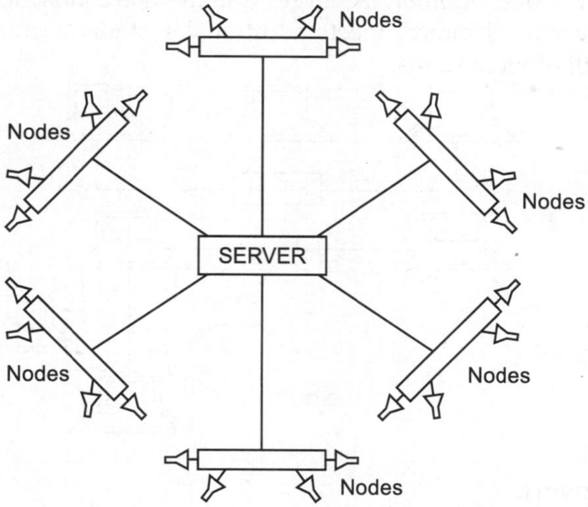

In star networks, terminals are connected by lines branching from a central node.

3. Ring Network: It is a local area network in which devices (nodes) are connected in a closed loop, or ring. Messages in a ring network pass in one direction, from node to node. As a message travels around the ring, each node examines the destination address attached to the message. If the address is the same as the address assigned to the node, the node accepts the message; otherwise, it regenerates the signal and passes the message along to the next node in the circle. Such regeneration allows a ring network to cover larger distances than star and bus networks. It can also be designed to bypass any malfunctioning

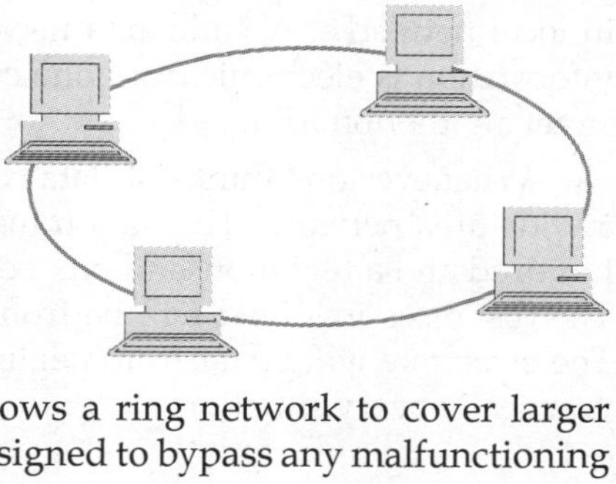

or failed node. Because of the closed loop, however, new nodes can be difficult to add. In the ring network, the central site, goes not handle data transmitted from the node to another. It can be seen as follows:

4. Token Ring Network: It is a type of local area network in ring topology in which all the computers are arranged in a circle A token is a special bit pattern and it travels around the circle. On a token ring network a token governing the right to transmit is passed from one station to the next in a physical circle. To send a message, a computer catches the token, attaches a message to it, and then lets it continue to travel around the network. The concept of token ring network can be seen as follows:

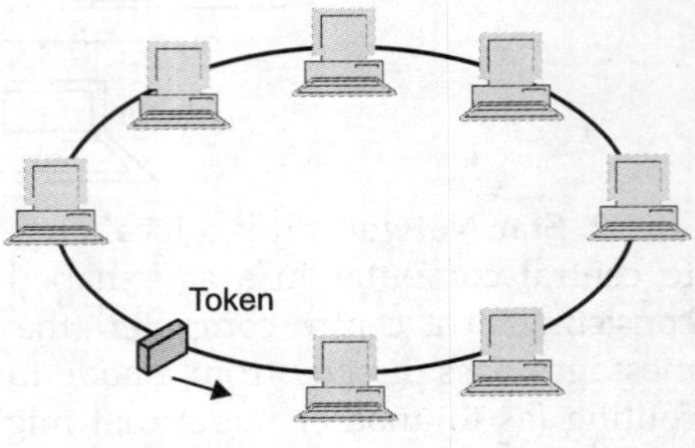

If a station has information to transmit, it "seizes" the token, marks it as being in use, and inserts the information. The "busy" token, plus message, is then passed around the circle, copies when it arrives at its destination, and eventually returned to the sender. The sender removes the attached message and then passes the freed token to the next station in line. Token ring networks are defined in the IEEE 802. 5 standards.

5. Hierarchical Networks: They are configured to have multiple levels of systems interconnected with one another. A large system interconnection with several other systems. Each lower level interconnects additional systems terminals. They in turn are connected with still other systems.

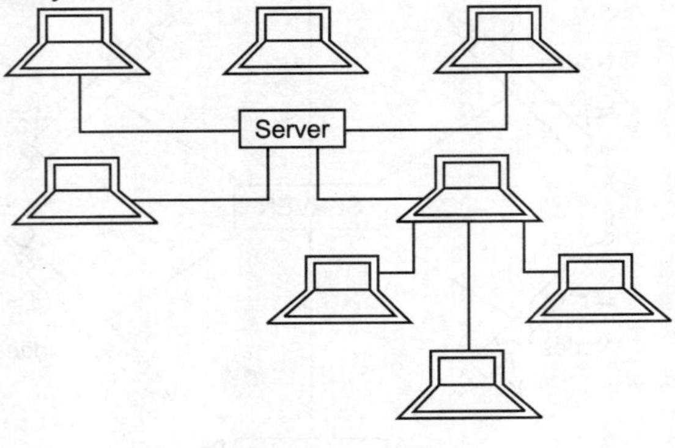

II. Wide Area Network

Wide area networks include all the networks which are involved in transporting information from one geographic location to another. The scale is much greater than in local networks. A wide area network will almost always by employed whenever the information is electronic from one cables leaves the site, even it is only to cross over the street another building.

Whenever one thinks of data communications network, one is normally thinking of a wide area network. The data transmission rates involved are generally between a few hundred and a few thousand bits per second with the usual maximum of about 50 KBPS. The distances involved will be from around 1 km to possibly thousands of kilometers. The error rate will be far from negligible and error detection procedures are essential for practically every situation.

A. Features of Wide Area Network

A wide area network (WAN) is used to connect LANs and nodes that are separated by great physical distance. Generally speaking it is larger version of LAN with several differences:

(*a*) It operates by means of the international telephone network

(*b*) Unlike LANs which owned by their users, WANs operate on public and leased telephone lines provided by licensed common carriers, or by other means such as satellite and microwave, which are regulated by government agencies.

(*c*) Data transmission is somewhere slower.

(*d*) The WAN compose any of the following system configurations:

(*i*) Single nodes

(*ii*) Clusters

(*iii*) LANs

Suppose a company has its central headquarters in Coimbatore and the Coimbatore site contains all departments and equipment for product manufacturing product distribution, accounting, and sales. The information pertaining to these operations is tracked by a single centralised database system. As the company becomes more profitable and expands, it established additional sales offices on Mumbai and Delhi. Each sales office maintains its own system to record and track customer orders for its region. At the same time the two sites are linked to the mode at corporate headquarters and relay each order for shipment and inventory and invoice processing.

B. Advantages of WAN

The integration of the local nodes into the distributed database linked by the WAN provides the following advantages:

1. The WAN allows access to database at remote sites, enabling exchange of data.
2. If a remote node fails, remaining nodes on the network can still exchange data.
3. If the network fails, the local mode can still access its own database.
4. The data used on daily basis by the sales offices resides at the local site, making it easier to retrieve quickly.
5. The local offices can maintain the data more effectively. The corporate office can access the data as needed.
6. As a site's database grows larger, its system's storage capacity can be easily upgraded without affecting the transfer of data between other nodes on the network.

One of the most significant aspects of a wide area network when comparing it with the freedom of a local area network is the involvement of a public telecommunications authority. Regardless of whether the network is made up from system, the controlling authority is almost always the public authority. In order to protect their equipment and employees, the authority lays down rules, which must be observed by anyone connecting to their lines. In most countries stringent requirements are also imposed on the characteristics of the data transmissions.

III. Metropolitan Area Network

A MAN (metropolitan area network) is a network that interconnects users with computer resources in a geographic area or region larger than that covered by even a large local area network but smaller than the area covered by a wide area network. The term is applied to the interconnection of networks in a city into a single larger network (which may then also offer efficient connection to a wide area network). It is also used to mean the interconnection of several local area networks by bridging them with backbone lines. The latter usage is also sometimes referred to as a *campus network.*

IV. Wireless Local Area Network (WLAN)

Wireless LANs uses radio frequency for transmit and receive data using air as a medium. In typical WLAN setup a transmitter/receiver (transceiver) device, known as access point, connects to wired network from a fixed location using standard cable. Access point receives buffers and transmits data between WLAN and wired network infrastructure. A single access point can support small number of user and function within a range of one hundred to several hundred feet. End user can access WLAN through wireless LAN adapter (Network Card), which are most famous a PC card/PCMCIA card in notebooks or palmtop computer.

A. Technologies of WLAN

WLAN uses the following technologies:

(*a*) **Narrowband:** A narrowband radio system transmits and receives information on a specific radio frequency (RF). Narrow band keeps the frequency as low as possible just to pass the information for security purpose and avoiding cross talk.

(*b*) **Spread Spectrum:** Most WLAN systems use spread-spectrum technology, developed by military for the use in reliable, secure, mission-critical communication systems. As compared to narrowband, spread-spectrum consumes more bandwidth but provide more security.

(*c*) **Infrared:** IR (Infrared) use very high frequency, just below visible light to carry data. IR cannot penetrate the opaque object. It is generally used for personal area network, and can function efficiently within the range of three feet.

B. Advantages WLAN

Wireless LANs provide the following advantages over the wired network.

1. **Mobility:** User can access the real time information anywhere in their organisations, this kind of mobility supports productivity and service opportunities not possible with wired networks.
2. **Speed:** Installation and implementation of WLAN is fast and easy over the wired LAN where you have to pull cables through walls and ceilings.
3. **Flexibility:** WLAN provide the flexibility by allowing the network to go places where wires cannot reach.
4. **Scalability:** WLAN systems can be configured in a variety of different topologies. Setup and configuration can be easily changed and set as peer - to - peer network for small number of users, to full infrastructure networks for thousands of users that enable roaming over a broad area.

C. Disadvantages of WLAN

1. **Crosstalk:** WLAN require the constant frequency to be set between transmitter and receiver, slight change in frequency or any external interference lead to crosstalk which cause loss of data.

2. **Speed:** WLAN mainly used for connectivity between two locations nearby or within the same complex, as distance increases the strength of signal becomes weaker. The maximum speed WLAN provide is between 1-2 MBPS.

In India, wireless LAN is extensively used for MAN (Metropolitan Area Network), using RF modems and WAN (Wide Area Network), using VSATs, but is not very popular for LAN application. As cables are used for LANs, it will initially be a little difficult for organisations to accept the WLAN. Pharmaceutical major Ranbaxy, has recently deployed a wireless LAN infrastructure solution for its Delhi office. But many corporate and organisations are looking WLAN as a viable option for LAN connectivity too.

10.5.2. Networks Based On Nature and Scope

On the basis of nature and scope, the networks can be classed as Intranet, extranet and internet.

I. INTRANET

An Intranet is a private network that is maintained within an enterprise. It may consist of many interlinked local area networks and also use leased lines in the wide area network. It can be used to access one or more internal website, which are located centrally or distributed among departments or divisions. They use internet technology to deliver an organisation's internal information. This includes integration of e-mail, FTP, mail server and web servers with the internal applications. Web browsers provide the user interface. Thus, intranet can be defined as "a computer network connecting an affiliated set of clients using standard internet protocols and an IP-based network of nodes behind a firewall, connected by secure networks".

Thus, an intranet is a corporate local area network or wide area network that is secured behind company's firewalls and it uses internet technologies. Although intranets are developed using the same TCP/IP protocol as the internet, they operate as private networks with limited access. Only employees who are issued passwords and access codes are able to use them. So, intranets are limited to information applicable to the company and contain exclusive and sensitive information. Firewalls protect intranets from unauthorized outside access. Intranets assist communication and efficiency in the areas of sales, marketing, service, training, human resources, filing, administration, and corporate culture-building.

A. Features of Intranet

Intranet has the following features:

(*i*) It is the use of Internet technologies for internal networks.

(*ii*) It uses TCP/ IP, hypertext transfer protocol and other Internet protocols.

(*iii*) It integrates the mail, file, web, audio, and video services.

(*iv*) It belongs to an organisation and is accessible only by the organisation's members, employees or others with authorization.

(*v*) It is not limited by physical locations.

(*vi*) It is protected by firewalls.

Thus Intranet refers to inward-facing or staff-facing systems. Intranets have some similarities to Internet - based Web sites, starting out as departmental or corporate e-mail systems and evolving into a broadcast medium for managing internal information, including Web - based documents as well as access to existing systems and data repositories.

B. Services of Intranet

An intranet has two fundamental functions: provide secure, customized access to relevant, up-to-date information found in transaction systems; and let users act on that information by managing how it flows through process systems. These applications are used within and across workgroups to manage product development, human resources, sales force automation and other internal business processes. The other services of the intranet are as follows:

(*a*) Makes it possible the Corporate or departmental web pages.
(*b*) Provides for database access.
(*c*) Facilities of search engines and directories are available.
(*d*) Ensures interactive communication like chatting, audio- and video -conferencing.
(*e*) Distribution of documents, software and there by ensures free workflow.
(*f*) Provides groupware such as e-mail discussion groups and bulletin boards.
(g) Makes it possible the facility of telephony.
(*h*) Integrates with e-Commerce -ie., interface with internet-based sales and purchasing.
(*i*) It enables group scheduling.
(*j*) It provides an easy front end to company's databases.
(*k*) It is platform independent.

C. The working of Intranet:

The working of intranet can be best understood with the following diagram.

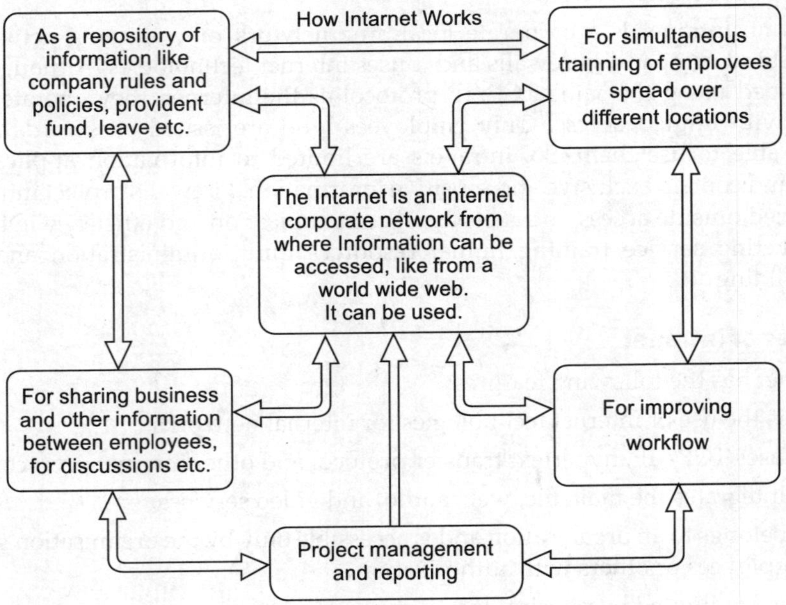

D. Advantages of Intranet:

The intranet provides the following advantages:

1. The employees feel working like a single location company although they are spread across many locations.

2. The intranet has other uses also for computer buffs. If someone wants new software installed in his machine, he just needs to logon to intranet and download. This is just like what happens in the internet.
3. Companies can use intranet for disseminating information.
4. Intranet can be used for training purpose and for improving the workflow.
5. The main purpose of the intranet is to share company information and computing resources among employees.
6. An intranet can also be used to facilitate working in group and for teleconferences.
7. Intranet allows for collaborative work.
8. It reduces the costs of printing, paper, software distribution, mailing, order processing, etc.
9. It reduces the telephone expense also.
10. Easy and quick access of technical and marketing information.
11. Easy access to remote locations.
12. Latest and updates research base.
13. Increase the competitive efficiency of the firms.
14. Increases the productivity and reduces the administrative workload.
15. It provides for securing the sensitive information.

E. Types of Internet:

The intranet can be designed for the followings;

(*i*) Human Resource Intranet.

(*ii*) Sales and Marketing Intranet.

(*iii*) Information System Intranet.

(*iv*) Executive or Corporate Intranet.

(*v*) Customer Service Intranet.

(*vi*) Finance Intranet.

II. EXTRANET

An Extranet is a private network that uses the internet protocol and the public telecommunication system to securely share part of business information or operations with suppliers, vendors, partners, customers, or other businesses. An Extranet can be viewed as part of a company's intranet that is extended to users outside the company. It has also been described as a "state of mind" in which the internet is perceived as a way to do business with other companies as well as to sell products to customers. Extranet extends the intranet from one location to another across the internet by securing data flow, to another intranet of a business partner. In these way intranets of business partners, suppliers, creditors, distributors, customers, and the like are connected to extranets by agreements.

An Extranet requires security and privacy. These require firewall server management, the issuance and use of digital certificate or similar means of user authentication, encryption of messages, and the use of virtual private networks that tunnel through the public network.

A. Characteristics of Extranet

The following are the important characteristics of the Extranet.

(*a*) It is an extended internet-private business networks located outside of the corporate firewall.

(*b*) It can be referred to an intranet that is partially accessible to authorized outsiders.

(*c*) It is a network that uses the internet to link businesses with others that share the common goals.

B. Uses of Extranet

Companies can use an Extranet to:

1. Exchange large volumes of data using Electronic Data Interchange.
2. Share product catalogs exclusively with wholesalers or those in the Trade.
3. Collaborate with other companies on joint development efforts.
4. Jointly develop and use training programs with other companies.
5. Provide or access services provided by one company to a group of other companies, such as an online banking application managed by one company on behalf or affiliated banks.
6. Share news of common interest exclusively with partner companies.
7. The manufacturing companies can coordinate the design manufacturing, scheduling and delivery across supply chain.
8. With extranet the technology firms can support for their customers and partners and makes it possible for remote access for employees.
9. The financial services firms by using extranet can reduce costs of proprietary networks.
10. With extranet the publishing companies can increase the speed of design and production cycles.
11. Other benefits:
    (*i*) Quicker turnaround time
    (*ii*) Improved communication
    (*iii*) Decreased paper flow
    (*iv*) Trackable correspondence
    (*v*) Better service
    (*vi*) Lower overhead and expenses
    (*vii*) Improved employee morale
    (*viii*) Increased Margins.
    (*ix*) Flexibility and scalability.
    (*x*) Redused transitional barriers.
    (*xi*) Versatility.

Business of business e-commerce is growing on extranets. The companies gain competitive efficiency and advantage through quick transactions and easy access to new markets. The extranets also facilitates quick transactions and easy access to new markets. The extranets also facilitates quick distribution of information products and services.

10.6. INTERNET VS INTRANET

Internet Vs Intranet

Parameter	The Internet	An Intranet
Security	Low or None	High
Speed	Low to Medium	High
Services	Almost unlimited	Specified by Organisation
Access Control	None or limited. Public encouraged to visit.	Account Name and Password. Generally no external (public) access.
Membership	Unlimited	Population of Organisation
Reliability	Low	High
Control	Low or None	High
Size	Enormous	Constrained Small, Medium or Large
Costs	Attachment: Low Presence: Medium	Medium to High
Benefits	What we see is what we get	Efficiencies and Productivities

10.7. BLUETOOTH

The name Bluetooth comes from the name of the king Harald Blatan of Denmark. In the 10th century, he united Denmark and Norway. Bluetooth is the English translation of his name. Ericsson (Scandinavian Company) was the first to develop this specification. Bluetooth is a technology that will be used to provide personal area networks connectivity between consumer electronics and devices. Invented by Ericsson, Bluetooth is, in essence, a set of radio wave communications, protocols and standards that enable low-cost, high speed communications among devices that are within 10 meters of each other (this distance can be increased to 100 meters with amplifiers or increasing the transmit power). Although Blue tooth cannot match the speed of infrared communication, it does not have infrared's line-of-sight limitation. Bluetooth can also transmit both data and voice communications.

Bluetooth is the official name of a specification of a growing technology and this technology lets the electronic devices communicate with each other using a secure radio frequency. With mobile multimedia and wireless networks, bluetooth technology provides a no-wire connection between the electronic devices like computers, mobile phones etc. transmits in the unlicensed 2.4 GHz band and uses a frequency hopping spread spectrum technique that changes its signal 1600times per second. If there is interference from other devices, the transmission does not stop, but its speed is downgraded.

The main benefit of blue tooth technology wireless is the mobile connections between devices providing ad hoc networking. Thus the devices equipped with Bluetooth technology are able to establish connections to other devices as soon as they are in range without user interaction.

Piconet: When two devices of Bluetooth technology are in range, they can link to form a mini-network called piconet. It supports point to point and point to multipoint connections. With this unique feature, many piconets can be formed and linked according tour requirements. Generally up to eight devices of Bluetooth technology can form a piconet. And up to ten piconets with in a range can form a scatter-net.

REVIEW QUESTIONS

Short Answer Questions

1. What is meant by network?
2. Explain the need for computer network.
3. Write a note on the components of computer network
4. Explain the following:
   (*a*) LAN (*b*) WAN
   (*c*) MAN (*d*) WLAN
5. What is meant by Bluetooth?
6. What is intranet?
7. Write a note on the features of intranet.
8. What is extranet?

Essay Type Questions:

1. Explain the different types of computer networks.
2. Explain about LAN with its different structures.
3. What do you know about WAN? Explain it detail.
4. Differentiate between intranet and internet.
5. Distinguish between intranet and extranet.
6. Explain the features and working of intranet
7. Describe the feature and uses of extranet.

CHAPTER

11

E-Commerce and Internet

11.1. E-COMMERCE

E-commerce refers to the paperless exchange of business information using network based technologies. It is a general term for any type of business, or commercial transaction, that involves the transfer of information across the Internet. In past, a consumer had ample time to go from store to store to locate a desired item, followed by bargaining, placing an order and finally getting the supply. This entire process could range from a few hours to weeks depending on the product, quantity, quality and source of purchase. But the entire scenario has changed. Everything in today's world is electronics whether it is EDI (Electronic Data Interchange), EFT (Electronic Funds Transfer), Ecash (Electronic Cash), E- Stamp (Electronic Stamp), E-mail (Electronic Mail), E-Business (Electronic Business) and E-Commerce (Electronic Commerce).

Differences between Traditional commerce and E-commerce:

Now we shall explain the differences between traditional commerce and e-commerce in the following table.

S. No.	Features	Traditional commerce	E-commerce
1.	Exchange of information.	Direct person-to-person contact, i.e., face-to-face, postal, or phone exchanges.	Through electronic medium.
2.	Method of purchasing involved.	Manual-individuals participating in all transactions manual presence is limited	Automated-Almost the entire process is automated and the
3.	Technology involved.	As facilitator.	As enabler.
4.	Factor of competitive edge.	Factor of differentiation.	Factor of speed.
5.	Chance of repudiation of a transaction.	It provides for both parties of a transaction to not be able to refuse or acknowledge a debt or contract.	Repudiation is possible.
6.	Strategy of Marketing	Mainly push strategy.	Pull strategy.
7.	Time of accessibility days.	Only limited time.	Round the clock on all

8.	Product characteristics	Customers can feel or touch the commodities to make their purchases.	It is not possible.
9.	Security	Participating entities are physically close, receipts and authentication are standard	Since non-repudiation is possible, authentication must be provided digitally.
10.	Socialisation	Provides for Socialisation and meeting people and friends.	Isolated from public.
11.	Support services	It does not have any specialised support services along with it.	It has a variety of support services, such as e-mail, online directories, ordering, settlement support systems, inventory control systems, etc.
12.	Experience	It provides for enjoying the urban life and experience entertainment	It is not possible.

11.1.1. Reasons for The Growth of E -Commerce

There have been a number of reasons, which have led to the growth of E-Commerce. A few of them are:

1. Age of competition
2. Globalization of economy
3. Commercialization and privatization of Internet
4. High labour cost and lesser available time.
5. Higher volumes of sales at lower profits.
6. Shorter product life cycles due to changes in technology.
7. Faster communication of information over computer networks the reducing distances world wide as a result of emergence of a new field Information Technology that is a combination of telecommunications and computer science.

Electronic Commerce is a critical action tool for competitive business strategies in international trade. Electronic Commerce encompasses the entire online process of developing, marketing, selling, delivering, servicing and paying for products and services. The Internet's Web Browser and client/server architecture and networks of hypermedia databases on the World Wide Web serve as the technology platform for electronic commerce among inter networked communities of customers and business partners. Since communication through Internet and other online services have become very popular and easy to operate traditional EC activities can now be conducted with new participants on a global scale.

Electronic Commerce uses the Internet Intranet and Extranets to accomplish online transactions with customers and business partners. EC means different things to different people. To some it may mean transfer of standardised and structured information between firms i.e., EDI (Electronic Data Interchange). To others it may mean shopping on the internet and to still others it may mean tracking & tracing the course of action through its journey in the value chain.

11.1.2. Features of E-Commerce:

E-Commerce has the following general features:

1. It is a business strategy to cut down costs, while improving quality and increasing the speed of delivery of goods/services.
2. It has ability to sell and purchase products/services/information on computer networks.
3. It is a solution for office automation and quick business transactions.
4. It is a tool to improve intra business functioning like business re-engineering.
5. It is a tool to improve inter business communication through easy and accurate interaction and information interchange.

11.1.3. Importance of E-Commerce

E-Commerce becomes inevitable because of the following:

1. Low setup cost

Any body can easily set up a website. In fact there are many organizations and training institutes who help customers in developing and launching websites. To market a product large retail showrooms are not required, just a web site showing the characteristics of the product including cost details are sufficient.

2. Global Free Market

Nobody can dominate the global market as presence on the internet is easy not only for global giants, but even small organisations can participate actively at low costs and compete with stiff competition.

3. Global Access

Since more than 200 countries are hooked onto the Internet, anybody who can afford a TV and a telephone can fully access the Internet and gain the information required.

4. Availability of Technology:

Since the same technology like web servers, browsers, engines, internet, etc., is used throughout the world therefore business can be easily conducted.

5. Multiple Opportunities:

By using E-Commerce multiple activities like selling, renting, purchasing etc. can be performed. In fact a whole variety of transactions can be provided all under one roof.

6. Others

E-commerce systems are being established for automating and enhancing many aspects of communications, publishing, marketing, sales and customer service such as:

- Customer Research;
- Pre-Sales Enquiries;
- Information Publishing and Dissemination;
- Sales;
- Advertising;
- Promotions;
- Public Relations;
- Purchasing;

- Transactions;
- Funds Transfer;
- Production;
- Delivery;
- After-Sales Service;
- Ongoing Relationship Management; and
- Customer Support.

The benefits of electronic commerce are not just available to large corporations and government departments, and many small to medium businesses are discovering new cost-effective opportunities to use Internet-related technology to help their business operations locally and internationally.

11.1.4. Objectives of E-Commerce

The objectives of E-Commerce can easily be understand with the help of the following diagram.

Objectives of E-Commerce

Conduct Distant Business	Streamline Procurement Process	Use of Competitive Processes
1. To acquire latest technologies and improvements in the filed	1. To cut down procurement time	1. To decrease the length of production cycle.
2. To help expand horizon of business and service	2. To cut down procurement cost	2. To create competitive edge in the respective fields.
3. To create new services and businesses	3. To simplify procurement process	3. To improve and maintain production quality.

11.1.5. Types of E - Commerce

The following are the important types of E - Commerce:

1. E - tailing or "virtual storefronts" on Web sites with online catalogs, sometimes gathered into a "virtual mail"
2. The gathering and use of demographic data through Web contacts
3. Electronic Data Interchange, the business-to-business exchange of data
4. E-mail and fax and their use as media for reaching prospects and established customers (for example, with newsletters)
5. Business to Consumer Commerce.

6. Business to Business Applications
7. Consumer to Consumer Applications
8. Internal Business Processes
9. The security of business transactions.

Let us discuss these items one by one:

1. E-tailing or The Virtual Storefront and the Virtual Mall

As a place for direct retail shopping, with its 24-hour availability, a global reach, the ability to interact and provide custom information and ordering, and multimedia prospects, the Web is rapidly becoming a multibillion-dollar source of revenue for the world's businesses. A number of businesses already report considerable success.

2. Market Research

In early 1999, it was widely recognized that because of the interactive nature of the internet, companies could gather data about prospects and customers in unprecedented amounts -through site registration, questionnaires, and as part of taking orders. The issue of whether data was being collected with the knowledge and permission of market subjects had been raised.

3. Electronic Data Interchange (EDI)

The business environment is moving fast than ever before. Increased competition at home and abroad means quality as well as profitability must be preserved. This picture has led to a reappraisal of accepted business practice in the search for greater efficiency. Traditional the response in the face of competitive threat been to reduce costs by rationalising production, shedding labour and restricting business, coupled with investment in technology to improve productivity.

But the huge bulk of commercial documents generated between companies in the trading cycle still remains locked in slow, antiquated, paperbound processes. Documents produced by one computer are printed and posted, only to be entered into the recipient's computer - a time - consuming, error - prone and costly exercise, estimated at between 4% and 7% of the value of the goods traded.

In a complex web of trading relationship in which each organisation is itself a customer of another, we can see that paperwork all too easily becomes a barrier to the trade it was designed to support. It is this area on which attention is now focused because it offers tremendous potential for improvement. Sales returns could be analysed and fed into the ordering process; orders could be raised to reflect both demand and known stock availability, instructions could be sent to distributors in parallel with the order to ensure fast delivery carriage by road, rail, sea or air could be booked simultaneously; customs clearance documentation could be available in advance of good arriving, avoiding holdups; payment instructions could be issued to banks to ensure prompt payment. And all without the mountain of paperwork surrounding today's business transactions.

Common business transaction, such as purchase orders and invoice, are often printed as standard paper forms. When business information is available in a standard format, we can transmit it direct to our trading partner's computer system for processing. This type of information transmission is known as Electronic Data Interchange. EDI lets we replace conventional paper documents with formatted, standardized business documents transmitted as electronic data.

The Importance of EDI: First, today's paper-based system for handling business-to-business information exchange presents several problems. Second, a number of large firms are moving rapidly to implement EDI and are sending the message that trading partners should be prepared to do EDI or face the loss of relationships. Some of the problems with paper-based information systems that EDI can address include the following:

(*a*) **Time delays:** In a paper-based transaction systems, a number of delays occur along the time line. The first source is transportation delay, caused by the mail system or by other system required to physically move paper documents between parties. The second source is manual processing delay caused by the need to key and re-key information along the time line. Delays in transporting, billing, payment, poor customer service and poor management information can be overcome by EDI.

(*b*) **Labour Costs:** In a paper-based system, manual processing is required for data keying, document storage and retrieval, document matching envelop stuffing etc. EDI reduces these types of paper costs.

(*c*) **Errors:** Because the same information is keyed multiple times, paper-based system is error-prone. This problem is effectively solved with EDI.

(*d*) **Inventory:** Because of delays and uncertainties in paper processing, inventory management can effectively be made with EDI.

(*e*) **Uncertainty:** Uncertainty exists in three areas. First, transportation and keying delays mean that timing is uncertain. Second, the sender does not know whether the transaction is received at all or whether the firm agrees with what was sent in for that transaction. Third, in the payment area, it is difficult to tell when a paper check will clear back to the disbursing bank.

(*f*) **Ensures quick order processing:** Since most purchasing transactions are routine, they can be handled automatically, freeing staff for more demanding and less routine tasks.

(*g*) **Make sales more easily:** With EDI, quotes, estimates, order entry and invoicing can be processed more smoothly and efficiently. Orders received electronically ensure that information is available virtually immediately. So the business firms can respond faster and become more competitive.

(*h*) **Ensures quicker payments:** Invoices received electronically can be reconciled automatically and entered in the accounting department sooner. This helps the purchasing department to negotiate better terms for faster payment.

(*i*) **Minimise capital ties up in inventory:** EDI helps the manufacturing organizations to minimise the capital invested in inventory. That is the firms can effectively administer their inventory levels and free from over investment in inventory.

(*j*) **Quick and Easy Enquiries:** Through EDI customers and suppliers make direct on-line enquires on product availability, or other non sensitive information.

(*k*) **Bulk updates to catalogues and parts listings :** The firms can provide updates of data files, such as catalogues to customers or part listings to franchisees.

EDI is the exchange of business data using an understood data format. It predates today's Internet. EDI involves data exchange among parties that know each other well and make arrangements for one-to-one (or point-to-point) connection, usually dial-up.

4. E-Mail, Fax, and Internet Telephony

E-commerce is also conducted through the more limited electronic forms of communication called e-mail, facsimile or fax, and the emerging use of telephone calls over the Internet. Most of this is business-to-business, with some companies attempting to use e-mail and fax for unsolicited ads (usually viewed as online junk mail or spam) to consumers and other business prospects. An increasing number of business Web sites offer e-mail newsletters for subscribers. A new trend is opt-in e-mail in which Web users voluntarily sign up to receive e-mail, usually sponsored or containing ads, about product categories or other subjects they are interested in.

5. Business to Consumer Commerce

Formerly whatever was sold in the market, consumers had to buy but the scenario has changed. Today the customers give their specifications and the manufacturers try and supply it. In fact it is because of choosy customers, more and more variety has to be offered. Therefore business houses have to set up attractive electronic market places to entice the customers. Since business houses may be remotely located and geographically spread over, they have to have the ability to retain customers. Hence they have to optimise on factors like performance service efficiency, personalisation, socialisation and offering of incentives. Some key factors which lead to the success of electronic marketing are:

(a) **Price attractiveness**

Overpricing will not help to make sales even though an effective advertisement is given and we can not force a customer to buy a particular product. Therefore offering discounts and value added products are easier to trade using e-commerce.

(b) **Attractive Web Sites**

No consumer would like to wait while transactions are performed. The Web Site should be attractive enough to hold the attention of the consumer by providing quick and easy access and user friendly ordering processes with instant acknowledgment.

(c) **Electronic Payment**

Since e-commerce does not rely on money and local cheques, there are many services introduced, which make payment easy.

(i) **Smart Card and Credit Services:** Online credit card services have made payment procedures easy. Large amount of security standards have been improvised so as to make the system foolproof.

(ii) **Electronic Checks:** This is an electronic version of paper cheques which ensures that instant clearing of checks takes place so that no 'bouncing back' possibility occurs.

(iii) **Micro Payments:** This is a service designed to support small payments/micro payments for information products over WWW.

(d) **Personalisation**

Some web sites keep track of the path followed by a customer in his former trip. So when he returns he is welcomed and guided on to those parts of the site he is attracted to. This makes a customer more comfortable and encourages him for return visits. Also a list of priorities can be made so that casual visitors, industrial customers and domestic consumers can be dealt with separately and in different way.

(e) **Socialising**

There are Chat and discussion groups available which let the customer know of the views of people already using a specific product. This enabling him to have a feeling of belongingness to a unique group of like minded individuals and thus helping to build up customer loyalty.

(f) **Global Marketing**

Setting up physical global distribution network and service centres will aid electronic commerce because E-commerce can only provide information and transmit messages but physical delivery is in the hands of business houses only.

(g) **New technology Products**

Since awareness rate is high on e-commerce, product life cycles become short with the arrival of new technology products. Launching of new products is faster using e-commerce as advertising is instant and immediate success or failure is known quickly.

(h) **Electronic Catalogs**

(i) They help in providing more information or simple ways to find products. Two way communication occurs in real time.

(ii) Changes in prices, repackaging, re-channeling and other minor adjustments are easily performed.

(iii) We can go from one part to catalog to another directly and any term requiring clarification can directly be dealt with first and then we can proceed sequentially.

(iv) Global presence of small organisations is felt at minimal cost on internet and other online services.

(i) **Convenience**

Through e-commerce shopping can be done from anywhere and at any time.

(j) **Time Saving**

Time lost in travelling to and fro the stores is saved. In fact if a consumer knows his requirement the entire process of ordering and payment takes a few seconds.

Shortcomings of On-line Shopping:

(i) **Visual Effects Only:** The web site may display the product but the user can not feel, taste or try the product.

(ii) **Time Lag:** It is difficult to find out the actual time of the arrival of the product.

(iii) **Internet Connectivity:** Technical delays due to heavy Internet traffic may cause lots of delay and problems.

(iv) **Slow Web Sites:** Web sites using a lot of graphics and images take a lot of time to download and is frustrating for the consumer as a lot of time is consumed.

(v) **Search Methods :** The customer may not know all search methods, therefore a lot of time may be wasted before the actual location is reached.

(vi) **Shipping and Handling Costs:** Sometimes shipping and handling costs may be higher than the cost of item purchased. Again if shipping costs are not known in advance then heavy amounts may have to be paid at the time of delivery.

6. Business to Business (Inter Organizational e-commerce)

Organization use e-commerce not only to interact better with their customers, for better co-ordination within the organization but also for inter organization relationships. A few of these business applications are:

(i) **Supplier Management**

Here the main objective is to provide purchase managers with better control over purchasing habits. The number of suppliers is reduced and business relationships are strengthened thus making strong virtual teams leading to reduced processing costs and cycle time.

(ii) **Inventory Management**

The purpose of e-commerce is lower the inventory levels by reducing out of stock circumstances and over stuffing of inventory. Again lead time is reduced so that the order-ship-bill cycle is reduced.

(*iii*) **Channel Management**

The use of open networks has enhanced inter business communication. No labour cost is needed to obtain accurate information. Communication on the internet is multipoint and therefore participants can limit themselves to their field of interest. This ensures channel management.

(*iv*) **Distribution Management**

As a result of EDI purchase orders, bills, shipping notices all contain accurate and sufficient data and are transmitted as shipping documents. This helps in distribution management.

(*v*) **Payment Management**

Electronic payments ensure that payments can be made between suppliers and organizations quickly thus reducing insecurities and processing costs.

(*vi*) **Financial Management**

E-commerce has enabled global companies to manage their money in various foreign exchange accounts.

(*vii*) **Sales force management**

Communication and flow of information among the sales force, customer service divisions etc., have improved considerably through e-commerce. This results into effective sales force management.

7. Consumer to Consumer Applications

In consumer to consumer commerce, the seller may sell his service or goods by providing its information on the net. This information may be evaluated by a consumer to carry out a transaction. Similarly, the buyer may also give his requirements to select the desired services.

8. Internal Business processes or Intra-organizational e-commerce

The purpose behind in the organizational e-commerce is to help a company maintain relationships, which are critical to delivering superior customer services. Many inter-networked enterprises are customer driven and market driven. Therefore constant monitoring and evaluation of data regarding customers, suppliers and competitors should be compiled from their web sites and discussion groups. The feedback got is used to shape the organisation's strategies in term of product design, advertising, customer services etc. E-commerce facilitates managers to communicate using video conferencing, e-mail and bulletin boards so that information is better disseminated and right decisions can be made.

Today large corporate Intranets have been installed so that information can be assessed and published. On line publishing helps to reduce costs as printing and distributing and faster delivery of current information takes place. Since information travels faster there is a better co-ordination between the various departments. In fact all efforts are being made to convert organizations into a paperless office.

9. The Security of Business Transactions

Security includes authenticating business transactions, controlling access to resources such as Web pages for registered or selected users, encrypting communications, and in general, ensuring the privacy and effectiveness of transactions.

11.2. INTERNET

The Internet is a worldwide network of networks. The Internet, sometimes called simply "the Net," is a worldwide system of computer networks. It is a configuration of smaller networks and other connected machines spanning the entire globe. Around the world, each country has at least one backbone network that operates network that operates at very high speed and carries the bulk of the traffic. Other smaller Networks connect to that backbone.

The internet, a global system of connected computers, was once available only to the government, academic, and research communities. Now the greatly publicised information superhighway is accessible to anyone with time, interest, and curiosity. Information on the internet, and opportunities to use it are growing at a phenomenal rate. The last decade has witnessed an explosion of internet activity. Many of these users are in Corporation, Universities, and Government Institutions. But the number of users connecting from home also continues to grow dramatically.

11.2.1. Meaning and Definition :

The Internet is a worldwide system of computer networks - a network of networks. It is a of connecting a computer to any other computer anywhere in the world via dedicated routers servers. It is a worldwide public network of computers on which people can join and multiple services such as sharing of information.

When two computers are connected over the Internet, they can send and receive all kind information such as text, graphics, voice, video, and computer programs. It consists of mill of private, public, academic, business, and government networks at global level and are linked a broad array of electronic and optical networking technologies.

11.2.2. Development of Internet

In 1969, the American defense Department wanted to connect all the computers in the department offices and military research institutions. When it was connected, the network was called ARPANET(Advanced Research Projects Agency network).It also included many universities doing military funded research. Later the span of this network expanded covering the whole of USA. As it was very successful, various research institutions and universities wanted to get connect themselves with the ARPANET.

Hence, the defense wanted to preserve its privacy and there by, divided the network in to two divisions, viz, ARPANET and MILNET (Military Network). These two divisions are connected with a technology called network protocol. Protocol means, a set of communication rules. In the network protocol means a set of rules to contact a person on the network. Hence we need a protocol to conta1ct a person on the other networks. The protocols in-between the networks are called internet protocols. Thus, internet protocol is a technical switching scheme, which enables a node of network to communicate with a node of another network. To control and monitor the network communications, the department of defense redesigned the existing protocol and thereby the protocols Transmission Control Protocol/Internet Protocol (TCP\IP) was developed.

At this stage, the "American National Science Foundation" developed another network of computers in AUSA. In this new network all universities and research institutions were allowed to join in to and provide their contributions in the development of super computer.

In early 1990, many institutions turn to "American National Science Foundation's" network and as a result ARPANET was shutdown. During 1994, many private organizations introduced global networks. They designed protocols and communicate between the nodes of different networks. This network of networks is called internet.

Evolution of Internet

The Internet as we know it today has revolutionised computing. Here an account of for the Internet evolution is given:

1957 The Sputnik

The Internet was conceived when the first artificial earth satellite, the Sputnik, was launched into the orbit on October 4 1957, and as a response the US Department of defense created the Advanced Research Projects Agency (ARPA).

1961 Packet Switching

The earliest models of networking used circuit switching. This required an unbroken connection between the communicating host. Circuit switching was not flexible and when made, the connection had to be maintained. Leonard Klein at MIT come up with packet switching, which was now dependent on a single unbroken line of communication. Packets could, in case of a broken connection, route themselves through other available routes. Packet switching is art the core of the Net as it exists today.

1962 Galactic Networks

In August 1962 JCR Lincklider of MIT wrote a series of memos discussing his concepts of a galactic network. He envisioned a globally interconnected set of computers through which everyone could quickly access data and programs from any site.

The same year, the first commercial communications satellite was placed in the orbit.

1965 First wide area network

Thomas Merril and Laurence G Roberts connected the TX-2 computer over a telephone line to create the first wide area network (WAN).

1966-67 Plans for ARPANET

In August 1968, after the overall structure and specification of the ARPANET were refined ARPA called for tenders for the development of one of the key components -the packet switch called the Interface Massage Processor (IMP). The contract was awarded to a group called Bolt, Beranek, and Newman(BBN) headed by Frank Heart.

Also the(NWG) networking group was formed to develop the various protocols for the planned network.

1969 ARPANET is created

In September 1969 BBN installed the first IMP at the Network Measurement Center, University of California, Los Angles (UCLA), and the first host node was established at the Stanford research institute (SRI), and the first host-to-host message was sent UCLA to SRI. Two more nodes were added at the University of California. Santa Barbara, and the University of Utah later that year.

1970 NCP - the first protocol for the net

The NWG presented NCP (network Communication Protocol), the first ever protocol for what was later to become the Internet.

1972 E-mail - the first "hot" application is developed

In March 1972, Rat Tomlinson at BBN wrote the basic e-mail send and receive program or the ARPANET, to enable easy coordination of activities between the four nodes. In July, Laurence Roberts ARPA expanded its utility by writing a program to list selectively read, forward, and responds to messages.

In October 1972, the ARPANET was demonstrated publicly at the international computer communication conference (ICCC) for the first time.

1973 ARPANET goes global

The University College of London, England and the Royal Radar Establishment of Norway connected to the ARPANET.

On May 22, Robert Metcalfe wrote a 13-page description of the Ethernet, which he later created both David Boggs. Ken Thompson and Dennis Ritchie presented their first paper of UNIX at the Symposium on Operating Systems Principles. Both of them, the Ethernet card and UNIX played vary significant roles on the evolution of the net.

1974 TCP

Vint Cerf and Bob Kahn published their paper "A protocol for packet network internet working", which established the Transmission Control Protocol (TCP). This was designed to provide transport and forwarding services on the Internet. (This was also the first time that the term "Internet" was used).

In the same year, BBN Kahn demonstrated the first commercial version of ARPANET.

1977 The first gateway

Vint Cerf and Bob Kahn demonstrated the first gateway system connecting packet radio and ARPANET.

1978 TCP and IP part ways

The TCP model worked fine for file transfers and remote login applications. But some of the early work on advanced network applications made it clearly that on some cases packet losses shouldn't be corrected by TCP, but should be left to the application to deal with. Vint Cerf, Steve Crocker, and Dannh Cohen separated TCP's routine functions into a separate protocol called the Internet protocol (IP) leaving error handling and data gram functions as a part of TCP.

1979 ICCB

DARPA (ARPA became Defense Advanced Research Projects or DARPA in 1972) formed the Internet Configuration Control Board (ICCB) to help the process of creating gateways between the hosts and the network.

1981 Xanadu

Ted Nelson conceptualized "xanadu", central pay per document hypertext database encompassing all written information. Xanadu is often called the largest running Vaporware project. Recently kperts of Xanadu were made Open Source.

1983 TCP/IP becomes the core protocol of the Internet

On January 1 the entire ARPANET shifted to TCP/IP from NCP. NSFNET was the first network to be completely on TCP/IP. ARPANET was split into Military and Civilian sections, making the Internet a reality. The military section was called the MLNET. ICCB was dissolved and in its place the Internet Activities Board (IAB) was created.

Paul Mockapetris of Information Sciences Institute outlined the "Domain Name Service". The first implementation of Pauls's DNS server was called "Jeeves".

1984 Increase in number of hostes

The numbers of hosts on the Internet crossed 1000. This numbers reached 10,000 by 1987 and 60,000 by 1988, when the "Worm" struck.

1988 The year of the Worm

1988 saw the dawn of worries about security and privacy in the connected world. New words like hacker, cracker, and electronic break-in where added to the dictionary.

These worries were justified when the Internet Worm struck. A malicious written by Robert Morris Jr., it attacked the distributed nature of the Internet and brought down approximately 6,000 of the estimated 60,000 hosts. The computer Emergency Response Team (CERT) is formed by DARPA to address security concerns raised by the Worm.

In the same year, the Internet Relay Char (IRC) was written by Jarko Oikarien, and Berbard Daines created the first Ethernet switch to add Ethernet Support to Nortel carrier-class telephone switches.

1990 Discontinuance of ARPANET

The ARPANET is discontinued in March, leaving vast networks, with more than 300,000 hosts. Archie - an easier way to files on the Net - was released Peter Deutsh, Alan Emtage, and Bill Heelan.

1991 WWW - the graphical browser

Till date, National Science Foundation (NSFNET), which served as the backbone of the Internet, had commercial use of the Internet. This ban was lifted, clearing the way for electronic commerce.

Paul Linder and Mark P McCahill at the University if Minnesota released "gopher", the first pointer-ad click way of finding files in the Internet.

Time Berners-Lee, working at CERN in Switzerland, posted the code of the World Wide Web in a relatively innocuous newgroup - alt.hypertex. The ability to combine words, pictures, and sounds on Web pages excited many computer programmers, who see the potential for easy publishing of information on the net.

Marc Andreesen and a group of student programmers at the National Center for super computing Application (NCSA), University of Illinois, developed Mosaic, the first graphical browser for the World Wide Web. The web is now open for general user.

1992 Surfing time

The Internet society (SOC) was chartered in January and Jean Armour Polly coined the term "surfing the Net".

1994

O' Reilly, Spry, etc announce "Internet in a box" product to bring the Web into homes.

1994 The World Wide Web consortium

The World Wide Web Consortium (W3C) is formed by Tim Berners Lee and AlVezza, and meets for the first time on December 14 in Cambridge.

1995 Apache

The Apache project was started "to address the concerns of a group of WWW providers and part time http programmers that http didn't behave as they wanted it to behave". The name Apache came from "A PatCHy server" as it was based on some existing code and some patch files.

National Science Federation announced that domain name registration would no longer be free, starting September 14, 1995.

Sun Micro systems released Java, a programming language for the Internet developed by James Gosling. The hot Java browser, the first application developed with Java, is also released.

11.2.3. Governing of the Internet

No governmental body, local, national or international or organization or corporation governs or rules the content of the Internet. It is totally self-governing. That is, many people and organizations voluntarily participate in task force groups who meet to develop standards for the many various technical needs of running the Internet. Decisions are made by consensus among all who choose to participate, and every point of view is heard in the long process of hashing out decisions and setting new standards. The lack of government on the internet causes problems in society. It does not matter whether the national government is a democracy or a dictatorial state, the internet provides free access to all for all. Some dictatorial states have taken substantial measures to block their citizens from free access to the internet.

Contrary to the fact that there is no oversight of internet content, there are some governing bodies overseeing the technical aspects of the internet. These are standards bodies that define how the internet works and how new technology is to be implemented. These bodies are standards organizations made up of representatives from various interested companies, governments, research organizations and interested individuals. These standards organizations include the following Key Management Structures :

1. Internet Configuration Control Board (ICCB)
2. Internet Activities Board (IAB)
3. Internet Engineering Task Force (IETF)
4. Internet Architecture Board (IAB)
5. Internet Society (ISOC)
6. Domain Name System (DNS)
7. Internet Corporation for Assigned Names and Numbers (ICANN)

ICAAN - Internet Corporation for Assigned Names and Numbers:- It is the private (non-government) non-profit corporation with responsibility for IP address space allocation, protocol parameter assignment, domain name system management, and root server system management functions, the services previously performed by the Internet Assigned Numbers Authority (IANA).

On November 2005, the World Summit on the Information Society, held in Tunis, established the Internet Governance Forum (IGF) to open an ongoing, non-binding conversation among multiple stakeholders about the future of Internet governance. Since the World Summit on the Information Society, the term "Internet governance" has been broadened beyond narrow technical concerns to include a wider range of Internet-related policy issues.

2009 - ICANN gains autonomy from the U.S government

Aspects of Internet Governance

(*a*) Infrastructure
(*b*) Copyright
(*c*) Content
(*d*) Trade Marks
(*e*) Standards
(*f*) Cyber crime
(*g*) Security
(*h*) Digital Divide
(*i*) Encryption
(*j*) Data and Consumer Protection

(*k*) Interconnection

(*l*) Transfer of technology

(*m*) Interoperability

(*n*) Moral and Cultural values

11.2.4. Transmission of Information and Resources

When information is transmitting in the form of text or pictures through internet, our information is split into small pieces called packets. They are routed through the internet. Route is a path or the beginning of a path through the internet to a node. Router is a specialized node, which selects the most efficient route for sending the information. The routes traffic across the Internet using internet provider addresses. The packets of information may travel through many routers before they reach their respective destinations. But first they have to go from us to our local Internet service provider (ISP). Our local ISP sends our packets of data to another ISP, which may send them to another ISP. Thus our packets pass through a chain of ISPs through nodal points to reach their destination. Our packets may pass through fiber optic cables in the ground, satellites in the sky, or undersea cables and the like. The internet protocols bind all of these links together, enabling our packets travel through the Internet. After our packets arrive at the web server, the web server sends responses back along a similar path.

If there is any problem like congestion, broken link, power outage, etc, that may cause the web server to seem slow or unresponsive to us. Problems in intervening parts of the Internet do not break the web server, which may well be accessible to other people, and may become accessible to us as soon as the various internet providers route our traffic around problems. Most of the rerouting in the internet is dynamic, and is done automatically. Some rerouting is not automatic. In particular, the biggest ISPs, frequently called backbones, cover vast geographical areas and carry large proportions of the internet's traffic. A failure in a backbone or in one of the major interconnection points between them can affect many internet users. And such a problem may take some time to be resolved, as the biggest ISPs often prefer to manually examine changes in major routes before implementing them. Internet providers use the same methods for routing packets for electronic mail or file transfers or remote login or voice or video.

11.2.5. Transmission Control Protocol/Internet Protocol (TCP/IP)

Transmission Control Protocol/Internet Protocol is the basic communication language or protocol of the Internet. TCP/IP is a two-layer program. The higher layer, Transmission Control Protocol, manages the assembling of a message or file into smaller packets that are transmitted over the Internet and received by a TCP layer that reassembles the packets into the original message. The lower layer, Internet Protocol, handles the address part of each packet so that it gets to the right destination. Each gateway computer on the network checks this address to see where to forward the message. Even though some packets from the same message are routed differently than others, they will be reassembled at the destination.

Many Internet users are familiar with the even higher layer application protocols that use TCP/IP to get to the Internet. These include the World Wide Web's Hypertext Transfer Protocol (HTTP), the File Transfer Protocol (FTP), Telnet (Telnet) which lets u logon to remote computers, and the Simple Mail Transfer Protocol (SMTP). These and other protocols are often packaged together with TCP/IP as a set.

11.2.6. Data Transfer

Data transfer over the Internet starts with an event. The event can be of anything, for example, we start the browser - a client program (in addition to the browser two other commonly used clients are - the FTP client and the Telnet client programs) on our computer and request for some information, for example, a HTML file, located on a remote computer. There are two important ways in which information is requested from a browser, (*i*) a URL is entered in the "Address" or "Location" field and (*ii*) a hyperlink is clicked. The even can also be generated from the instructions in a program. Thus, we can automate uploading and downloading of files (data transfer) with the help of a program.

For example, we have requested for an HTML document from a remote computer using a web browser. The browser searches for the remote computer and on locating it, passes the request to a program called the 'server' running on this distant computer. The server then checks up our request and tries to locate the HTML file on its hard disk. On finding it, the server sends this file to our computer. If this HTML document has embedded image, video, and/or sound files, the information and the content of such files are also passed to the browser. On receiving data from the server, the client (the browser in our example) starts to display the HTML page. The client (browser) holds the sole prerogative on document display, with no involvement from the servers' side. Once it sends the data to the remote computer, the action of the server will be over. On receipt of all requested data, the client-server connection is lost. Thus, when the next time this client asks for some information from the server, the server will treat it as a new request without any recollection of previous requests. This means that client-server interaction is "stateless" with every new request generating a new response.

11.2.7. The Development of Information Transfer on the Internet:

The information transfer history on the Internet can be traced and divided into six main stages. They are as follows:

1. FTP: The first stage.
2. Archie: The second stage.
3. Gopher: The third stage.
4. Veronica: The fourth stage.
5. Jughead: The fifth stage.
6. The World Wide Web: The sixth stage.

1. File Transfer Protocol (FTP): The first technology that the people used was File Transfer Protocol (FTP). The FTPs are of two types. They can be any one of the following:

(*i*) **Anonymous FTP:** This service is opened to everybody on the net. And the user can log on to this type of FTP server without opening an account on the server. The user can log on with the user ID 'anonymous'. Now the system will respond and ask e-mail address and password. After this process the user can download the file from the concerned FTP server.

(*ii*) **Non-anonymous FTP:** In non-anonymous FTP, the user can download a file only if he has created an account with the respective FTP server. That is the user must already have an account with the FTP server and he should have user ID and password to download a file.

2. Archie: The FTP service was found to be efficient for information sharing and downloading of files. However, the FTP user had initially to know the location of the files.

Browsing of information is not possible in FTP. Hence it was very difficult to locate the files. Then, a group of people at McGill University in Canada got together and created a query system called archie. It was originally formed to be a quick and easy way to scan the offerings of the many anonymous FTP sites that are maintained around the world. As time progressed, archie grew to include other valuable services as well. The files available on FTP were called FTP space. Archie helped users to search files available on FTP. It was possible by using key words. Archie was not a part of FTP service and it is different from FTP. The user can first search for a file in FTP space using Archie and then download it using FTP.

3. Gopher: In order to locate the files and information more easily, the University of Minnesota invented a new service called Gopher in 1991. Gopher is a menu-driven Internet client. It allows the user to find information by clicking on a selection of choices. These choices may be links to other servers, or directories, or files. The files can be text or graphics, or even music files. Gopher allows the user to hop around the globe looking for information in various or servers. Gopher's inter connected menus allow us to "burrow" deeper and deeper until we find the information that we are looking for. Now imagine if thousands of these specialized libraries were interconnected. That is what Gopher does, and all of these interconnected Gopher libraries make up what is called "Gopherspace".

A Gopher is a menu system that simplifies locating and using Internet resources. Each Gopher menu at each Gopher site is unique. Gopher menus usually include the other familiar features of the Internet. Gopher software allows us to search for and retrieve files from Gopher servers anywhere in the world on the Internet. It is organized in a more hierarchical, tree-like structure and does not have graphical display capabilities. Information is presented as a series of nested menus similar to the organization of a directory with subdirectories and files. Using a mouse or the keyboard to select from the menu, our Gopher client will then contact a gopher server for the information. Gopher servers on the Internet is free and for public use.

Archie just tells us where the information that we want can be found, but gopher actually goes out, gets the information that we want and puts the information on to our computer screen.

4. Veronica: After the development of Gopher, the location of files became easy. To make it more effective and efficient, a new search facility named veronica was developed. Veronica stands meaning: "Very Easy Rodent-Oriented Netwide Index to Computerized Archives". Gopher and veronica are not two different services they are bound together. If a user wants to search gopher servers, the tool veronica can be used. Veronica is a collection of menus from most Gopher sites. The Veronica database of all Gopher menu items is called Gopher space. Veronica is a gopher based search engine that we can use to search Gopher space for a specific topic. When we do a Veronica search, we are searching menu items. In the course of the search, Veronica builds an on-the-spot menu consisting of just those items that match our request. When the search is finished, Veronica will present us with a customized Gopher menu. Veronica is fairly easy to use. Many gopher menus include a selection called Search titles in Gopher space using veronica.

5. Jughead: After veronica another search facility Jughead was developed. It is similar to veronica except it is designed to search only one server at a time instead of all of gopher space. It was developed by R. Jones. He later restructure the program "Jonzy's Universal Gopher Hierarchy Excavation And Display"(Jughead). Jughead is available at some Gopher sites and uses the menu items on a single Gopher menu as its database. Since the search is more confined, the results are faster than veronica.

6. Development of WWW: Since the Gopher resources are arranged in simple linear forms, searching of files takes more time. Hence the information searching gets delayed. Besides, both of the resource locators FTP and Gopher mainly have text-based resources and they do not support multimedia features including graphics. Hence a unique and effective technology www has been developed incorporating all these facilities.

11.3. WORLD WIDE WEB-W3

WWW is the acronym for the World Wide Web. It is also commonly known as 'The Web'. World Wide Web can be defined as "all the resources on the internet that are using the Hypertext Transfer Protocol (HTTP)". A broader definition comes from the organization World Wide Web Consortium as: "The World Wide Web is the universe of network-accessible information, an embodiment of human knowledge."

The web may be the m*ost* complete realization of the Internet to date. It was developed in the early 1990s at the European Centre for Nuclear Research as an environment in which scientists in Geneva, Switzerland could share information. It has evolved into a medium that consists of text, graphics/audio, animation, and video. The World Wide Web is a graphical environment that can be navigated through hyperlinks. From one site we click on hyperlinks to go to any number of related sites.

The WWW is hypertext based information retrieval tool. The www is a collection of pages maintained on the internet using a technique called hyper-text. Hypertext is a document containing words that connect to other documents. That is, a hyper-text is of more than two dimensions. In hypertext, the two dimensions of the text/i.e., left to right and top to bottom, are shown on the screen. In the text certain words may be highlighted. If we click these highlighted words, more information about the words appears in another window. We can call it as the third dimension of the text since it goes deeper in to it. One can easily surf the Web by jumping from one document to another using the links in those documents. These documents can be in many formats, such as text, graphics, animation, sound and video. They may also be a combination of all these. All the information on Internet are presented to the user as a document or more popularly known as Web Page, All these web pages are link to each other or even to section within a Web Page. And tfiese links are known as Hyper Links. The address of a Web site usually begins with http:// WWW.

The tool used to view these web pages on internet is known as internet browser or simply browser, It is a software program specifically developed to extract information on user request from the Internet and present them as Web Page to the viewer. There are several browsers available in the market. However the most popular are Internet Explorer from Microsoft and Netscape from Netscape Inc. The process of using browser to view information on Internet is known as *Browsing or surfing*.

11.3.1. Working of the World Wide Web:

WWW servers supports hypertext to access several Internet protocols on a single interface. Almost every protocol type available on the Internet is accessible on the Web, In addition to these, the World Wide Web has its own protocol: Hypertext Transfer Protocol, or http. The World Wide Web provides a single interface for accessing all these protocols. This creates a convenient and user-friendly environment. It is no longer necessary to be conversant in these protocols within separate, command-level environments. The Web gathers together these protocols into a single system. Because of this feature, and because of the Web's ability to work with multimedia and advanced programming languages, the World Wide Web is the fastest-growing component of the Internet.

The Internet involves three fundamental elements: server, client, and network. A server is a computer program that makes data available to other programs on the same or other computers-it "serves" them. A client is a computer that requests data from a server. A network is an interconnected system in which multiple computers can communicate. The communication may be via copper wire, coaxial cable, fiber-optic cable, satellite transmission, etc. The software by which we access internet resources is the browser. When we go to site on the world wide web, we access the site's files.

Here are the steps in opening and accessing a file:

- In the browser, specify the address, or Uniform Resource Locator (URL) of the Web site.
- The browser sends our request to the Internet service provider's server,
- That server sends the request to the server at the specified URL
- The file is sent to the internet service provider's server, which sends the file back to the browser, which display the file,

The Web provides a vast array of facilities including multimedia presentations, real-time collaboration, interactive pages, etc. Programming languages such as Java, Java Script, Visual Basic, and XML are extending the capabilities of the Web. A growing amount of information on the Web is served dynamically from content stored in databases. The Web is therefore not a fixed thing, but the one that is in a constant state of development.

11.3.2. Web Page

A web page is the representation of a document, which resides at a remote site. This is a means to understanding what the web itself is and its implications. It is a single unit of information, often called a document that is available via the World Wide Web (WWW). A web page can be longer than one computer screen and can use more than one piece of paper when it is printed-out. If a "web" document resides on the machine we are working from, the document is called an HTML document, A web page becomes a document that is accessible over the internet because it is written in HTML (Hypertext Markup Language).

In simple words a web page is "an electronic document created using HTML, which conveys information through a browser, in the form of text, graphics, video and sound. It is stored on a server that is connected to the internet. In other words, it is written in a particular format called HTML and is readable by any other computer also connected to the internet by using a web browser (a program used to read HTML documents). HTML is simply a set of tags used to tell the web browser how to present the document.

11.3.3 Anatomy of a Web Page:

A web page is an electronic document written in a computer language called HTML, short for Hypertext Markup Language. Each web page has a unique address, called a URL or Uniform Resource Locator that identifies its location on the network. A website has one or more related web pages, depending on how it is designed. Web pages on a site are linked together through a system of hyperlinks, enabling us to Jump between them by clicking on a link. Web pages vary wildly in design and content. On the Web, we can navigate through pages of information according to our interests.

When we browse the World Wide Web, we can see the term 'home page' very often. A home page can be considered as the starting point of a website. Like the table of contents of a book, the home page usually provides an overview of what we can find at the website. A site can have one page, many pages or a few long ones. If a lot of information is not there, the home page may be the only page. But usually we can find at least n few other pages.

Text links are appearing in a different color from the rest of the text – typically in blue and underlined. When we move our cursor over a text link or over a graphic link, it will change from an arrow to a hand. The hypertext words often give a hint at what we are linked to. When we are return to a page with a link we have already visited, the hypertext words will often be in a different color. With this we know that we have already seen the page. If the next time we visit the same page, it looks different and the information has changed. The Web is a dynamic medium. To encourage visitors to return to a site, some web publishers update' pages often. That is what makes browsing the Web so exciting.

11.3.4. Technology for World Wide Web

The World Wide Web is based on the following technologies:

Technology for World Wide Web

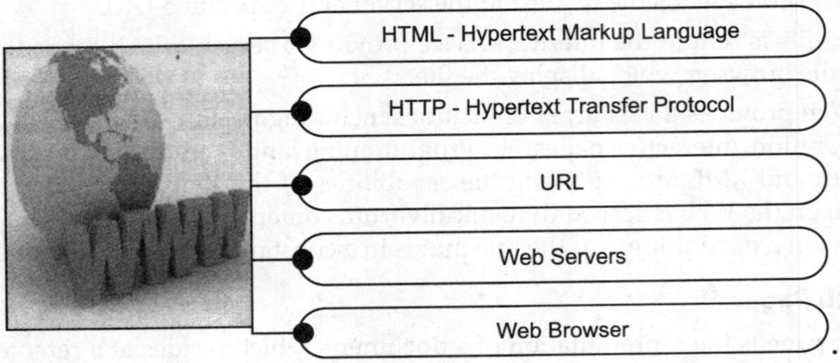

1. **HTTP - Hypertext Transfer Protocol**

Hypertext - It is and electronic document text that is connected (hyperlinked) to the other portions of text (or graphical elements) to which the user is transferred by a mouse click. It is usually differentiated from the normal text by a different color, by underlining, or by both. Hypertext is non-liner. That is, the user can jump from anywhere to anywhere while browsing on the web.

HTTP - A web page is transferred to a user's computer via the hypertext transfer protocol (HTTP). HTTP is the method through which hypertext files, such as web pages, are transferred over the Internet. HTTP is a client/server based Internet protocol, or set of rules. Web pages generally reside on HTTP servers. A user requests a web page from an HTTP (web) server through his or her web browser client software, either by clicking on a hypertext link or designating a particular URL (Uniform Resource Locator). The server then sends the requested information to the user's computer. The browser software interprets the HTML codes and presents the information contained in the web page in a readable format on the user's computer.

2. **HTML - Hypertext Markup Language**

HTML (Hyper Text Markup Language) is the language of the Internet. Hypertext means that some text in the HTML document carries a link to a different location, which can be on the same page or another page. On clicking this 'hot spot', the viewer is transferred to that location. Markup means that specific portions of a document are marked up to indicate how they should be displayed in the browser.

The main purpose of HTML is to describe the structure of a document. Formatting of HTML solely depends on the browser. It is well known that even different versions of the same browser do not display HTML alike. Structuring means describing different parts that make a document. The various parts of an HTML document can be tables, lists, links, blocks of text such as paragraphs etc. HTML was not designed for document layout, but

HTML pages can now be formatted using many traditional design elements such as line spacing, kerning, character spacing, padding etc.

3. URL

URL stands for Uniform Resource Locator. An URL is similar to our street address for our home. Just as our street address is used to find our home, a web page's URL helps it to be found by any other computer connected to the internet. The URL of a web page takes a particular form.

Example for the URL of a particular page is given below:

http://www.bharathi.edu/

Here, the parts of the URL mean:

- **http://** - tells the web browser that the URL is of a web page
- **www.bharathi.edu** - is the domain name of the server where the web page is stored.

4. Web Servers

A Web server is a program that generates and transmits responses to client requests for Web resources. Web server using the client/server model and the World Wide Web's Hypertext Transfer Protocol (HTTP) and serves the files form Web pages to Web users. It is an advanced application which runs on a server and does the following:

1. It provides connections to remote computers.
2. It sends web pages to remote computers via internet.

Web site and Web server are different in the way that a Web site consists of a collection of Web pages associated with a particular host name where as a Web server is a program to satisfy client requests for Web resources.

5. Web Browsers

A web browser is a program that helps users to access web pages on the World Wide Web. It is used to read documents written in HTML to access the World Wide Web. Most of the modern browsers present the user with a flat document that contains text and pictures, according to the HTML page received.

Examples of the web browsers can be seen below:

11.3.5. Advancement in Web Technology:

Web 1.0: Under Web 1.0 the information published on the web is in a static manner. It is like our word document on the web with pictures and formatted. Hyper-linking the web-pages and bookmarking are the two main aspects of Web 1.0 world. Today the most used technology is Web 1.0.

Web 2.0: The term Web 2.0 was coined by Tim O'Reilly. It is the second generation of the World Wide Web technology. The information published in web 2.0 world is very different from web 1.0. Importance is given on usability and sharing. Under Web 2.0, the information published on the web is not in the form of static HTML Web pages, but they are in the form of more dynamic Web. In Web 2.0 the web pages are well organized and it facilitates more open sharing of information.

Web 3.0 is the technology of connecting intelligence, data, concepts, applications and people and it is in the process.

11.4. INTERNET ADDRESSING

World Wide Web is a network of electronic files stored on millions of computers all around the globe. Hypertext links these resources together and the Uniform Resource Locators (URLs) are the addresses used to locate the files. Every URL is unique and identifies one specific file. Let us see the parts involved in internet addressing here in below:

Parts to an internet name

There are several parts to an internet name. They include:

1. Top Level Domain
2. Domain Name
3. Host Name
4. Method/Scheme

We see these parts with an example:

Example - The home Page of Bharathiar University

http://www.b-u.ac.in/

In the above example:

http://- method for receiving - This is the method used for the communication. It is usually a few letters followed by a colon and two forward slashes.

www- Type of the page

b-u. - Internet Domain of website

ac - is for academic institution

in - for India

Parts of WEB Address can be seen as follows:

1. **Top Level Domain**

This is the last part of the name. It can be .com for companies, .org for non profit organizations, .net for network infrastructure providers, .edu for educational institutions, .mil for military, gov for government, or a code for a country, for example, .us for United States or .in for India.

2. **Domain Name**

This is the middle part of the name and often the most important. It is specific to the company/organization. Every computer that hosts data on the internet has a unique numerical address like 198.187.121.010. But it is difficult for the people to remember the long strings of numbers. Hence, to make it easier the Domain Name System was invented. And the domain name links a numerical address to a name in the form of word. For getting access to the university website, we need not type its numerical address but we can just type its domain name (b-u.) in the address box.

3. Host Name

This is the name of the server within the company, usually named after the service provided. Example: www, ftp, news, mail.

4. Method/Scheme

This is the method used for the communication. It is usually a few letters followed by a colon and two forward slashes. Example: http:// for web connections, ftp:// for ftp connections.

11.5. INTERNET CONNECTION AND ACCESS

Internet Service providers offer different levels of Internet access. The types of access to internet are as follows:

1. Dial-up Access
2. ISDN (Integrated Services Digital Network) Access
3. DSL (Digital Subscriber Line) Access
4. Cable Modem Access
5. Broadband Wireless (WI-FI)
6. Mobile Broadband -GSM (Global System for Mobile Communications)

Broadband: Broadband is a general term used for mentioning higher-speed Internet. It is a telecommunications channel that is capable of carrying high volumes of text, pictures, sound and video data in very short periods of time.

Bandwidth: means the maximum data transfer rate of a internet connection. It measures how much data can be sent over a specific connection in a given amount of time.

Let us see these methods in brief below:

1. Dial-up Access: Old method of connecting with dedicated telephone lines:

Advantages:

1. Uses existing phone lines.
2. Lower cost,

Limitations:

1. Dial-up connection uses existing phone line, making it impossible to receive phone calls unless another line is installed. Uses existing phone lines.
2. Slow - Can be limited to speeds of 28.8 K to 33.6 K. Upload speeds can be limited to as low as 28.8, with download speeds approaching 56K under only perfect conditions.
3. Service can be somewhat unreliable (busy signals, spontaneously terminated sessions, etc).

2. ISDN (Integrated Services Digital Network) Access: Faster than dial-up, but every ISP does not support ISDN

Advantages:

- Can provide 2-4 times the speed of a 56K modem.
- Uses digital rather than analog signals to transmit data.

Limitations:

- Requires special equipment that can drive up cost,
- Data is not compressed so transmission rates can be comparable to 56k-at more cost.

3. DSL (Digital Subscriber Line) Access: Newer technologies such as DSL use an ISP to connect to the Internet and allow faster connections.

Advantages:

- Can fall back to slower speeds if the line cannot handle the modern's fastest speed.
- Uses the existing phone line in most cases.
- Does not tie up existing phone line, leading to "always on" access.
- More bandwidth results in improved streaming audio/video, online games, application programs, telephone calling, video conferencing and other high-bandwidth services.
- Can connect multiple computers-on-single line.
- Faster than a 56K dial-up modem.

Limitations:

- Availability-limited to homes/businesses with a dedicated copper wire running between it and the phone company's nearest central office.
- Cost-includes installation fees and monthly charges
- Need a firewall to ensure home network security. (additional cost)
- Service is not infallible.

4. Cable Modem Access: Cable modems, another newer technology that uses an ISP to connect to the Internet, allows faster connections.

Advantages.

- Uses coaxial and/or fiber-optic cable rather than phone lines for data transmission, so performance doesn't depend on your distance from a central cable office.
- Can fall back to slower speeds if the Sine cannot handle the modem's fastest speed.
- Convenient for homes already wired with cable access.
- Does not tie up existing phone line, leading to "always on" access.
- More bandwidth results in improved streaming audio/video, online games, application programs, telephone calling, video conferencing and other high-bandwidth services.
- Can connect multiple computers on a single line.

Limitations:

- Availability-limited to homes/businesses with cable access.
- Cost-includes installation fees and monthly charges
- Often requires commitment to a cable TV package.
- A firewall is necessary to ensure home network security (additional cost),
- Service *is* not infallible.

5. Wireless Broadband: Wireless broadband is mainly for the mobile users. The wireless technology is used in the connection to home, office and mainly laptop and PDAs.

Features:

(*a*) Always on connection when connected.

(*b*) Requires the user to be in a wireless hotspot.

(*c*) Does not support wireless roaming

(*d*) Large choice of service providers (ISPs)

(*e*) Speed varies depending on signal quality

6. Mobile Broadband -GSM: For mobile phones the 2G and 3G (generations of mobile telecommunication technologies) network connections are used.

11.6. SEARCHING ON THE NET

Searching on the net can be of time consuming and frustrating for the people who are new to it and having no previous exposure and experience on this. The search process is made all the more difficult because of the large number of search tools, their differing information content and the lack of industry standards. But, by practice it can be done very easy and will become a pleasant experience and exercise.

11.6.1. Search Engines

Search Engine is a program that searches documents for specified keywords and returns a list of the documents where the keywords were found. Although search engine is really a general class of programs, the term is often used to specifically describe systems like Google, Yahoo, Alta Vista etc , that enable users to search for documents on the World Wide Web and USENET newsgroups.

Typically, a search engine works by sending out a spider to fetch as many documents as possible. Then, another program, called an indexer, reads these documents and creates an index based on the words contained in each document. Each search engine uses a proprietary algorithm to create its indices such that, ideally, only meaningful results are returned for each query.

The commonly used Search Engines includes the following:

AltaVista - searches Web sites with advanced Boolean and field search options.

Ask.com - general search engine enhanced by a number of specialty searches including a dictionary, thesaurus, currency converter, encyclopedia, maps, news and more

Google - It is the most popular search engine and it uses PageRank and other methods to rank results. Google offers a number of Services

Lycos - general search engine that also offers searches of a few deep Web content sources including people look-up, yellow pages, and multimedia

Yahoo! - portal with a general Web search and many other content services

There are many other search engines available for effective browsing.

11.7. BASICS OF SEARCH TOOLS AND METHODS:

Let us see the searching tools and methods in detail below:

1. Search Tools and Methods:

A search tool is a computer program that performs searches. A search method is the way a search tool requests and retrieves information from its Web site. A search begins at a selected search tool's Web site, reached by means of its address or URL. Each tool's Web site comprises a store of information called a database. This database has links to other databases at other Web sites, and the other Web sites have links to still other Web sites and so on. Thus, each search tool has extended search capabilities by means of a worldwide system of links.

Types of Search Tools :

There are four basic types of search tools. They have their own search method. They are as follows :

(*i*) **Directory search tool:** It searches for information by subject matter. It is a hierarchic; search that starts with a general subject heading and follows with a succession of increasingly more specific sub-headings. The search method it employs is known as subject search. For using this tool, we have to choose a subject search when we want general information on a subject or topic. We can find links in the references provided that will lead to specific information we want. It is easy to use. But the directory databases are comparatively small and their updating frequency is relatively low and descriptive information about each site is limited and general.

(*ii*) **Search engine tool:** It searches for information through use of keywords and responds with a list of references or hits. The search method it employs is known as a keyword search. For this, we have to choose a keyword search to obtain specific information, since its extensive database is likely to contain the information sought. The main benefit of this is the information content or database is substantially larger and more current than that of a directory search tool. But, it is not very exacting in the way it indexes and retrieves information in its database. This makes finding relevant documents more difficult. Besides, Keyword searches require far more explanation than subject searches, because of their broader scope and greater complexity.

(*iii*) **Directory with search engine:** It uses both the subject and keyword search methods interactively as described above. In the directory search part, the search follows the directory path through increasingly more specific subject matter. At each stop along the path, a search engine option is provided to enable the searcher to convert to a keyword search. In this way the subject and keyword search are coordinated. It can be used when we are uncertain whether a subject or keyword search will provide the best results. The main advantage of this tool is its ability to narrow the search field to obtain better results. But, this search method may not succeed for difficult searches. Some search tools use search engine and directory searches independently. They are said to be non-coordinated.

(*iv*) **Multi-engine search tool (meta-search):** It utilises a number of search engines in parallel. The search is conducted via keywords employing commonly used operators or plain language. It then lists the hits either by search engine employed or by integrating the results into a single listing. The search method it employs is known as a meta search. This tool can be used to speed up the search process and to avoid redundant hits. The main advantage of this tool is that it's forbearing of imprecise search questions and provides fewer hits of likely greater relevance. But it is not as effective as a search engine for difficult searches.

Search Tools: A search tool employs a computer program to access Web sites and retrieve information. Each search tool is owned by a single entity, such as person, company or organization, which operates it from a master computer. When we use a search tool, our request travels to the tool's Web site. There, it conducts a search of its database and directs the response back to our computer. There are hundred's of search tools available for searching. The important and commonly used search tools are as follows:

Basic Search Tools

Directory [Subject Search]	Search Engine [Keyword Search]	[Meta Search] Multi-Engine
Encyclopedia Britannica	Alta Vista	Dog pile Excite
Go (Info seek) Look smart	All theWeb (Fast)	Mamma Hot bot
One Key (Provides coordinated searches) MSNBC (Snap)	Google	Metacrawler
Yahoo (Provides coordinated searches)	Northern Light	Search (Savvy Search)

2. Keyword - Search Operators:

The operators are the rules or specific instructions used for composing a query in a keyword search. A well-defined query greatly improves the chances of finding the mosl relevant information that we are looking for. While each search engine has its owr operators, some operators are used in common by a number of search engines. The commonly used operators as follows:

(i) **Boolean:** It employs AND, OR, NEAR and NOT to connect terms in the query. The meanings of them are:

- AND requires that both terms are present somewhere within thi document being sought.
- NEAR requires that one term must be found within a certain number of words of the other term.
- OR requires that at least one of the terms is present.
- NOT excludes any document containing the term. When using these operators, remember to capitalize them as shown above.

(ii) **Plus/Minus:** It employs [+] before a term to retrieve only the documents containing that term (it is similar to the Boolean AND). It uses [–] before a term to exclude that term from the search (it is similar to the Boolean NOT). The space is not given between the operators.

(iii) **Phrases:** Words enclosed within double quote marks [" "] denote an exact phrase, or reasonably close to it. It is sometimes similar to the Boolean NEAR. More often, it is treated like a single term.

(iv) **Stemming:** The use of the stem or the main part of a word to search for variations of the word. For example, the stem "act" searches act, actor, actress, acting and action. Stemming can be automatic, or it may require use of a wild card, symbolized by an asterisk [*] mark to initiate. For example, act*.

(v) **Case Sensitive:** Lower case letters are to be used for query terms except for proper names. The adjacent capitalized words are treated as a single proper name, for example Peter Drucker. Proper names are separated from each other a comma for example Peter Drucker, Elton Mayo.

3. Planning and Conducting a Search:

Our search for a specific item in a world of information can be difficult, especially if the search is done without any planning. For conducting a search in an orderly way the following methods can be used:

1. First we shall develop a general understanding of the search tools, process and language. However, it is not necessary to know everything at the beginning. We can start with the information that we need to search subjects of interest. Later we can find that our understanding will be built as our experience broadens.
2. We should avoid searching for obscure information not likely to be found without use of sophisticated search methods. Once we become familiar with the use of operators, we can move toward the more complex searches.
3. In keyword searches, we shall start by working with no more than two or three search tools until we gain some mastery over them. A search tool's Help section usually describes its current keyword search practices. From these we can learn how best to compose a query and focus the search.
4. The enormous amount of information on the internet, the many search tools, and the complexities of their use may threaten us. But it can be overcome by just focusing on the subject we wish to pursue, developing a search plan and going about finding the desired information.

11.8. BENEFITS OF THE INTERNET

The Internet is an arrangement of connected computers, which lets the computer users all over the globe exchange data. The principal components of the Internet are the World Wide Web and e-mail. With the passage of time, the Internet has become the most effective business tool in the contemporary world. The following are the important benefits of the Internet.

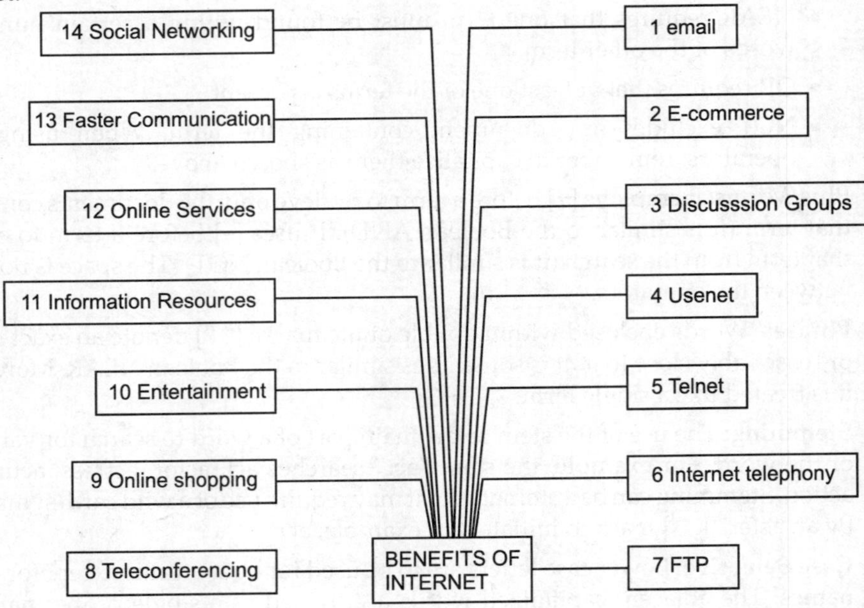

1. Email

The rapid development of the Internet can be attributed to the immense popularity of email. Email has been the most widely used Internet service because it has revolutionized messaging. Messages over email can be received almost instantly and can include images, video and sound in addition to text. Furthermore, interactive emails can be created using HTML.

2. E-commerce

Internet facilitates electronic commerce. It is the process of buying and selling through electronic communication; these transactions, such as credit purchase, are carried out on the Internet. By incorporating e-commerce into web sites, internet could provide business institutions with the capability to achieve large volume of sales, wider market, and generating additional revenue.

3. Discussion Groups

One of the benefits of the Internet is the opportunity it offers to people worldwide to communicate via e-mail. The Internet is home to a large community of individuals who carry out active discussions organized around topic-oriented forums distributed by e-mail. Software programs administer these discussions.

Here a number of people can participate in different types of debates and discussions, express their views and gather valuable knowledge.

4. Usenet

While mail lets one person to send a message to another specific person or group, network news lets him send a message on an electronic bulletin board for anyone to see. Usenet is the international meeting place, where people gather to meet their friends, discuss the day's events, keep up with computer trends or talk, about whatever's on their mind. Usenet is the set of machines that exchange articles tagged with one or more universally recognized labels, called newsgroups.

Usenet itself is a set of machines that exchanges- messages, or articles, from Usenet discussion forums, called newsgroups. Usenet administrators control their own sites, and decide which newsgroups to sponsor and which remote newsgroups to allow into the system.

Usenet News is a global electronic bulletin board system in which millions of computer users exchange information on a vast range of topics. The major difference between Usenet News and e-mail discussion groups is the fact that Usenet messages are stored on central computers, and users must connect to these computers to read or download the messages posted to these groups.

This is distinct from e-mail distribution, in which messages arrive in the electronic mailboxes of each list member.

The transmission of Usenet news is entirely cooperative. Information is generally provided out of good will and the desire to distribute news everywhere. There are places, which provide information for a fee, but for the large part no exchange of money is involved. There are two major transport methods, UUCP and NNTP. The first is mainly modem-based and involves the normal charges for telephone calls. The second, NNTP, is the primary method for distributing news over the Internet.

There are thousands of Usenet newsgroups in existence. While many are academic in nature, numerous newsgroups are organized around recreational topics. Much serious computer-related work takes place in Usenet discussions. A small number of e-mail discussion groups also exist as Usenet newsgroups.

5. Telnet

Telnet is the main Internet protocol for creating a connection with a remote computer. It gives the user the opportunity to be on one computer system and do work on another, which may be across the street or thousands of miles away. Where modems are limited by the quality of telephone lines and a single connection, telnet provides a connection that is error-free and nearly always faster than the latest conventional modems.

Thus, telnet allows us to log into computers on the Internet and use online databases, library catalogs, chat services, and more. There are no graphics in Telnet sessions, just text. To Telnet to a computer, we must know its address. This can consist of words or numbers.

Telnet is available on the World Wide Web. Probably the most common Web-based resources available through Telnet are library catalogs. A link to a Telnet resource may look like any other link, but it will launch a Telnet session to make the connection. A Telnet program must be installed in our local computer and configured to our Web browser in order to work. With the increasing popularity of the Web, Telnet has become less frequently used as a means of access to information on the Internet.

6. FTP

File transfer protocol (FTP) is a tool as the name suggests copying files from remote host to our host and vice versa. Hundreds of systems connected to the Internet have file libraries. Much of this consists of free or low cost computer program for virtually every make of computer.

There are also libraries of documents as well. If we want a copy of historical documents, song lyrics, etc., it can easily be made. We can also find extensive files detailing everything you could possible want to know about the Internet.

Objectives of FTP

The basic objectives of FTP are:

(*a*) To give flexibility and promote sharing of computer programs, files and data.

(*b*) To transfer data reliably and more efficiently over network.

(*c*) To encourage implicit or indirect use of remote computers using Internet.

(*d*) To shield a user from variations in file storage systems among the hosts.

7. Internet Telephony

This duplicates the definition telephony. Telephony is the technology associated with the electronic transmission of voice, fax, or other information between distant parties using systems historically associated with the telephone, a handheld device containing both a speaker and transmitter and a receiver. With the arrival of computers and transmittal of digital information over telephone systems and the use of radio to transmit telephone signals, the distinction between telephony and telecommunication has become, difficult to find. However, we believe that telephony does connote voice or spoken and heard information and it usually assumes a point-to-point connection. It also tends to assume a temporarily dedicated connection.

Internet telephony is the use of the internet rather than the traditional telephone company infrastructure. Since access to the internet is available at lesser cost, an international or other long distance call will be much less expensive than through the traditional call arrangement.

On the Internet, three new services are available:

(*a*) The ability to make a normal voice phone call

(*b*) The ability to send fax transmissions at very low cost

(*c*) The ability to leave voice mail at a called number.

8. Teleconferencing

Teleconferencing allows two or more people to meet through electronic transmission. There are several forms of teleconferencing.

Computer Conferencing: It allows discussion through text messages typed into computers from various locations

Video Conferencing: It is the extension of computer conferencing where participants can see each other through separate video conferencing windows displayed on screen.

9. On-Line Shopping

Internet provides for the service of on-line shopping. We can place our orders for goods and services on the net from our home. So many household items can be bought on the net without any tiresome travel and waste of time.

10. Entertainment

We can use the Internet for entertainment also. .

- To exchange electronic mail instantly with friends or family, such as a student away at college.
- To find educational tools. Universities around the world, bookstores, libraries, etc.
- To read about interesting sports and leisure events.
- MUD: MUD stands for Multi User Dimension. MUDs are multi-user virtual reality games based on simulated worlds. There are MUDs of all kinds on the Interne, and many can be joined free of charge.

11. Information Resources

Information is main advantage that internet offers. Internet is a virtual treasure of all kinds of information.

12. Online Services

Internet has made life very convenient. With numerous online services we can now perform all our transactions both personal and office online.

13. Faster Communication:

The main aim of internet is speedy communication. Now, we can communicate in Nano second with a person who is in the other place or country.

14. Social Networking:

With internet today social networking has grown up to a very larger level. Such social networks through internet includes Face Book, Orkut, twitter etc.

11.9. E -MAIL

Letter writing was dying out as the pace of modern life has gotten faster and faster. E-mail on the other hand, requires no trip to the post office or having to paste stamps or having to wait several days to a week for our recipient to get our message. Besides, we can reply to a message or forward a message with a minimum of time and effort. *E-mail is the most important* reason and application on the Internet. We type a message into our computer, and it travels instantly over the network to whomever we wish. *Electronic mail is a system of* electronic correspondence by which users send and receive messages over a network of computers and telecommunication links. In e-mail messages are automatically passed from one computer user to another, often through computer networks and/or via modems over telephone lines. The messages may consist of short notes or extensive text files plus graphic and photographic images, video clips, or sound.

Emails allow users to communicate with each other almost instantly. Just as a letter makes stops at different postal stations along its way, e-mail passes from one computer, known as a mail server, to another as it travels over the Internet. Once it arrives at the destination mail server, it is stored in an electronic mailbox until the recipient retrieves it. This whole process can take seconds, allowing us to quickly communicate with people around the world at any time of the day or night. Daily, millions of emails are sent from one part of the globe to the other. We can receive and send emails from all systems irrespective of the operating system used, i.e., whether it is a Windows PC or a Unix machine. Employing MIME (Multipurpose Internet Mail Extensions), we can send video, pictures or sounds with text messages via email.

11.9.1. Types of e-mail Accounts

E-mails can be classified on the following bases:

1. **Web-based e-mail:** With a Web-based e-mail account, we can mail from any computer connected to the net anywhere on the earth. Web-based e-mail address can be used for life. Once we have an account, even if we change companies or switch Internet service providers, the address remains ours. With Web-based e-mail, to send and receive messages, we have to access a web site, so all we need is internet access and a web browser.

For using the web-based e-mail, first we log on to the site by entering our account name (user name) and password. Now we can read our messages, send replies, forward messages, and send and view attachments. Most services offer online address books to store our e-mail addresses and contact information. We can also set up folders to manage our messages. But many free Web-based e-mail services limit the amount of storage that they provide. For example, Yahoo Mail provides 6.0 MB limit and Rediffmail provides 1 GB limit. If we receive much number of mails and if they include attachments like photos, we will have to delete them periodically to stay below the limit or pay for additional storage.

2. **Client-Based E-Mail:** With client-based e-mail, like Outlook Express, a software program running on our computer accesses a remote mail server. Our email account would most probably reside on a remote computer. Email clients are programs that download emails from the remote server and store them on our computer. This saves online time as we can download all emails at one go, close the Internet connection and read the mails at our leisure. Email clients also help we to write our email offline. On subsequent connection to the Internet we can instruct the client to send the emails we have written.

An email client typically has the following features:

- Ability to send and receive email quickly.
- An address book in which we can store email addresses of our friends and other contacts.
- The ability to easily attach other non-text based files using MIME. We can, thus, send pictures, sounds etc. with our email.
- Add signatures to outgoing emails.

11.9.2. Sending and Receiving Messages in e-mail:

To receive e-mail, we must have an account on a mail server. This is similar to having an address where we receive letters. One advantage over regular mail is that we can retrieve our e-mail from anywhere location. Once we connect to our mail server, we download our messages in to our computer. To send e-mail, we need a connection to the Internet and access to a mail server that forwards our mail. The standard protocol used for sending Internet e-mail is called SMTP(Simple Mail Transfer Protocol). When we send an e-mail message, our computer routes it to an SMTP server. The server looks at the e-mail address (similar to the address on an envelope), then forwards it to the recipient's mail server, where it is stored until the addressee retrieves it. We can send e-mail anywhere in the world to anyone who has an e-mail address.

11.9.3. Main Parts of E-mail Address

E-mail messages are similar to letters, with two main parts:

- The header contains the name and address of the recipient, the name and address of anyone who is being copied, and the subject of the message. Some e-mail programs also display our name and address and the date of the message.
- The body contains the message itself.

For sending a mail we need the correct address. If we use the wrong address or mistype it, our message will bounce back to us. When we receive mail, the header tells us where it came from, how it was sent, and when. It is like an electronic postmark. Unlike a letter, which is sealed in an envelope, e-mail is not that much private. It is more like a post card. Messages can be intercepted and read by people who really should not be looking at it. Hence, it is better to avoid including any confidential information unless we have a way to encrypt it.

General Format for an Email Address:

Each email account has a unique address. A general format for an email address is: Our-name@some-computer-name

Where 'our-name' is our user name we use to log at the email server. This is followed by a '@' sign and the name of the computer on which our email service resides. A few examples would be:

tsen@yahoo.co.in

saravan@hotmail.com

Components of the E-mail Address:

As in the case of normal mail system, e-mail is also based upon the concept of a recipient address. The email address provides all of the information required to get a message to the recipient from anywhere in the world. For example consider the following e-mail ID.

saravan@hotmail.com

In example above, "saravan" is the local part, which is the name of a mailbox on the destination computer, where finally the mail will be delivered. Then there is an at sign (@). Next comes the host name (Hotmail), also called the domain name. This refers to the mail server, the computer where the recipient has an electronic mailbox that is where the mailbox "saravan" exists. It is usually the name of a company or organization. The end of the domain name consists of a dot (".") followed by three or more letters (such as .com and .gov) that indicate the top-level domain (TLD). This part of the domain name indicates the type of organization or the country where the host server is located.

- The following are the popular domains:

Domain	Description
.com	A Commercial institution or organization or business
.edu	Educational institutions and universities
.gov	Government entity
.mil	Military organisation
.net	A network administration A
.org	Other Private organizations
.coop	Cooperatives
.info	For all use
.net	For networks; usually reserved for organizations like Internet service providers

11.9.4. Contents of E-mail

Each email consists of a header and a body. The header contains the following information:

- Recipient email address
- Senders email address
- Email address of the people to whom a carbon copy (Cc) and blind carbon copy (Bcc) has been sent.
- The subject line
- The main text message resides in the email body: The underlying rules governing email transmission are highly standardized, but there are a large number of different software programs that can be used to read email. It is quite possible that the message we send will not look at all the same when displayed on our correspondent's screen. We therefore have to be careful about how we present our text.

Emails can be sent by typing the recipients' email address in the 'Send to' field. Any additional recipients can be specified using the Cc or the Bcc. It can be seen from the following.

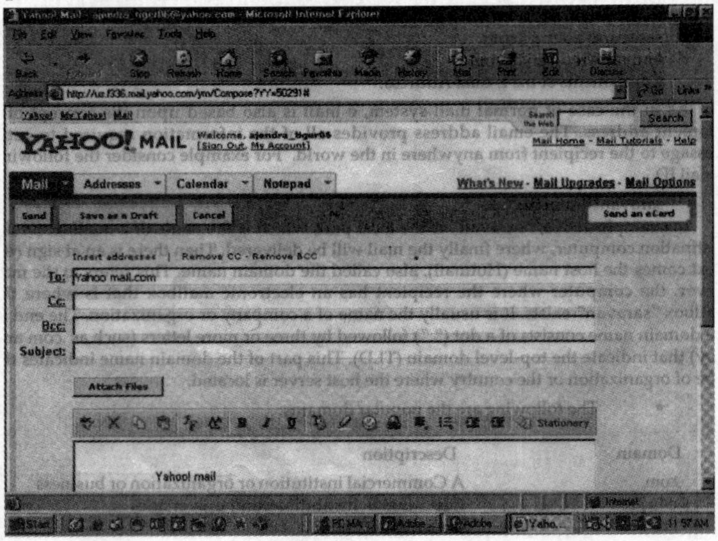

11.9.5. Working of e-mail:

The e-mails of corporates, Universities, and Governments travel to internal recipients over the dedicated high-speed line of their private local area networks. For external recipients, e-mail is sent via a wide area network or the Internet, which directs messages through a network of computers and transmission media. External e-mail from small businesses and homes generally travels from the user's computer via a modem over local telephone lines to an Internet access provider. On both public and private networks, e-mail is routed to a central computer server that stores e-mail in a "mailbox" assigned to the recipient; the messages are held there to be retrieved at the recipient's convenience.

An user can send the same message to several recipients by keying in their address one after another; a massage can also be sent automatically to a fixed distribution list by combining all address under a single address, called an alias. Most mailers will store frequently used address and distribution lists so that the sender simply clicks on the recipient's name on the computer screen to forward the message.

After retrieving a message from the mailbox the recipient can read it, print it, or save it. When 'reply' is clicked on the computer screen, the mailer program automatically addresses the reply to the originator (including in the reply a copy of the originator's message if desired). When "forward" is clicking, the message is sent to another recipient or group of recipients.

For example we consider the following. If we open the yahoo mail the screen will appear as follows.

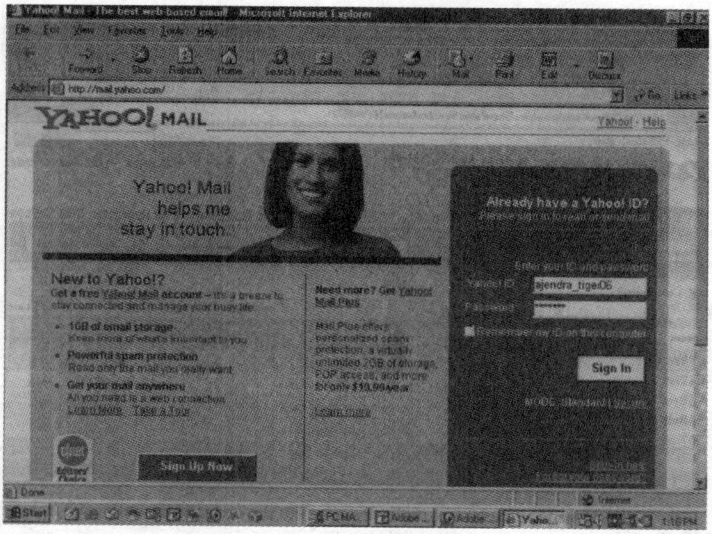

After entering our ID and password in the respective boxes and click the 'sign in' the mail box will be opened as follows:

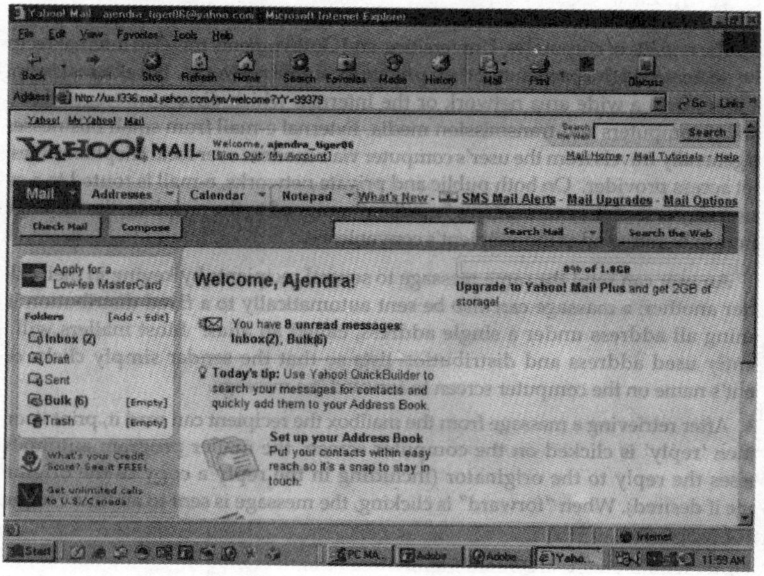

It shows the number of unread (new) mails in the mailbox (inbox) and other folders such as Draft, Sent and Trash. By clicking the 'Inbox' the screen opens like the following:

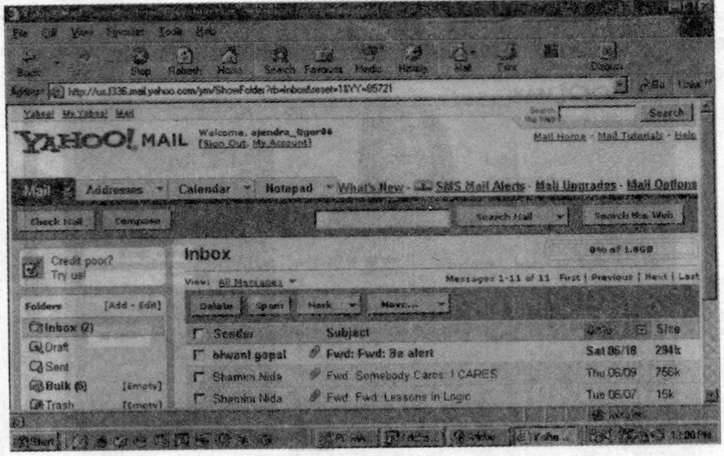

Here in the screen the incoming mails are given in the order of time they are being sent along with the senders name and respective subject. If we want to read a mail, we just click the respective mail and the mail opens like the following:

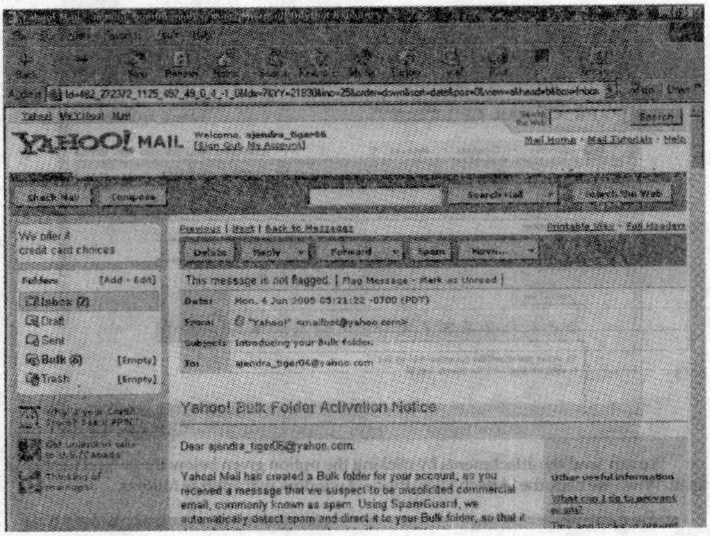

It contains the date of the mail, from whom it is received (sender's mail address), subject of the mail (it may or may not be given in the mails) and to whom it is sent (our mail ID). After reading the mails, they may be deleted or move to the folders where we like to have it. If we delete a mail it will goes to the Trash folder. The Trash folder is cleared in periodical intervals. If we wrongly delete a mail, we can find it in the Trash folder and it can be moved back to inbox or to the folder that we like. The draft folder is used to have a draft of the mails that we sent for future references. The 'Sent' folders contain the mails that we sent. But it is cleared in periodical intervals.

Attachments:

Data files may be attached to e-mail messages. Some mailers support "attachments", where we can specify a document to send through email. This allows people to share essentially any file in any format. GIF-encoded images, JPEG-encoded images, Word documents, WordPerfect documents, Photoshop files, Excel spreadsheets, and executable files are just a few of the types of documents that can be sent. Originally, attachments could be only text or executable software in plain alphanumeric characters, or ASCII format. Most mailers today support MIME (Multipurpose Internet Mail Extensions), a technology that preserves the original formatting of the attached file. MIME attachments may be word processor documents, graphic images, sound ("wave") files, animations, or video clips.

Let see the procedure of sending attachments with the mail.

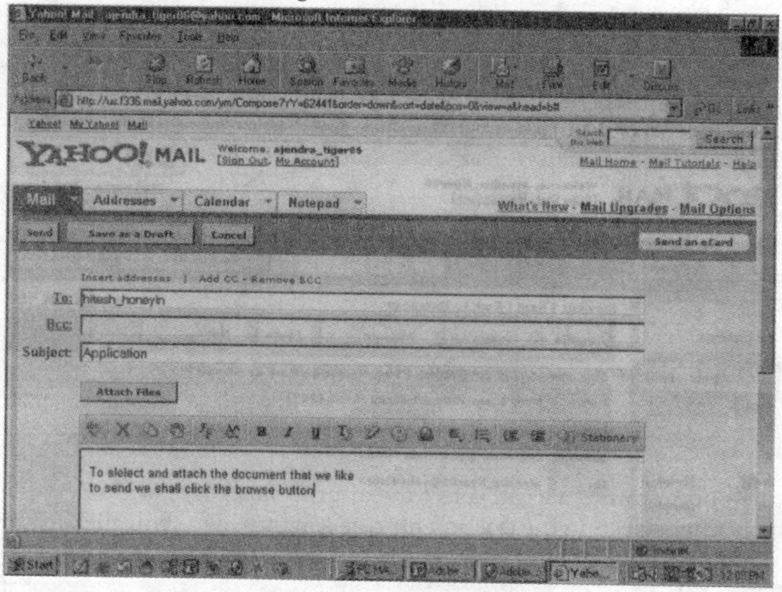

We can send the attachments by clicking the option given below the subject field of the mail. When we click the 'Attach Files' the next window will open as follows:

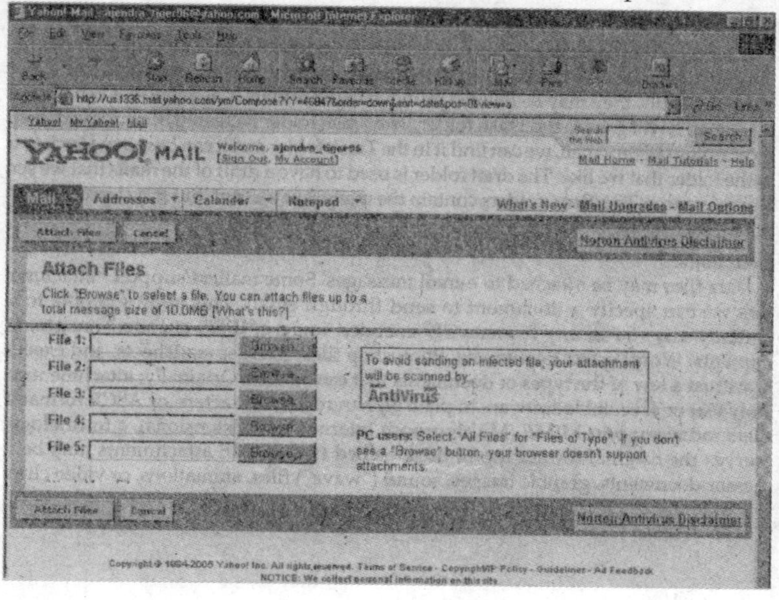

To select and attach the document that we like to send we shall click the 'Browse button, then the next window opens as follows:

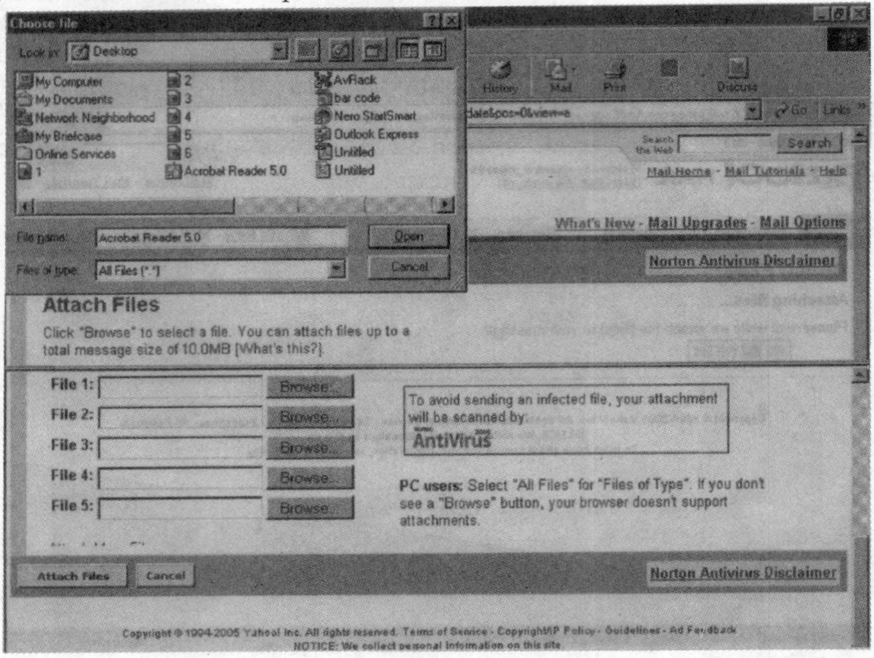

From the pop in frame we can select the appropriate drive and select the document to be attached. After selecting the document to be sent now we shall click the open button. Then the following frame will be opened.

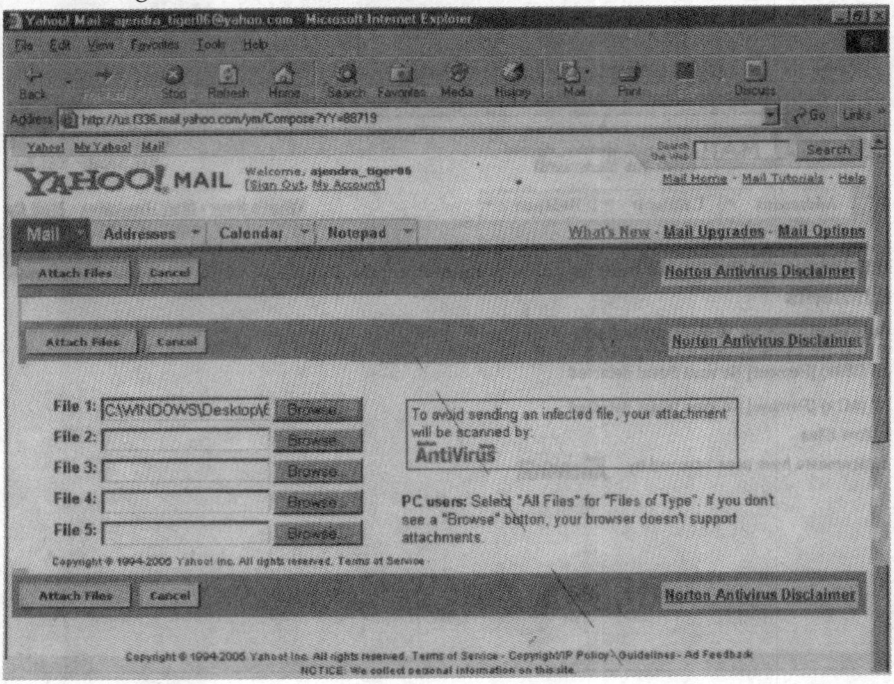

After this step, we shall now just click the 'Attach files' button given below the browse fields. Then the attachment process will begin as follows :

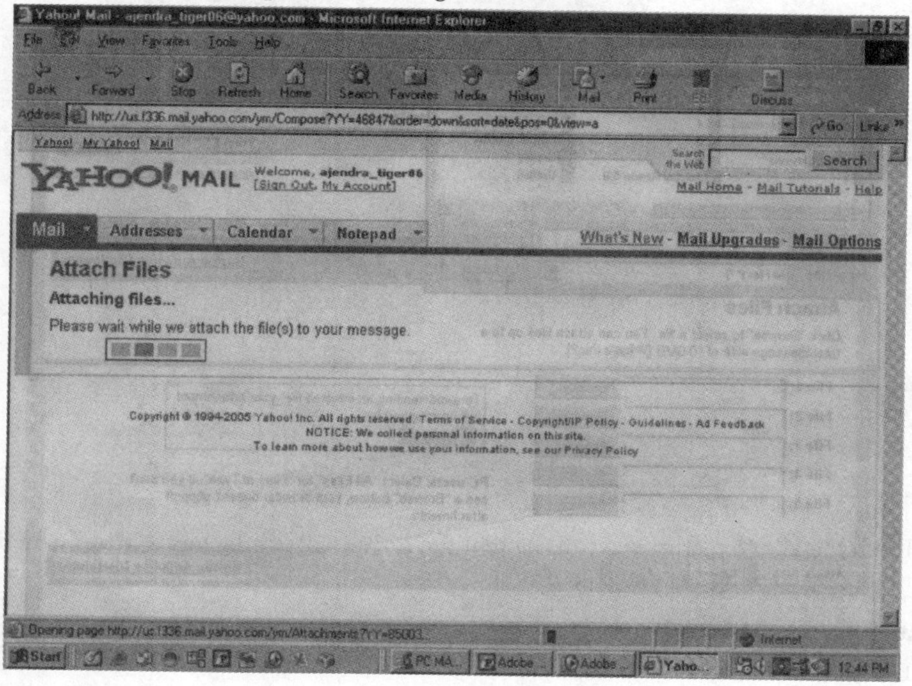

After the process of attachment is over, the screen will be as follows:

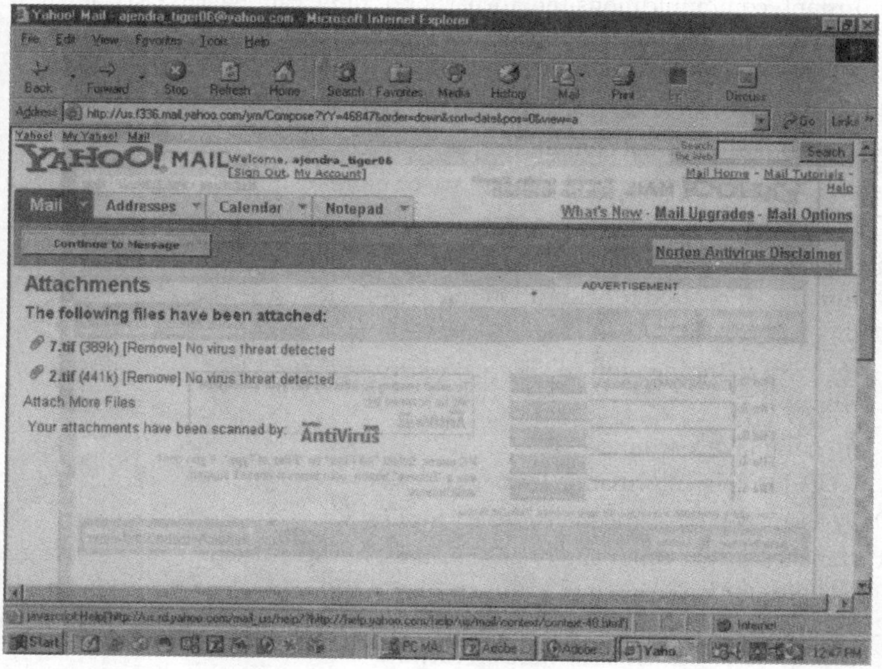

Now, by clicking the Done button, the mail is ready with the attachment as follow:

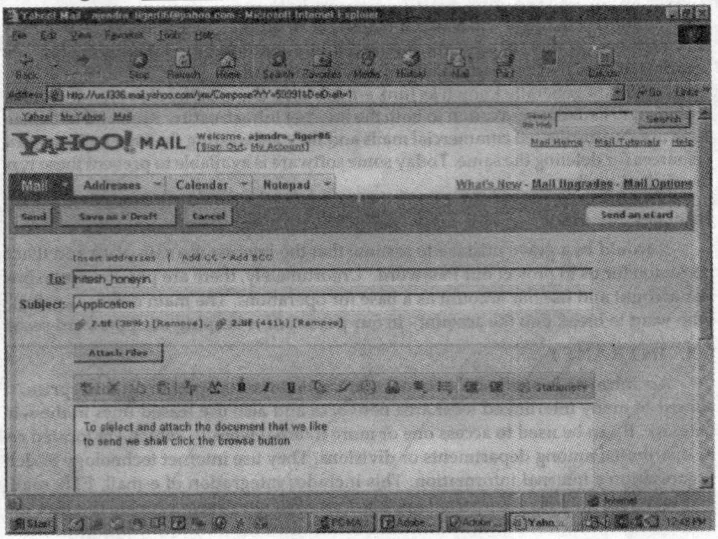

From the above picture we can see that the document is attached. Now, the mail can be sent just by clicking the 'Send' button.

11.9.6. Benefits of E-mail

E-mail provides the following services:

1. One-to-one or one-to-many communications.
2. Instant communications-the turnaround time can be so fast, email is more conversational than traditional paper-based media.
3. Physical presence of recipient is not required.
4. Most inexpensive mail service, 24-hours a day and seven days a week.
5. Encourages informal communication.
6. The same messages can be sent to one or more people.
7. In e-mail previous pages can be quoted.
8. Typographical symbols called smilies can be used to convey emotion.
9. E-mail can be used for education purposes as follows:
   (*a*) Corresponding with other teachers.
   (*b*) Corresponding with subject matter experts.
   (*c*) Pen pals.
   (*d*) Language learning.
   (*e*) Cultural or information exchange.
10. We can keep the same mail address for life.
11. It makes sure that our spelling is faultless, our words eloquent, and our grammar beyond reproach.
12. With a Web-based e-mail account, we can check our mails from any computer connected to the net,anywhere on earth.
13. Attachment of text, graphics, audio and video files.
14. Facilitates on line submission of application, reports etc.

15. Emails can be quoted as legal evidence.

Spam (Junk e-mail)

Spam is threatening to kill the quality and purpose of the regular email. Email important element of electronic commerce today. It modified today's office environment to a considerable level. Email has attained that status of quicker communication than the normal fax machines. Today, People are interested in e-mail and are signing up for free email accounts at sites like hotmail, rediffmail and yahoo mail.

Spam generally known as Junk e-mail, costs the unscrupulous sender virtually nothing and causes aggravation to both the internet infrastructure itself and to the end user. They are the unsolicited commercial mails and they are wasting the time and computer resources for deleting the same. Today some software is available to prevent these types of unsolicited mails.

Internet Security

It would be a grave mistake to assume that the internet is a safe place and that there is no reason for us to protect our Password. Unfortunately, there are possibilities to break into our account and use our account as a base for operations. The main defense against people who want to break into the account - in our password is keeping our password secure.

REVIEW QUESTIONS

Short Answer Questions

1. What is meant by e-commerce?
2. Give the reasons for the growth of e-commerce.
3. Differentiate between traditional commerce and e-commerce.
4. What is meant by e-mail?
5. Define internet.
6. Explain the following:
   (*a*) FTP (*b*) HTML (*c*) HTIP
7. What do you mean by WWW?
8. Give a short on Usenet.
9. What does Telnet mean?
10. What is internet telephony?
11. Give the meaning of Teleconferencing.
12. Define internet.
13. What are the features of internet?
14. Write a note on the governance of internet.
15. Give the meaning of WWW.
16. Give a note on web browsers with examples.
17. What are search engines?
18. Explain briefly on internet access.
19. Write a brief note on URL.
20. What are the types of e-mail accounts?
21. What do you know about scam in e-mail?

Essay Type Questions:

1. Explain the meaning of e-commerce. Give the importance of e-commerce.
2. What are the objectives of e-commerce?
3. What are the different types of e-commerce?
4. Explain the different applications of e-commerce?
5. Explain the meaning and evolution of internet.
6. Write a note on transmission of information on internet.
7. What are the different benefits of internet?
8. Explain the meaning and working of e-mail?
9. Explain the working of the WWW.
10. Write a detailed note on the technology of WWW.
11. Give a detailed note on the searching methods of internet.
12. Explain the benefits of e-mail.

CHAPTER

12

Computer Based Information Systems

12.1. INTRODUCTION TO INFORMATION SYSTEMS

Information is the data that has been processed and is meaningful to the user. It is a resource, produced by information systems and is important to the operation and management of organisations. It should be noted that information is neither a natural resource, such as oil and coal nor a resource that is acquired from the external environment to the organisation such as raw material or personnel. If it is designed suitably and properly managed, it can be the most effective resource of the organization.

12.2. FEATURES OF QUALITY INFORMATION

The main features of good quality information include the following:

FEATURES OF QUALITY INFORMATION	
Features	Meaning
Completeness	All needs of the user are include
Accuracy	Correctness and representing without any error
Timeliness	Up to date and available when needed
Consistency	A degree of firmness - stands together as a united whole - a combination
Validity	Unbiased, representative and verifiable
Appropriateness	The degree and level of details are based on the situation in question in all respects
Relevance	Information should directly be based on the situation in question
Precision	Provides exact information of quantitative nature based on the data used
Accessibility	User can access to any part of the information quickly and easily-scope to easy access

12.3. THE INFORMATION PROCESSING CYCLE

The information processing cycle includes the following steps:

1. Acquisition
2. Input
3. Validation

4. Processing (manipulation)
5. Storage
6. Retrieval
7. Output
8. Communication
9. Disposal/Archiving.

Let us these steps one by one here under.

1. **Acquisition:** It is the collection of raw data from the outside world so it can be put into an information system.
2. **Input:** It is putting the acquired data into the information system.
3. **Validation**: It is checking the quality of the data before it is processed. Processing invalid data gives waste information.
4. **Processing (manipulation):** This is a key point. At this stage data is converted into information.
5. **Storage**: Unless we want to input the data every time we process it, it is useful to store the data. We also may want to store information that we have produced so we need not have to keep repeating work.
6. **Retrieval:** This involves the reverse process of storage. The stored data or processed information can be taken back for further use. It is called as retrieval.
7. **Output:** All the previous steps are used to produce the results. The important output devices include the following:

   (*a*) Monitors (*b*) Printers (*c*) Sound cards/speakers (*d*) Plotters
8. **Communication:** this is nothing but sending data or information to another place. This usually involves LANs (local area networks), WANS (wide area networks - LANs joined together), and the internet.
9. **Disposal:** This involves deleting data or archiving data. Issues involve the security of deleted data. When data is no longer needed it can be deleted. Very sensitive data may need more: when PCs delete data, they do not actually remove it from the disk. They just mark that part of the disk as "available for saving on". Thus data can stay on the disk and be easily restored by snoops. To really delete sensitive data it should be wiped out. That is overwritten with trash until it is no longer readable.

   Archiving means that taking the data from the main storage and storing it offline usually on CDs. If in the future the data were needed again, it is still available and it is not taking up important hard disk space. Businesses tend to archive rather than delete data - just in case.

12.4. NEED FOR COMPUTER BASED INFORMATION SYSTEM

The computer based information system is required because of the following reasons:

1. Information is a valuable source to gain competitive advantage.
2. Information helps line managers in taking effective control of operations.
3. Information makes the planning more realistic.
4. Information enhances customer relationship.
5. Information paves the way for outsourcing certain activities like installation and maintenance of equipment, etc.
6. Information helps in decision making process.

7. Information helps in implementing business re-engineering.
8. Administrators need information for the survival of the organization and also improve the efficiency.
9. Management needs information to reduce the uncertainty in decision- making.
10. Computer operations need information to process the data correctly and produce the desirable output.
11. Individuals need information to manage and operate in the organization.
12. Organization needs information to improve the performance and growth
13. Banker needs information to provide loans or granting credit.
14. Investors need information to know the financial status and the future prospects of the business firms.
15. Government agencies need information systems for calculating taxation and taking regulatory measures.

12.5. INFORMATION SYSTEMS

The information requirements in business firms differ on the level of management. It is greatly depends on the paradigm of routine and exceptional. It can be seen easily from the following diagram:

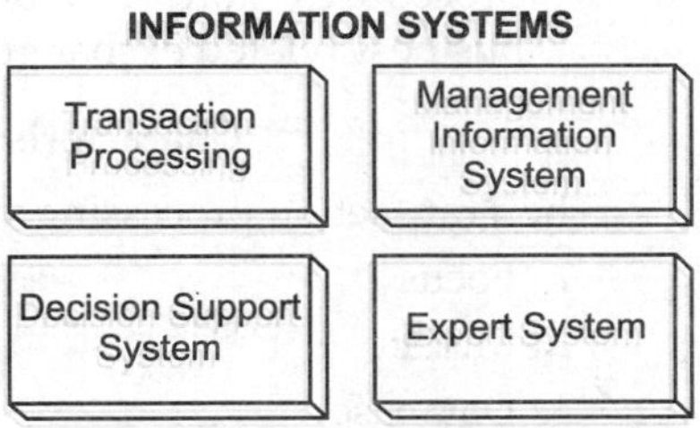

We shall discuss these information systems below:

12.5.1. Transaction Processing System

In large organizations, every day thousands of activities are being taking place. Each activity involves one or more transactions. The transactions may be recorded manually or mechanically or electronically. The recorded transactions form the data are processed to obtain the required information, because, it must be processed and converted into information. Such a great task can be accomplished through the transaction processing system.

A transaction is "a unit of work having qualities of consistency, durability and isolation". Consistency here means that a transaction should transform the system from one consistent state to another consistent state. Whereas isolation denotes that each and every transaction should be executed independently of other transactions that may be executing concurrently in the same environment.

The concept of *transaction processing* services evolved from the requirement of database applications. A *transaction* is an update (i.e., change) made to information in a database. Many transactions involve a query as well. The database is queried, a decision made on the basis of the information obtained from the query, and then a change made to the database. An application maintaining a database on a serve in a heterogeneous computing environment must be capable of managing transactions, which arrive virtually simultaneously from clients, in a manner which insures the integrity of the information.

In a heterogeneous computing environment, transaction processing services are provided in order to meet the special needs of distributed database applications. A transaction applied against a database on a server can cause the server to generate transactions against databases on other servers, and so on. The initial transaction generates a flow of transactions, which may be depicted as a flow through a tree structure. Each leaf of the tree represents a server running an application maintaining a database. Transaction processing services help the server database application control and synchronize these transaction flows so that the information contained in all of the databases is reliable and up-to-date.

In electronic data processing, data is processed in the computers automatically. The employees are having the knowledge only to operate the system. The transactions are carried out automatically through computers are called Transaction Processing System. The transaction processing system supports the day-to-day operations. Thus, the transaction processing system can be defined as "the Computerised system that process and records the routine day-to-day transactions necessary to carry out the business and this system serves the people at operational level of the organization. Payroll, inventory, invoices are some of the transaction processing system. Transaction is nothing but the representations of these operations.

12.5.1.1. Characteristics of Transaction Processing System

The transaction processing system has the following characteristic features.

1. Transaction - Any business-related exchange - E.g., generating a weekly payroll
2. Transaction processing system (TPS) - An organized collection of people, procedures, software, databases, and devices used to record completed for business related exchanges

Characteristics of Transaction Processing System

The Transaction processing system has the following characteristic features.

1. Focus	-	The TPS focuses on data transactions.
2. Impact	-	In TPS, the impact in one expediency.
3. Database	-	The database in TPS in unique to each application and in updated on batch mode.
4. Manipulation	-	In TPS, serves the need of sub-managerial and lower management levels.
5. Level of Management	-	The TPS, serves the need of sub-managerial and lower management levels.
6. Decision-capability	-	In TPS no decision in made. At times simple decision models may be made.
7. Information	-	The information provided by the TPS is in the form of summary reports and operational reports.
8. Applications	-	The TPS is commonly used in the areas of inventory, record keeping, sales, payroll etc.
9. Models of operation	-	The TPS can be operated on batch as well as on-line modes.
10. Path of Transaction	-	Transaction processing is done through the stages processing of recording and data collection, data conversion, data verification, data validation, file updating and processing, and reporting. That is the transaction processing is done as local or remote processing.

12.5.1.2. Transaction Processing Model and Cycle

Transaction Processing Systems are designed to capture and process data resulting from business transactions (e.g., sales, inventory changes, payments, refunds, etc.). Accurate and efficient processing of these business transactions form the basis for organizational operations and for most other types of information systems.

Model of Transaction Processing

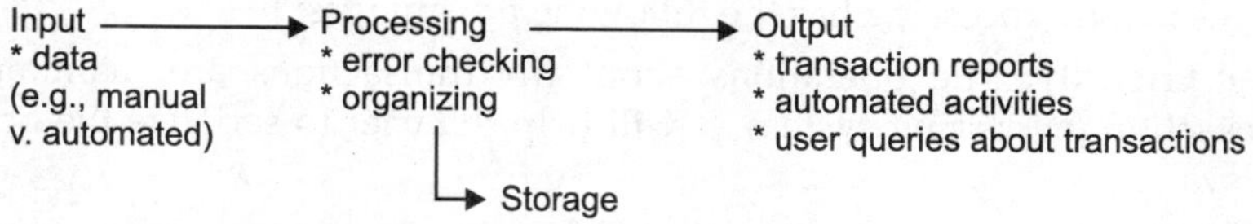

Transaction Processing Cycle

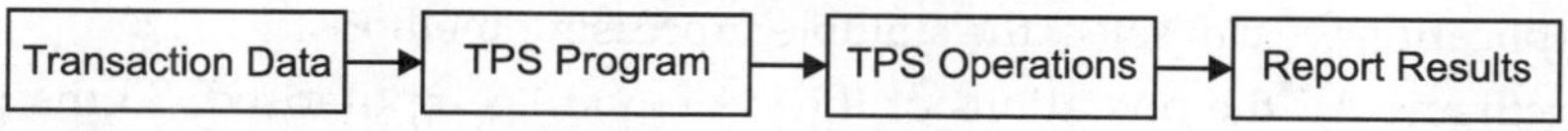

Basic Approaches to Data Entry: The data entry in the TPS, can be classified as follows:

1. The traditional approach in which paper-based source documents are generated at the time of the transaction and entered into the computer at a later point in time.
2. Automated data entry - source data automation - in which the transaction is entered into the computer system as soon as possible after the transaction has occurred by automating the entry process and eliminating as many unnecessary steps as possible.

Basic Approaches to Data Processing: The EDP systems focused on high volume applications and well defined rules. These two constraints are managed by the transaction processing system. This will help the business computerize the details. These are two types of transaction processing.

1. Online Transaction Processing
2. Batch Transaction Processing

1. **Online Transaction Processing:** This is the direct communication method between the operator and the transaction program. It will provide immediate results. In this method the transactions are processed to update a file or to make modifications in a file immediately after the transactions that occur in this real world. It will process only a single transaction at a time. It will be very suitable for airline reservation and railway reservation system.
2. **Batch Transaction Processing:** The transactions are grouped together and processed periodically on a sequential basis. The transactions are grouped into a transaction file and sorted. The units are read in order by the transaction processing system program. It will collect the data from the old file and process the transactions and creates the new file to store the data. This method is very much useful for sequential access method.

Example: Payroll system

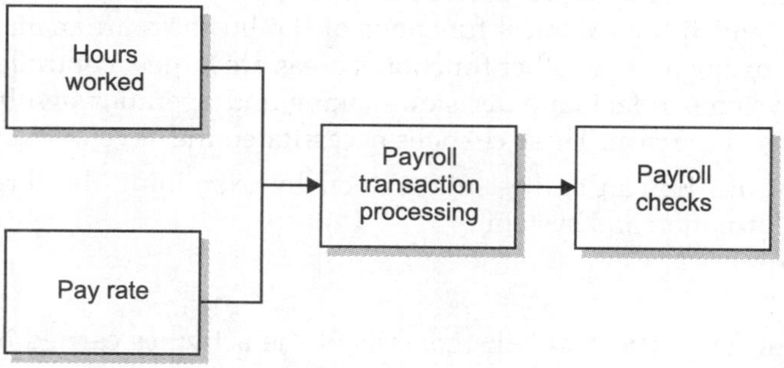

12.5.1. 3. Advantages of Transaction Processing

The Transaction Processing has the following advantages:

1. **User Friendly:** The operations about the transactions are maintained in the transaction processing system. It will help the user to serialize the operations of the system.
2. **Processing Speed:** The Transaction Processing System processes the date in two ways: Online or Batch Processing. The processing speed is increased because each application we can select the suitable processing methods.
3. **Accuracy:** All the operations of the system are computerised. So the results are more accurate and efficient.
4. **Easy Retrieval:** The data stored in the transaction processing method. It is easy to retrieve the data, because all processes are done automatically.
5. **Easy Reporting:** It will produce the printed documents. The documents provided by the transaction processing system should be very neat and easily understandable. It is possible to take as many reports as possible with less time.
6. **Completeness:** In transaction process transaction is executed completely and it do most leave any partial results.
7. **Individuality:** In transaction processing each and every transaction is processed as if it were running alone, even though the transactions are processed concurrently to improve the performance.
8. **Consistency:** In transaction processing, after completion, each transaction moves the system from one state to another.
9. **Durability:** In transaction processing, after the completion of a transaction to the system failure or the other.

12.5.2. Management Information System

The increasing complexities of modern organizations demand new dimensions in modern management. Perhaps, the most profound and promising of these dimensions is the emerging utilization of more advanced information systems. These systems are changing the process of management in several ways.

First, the basic functions of planning and control now depend to an increasingly greater extent on access to computer-based information systems as decision-making becomes more structured and relies most and more on the flow of information to and between decision centres. Second, the organization is changing to accommodate information technology. The structure and composition of organizational resources are beginning to reflect a new approach to organizational design caused by the decision approach. The third major change is the manner in which the technical functions of the business are managed, marketing, finance, manufacturing and the other functional areas are largely controlled by the design of information systems to facilitate decision-making and operations within and between these sub-systems of the firm. These changes necessitated the development of MIS.

The concept of MIS can be best understood by examining the three basic terms : management, information and system.

Management:

Management for purpose of MIS, consists of the activities carried out by manager. They plan organise and control the major activities of the business and initiate action.

Because decision making is a major requirement for each of the managerial functions, MIS becomes a facilitating system for developing decisions in planning, organizing controlling and execution. This precisely server the basic aim of MIS.

Information:

Information is different from Data and distinction between the two is very important. Data are facts and figures which are not directly used in the decision process. But information consists of classified and interpreted data and is being used for decision making. For example, record of shipments to customers, over the past years when lying in files, represents data. These figures, when classified by customer, location and cumulative sales distribution among customers and used by management for the purpose of deciding the future marketing programs, they are called information.

System:

A system is a set of two or more elements, such as people, things and concepts, which are joined together to attain a common objective. A system consists of a number of smaller systems, which are called subsystems. A properly functioning system is characterized by its synergy. That is, all subsystems or elements work more effectively together in the system than when they were operating independently. The output of the integrated system cumulatively will be expected to be far greater than the sum of the outputs of the subsystems taken separately.

A system is a set of components working together toward a defined goal. A stereo system, for example is a set of components – speakers, amplifiers, turner, cassette deck, record player – working together to provide quality sound. The term system can be defined as follows:

"A system is a set of elements forming an activity or processing procedure seeking a common goal by operating on data in a time reference to yield information".

Management Information System

Management information system is a general term for the computer systems in an enterprise that provide information about its business operations. It is also used to refer to the people who manage these systems. Typically, in a large organisation MIS refers to a centrally coordinated system of computer expertise and management, including mainframe systems and the entire network of computer resources.

In the beginning, business computers were used for the practical business of computing the payroll and keeping track of accounts payable and receivable. As applications were developed that provided managers with information about sales, inventories, and other data that would help in managing the enterprise, the term "MIS" arose to described these kinds of applications. Today, the term is used broadly in a number of contexts and includes: decision support systems, resource and people management applications, project management, and database retrieval applications.

Thus, MIS can be defined as "a set of inter related elements which work together to render classified and interpreted data that are usable and used by managers in the process of planning, organising, staffing, directing and controlling the major activities of business".

12.5.2.1. Evolution of MIS

The Management Information System is a formal method of making available the accurate and timely information necessary for decision making process and enable the management to plan, execute, control and co-ordinate the necessary functions effectively. Initially, the organisations had some kind of management information systems even when it was not recognised as such. Let us have a look into the evolution of MIS right from the beginning.

Year	Perception of MIS
Early period of 20th Century	Information (Highly Informal) was available but it was not recognised as MIS. Before the advent of computers Manual Processing - MIS was determined by the ability to process and condense large volume of data.
1950s	MIS was organised under separate department called Computer Department.
	Computer Manager and MIS Manager became synonymous
1960s	Computer Department was called as EDP (Electronic Data Processing)
1970s	The System concept was introduced in management of EDP.
	The focus of EDP was computer in 1960s and got shifted to information by 1970s
1980s	The growth of EDP led to the emergence of the concept of computer based information systems
1990s	Decision Support System has emerged. Recent advances in computer hardware and software have made it possible for the managers to gain on-line or real-time access to the databases in MIS
21st Century	Artificial Intelligence will be used for designing Expert Systems to cater managerial information needs.

12.5.2.2. MIS Cycle

The objectives of an MIS is to provide summary information for planning, controlling and organizing the activities of the system and also used for solving problems and making decision.

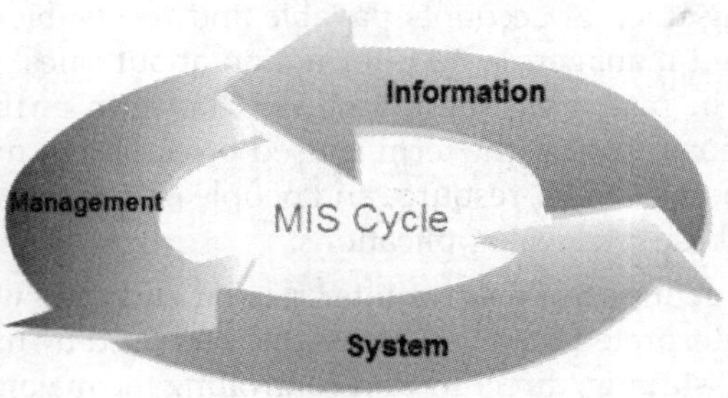

MIS applications, process the data which is generated by the internal and external information sources. The processed data is called information. The information is transferred to the managers to make decisions.

Schematic of MIS

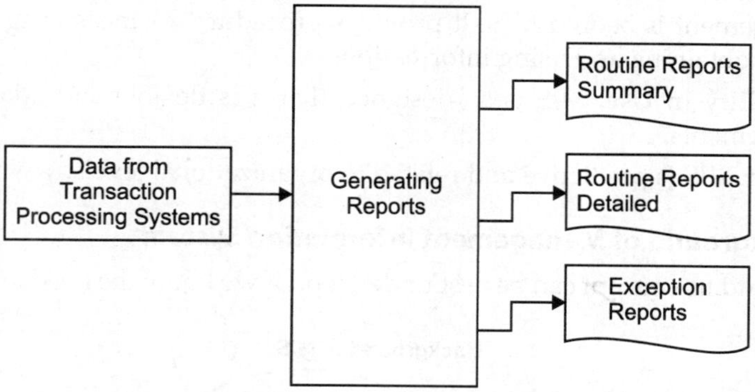

The data from transaction processing systems are processed in Management information system to generate the following reports:

- Routine reports - information for routine decisions
- Detailed reports - information for managerial activities
- Exception reports – information on exceptions-demands special attention and efficient managerial activity

12.5.2.3. Characteristics of MIS

MIS generally has the following characteristics:

1. **Management Oriented:** Beyond any doubt is the fact that MIS is a management oriented system. This could be understood from the terminology itself. The information processing carried out by MIS is always attempting at helping the management.
2. **Management Directed:** Similarly, all the activities of MIS are initiated by the management. It is the management's need that the MIS strives to satisfy. Hence, MIS is management directed.
3. **User – machine System:** The concept of user-machine system implies that some tasks of MIS are done by the users while others are best done by machines. There is co-existence of both men and machines in MIS.
4. **Integrated System:** MIS provides the basis for the integration of information processing. This leads to common data flows. Even though applications in a system are implemented one at a time, their design is guided by an overall plan. In essence information system is designed as a federation of small systems.
5. **Involves Large Planning:** The concepts of MIS goes only with planning. There is a huge amount of planning coupled with the installation and maintenance of MIS.
6. **Sub Systems:** Naturally, a vast system like the MIS will be having plenty of subsystems which are mutually related with defined with definite relationships and properly ordered. It is based on subsystem concept.
7. **Use of Models:** MIS uses scientific and mathematical models for planning, organizing, directing and controlling for its analysis.
8. **Data Base:** One of the pre-requisites for installing, implementing and successful operating of MIS is data. Hence, there has to be a way to maintain data in data bases and there has to be a central data base.

9. **Information as a Resource:** MIS transforms Data into information and the management is behind MIS. It provides procedure for measuring and matching cost of obtaining and using information.
10. **Flexibility in Use:** MIS is so designed that it is flexible and adaptable to user requirements.
11. **Others:** MIS is predictive and related to organizational levels.

12.5.2.4. Background of Management Information System

The MIS and its concept can be best understood if we know the need and background of MIS.

Background of MIS

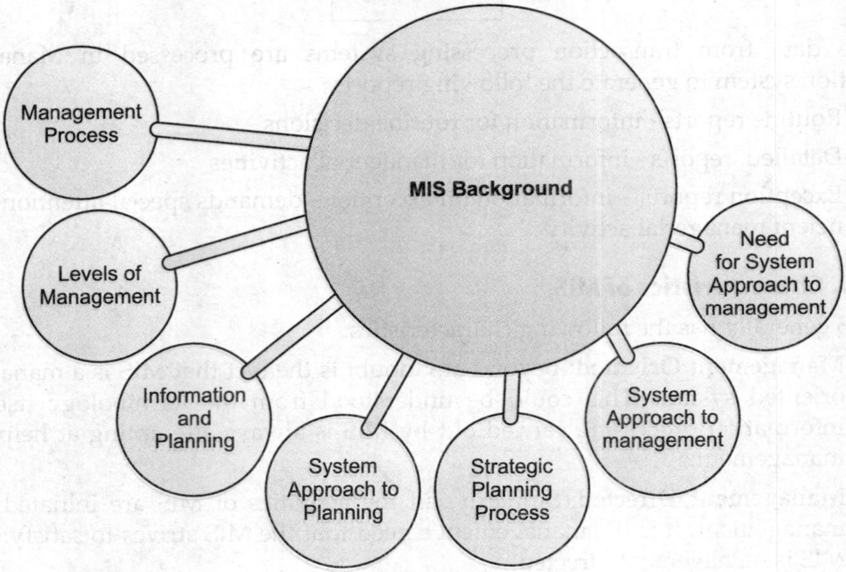

A. Management Process:

The functions of management are not performed sequentially. Planning is involved in organising and controlling. Similarly, organizing is required for planning and controlling. Each function interacts with the other to form the management process. The general model of management process is shown below:

Management Process Model

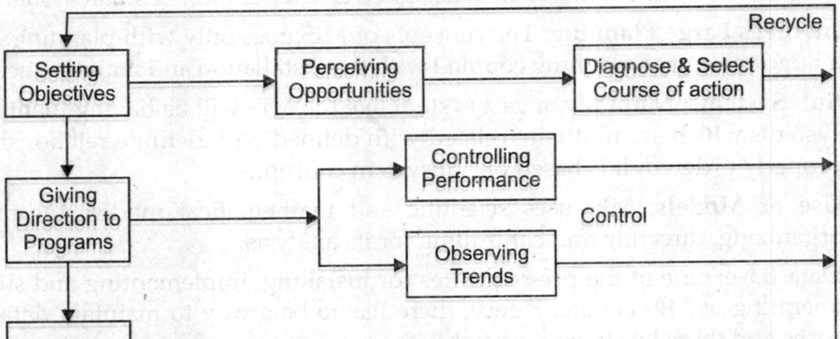

The functions involved in the management process are briefly explained hereunder.

Planning: Planning includes the following:

1. Setting of objectives for the manager's area of activity.
2. Perception of opportunities, problems and alternatives to achieve objectives.
3. Diagnosis of opportunities, analysis of objectives and selection of a course of action.
4. Design of program of action to achieve the objective.

Directing: It involves leadership required to achieve the planned objectives, including communication and motivation.

Organising: It includes supervision of action planning where the relationship between individuals are defined and understood.

Controlling: It involves the observation and measurement of performance against standards for achieving the plan and take corrective action in case of deviations. For controlling, observing the trends is required. The objectives may be modified if necessary.

Feedback: It involves recycling of information concerning plans, actions and progress at different stages of the management process to ensure that proper programming to achieve the objective is being accomplished.

B. Levels of Management:

Each organization is made up of several levels. These could be classified at least in three main groups - top middle and lower levels. The top level is primarily interested in strategic planning and would thus require the other two levels to provide a support in the form of processed information. The 'middle level' would be interested in tactical planning and operational control and would need information to support these managerial functions so that the organization runs smoothly. The 'junior level' involved in day-to-day information transactions and needs information for its working, the process being called as 'operational control'.

The three levels of managerial activity in the organization are:

LEVELS OF MANAGEMENT AND DECISIONS

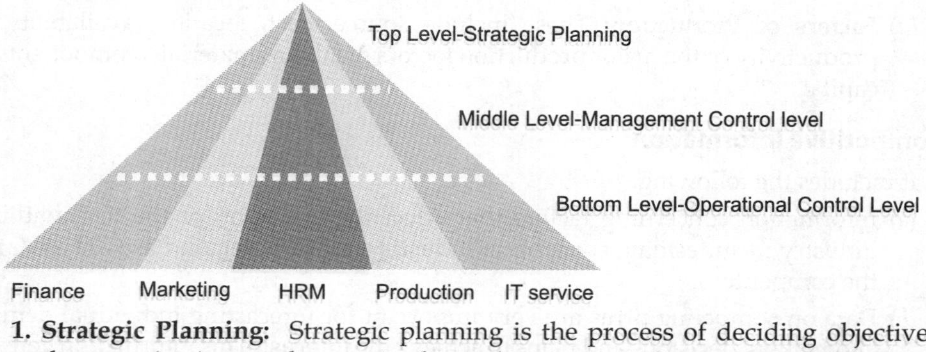

1. **Strategic Planning:** Strategic planning is the process of deciding objectives of the organization or changes in these objectives, or the resources used to attain these objectives, and on the policies that are to govern the acquisition, use and disposition of these resources.
2. **Management Control:** Operational control is the process of assuring that specific tasks are carried out effectively and efficiently. Thus a top manager in an organization will devote most of his time in strategic planning while a

supervisor/manager at the operational level will spend most of his time on operational planning and control. Management control is the process by which managers assure that resources are obtained and used effectively and efficiently in the accomplishment of the objectives of the organization.

3. **Operational Control:** Operational control is the process of assuring that specific tasks carried out effectively. Thus a manager at top level devotes most of his time in strategic planning while a supervisor at the operational level will spend most of his time on operational planning and control.

C. Information and Planning

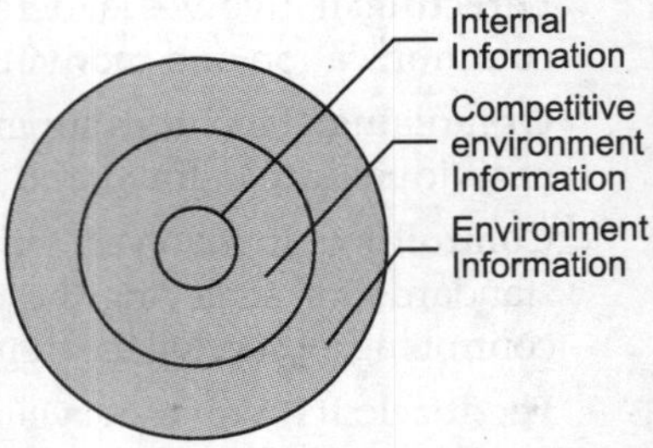

Planning is, deciding in advance, what has to be done, who has to do it, when it has to be done, and how it is to be done. It bridges the gap from where we are and where we want to go. A manager plans for the allocation of resources and the work of other people, in contrast to the non-manager's who plan only their individual activities.

The planning needs of an organization can be classified into three broad types:

1. Environment Information:

Environmental information needs can be classified and described as follows:

(*a*) **Political and Governmental Considerations:** Some information on political stability is important for forecasting plans. Additionally, the nature and extent of Government controls and their effect on the organization must be taken into account. A third factor is the important role played by government financial and tax policies as they have a very significant effect on many planning decisions.

(*b*) **Demographic & Special Trends:** Included herein would be the GNP level and trend, consumer disposable income, price and wage levels, whose effects are vital to almost all organisations, regardless of, product or service.

(*c*) **Technological Environment:** Rapid technical changes and their consequences should be considered.

(*d*) **Factors of Production:** These include source, cost, location, availability and productivity of the major production factors of labour, materials, components and capital.

2. Competitive Information:

It includes the following:

(*a*) Information concerning factors that affect the operation of the firm within an industry includes data concerning industry and firm demand as well as data on the competitors.

(*b*) Data on competing firms are very important for forecasting individual demands and making decisions and plans to achieve the forecast. This information generally falls into three types.

- Past performance i.e., Profitability, return on investment, share of the Market etc.
- Present activity i.e., Developments concerning price, strategy, advertising, changes in the distribution channels etc.
- Future plans i.e., Information concerning new products, acquisitions, R & D efforts etc.

3. Internal Information:

Internal premises affect the planning decisions at many levels in the organization. In some respects they are more important than the external information. As they relate to the total planning process, internal data are aimed at identification of the organisation strength and weakness. MIS master plans are of the following types:

(*a*) **Sales Forecast:** This is perhaps the simplest important planning document in the organization, because the allocation of the entire company's resources is a function of the sales plan. It sets the framework, on which, most other internal plans are constructed.

(*b*) **The Financial Plan:** The financial plan frequently called the budget, involves the entire organization and when completed, provides subsidiary planning information for a variety of sub-plans throughout the company. It is a system that links all activities of the company together.

(*c*) **Supply Factors:** Labour, capital, plant and equipment, organization and other supply factors are vital planning premises that provide constraints or boundaries within which planning takes place. These factors are controllable to a large extent by the firm, but their availability and limitations must be taken into account in developing the financial plan and subsidiary plans for achieving objectives.

(*d*) **Policies:** Basic policies are relatively fixed for long run purposes and cannot be readily changed to permit flexibility in developing alternative courses of action in the short run. To the extent, that product, marketing, financial, personnel and other basic policies remains unchanged in the short run, they provide constraints to planning in much the same way as do supply factors.

D. System Approach to Planning:

The System approach to planning can be depicted as follows:

System Approach to Planning

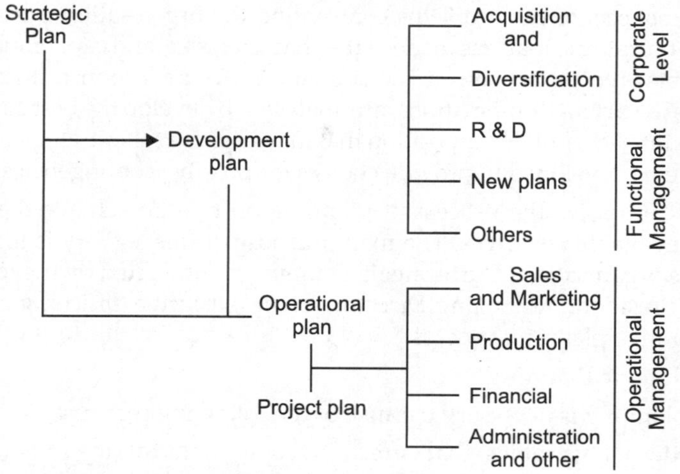

The four special reasons for system planning are:

(*i*) To offset uncertainty

(*ii*) To improve economy of operations.

(*iii*) To focus on objectives.

(*iv*) To provide a device for control of operations.

E. Strategic Planning Process:

When the system approach is made to planning, particularly the strategic planning, it involves the following process.

Strategic Planning Process

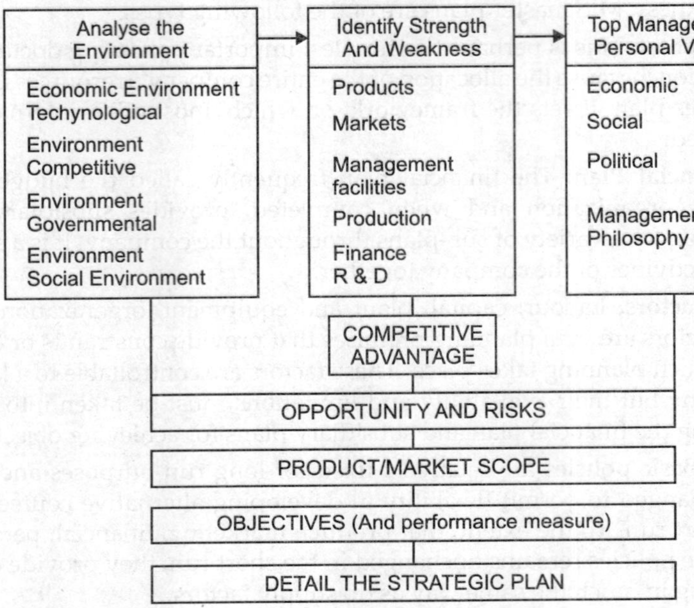

Strategy involves the use and close integration of economic, political, cultural, social, moral, spiritual, and psychological power. Strategy can be formulated only after the objectives to be accomplished have been determined. Thus, corporate objectives and corporate power are the irreducible elements of corporate strategy. After corporate objectives have been determined, all aspects of the problems confronting the organisation must be thoroughly examined and accurate evaluations made of the character, size, and capabilities of the various available elements of corporate power. Then possible courses of action, utilizing the corporate power elements in varying combinations, are analysed to develop the best corporate strategy possible, taking into account the opposition that may be met as the strategy unfolds. Options should therefore be developed to provide choices for possible contingencies.

Strategic Planning is the process of planning on how to achieve the organisational goals with the available resources. The main purpose of this activity is to accomplish the objectives of the organisation. The Strategic Planning is conducted by the top management which include President, Managing Director, Chief Executive Officer, General Manager, etc. It is a long range planning process.

Reasons for Strategic Planning:

Strategic planning is necessary because of the following reasons:

1. The external variables that affect the operations of the organisation do not remain constant. These variables include technological changes, international environment, political and government policies, economic trends, etc. Necessary provisions to be made in strategic plans to cope with these situations.
2. As all natural resources are becoming scarce, the management must decide on how to allocate them properly. A proper redistribution of resources must be planned accordingly.

3. Information explosion has necessitated increase in knowledge and ability to plan effectively. All competitive forces generate an absolute necessity to introduce strategic planning in most companies.

Strategic planning activity consists of the following steps:

1. Express and define clearly the mission and vision of the organisation
2. Ascertain long-range goals and objectives.
3. Formulate long-range plans.
4. Formulate short-range plans.
5. Make predictions about the economic environment in the future.

For the above said strategies, specific structured information is required. So it is the responsibility of the Information Systems Division to provide the details in the required manner.

F. System Approach to Management

A system is a set of interdependent components that create a whole entity. The components are dynamically linked. That is, each one affects the other components in the system. The systems approach is concerned with a logistic entity, but does not neglect the components of the entity. It recognizes the activities of the components while simultaneously considering the activity of the whole system that contains them. The systems approach is primarily a philosophy of structure that co-ordinates in an efficient and optimum manner the activities and operations within any system.

It is designed to utilise scientific analysis in the organisation for :

(*a*) Developing and managing operating system.

(*b*) Designing information system for decision-making.

Characteristics of system approach to management:

The system approach to MIS has the following features.

(1) **Organised:** It combines various facts of the problem. Problem diagnosis is most important in the systems approach, as it determines the information needs and the system objectives.

(2) **Theoretical:** It is based on scientific methods which provide theoretical frame work.

(3) **Empirical:** Only the relevant data must be used.

(4) **Pragmatic:** The system must be feasible and operative.

(5) **Creative:** The system approach must focus on goals first and methods afterwards. It must be creative because:-

(*a*) Problems are complex and ill structured and there is no unique formulation or solution.

(*b*) Data available is incomplete.

(*c*) Traditional, functional and disciplinary barriers must be subordinated to the synthesis of solution.

G. Need for System approach to management

System approach to management is needed because of the following reasons:

1. The growing size of the business.
2. The organisations are becoming more and more complex.
3. Growing environmental constraints – laws, pollution.
4. Technological Revolution.
5. Increasing expenditure on R & D.
6. Product change.
7. Intensive competition.
8. International markets.
9. Increasing consumerism
10. Increasing government intervention etc.

12.5.2.5. Designing of MIS

The basic decision has to take into account a general approach, so that suitable systems can be developed for different organisations depending upon their role, functions and decision making requirement. In each organisation, data gets generated at different levels. This data when processed and analysed becomes information which, when properly communicated in time for the decision making can result in decision actions.

Designing of MIS involves the following steps:

STEPS IN DESIGNING MIS

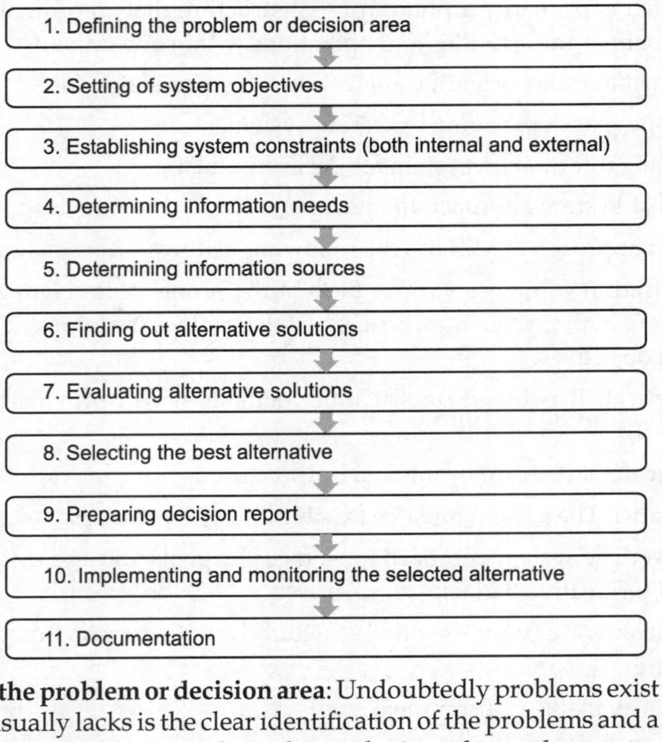

1. Defining the problem or decision area: Undoubtedly problems exist in any dynamic business. What usually lacks is the clear identification of the problems and a priority system for their solution. The problem may be in the marketing where sales are poor or there could be problems in the inventory area where large stocks exist and every year it is increasing. Therefore, management must take the first step in MIS designing by formulating problems to be solved. The precise definition of the problem is crucial. Otherwise, the problem solver would be restricted to a solution or a system that is suboptimal or that encompasses more than it is needed.

2. System objectives: The system objective should clearly be stated in terms of the functions the information system is to perform. The objectives could be to cater specifically for information needs of finance, personnel, material or any other specific area of business. It could also be to meet the total information needs of the organization. In short, system objective should be stated in terms of what managers can do and how effectively they would be able to function after their information requirements have been met. To give an example, in the field of inventory, the objective could be to design better decision rules so that various levels of inventory could adequately be controlled.

The following questions should be answered while laying down the objectives of MIS design:

(*a*) What is the purpose of the system?

(*b*) What is it expected to do?

(*c*) Why is it needed?

(*d*) What are the users and what are their objectives?

The objectives of MIS system design have to match the organisation objectives. The aim being to improve decision making, lower cost, meet customer demands and improve the image of the organization.

3. Establishing system constraints: In designing MIS the designer has to face certain limitations; sometimes called problem boundaries or restrictions. Constraints enable the designer to stipulate the conditions under which objectives may be attained and help to consider the limitations that restrict the design. To state it in another way, constraints, which are provided by the manager, user or the designer himself, limit freedom of action in designing a system to achieve the objective.

Constraints may be classified as (*a*) internal or (*b*) external to the organisations as shown in figure:

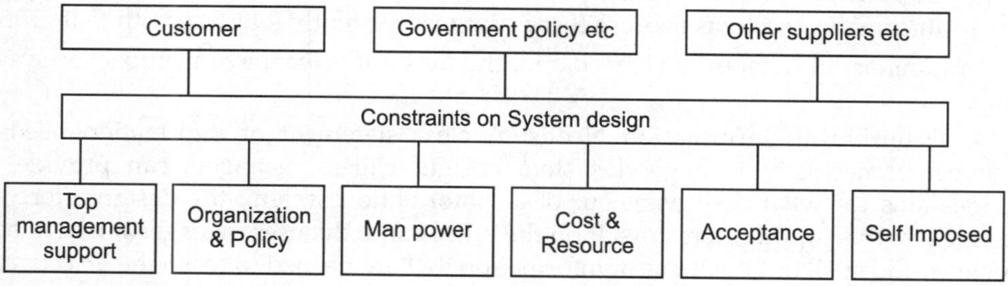

(*a*) **Internal constraints:**

(*i*) **Top Management Support:** It is very essential for MIS system. A good environment for information system must be set. Approval and support of top management should be taken. Their feedback and guidelines definitely influence the kind of system managers may design.

(*ii*) **Organizational Policy:** Considerations frequently set limits on objectives and modify an intended approval for design of a system. In every organization managers occupying various positions, influence information flow, particularly in a decentralized system. Also company policies frequently define or limit the approach to system design. Among these policies are those concerned with product and service, R & D, Marketing, Finance and Personnel.

(*iii*) **Man Power:** Perhaps the most significant constraint of all is the one concerning people or MANPOWER. Men problem is probably the fact, most often mentioned where failure to achieve expected results is concerned. Here we have the difficulties associated with the natural human reaction to change, the lack of interest and support, frequently met in systems design and operation.

(*iv*) **Cost:** It is a major resource limitation. The cost to achieve an objective should be compared with the benefits to be derived. The other resource requirements could be space, air conditioning, power etc., and other facilities for setting up the information system. Inadequacy of resources can greatly limit the system design.

(*v*) **Acceptance:** Acceptance of the computerized MIS system perhaps presents the most difficult aspect of the problem in organizations, as it causes a natural human reaction against the change.

(*vi*) **Self-Imposed restrictions:** These are those placed on the design by the manager or the designer. The data requirements, the data volume and the rate of processing are constraints imposed by the immediate users.

(*b*) **External constraints:**

(*i*) **Customer:** Foremost among the consideration surrounding the external environments are those concerning the customer. Order entry, billing, and other systems that interface with systems of the customer must be designed with the customer's needs in mind. If certain outputs from the system are not acceptable to the customer, a definite limitation is to be faced.

(*ii*) **Government:** A variety of additional external constraints should be considered in addition to the customer. The government (central, state, local) imposes certain restrictions on the processing of data, in maintaining and in the conduct of business like taxes and reporting.

(*iii*) **Unions:** Unions can affect the operation of systems involving members in matters such as compensation, grievances and working conditions.

(*iv*) **Suppliers:** They are also an important group to be considered when designing information systems because these systems frequently interface with that group.

In summary, it is important to recognize the constraints that have an impact on system design.

4. Determining Information Needs: A clear statement of information needs is fundamental necessity to a good system design. Unless managers can provide the specifications for what they want out of an information system, the design effort will produce less than optimum results. If on the other hand, the user manager can define the objectives and spell out the items of information that are needed to reach the objective, he or she is, then, at least half way through in system.

A manager needs information for a variety of reasons concerned with the management process. The type of need that he or she will have at various times and for various purposes depends largely upon following factors:

(*i*) **Personal Attributes** such as

(*a*) knowledge of information systems

(*b*) Managerial style i.e., Leadership style and decision making ability

(*c*) Manager's perception of information needs.

(*ii*) **Organisational Environment** such as

(*a*) Nature of the company,

(*b*) Level of management and

(*c*) Structure of the organisation.

5. Determination of Information Sources: The step for determining information needs is hardly completed, before we consider the information sources. Although some systems require considerable external information, for the most part, the natural place to turn for information is inside the firm-books, records, files, accounting documents etc. Thus most analysis refers to the step of determining information requirements on analysing the present system. We must not only uncover information sources for the particular subsystem under consideration but also take into account how they fit into the overall integrated sources of information and techniques of analysis.

6. Finding out Alternative Solutions: Once the problem has been understood, the solutions for the problem are to be found out. Ideally, one has to attempt to find out more than one alternative solution, but it should not be much more. It should be narrow down to a few. Because having too many alternatives affects the problem solving process, increase costs and become unmanageable.

7. Evaluating Alternative Solutions: Each alternative has its own advantages and disadvantages that contribute to solving the problem in question. These must be evaluated and attached to the proposed alternative. In certain business problems, the costs and benefits are partly intangible or immeasurable. In such a situation the problem solver should make approximations using surrogate measures and probabilities.

8. Selecting the Best Alternative: In this stage, the problem solver may have many alternatives which have more benefits than costs. In such a situation he applies a decision-rule or a yardstick (e.g., rate of return or time etc.) to summerise and rank the alternatives. Finally the best alternative is chosen.

9. Preparation of Design Report: The conceptual design report is, in a sense, a proposal for the expenditure of funds and for organizational changes. Because it is directed to management, it should have a concise summary of the problems that constitutes the system, the objectives, the general nature of the system, reasons why the concept was selected over others, and the time and resources required to design and implement the system.

10. Implementing and Monitoring the Selected Alternative: Once, the best alternative or system has been selected it must be implemented and followed up. If it does not perform well and incurs more costs than estimated, then the next best alternative should be chosen and implemented and controlled.

11. DOCUMENTATION: For the smooth running of the MIS it is necessary that the following types of documentations are to be prepared:

(*a*) For those providing input, a simple overview of the system, a clear description of exactly what input is expected and a note above what input is not acceptable.

(*b*) For those running and maintaining the system, all the technical documentation generated during the development process.

(*c*) For those using the output, a simple overview of the system, a clear description of what the output means and a note about its limitations.

12.5.2.6. Benefits of MIS

Information is needed in virtually every field, thought and action. But besides being essential to individuals who use it to achieve personal ends; information is also needed by managers in organisations. Managers at all levels must perform such basic tasks as staffing, directing and controlling. The success of any business is determined by the success of its managers in performing their activities. Activities in turn are being affected by the excellence in decision-making. The blood pool of better decisions is information. Decision making must be supported by quality information.

In short, quality information leads to better decisions. Better decisions enhance better managerial activities and, effective managerial performance leads to organizational effectiveness. It is MIS which is the supplier of information to the managers. Hence, the role of MIS is very important in every organisation.

The following diagram explains the role of MIS in the process or organizational effectiveness.

Role of MIS

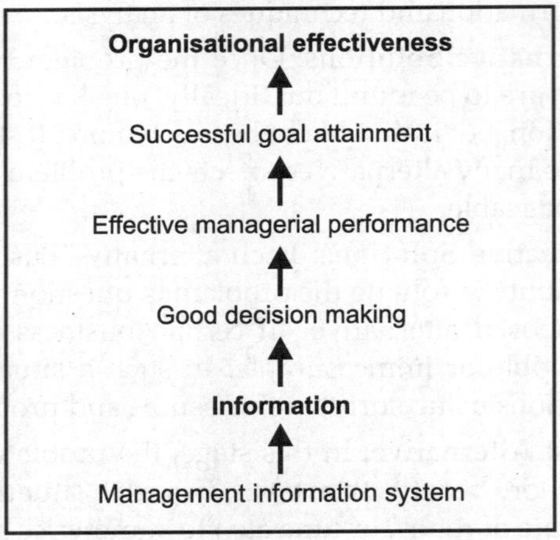

The analysis, design and implementation of MIS is more expensive and difficult. Even though expensive it is justified for several reasons.

1. **Timeliness:** Managers make decisions more quickly and take less time to solve the problems and give satisfactory solutions to the management.
2. **Accuracy:** Normally the organizations are in position to provide variety of regular reports, for the increased government regulations. Also the organizations have variety of customers, requires variety of reports. These reports are organized by the management accurately with the effective MIS.
3. **Reduction in inventory levels:** With effective MIS the inventory levels can be maintained at an optimum level which results into cost reduction.
4. **Better Liquidity:** MIS provides for better liquidity by justifying account receivable, cash flow or living systems.
5. **Better work allocation:** MIS ensures the better allocation of work by evaluating the benefits of personnel allocation, maintenance control and production scheduling system. This results into reduction in work hours which lead to monetary benefits to the firms.
6. **Increase in sales:** Through effective MIS, one can assess the profitability of distribution, marketing, finished goods, inventory control, and customer order systems. This may result into increase in sales.
7. **Reduction in maintenance costs:** MIS can be used as a measure for evaluating maintenance control system and spare parts inventory control systems. It ensures reduction in maintenance costs.
8. **Completeness**: In MIS, the system managers understand the management technique and the procedures. So they are able to produce the complete report of a system.

9. **Accurate reports:** The MIS has the ability to provide the complete and concise reports. For example,

(*a*) Summary Reports	-	Summaries all activities of the organisation and present in the form of summary report.
(*b*) Demand Reports	-	This report will be prepared only when they are requested by the management.
(*c*) Customer Reports	-	According to the specifications of the management it will be prepared.
(*d*) Exception Reports	-	According to the conditions or exceptions the report is prepared.
(*e*) Responsibility	-	The MIS structure provides the boundaries of management responsibilities.

10. **Other benefits:** MIS provides the following other benefits.
    (*i*) Ensures shorter response time.
    (*ii*) Reduces the number of negative responses to customers.
    (*iii*) Improves decision-making process.
    (*iv*) Widens information bases for decision-making.
    (*v*) Facilitates data integration.
    (*vi*) Simple and easy to understand.
    (*vii*) Saves the precious time of managers.
    (*viii*) Saves manpower
    (*ix*) Enhances the quality of decisions
    (*x*) Easy accessibility
    (*xi*) Reduces data redundancy
    (*xii*) Improves productivity

12.5.3. Decision Support System

The meaning of the term 'decision' varies widely. The important broad classification of this concept can be made as follows:

(*a*) **Decision Logic:** Here a "decision" is defined as an abstract, timeless, context free "act of choice". Here it is the combination of action, state, event, utility and probability. The decision logic is a purely formal, mathematical or logical theory, focusing on rationality in acts of choice.

(*b*) **Cognitive decision theory:** This is an empirical, descriptive, non-statistical, context related process theory. It considers a "decision" as a decision making process very similar to a problem solving process, which is a special, time consuming, context dependent information processing process. Here the data and knowledge has to be fed into the system and the type of information processing determines the outcome.

(*c*) **The connectionist paradigm:** Neural network is a model for information processing, but on a more physical and not so functional level. Information is processed from input to output layers of artificial neurons. One of the differences between the "cognitive" and the "neural" decision model is, that the latter includes capacity and even concentrates on learning and on topological features, while the former does not exclude learning but does not consider it as one of the points of major interest.

Based on these broad classifications, the decisions at an organizational level can be further categorized as follows:

1. **Structured decision:** It is a type of decision in which all steps in the decision-making process are structured.
2. **Semi-structured decision:** It is a decision in which some of the decision-making processes are structured and some are unstructured.
3. **Unstructured decision:** It is a decision in which all the steps in the decision- making process are unstructured.

In a nutshell, the process of making structured decision is algorithmic and that of the unstructured decision is heuristic. Decision making is not made at a specific point of time but it is a step wise process. It involves the following three steps:

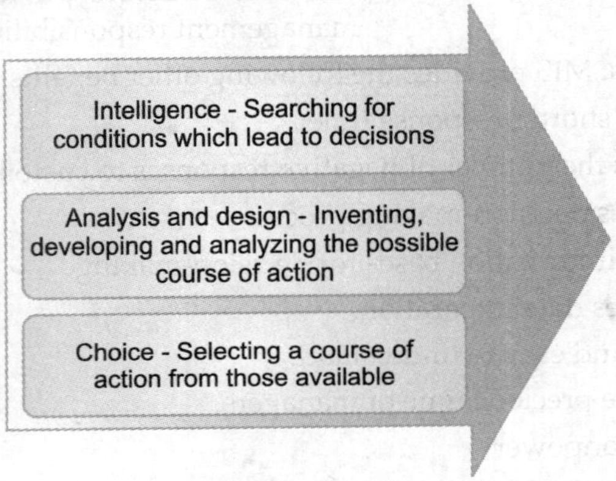

Moreover, the decision-making process lies in between highly structured decisions to highly unstructured decisions. For the structured or routine problems, standard solutions are available. But, for the unstructured or complex problems, such solutions are not available. Thus, in the large organizations, DSS is necessitated due to the following reasons.

The decision-making process is an interactive human-machine process.

The computer system provides supporting information to the decision-maker by accessing and using database and model base.

At the top management level, many decisions are unstructured or semi structured.

The decision-makers at this level have to depend on assumptions, intuition and experience.

The internal data base may have to be augmented by external data.

The interactive process is to be made in a relatively lesser times.

12.5.3.1. Definitions of DSS

The decision support system has been defined by various experts as follows :

(*i*) DSS is "an interactive, computer-based system which supports managers in making unstructured decisions".

(*ii*) DSS is "an interactive computer-based system, which helps decision- makers in utilise data and models to solve unstructured and semi-structured problems".

(*iii*) DSS is "a computer-based information system used to support decision-making activities in situations where it is not possible or not desirable to have an automated system perform the entire decision process".

Thus, a Decision Support System is a computer program application that analyses business data and presents it so that users can make business decisions more easily. It is an "informational application" (in distinction to an "operational application" that collects the data in the course of normal business operation).

The decision support system may present information graphically and may include an expert system or artificial intelligence. It may be aimed at business executives or some other group of knowledge workers. Decision support systems provides (*i*) facilities that are useful during decision making (*ii*) data management capabilities for collecting, organizing and processing data relevant to the problem and (*iii*) modeling capabilities for developing computer-based models for analyzing decision problems.

12.5.3.2. Nature of DSS

The above discussion gives the following aspects of DSS.

(*i*) Objective	-	To enhance human decision-making by providing intellectual support.
(*ii*) Philosophy	-	Amplify a decision-maker's capability of control by providing resources and facilities.
(*iii*) Machine	-	Shared expertise and labour supplements human expertise and capabilities.
(*iv*) Roll of human	-	Shared expertise and roles. Human may not be the expert but quite capable of solving problems on his own.
(*v*) Orientation	-	Information to the right people, at the right time and in right place.

12.5.3.3. DSS Characteristics

DSS is an information system whose focus is on decision making with the following characteristics:

1. Man-machine working together for solving problems.
2. Functional capabilities together for solving decision problems.
3. Emphasize flexibility and adaptability to accommodate change in decision-making.
4. Focus is on improving the effectiveness rather than efficiency of decision - making.
5. Usually it is adhoc system designed for specific non-recurring decision problem.
6. User friendly systems with emphasis on interactive user interfaces.
7. Most DSS tools afford goal testing rather than goal seeking.
8. DSS supports the managerial judgment and it does not replace it.
9. Unstructured: DSS are not structured. They do not have clear procedures to solve the problem and they are designed to assist managers in their decision processes in semi-structured or unstructured tasks.
10. Dynamic: DSS models are complex and dynamic. The user can friendly change the models according to the specifications of the users.
11. Corporate Database: DSS can move the data from one or more departments. Each department in the company has their own database. This can be used by the DSS for doing some analysis.

12. Local Database: The DSS can store the data from the external sources and also maintained its own data model.
13. Database Model: The models are created or adjusted and data is manipulated according to the convenient of the DSS users. It is a collection of statistical and optimization programs.
14. DSS Outputs: DSS outputs are structured reports or graphics report that will help the user to use the system effectively.
15. DSS Support Facilities: DSS includes spreadsheets, word-processing, graphics and DBMS programs.
16. Real time data processing System: The DSS Systems are real time processing systems which is very much useful for the organization.
17. DSS Concept: Decision support system is a tool for managers which assist them in making decisions. It provides the facility for changing the parameters and studying its effect on other quantities. Manager goes on changing the parameters till he is satisfied with the outcome.

An interaction of this tool and the manager has been shown in the following diagram:

Concept of Decision Support System

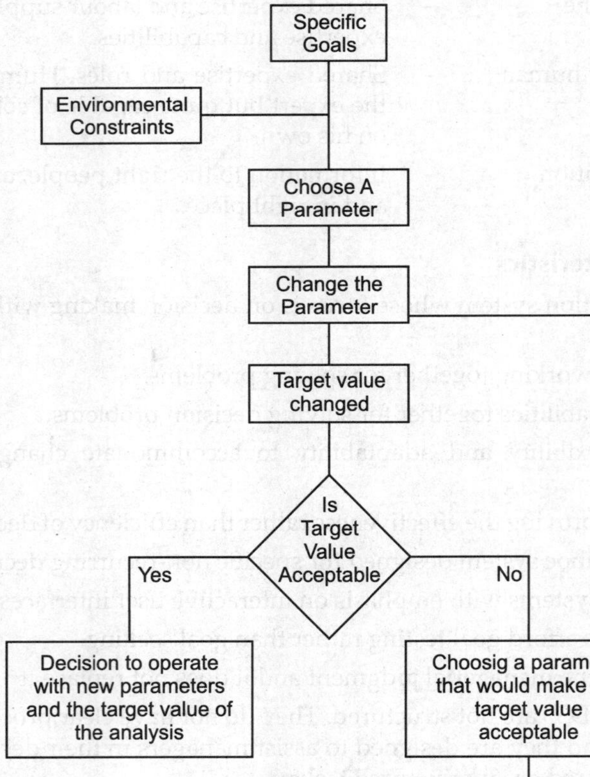

In the above diagram, the company's target is to set and achieve goals in a specified time period. For this, a plan is laid out and all the activities are performed accordingly, but the path of action is not simple. Environmental change affects the working and hence becomes a problem for achieving the goal. At this time manager has to review the situation and make changes in the working parameters. Changes in the working parameters may ultimately affect the overall goal. At this stage he has to decide whether he would like to go ahead with the modified goal or impose other internal constraints to overcome the effect of changes. The choice of path totally depends upon the quality, knowledge and experience of the manager. A less enterprising manager would like to work with modified goals and new parameters while a dynamic manager would keep the goals unaltered and change parameters. He goes on changing the parameters till he is satisfied with the outcome. The outcome of this analysis is finally used for decision-making and it will be the goal and guidelines for working.

12.5.3.4. Comparative Analysis of Information Support Systems

To have an understanding about the different information support systems, a comparative analysis will be helpful. Hereunder, a brief description of such systems is given:

Comparative Analysis work of Information Support Systems

Decision	Planning			Support System
	Operational	Managerial	Strategic	
Structured Decision	Debt Management, Accounts receivable, Order entry etc.	Budget analysis, Make or buy analysis, purchasing or leasing analysis, Short-term forecasting etc.	Financial Management Plant location, Warehouse Distribution channel system etc.	Transaction Processing and Management Information System.
Semi structural Decision	Inventory Management Production planning etc.	Debt analysis, Preparation of budgets, Project Planning	Construction of new plant, Amalgamations and mergers, New product development, Quality Assurance planning etc.	Decision Support System
Unstructured Decision	Selection a decision for the new package, Selecting a software, Extending credit to new customers etc.	New order negotiations, selecting a hareware and live ware	Development of new technical know-how, Research and development etc.	DSS and Expert Systems

12.5.3.5. Differences between MIS and DSS

The important differences between MIS and DSS are discussed below:

MIS	DSS
1. INPUT	
In MIS, little entry is required and external data may be transferred. The reports may be transferred. The data sources are largely internal.	Most of the DSS data come from transaction processing and some input data are given as parameters. The data sources are largely external.
2. OUTPUT	
MIS, output is in the form of query responses and reports. The reports may be detail, exception, summary, or demand reports.	DSS outputs are in the form of analysis reports. It may be in table or graphical form. They are in the nature of summary, exception or demand or adhoc reports.
3. STORAGE	
In MIS data are stores in files, but Mostly databases.	In DSS, data usually stored in databases, may be a data werehouse.
4. PROCESSING	
MIS normally involves simple computation. Here, it involves data accumulation and totalling.	The processing in DSS may be very complex. It involves statistical analysis.
5. SOFTWARE	
In MIS, the software may be written Using business programming languages such as SQL, client-server software, etc.	In DSS, the software is required for analysis work. Hence, they include statistical packages, etc. They do data mining searching for patterns in large amounts of data to determine business practices.
6. ENVIRONMENT	
In MIS, the environment of the decision-marker is constant, steady and relatively simple.	In DSS, such environment is charging dynamic and complex.
7. LEVEL OF MANAGEMENT	
In MIS, the level of decision maker is operational.	In DSS, the level is strategic.
8. EFFECT	
In MIS, the system development initiative is pushed to decision maker. That is, it has push effect.	In DSS, it comes from the decision maker, i.e., it has pull effect.
9. STYLE OF DECISION-MAKING	
In MIS, the decision-making style is predetermined, universal and impersonal.	In DSS, the style of decision-making is individual, personal and subjective.
10. STRUCTUREDNESS	
In MIS the decisions are structured.	Here, they are unstructured or semi structured.

11. TIME ORIENTATION	
MIS has historical and past orientation.	DSS has future orientation.
12. NATURE OF USE	
The use of MIS is routine and regular.	Here, the use of DSS is not routine and it is unique.
13. DECISION-MAKING PROCESS	
The process of decision-making in MIS is algorithmic and well defined.	But DSS, it is heuristic.
14. SCOPE OF SUPPORT	
In MIS the decision process supports all phases.	In DSS, the decision process supports some phases.
15. SYSTEM DESIGN	
In MIS, the system design is data-oriented	In DSS, the system decision is decision model oriented.

12.5.3.6. Components of DSS

The DSS has a specific decision environment. It has some internal structure comprising of components and their inter relationships i.e., arrangements. Let us explain these components from the following diagram.

Components of DSS

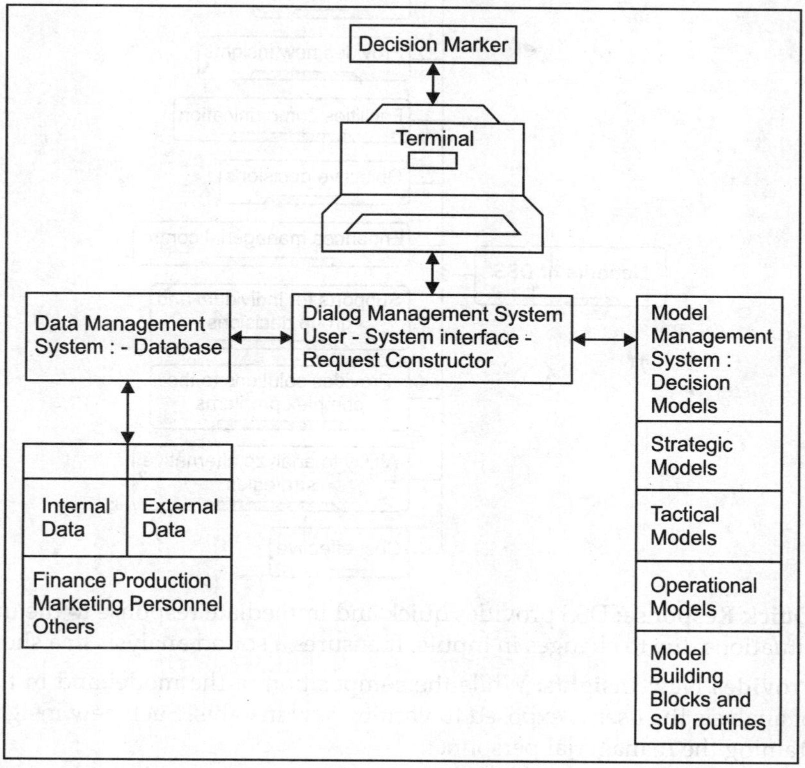

12.5.3.7. Resources of DSS

The following are considered as the resources of a decision support system.

1. **Data:** The data required for the DSS can be internal, external, operational and maintained by the transaction processing system.
2. **Software:** There has been a variety of software available for the DSS. Such software may be developed internally or purchased externally or formulated by the users themselves. It includes the following:
   (*a*) **Specific Software Systems**: Systems developed to specific decision situation of particular users.
   (*b*) **DSS Tools:** These software includes spread sheet, database management system, modeling software, statistical analysis packages, graphic packages etc.
   (*c*) **Generalised DSS:** Software packages which provide support for many kinds of problems.
3. **Hardware:** The hardware includes terminals, processors, storage devices and communication networks.
4. **Liveware:** Human beings are the main resources for DSS design and operational activities.

12.5.3.8. Benefits of DSS

Decision support system provides the following benefits:

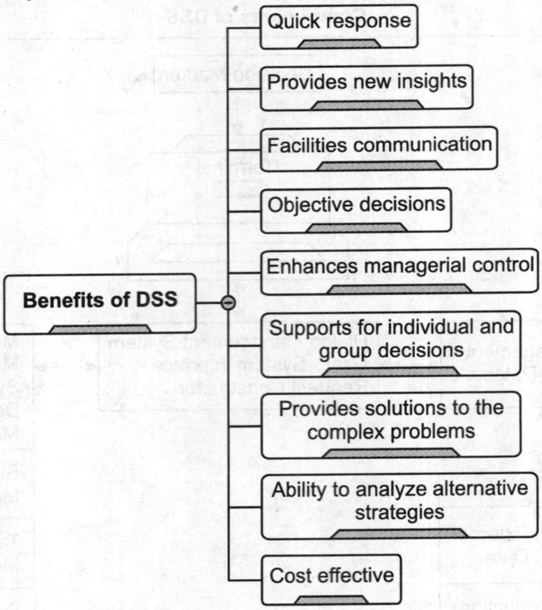

1. **Quick Response:** DSS provides quick and immediate response to the unexpected situations due to changes in inputs. It ensures a sound analysis in a short time.
2. **Provides New Insights:** While the composition of the model and in the process of analysis the user is exposed to various new insights. Such new insights help in training the managerial personnel.
3. **Enhances Team Work:** DSS enhances the team-work by facilitating communication among managerial personnel while constructing and experimenting the models for DSS. It ensures their support in organizational decisions.

4. **Ensures Effective Decisions:** By using DSS, the decisions are made on the basis of analysis and are executed with greater participation of the individuals (affected by the decisions). Thus, it ensures effective decisions and successful implementation.
5. **Enhances Managerial Control and Effectiveness:** By using the DSS, the management increase the control over the expenditure. This will increase the operational efficiency and thereby the overall performance of the organization.
6. **Provides Solutions to The Complex Problems:** DSS provides solutions for the complex problems which is not possible with other ordinary information systems.
7. **Supports For Individual And Group Decisions:** DSS has the ability to analyze and try various alternative strategies very quickly so that, each alternative can be evaluated and the best can be chosen.
8. **Cost Effective:** Through DSS, one can select the best decision which eliminates the cost of using choice. Moreover, through DSS one can reduce the overall expenditure at a considerable level. This ensures cost effectiveness in the organization.
9. **Enhances the Competitive Efficiency:** DSS increases the overall operational efficiency and it results in the reduction of cost. It provides a competitive edge to the firms.

EXAMPLE of DSS:

We can explain the concept of DSS with the help of the following example.

Organizational Goal:

A company sells three products namely A_1, A_2 and A_3. The company has targeted for profit of fifty lacks in this financial year. To achieve this target it has decided that it will sell quantity Q_1, Q_2 and Q_3 of these products respectively at the price P_1, P_2 and P_3.

Profit:

Profit = selling price – (production cost + working cost)

Production Cost:

Production cost = cost of raw material + labour cost + packaging cost + Freight and forwarding cost.

Working Cost:

Working cost = traveling cost + electricity charges + Miscellaneous charges.

Environmental Constraints and Choosing the Parameters:

Competitors have reduced the price of product A1, so this company also has to reduce the price else the product will not sell.

Changing the Parameters:

Manager reduces the selling price P1 of item A1, say by 10%.

DSS Response:

Shows that now we will have to work for lesser profit for example Rs.30 lacks

Manager A:

He is less enterprising and chooses to operate with lower selling price and less profit.

Manager B:

He is enterprising and wants to see that if packaging cost is reduced by 5%, will the profit still be ₹ 50 lacks.

DSS Response:

DSS shows that by reducing the selling price by 10% and packaging by 5% the net profit will be ₹ 40 lacks.

Now he has to look forward for another parameter which can be changed.

Another Change in Parameter:

He chooses that if electricity cost is reduced by 10% then what will be the effect on profit.

DSS Response:

DSS shows that now the profit will be ₹ 55 lacks.

Decision:

He issues the order to

1. All the offices to sell the product at 10% reduced cost and operate in such a way that electricity bills are reduced by 10%.
2. Production department to use less expensive material so that the cost of packaging is reduced by 5%.

12.5.3.9. Group Decision Support System

In large scale organizations, decision making involves groups to executives. This necessitates the need for a new decision support system which can accommodate a multi-user environment. Because of this requirement, the concept of "group decision support system" has been developed. The group decision support system can be defined as "a computer based system which supports the multi-user environment and collective problem solving and decision-making.

Concept of Group Decision Support System (GDSS):

In GDSS, the decision is made collectively. In this system, there are two or more persons engaging in problem solving.

1. The persons involving in decision-making have their own attitudes, perceptions and personalities.
2. The persons realise the existence of common problems and goals.
3. They attempt to reach a collective decision.
4. One of them acts as a chair person and others act as technical experts.
5. It implements DSS technology into the group decision setting.
6. GDSS can support group by structuring the process.
7. It enlarges participation and creativity.
8. Examples of GDSS are electronic voting, ranking, brain storming etc.

Thus, group decision support system can be defined as, "the interactive computer-based system facilities solutions of unstructured problems by decision makers working as group".

Tools of Group Decision Support System:

The following are the important software tools of group decision support system.

1. Electronic brain-storming.

2. Idea organizers.
3. Questionnaire evaluation tools.
4. Tools voting and setting priorities.
5. Stock holder identification analysis.
6. Policy formation tools.
7. Group dictionaries etc.

Advantages of the Group Decision Support System:

The GDSS allows the participants to feel much freer to voice their true opinion. With a GDSS, it is virtually impossible for a single participant to "hold the floor" as all participants are conveying their ideas simultaneously. The GDSS has the following advantages.

1. GDSS improves the pre-planning process.
2. It increases the group participation.
3. It creates an open and collaborative atmosphere.
4. It induces idea generation free of criticism.
5. It ensures evaluation objectivity.
6. It provides for setting of priorities and decision making.
7. It provides for the documentation of meetings.
8. By GDSS external information can be accessed.
9. It helps in the preservation of organizational money.
10. It makes possible of electronic questionnaires.
11. The GDSS uses information technology to make group meeting more productive.
12. It facilitates effective communication for better decision-making.

12.5.4. Expert System

An expert system is a computer application that stimulates the procedures and thought processes of a human expert on some subject in making a specialized decision or reaching a conclusion. This system functions like a human expert. It assimilates data and then applies rules and conditions to the data to reach a goal or conclusion. In other words, the expert system is a computer program that emulates the judgment and behaviour of a human or an organization that has expert knowledge and experience in a particular field. Typically, such a system contains a knowledge base containing accumulated experience and a set of rules for applying the knowledge base to each particular situation that is described to the program. Thus, it can be defined as follows:

"An Expert System is a computer system that facilitates solving problem in a given field or application by drawing inference from a knowledge base developed from human expertise."

A wide variety of definitions on expert system are given by the different institutes. Some of them are:

(*i*) "It is a computer program that behaves like a human expert in some useful ways".

(*ii*) "It is a system that solves problems efficiently and effectively in a narrow problem area".

(*iii*) "It is a system which typically pertains to problems that can be symbolically represented".

(*iv*) "It is an application of expert knowledge to difficult real world problems".

(*v*) "An Expert System solves problems that are difficult enough to require significant human expertise for their solution".

(*vi*) "Expert System is a program that mimics the advice-giving capabilities of human experts.

(*vii*) "It is a system that can offer intelligent advice or make an intelligent decision about a processing function".

(*viii*) "It is a system that allows a user to access the expertise in a way similar to that in which one might consult a human expert, with a similar results".

(*ix*) "It is a system that has the capability to justify its own line of reasoning in a manner directly intelligible to the enquirer".

(*x*) "It is a system that incorporates the explanation processes to the problem situations.

(*xi*) "It is a system that uses the programming techniques of artificial intelligence, especially those techniques developed for problem solving".

(*xii*) "Expert System is a the embodiment within a computer of a knowledge-based component, from an expert skill and in which representations of expertise are stored".

(*xiii*) "Expert System is a sophisticated computer programs that manipulate knowledge to solve problems".

(*xiv*) "It is a system that makes domain knowledge explicit and separate from the rest of the system".

(*xv*) "It is an intelligent computer program that uses knowledge and inference procedures and the style adopted to attain these characteristics is rule-based programming".

(*xvi*) "An Expert System is a representation of domain-specific knowledge in the manner in which the expert thinks and such a system can be thought of as a model of the expertise of the best practitioners of the field.

A wide variety of expert systems have been developed over the years on subjects ranging from computer configuration specification to product defect analysis to medical diagnosis etc. Expert Systems contain inference engines designed to take the rules about a decision making process and the data about a specific instance in the subject area and reach a conclusion about that instance. Expert Systems are either developed from scratch or from expert system shells containing generalized inference engines designed to evaluate data and rules on any subject.

12.5.4.1. Components Of Expert System

The main components of the Expert System can be explained with the help of the following diagram:

EXPERT SYSTEM COMPONENTS

USER INTERFACE

- Friendly
- Intelligent
  - (*i*) Knowledge of how to present information
  - (*ii*) Knowledge of user preferences

Inference Engine

- general problem - solving knowledge or methods
- interpreter analyses and processes the rules
- scheduler determines which rule to look at next
- the search portion of a rule-based system
  - (*i*) takes advantage of heuristic information
  - (*ii*) otherwise, the time to solve a problem could become prohibitively long
  - (*iii*) this problem is called the combinational explosion
- expert-system shell provides customizable inference engine

Database

- Contains some of the data of interest to the system
- May be connected to on-line company or public database
- Human user may be considered a database

Knowledge Base (rule base)

- Contains much of the problem solving knowledge
- Rules are of the form IF condition THEN action
  - (*i*) condition portion of the rule is usually a fact - (if some particular fact is in the database then perform this action)
  - (*ii*) action portion of the rule can include
    - (*a*) actions that affect the outside world (terminal)
    - (*b*) test another rule (check rule no. 64 next)
    - (*c*) add a new fact to the database
- Rules can be specific, a priori rule (e.g., tax law... so much for each exemption) - represent laws and codified rules

The components of expert system can be discussed briefly as follows :

1. **User Interface:**

   The first component of expert system is user interface mechanism. Here the user-system interface is designed in such a way so that the user can easily communicate with the system by answering to the queries. It includes the knowledge of user preferences etc.

2. **Inference System -Inference Engine :**

   The main part of the expert system is the inference system. It is also called as inference engine or control structure or the rule interpreter. Inference engine is a computer program which provides methods for reasoning about information stored in knowledge base. It also provides methods for formulating conclusions.

   Inference engine includes the following elements:

   (*a*) General Problem - solving or methods

   (*b*) Interpreter - analyses and processes the rules

   (*c*) Scheduler - determines which rule to look at next

   (*d*) Consistency enforcer – maintains a consistent-representation of the emerging solution.

   (*e*) Expert – system shell – provides customizable inference engine.

3. **Database:**

   Database involves the facts such as the problem situation, general theories about the problem area etc. The database generally includes the following:

   (*a*) The data of interest to the system and the problem.

   (*b*) It may have on-line connections to company or public databases.

4. **Knowledge-base:**

   The knowledge base includes all necessary information for recognizing, formulating and solving problem. It includes the following:

   (*a*) It contains all knowledge required for problem solving.

   (*b*) It includes the rules which are in the form "IF condition THEN action".

   (*c*) The condition portion of the rule is usually a fact.

   (*d*) The action portion of the rule can include actions that are useful to the outside world (output a message on the terminal).

   (*e*) The rules can be specific and priori rules – represent laws and codified rules.

   (*f*) The rules can be heuristics – rules of the thumb.

   (*g*) The rules can be connected together like a chain: A $\rightarrow$ B $\rightarrow$ C.

12.5.4.2. Requirements Of Expert Systems

Expert system is a branch of applied artificial intelligence. The basic requirements of expert systems are:

(*i*) Experts - Persons with special knowledge skills or training to solve the problems. It includes the ability to recognise and solve the problems quickly, explaining the solution, learn from experience, restructuring knowledge etc.

(*ii*) Expertise - The extensive and task specific knowledge acquired from reading, field training and experience. It includes the facts, theories and rules about problem area, general strategies for solving these types of problems etc.

(*iii*) Transferring Expertise - Transferring the expertise from the experts to computer and transferring such applications to general public. It includes knowledge acquisition and knowledge representations.

(*iv*) Reasoning - Ability to reason out. That is, when the expertise is transferred and stored in the computer *i.e.*, in knowledge base, the system is designed to make inferences from the knowledge base. The component in which such inferences are made, is called 'inference engine'.

(*v*) Rules - Expert systems are generally rule based *i.e.*, knowledge is stored in the form of rules and problem solving procedures.

(*vi*) Explanation capacity - The ability to explain the suggestions and recommendations. Sometimes it has to justify the reasons for not recommending certain course or activities.

12.5.4.3. Differences between Traditional Systems and Knowledge based Expert Systems:

The expert system is different from the traditional system in various respects. They are given below:

Traditional System	Expert System
1. In traditional system the knowledge and processing are combined in one sequential program.	In expert system they are separated, i.e., knowledge base and inference engine are separate.
2. In traditional system there is no possibility for mistakes in the performance. That is, the programs do not commit any mistakes.	In expert system that is not so. Here the program may make mistakes.
3. It does not explain how the conclusions were drawn and why certain types of input data are required etc.	Such explanation is the special feature of an expert system.
4. It performs only when all of its requirements are completed.	In expert system, it performs even with a few rules.
5. It effectively manipulates large data bases.	It can effectively manipulate large knowledge bases.
6. It represents and uses data.	It represents and uses knowledge.

7. In traditional system changes in the knowledge is not easy to accomplish.	In expert system changes in the rules are easy to carry out.
8. It can easily deal with quantitative data.	It can easily deal with quantitative data.
9. In traditional system execution is done on algorithmic basis, *i.e.,* on a step-by-step basis.	In expert system the execution is done by using logic and rules.
10. It aims at efficiency.	It aims at effectiveness.

12.5.4.4. Construction and Development of Expert System

In almost all types of organizations, same sort of expert system is needed. Hence, it is to be developed accordingly. The development and construction of expert system involves the following steps.

Expert System-Steps

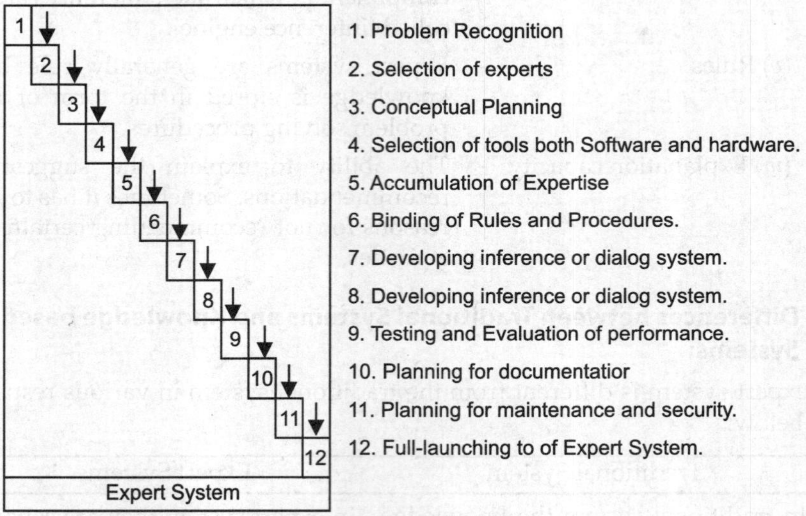

Let us discuss these steps one by one hereunder:

1. **Problem Recognition:** In this step a problem which warrants special expertise is identified and selected. It is the basic and fundamental activity because all the developmental processes centred on the problem selected. The problem may be of any nature or in any field. For example, it may be related to automated diagnosis, engineering consultant, sensor validation, process automation or credit analysis or security and portfolio analysis, or problems related insurance and banking or other financial services etc.
2. **Selection of Experts:** Once the problem is selected, the next step involves the selection of experts in the relevant field. They might have acquired such knowledge and expertise through education, training and experience.
3. **Conceptual Planning:** After the selection of experts, the development process of expert system involves conceptual planning. This step includes the determination of the requirements for an expert system at a conceptual level. This step visualizes the further requirements and possibilities for variations at the user level etc. This is the core part of the process since the standard of the expert system depend upon the plans arrived at this stage.

4. **Selection of Required Tools:** The next step involves the careful selection of necessary software and hardware tools for the fulfilment of the expert system. Though various software and hardware tools are available for the accomplishment of a particular task, utmost care should be taken while selecting the appropriate tools. Then only, there will be no deviation or errors which may block the efficient result of the expert system.
5. **Accumulation of the Expertise:** After selecting the appropriate hardware and software tools, the required expertise or knowledge is to be acquisitional from the experts based on the conceptual plans arrived at the third step. This step involves the extraction of knowledge from the experts selected at the first step. Here knowledge includes the facts, rules and procedures. The knowledge can be accumulated through interviews and discussions with experts, observation of the experts at work etc. Thus, this step involves the transformation of problem - solving expertise from the same knowledge source to a computer program.
6. **Building Rules and Procedures:** Like obtaining knowledge in the earlier step, here, the rules and procedures for the expert system is developed. It can be designed by analysing and observing the various example cases. By analysing the available examples whose outcomes are known, the knowledge engineer can formulate rules and procedures for the present expert system whose outcome is not known.
7. **Development of Inference System:** The inference system is also called as inference engine. This step involves the development of inference system which solves problems or provides advice by building up a long chain of logic and reasoning which lead from the basic assumptions to a conclusion. The inference system is built by combining a set of inference rules and knowledge about problem solving to guide the application of these rules.
8. **Development of Interface or Dialog System:** The next involves the development of input and output interface between the user and other components. It is the set of procedures that provide an appropriate action on the basis of the knowledge base and specific problem data. It can advise the user and explain the reasoning behind the advice. In short, here the user and system dialog interface is developed.
9. **Testing and Evaluation of Performance:** In this step, the results obtained in earlier steps are tested and evaluated. In this stage the expert system is applied to test the example cases or problems whose outcomes are known. On the basis of the test results, the system can be refined or improved. Thereafter, the present expert system is experimented. Such experiment ensures the quality of advice given by the system.
10. **Planning for documentation:** Knowledge and expertise cannot be exhausted. Hence, the expert system needs to be continually be developed and upgraded. For such regular and continued updation of quality of the system requires proper documentation. Hence in this stage, it is necessary to develop plans for documentation.
11. **Planning for Maintenance and Security:** The next step involves the development of plans for the maintenance and security of the system. Unless it is properly maintained, it may not be useful in long-run and not available in times of need. Likewise security is the crucial aspect in the construction of an expert system. If there is no sound security system, the unauthorized access may corrupt the end results and also it may reduce the value of the expert system developed. Hence, proper and suitable software has to be developed for the maintenance and security issue of the expert system.
12. **Field - Launching of the Expert System:** after completing all the above stages, the present expert system is ready to use. It can be put into use in the organization. But, it should be noted that the system has to be conditionally updated and developments

f the expertise in the relevant fields, is to be incorporated. And at the same time, the system has to be tested and evaluated with the results of other available examples so as to suitably modify and to improve and to ensure the quality of the end product.

12.5.4.5. Practical Applications of Expert System

An expert system can advise, analyse, categories, communicate, consult, design, diagnose, explain, explore, forecast, form concepts, facts etc., included in the knowledge base. The expert system can be applied to all fields. Some practical applications are given below:

1. **Automated Diagnosis:** An expert system was developed for automated diagnostic system to perform non-invasive checkout of a launch vehicle propulsion system.
2. **Process Automation:** An expert system can effectively be applied in process automation. It can provide automated comprehensive and continuous data monitoring, control the movement of parts through a manufacturing cell etc., and it can provide for the control of various processes and subsystems.
3. **Engineering Consultancy :** The expert system can help engineers in performing tasks such as structural damage assessments, finite element analysis, critique chip designs, evaluate software, identify the root cause of problems, perform capacity planning and inventory management.
4. **Sensor Validation:** Expert system can be applied in sensor validation. It can provide validation of sensors by monitoring sensor measurements and analyzing the propagation and affects of the predicted and actual performance throughout the system.
5. **Credit Analysis:** The business firms can use expert systems to assist with credit analysis. Because, while applying expert system in such analysis, it provides speed and accuracy.
6. **Security and Portfolio Analysis:** Expert system can effectively be applied in security trading and portfolio analysis. The expert system can easily evaluate rate of return and the live.
7. **Insurance Analysis:** Expert system can be used to assist actuaries in evaluating risk and claims on insurance policies, and aid in policy maintenance and administration.
8. **Financial Planning:** Financial plans can help individuals in investments, Income-tax, real estate planning, debt management and the like. Expert system can be applied to effectively making out these types of plans.

Moreover the expert system reduces the cost of providing financial services by the companies. It makes the planning process quicker, easier and more consistent. Now-a-days employers use expert systems to offer this service to their employees more easily.

12.5.4.6. Merits of Expert Systems

Expert systems provide the following merits to users:

1. Efficient in performance.
2. Managing large number of rules.
3. Increase quality.
4. Collecting scarce expertise.
5. Easy to operate.
6. Quick response.
7. Operating with incomplete information.

8. Documentation.
9. Security measures.
10. Flexibility.
11. Able to operate in dangerous environments.
12. Increase the ability of problem solving.
13. Educational value.
14. Transferability of knowledge.
15. Economy.

Let us discuss these points one by one.

1. **Efficient in performance:** Expert systems are more efficient in operation when comparing with human beings. It can work faster and many copies of an expert system can be made but training such number of new human experts are expensive and time consuming.
2. **Managing large number of rules:** Expert systems can manage effectively a large number of rules and procedures more effectively. When there is more number of rules as in the case of taxation etc., the expert system can easily manage and solve the problems.
3. **Increase quality:** Whatever may be the nature of the problem situation the expert system can manage easily and can provide consistent advice. Such expert advice certainly will reduce the error rate and increase the quality of the result.
4. **Collecting scarce expertise:** In real life situation each and every organization cannot search and gather expert advice due to various reasons such as the retirement and migration of experts from one place to another etc. But, when such scarce expertise is put in an expert system, it can be used by the organizations all over the world. Thus, the knowledge of multiple human experts can be combined to give a system more breadth.
5. **Easy to operate:** The expert systems are designed and developed in such a way so as to manage and operate the complex equipment very easily. Simply, by interact with the expert system using the dialog or interface system one can easily operate.
6. **Quick response:** In expert system errors can be prevented and the necessary information is quickly available for decision making. Hence, it can respond much faster than human beings when it works with a large volume of data.
7. **Able to operate with incomplete information:** The traditional computer systems can work only when all the relevant information are available. But expert system can do it with even incomplete and uncertain information. That is, while conversing with the expert system through its dialog system, the expert system will ask questions for information relating to the problem in question. If the user is not able to provide information for some questions and answer "don't know", the expert system will still be able to provide a possible answer. That is, depending on the capability of the inference system, an expert system can operate with probabilities.
8. **Facility of Documentation:** Expert systems provide permanent documentation of the decision process. Such documentation will be very helpful for the future reference and further development and updation.
9. **Securing measures:** Expert systems can help the firms in creating entry barriers for potential competitions. This can serve as entry barriers.
10. **Flexibility:** Expert systems are highly flexible in providing services. Such flexibility enhances the operational efficiency of the firms.

11. **Able to operate in dangerous environments:** In various organizations, people are engaged to work in hot, humid or toxic environments. In such organizations, the expert system may enable them to avoid such environments. Such facility is highly useful in defence activities also.
12. **Increases the profile on solving capacity:** The expert system makes available the advice of the experts in the analysis. Besides, it provides explanations to users and thus enhancing their understanding and supports them in solving problems. This process certainly will increase the problem solving capacity in the organization.
13. **Educational value:** Today expert system concepts are being taught as a separate field of education particularly in computer technology. By working with expert systems a layman can become more experienced. Hence, it can rightly be said that it has educational value.
14. **Transferability of knowledge:** Through expert systems the knowledge and expertise available in developed entries may be transferred to developing entries which are not able to pay for such human experts. Such transferability involves almost all fields live medicine, engineering, physical science, business science etc.
15. **Economy:** Expert systems increase productivity and reduce personnel costs. It includes the following:
    (*a*) Though expert systems are expensive to build and maintain, they are inexpensive to operate.
    (*b*) The development and maintenance costs can be spread over many users.
    (*c*) The overall cost is reasonable when compared to expensive and scarce human experts.
    (*d*) Reduces the labor costs i.e., expert system reduces the number of workers in the organization. Thus, expert system results in to economy.

12.5.4.7. Limitations of Expert Systems

The expert systems are not free from limitations. The following are the drawbacks of an expert system.

1. **Lack of common sense:** In addition to a great deal of technical knowledge, human experts have common sense. But such common sense is not available in expert system.
2. **Lack of creativity:** Human experts can respond creatively to unusual situations. But expert systems can not provide such creativity.
3. **Lack of sensory experience:** Human experts have a wide range of sensory experience. But the expert systems are currently dependent on symbolic input.
4. **Not able to learn:** Human experts automatically adapt to changing environments. But expert systems must be explicitly updated.
5. **Lack of quality :** Expert systems are not effectively recognizing when the answers like "Don't know" or "Not sure" etc., exists or when the problem is outside their area of expertise i.e., it can work well only in a narrow domain.
6. **Other drawbacks:** Besides the above, the expert system involves the following other limitations.
    (*a*) Knowledge is not always readily available.
    (*b*) It is not easy to extract expertise from human beings.
    (*c*) Complex vocabulary used by experts may not be understood by others.

(*d*) It involves high initial cost and the help of knowledge engineers are frequently removed which makes it more costly.

12.5.4.8. Differences Between DSS and Expert System

Decision Support Systems, as successors of Management Information Systems, traditionally follow the decision logic line of thinking and include in MIS algorithmic tools to improve the choice activity of decision makers. This includes optimization methods, mathematical programming, multi criteria models etc. They are "structure related", normally assume that the decision problem can be formulated mathematically and do not stress information processing and display.

By contrast to DSS, Expert System or knowledge-based systems, as successors of the "General Problem Solver" follow more the process paradigm of cognitive decision theory; they not necessarily assume that the decision problems can be formulated as mathematical models; they substitute human expertise for missing efficient algorithms and they are not structure-but context related, with much smaller domains of application than DSS. "Knowledge" is represented in many different ways, such as, frames, semantic nets, rules etc. Knowledge is processed in inference machines, which normally perform symbol processing, i.e. truth values of antecedents, conclusions etc. In the more recent past the border between DSS and ES has become pretty fuzzy. Some experts consider ES as part of DSS, others see DSS and ES as basically different systems and others combine the two approaches into "knowledge-based DSS".

Let us discuss the important differences between the two as follows:

DSS	Expert System
1. Decision Support	
DSS assists human decision-making.	Expert system minimizes human decision - making.
2. Decision-making	
In DSS, human beings make decisions.	In Expert System, the system itself can make decision.
3. Orientation	
DSS oriented to decision making only. It focuses on decisions, flexibility and user friendliness.	Expert System oriented toward advice, transfer of expertise etc. It focuses on inference and transfer expertise.
4. Database	
DSS includes DBMS, interactive access and factual knowledge.	E.S. includes procedural and factual knowledge. Here knowledge base includes facts, fules, procedures etc.
5. Decision capabilities	
DSS supports the decisions for semi structured problems and models.	Expert System supports complex and unstructured decisions.
6. Nature of Information	
In DSS, information supports specific or ad-hoc decisions.	In Expert System information provides advices and explanations on request.
7. Nature of Query	
DSS is queried by the user.	Expert System queries the user.
8. Manipulation	
DSS manipulates numbers and data (facts).	Expert System manipulates symbols (knowledge).

9. Scope	
DSS can handle broad domain. It involves large-range strategic planning, complex and integrated problem areas.	E.S. handles narrow domain. It involves diagnosis, strategic planning, maintenance, strategies and the like areas.
10. Reasoning	
DSS can not explain reasoning.	E.S. can explain reasoning.
11. Impact	
DSS concentrates on effectiveness	E.S. concentrates on effectiveness and Efficiency.

REVIEW QUESTIONS

Short Answer Questions:

1. What is meant by information system?
2. Give the meaning of transaction processing cycle.
3. What are the characteristics of transaction processing cycle?
4. Write a note on transaction processing cycle?
5. What does MIS mean?
6. Give the MIS cycle.
7. Mention about the characteristics of MIS.
8. What is meant by DSS?
9. Give a short note on the features of DSS.
10. What are the resources of DSS?
11. Give the meaning of group DSS.
12. Define expert system.
13. What are the requirements of expert system?
14. Mention about the components of expert system.

Essay Type Questions:

1. Explain the features of quality information.
2. Explain the meaning and need of computer based information systems.
3. Give a detailed note on transaction processing system along with its advantages.
4. Explain the meaning of MIS along with the steps involved in designing it.
5. What are the benefits of MIS?
6. Explain DSS along with its merits.
7. What are the differences between the MIS and DSS?
8. Give a detailed explanation on the components of DSS.
9. What do you know about group DSS? What are its advantages?
10. Explain the meaning of Expert system. What are its components?
11. Differentiate between traditional information system and expert system.
12. Explain the steps involved in the construction of the expert system.
13. What are the merits and limitations of expert system?
14. Explain the differences between DSS and Expert system.

CHAPTER

13

Functional Management Information Systems

To understand automation in an organization, we have to first understand what an organization is. The word organization is derived from the term organizing which in turn is derived from the word organism. Organism is an entity with its parts so integrated that the individual parts have no meaning. Their relation to each other is governed by their relation to the whole. Similarly when two or more persons get closely associated and work together for achieving a common goal the group is called an organization. Organization is made up of many people and it becomes necessary that the following should be identified:

(*a*) What should be done in order to achieve the goal?

(*b*) Who should do what?

(*c*) How should people interact with each other and work together?

(*d*) When a problem arises what is to be done?

All these activities relate to organizing the work. That means for effective working in an organization there has to be an existing activity of organizing the work and then only the common goal would be achieved, else it might lead to confusions and undesired results. Thus, the structure of the organization is the way in which all employees are organized. Each employee is allocated to a specific department within the organization. The departments of an organization are also referred to as the functional areas.

13.1. FUNCTIONAL AREAS OF BUSINESS ORGANIZATION

Today, in this competitive environment all businesses have different needs for information. Managers at top level need information to help with their business planning. Middle management needs more detailed information to help them monitor and control business activities. At operational levels people need information to help them carry out their duties. As a result, businesses tend to have several information systems operating at the same time. The functional areas in an organization include:

Advances in computer technology often leads to advances in business and industries. For example there was a time when, only single user systems were available in the market and all the industries were making use of batch applications. In batch applications the data was collected from various departments (situated at different geographical locations) and for processing it had to undergo the following cycle:

(*a*) Master file maintenance

(*b*) Transaction file maintenance

(*c*) Updation of master file from transaction files data

(*d*) Report generation - routine and exception

In these types of applications the data collection was a time consuming process and information supplied was not of the time when it was produced, but was quite old (possibly few hours, days or even weeks). As the computer technology advanced, the multi-user systems came and now it is possible to develop on line applications in which transaction entry itself updated all the information. In these systems, information processing is quite up to date, and reports give most recent information. Through networking and distributed data base systems it is possible to link multiple units of an organization which were even situated in different cities. And it is possible to produce comprehensive reports which reflect up-to-date information of different branches also.

We can see that a large spectrum of computer and supported technologies are available in the market and any organization can choose any option according to its choice and needs. There are variety of ways in which computerization can be implemented in an organization. One way is that each department which is facing problem purchases its own computer and computerizes its activities independently. Another way is that computerization activity is centralized. In this approach a separate IS\EDP department is created. All the departments send their data for processing to the IS\E.D.P. department which processes the data received and takes out the reports and sends them to relevant departments.

13.2. CATEGORIES OF INFORMATION SYSTEMS

Information systems of a company can be said to play a critical role in supporting the activities of the company. Information systems are systems whose ultimate purpose is to store and manage information. They are basic infrastructures of the modern business organization and they co-ordinate the resources and activities of the input, process and output subsystems of the organization, thus monitoring and ensuring internal efficiency. Furthermore, they can be used to scan the external environment and internal operations continuously to ensure that organizational effectiveness is achieved. There are four categories of information systems. They are:

Categories of Information Systems

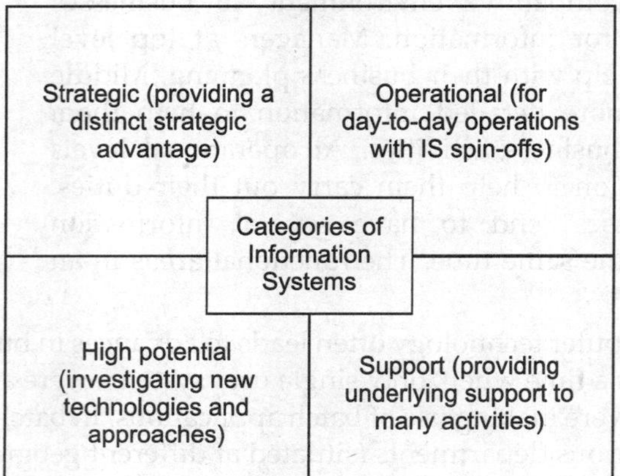

Strategic (Providing a Distinct Strategic Advantage) - for an information system to be strategic, it has to directly support and shape the competitive strategy of an organization. Furthermore, it may function as a management information system or a management support system. Strategic computer-based information systems strengthen the competitive position of the companies by providing quality service to consumers and suppliers. And they are made to improve the performance of the company.

Operational (for day-to-day operations with IS spin-offs) - an Operational Information System is a large-scale, distributed system that provides continuous support for a company or organization's daily operations. For example IS run by some Air Lines, provides the company with up-to-date information about all of its operations, including flights, crews, passenger, baggage etc. The tasks of the company's OIS is to integrate such data events, by applying to them relevant 'business logic'. Another important task is to make the 'business events' produced by such logic available to a potentially large number of remote subscribers, such as airport flight displays and gate agents. Another example of OIS addresses the unique needs of every employee in a business organization by providing them intranet-based information about the different operations of the company including schedules, meetings, etc.

High potential (Investigating New Technologies and Approaches) - systems that investigate new technologies and approaches. The collaboration between companies for outsourcing development and maintenance of corporate and commercial applications etc., is an example in this regard.

Support (Providing underlying Support to many Activities) - It helps the company perform several activities faster and more convenient and effective. For instance, the use of software technologies such as word processors, spread sheets, and other computer tools support the company in performing daily business tasks.

13.3. MIS AND FUNCTIONAL INFORMATION SYSTEMS

In order to find out the scope of computerization and application of information systems in business organizations, we shall discuss the main functional areas in detail here in below:

MIS and Functional Information System

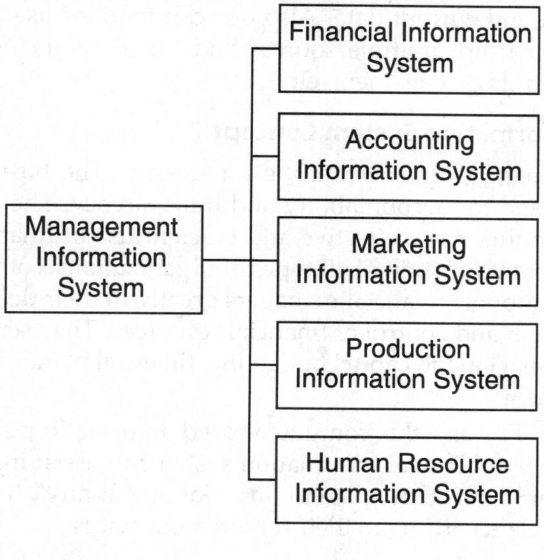

13.4. FINANCIAL INFORMATION SYSTEM

Finance is used by individuals (personal finance), by governments (public finance), by businesses (corporate finance), as well as by a wide variety of organizations including schools and non-profit organizations. In general, the goals of each of the above activities are achieved through the use of appropriate financial instruments, with consideration to their institutional setting.

Finance is one of the most important aspects of business management. Without proper financial planning a new enterprise is unlikely to be successful. Managing money (a liquid asset) is essential to ensure a secure future, both for the individual and an organization. "Finance" refers to the application of general principles of management to the specific core finance area of business enterprises.

The term 'Finance' is the application of economic principles and concepts to business decision making. It is the central function of business enterprises, which ensures careful selection of sources of capital and judicious use of funds raised. It provides proper direction to the firms in accomplishing their goals. Every decision that a business makes has financial implications, and any decision which affects the finances of a business is a finance decision. Thus, Business finance is the study of ways to answer the following four basic questions.

1. What long-term investments should the business enterprises employ-kind of buildings, machinery, and equipment needed?
2. Where will the business enterprises get the long-term financing to pay for their investments? - owners money or borrowed money?
3. How will the business enterprises manage their daily financial activities including the collection from customers and paying to suppliers?
4. How will the business enterprises determine the dividend payouts?

Answer to these questions can best be achieved through effective financial information system. The financial system is the most important management information system in a business organization and in most companies it is the oldest and the best developed. The financial information system takes care of every rupee that flows in and out of the organization.

Financial information systems include a full range of management reports so a business can achieve its goals successfully and cost-effectively. With Financial MIS, one can analyse historical and current data. Also one can monitor use of funds. Financial IS integrates information from multiple sources and functions including, costing, P & L reporting, auditing, funds management, etc.

13.4.1. Financial Information System Concept

Today, strong financial management is a necessity. The business units are in the era of increased demand for accountability and transparency. The "stakeholders" of the companies are demanding more effective and efficient use of financial resources. Since, financing is the important function of all types of organizations, computer based financial information systems support financial managers greatly in their decision making process relating to the allocation and control of financial resources. They serve information to the managers for cash management, capital budgeting, financial planning and forecasting and investment management.

We can see the FIS as "the computer-based information system that works in concurrence with other functional information systems to assist managerial decisions at all levels in solving problems that relate to financial operations". It provides information to managers at all levels according to their requirement status.

13.4.2. Financial Information System Structure:

FIS is designed to:

(*a*) Support all financial operations

(*b*) Collect accurate, timely, complete, reliable and consistent information on all financial events of the organization

(*c*) Provide adequate management reporting

(*d*) Support policy decisions

(*e*) Produce auditable financial statements

The conceptual model of Financial Information System can be seen as given in the following diagram:

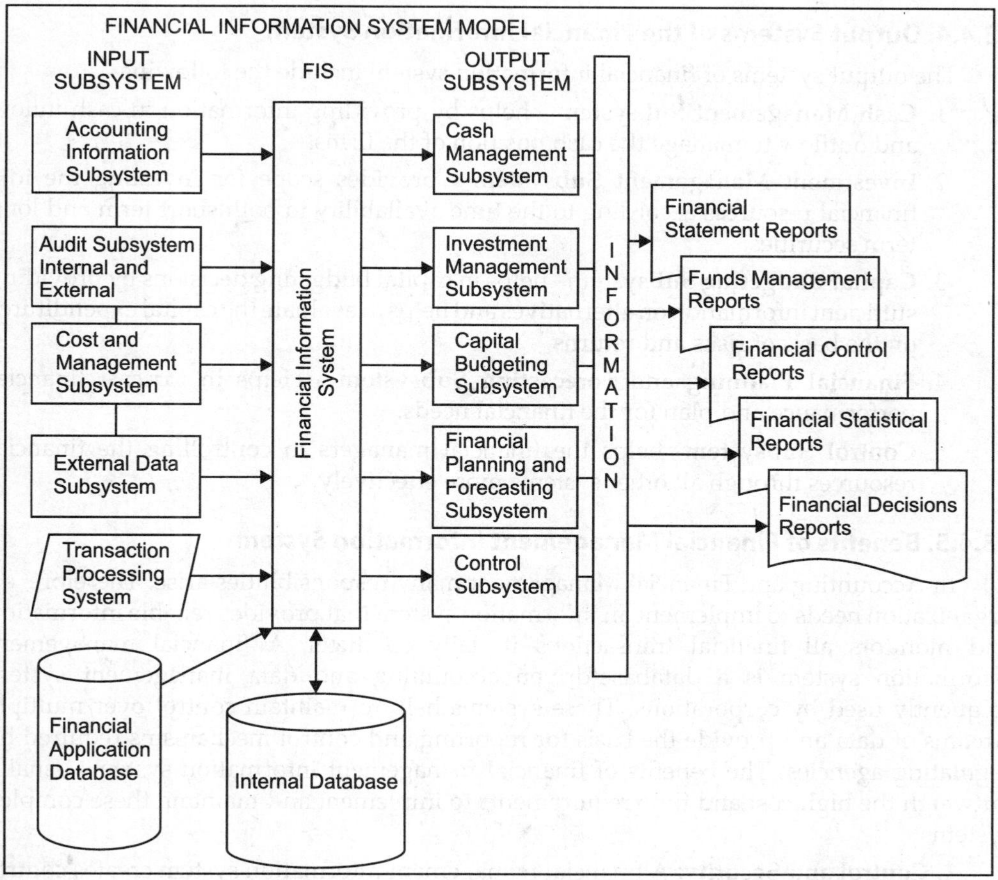

13.4.3. Inputs to the Financial Information System

The efficiency and effectiveness of Financial Information System is based on the inputs given and such input subsystems include the following:

1. Accounting Information Subsystem Profit and Loss Accounts and other financial statement including cash flow statements etc
2. Audit Subsystem- Internal and external audit reports
3. Cost and Management Sub system - Cost and management based information and reports.

4. External Data Subsystem - gathering external data including financial market trends, interest rate, rate of expected dividend, government policy, Annual reports and financial statements of competitors and general news items etc.
5. In addition to these subsystems, input data is gathered real time through transaction processing systems. Important financial information collected from almost every TPS - payroll, inventory control, order processing, accounts payable, accounts receivable, general ledger etc.
6. The financial applications data base is also used.
7. In addition to the entire internal database is also included in the input system for the data stored previously, strategic plan or corporate policies - Contains major financial objectives and often projects financial needs etc.

13.4.4. Output Systems of the Financial Information System

The output systems of financial information system include the following:

1. **Cash Management Subsystem -** helps by providing information in cash inflow and outflow to manage the cash position of the firms.
2. **Investment Management Subsystem -** provides scope for investing the idle financial resources according to the time availability in both short term and long term securities.
3. **Capital Budgeting Subsystem -** helps in capital budgeting decisions by providing sufficient information on alternatives and helps in evaluate the capital expenditures on the basis of risks and returns.
4. **Financial Planning and Forecasting Subsystem** - Helps in forecast financial performance and plan for the financial needs.
5. **Control Subsystem**- helps the financial managers in controlling the financial resources through all other systems more effectively.

13.4.5. Benefits of Financial Management Information System

In Accounting and Financial Management many responsibilities arise. Therefore, an organization needs to implement an information system that provides reliable information and monitors all financial transactions it daily conducts. A financial management information system is a database-driven accounting and data management system frequently used by corporations. These systems help to maintain control over multiple streams of data and provide the basis for reporting and control mechanisms required by regulating agencies. The benefits of financial management information systems usually outweigh the high cost and time requirements to implement and maintain these complex systems.

1. Control and Security: A financial management information system creates control and security on financial information and data through built-in security and management controls.

2. Accounting Benefits: Reporting for accounting reporting cycles such as month-end, and quarter-end requirements are simpler with a financial management information system that can automatically generate reports, data and analysis.

3. Reporting Ability: Routine reports and ad-hoc reporting are streamlined with a financial management information system. The ease of data access and reliability is systematically increased.

4. Improved Executive Performance: Executives benefit from a financial management information system through increased reliability in data, faster reporting, and decreased possibility of fraudulent or misleading information.

5. Compliance with other subsystems: Most financial management information systems can help maintain compliance to the other subsystems such as accounting and system control requirements.

Examples of Financial Management Information Systems:

The benefits of financial management information systems can be found in popular packages include the following:

- People Soft Financials
- SAP Business One
- Microsoft Dynamics GP/Nav
- Oracle Enterprise Financials
- Sage ERP
- Microsoft Dynamics Greentree

13.5. ACCOUNTING INFORMATION SYSTEM

In the modern competitive world, the business organizations consider using the computerized accounting information system to help their work. The system not only increases the efficiency of accounting process, but also the effectiveness. Companies use computerized accounting information systems to maintain and even to create the competitive advantages. There are some essential critical factors to help the companies adopt a computerized information system such as top management support, the clear goal and objectives, the business process reengineering etc.

Keeping accurate accounting records is a vital part of managing an organization. Apart from helping to keep it afloat financially and legally, it is also a requirement of funding bodies. Smaller groups can usually manage with simple book-keeping procedures but bigger groups dealing with larger volume of money and more complex financial transactions may find their workload eased by using a accounting information system. Being an information system, an accounting information system must have a target system. It should be obvious that the target system must be business operations in a narrow sense. Other non-accounting aspects of business operations are covered by information systems such as Human Resources Information System, Management Information System, Production Planning/Scheduling System, Strategic Planning System, and so on.

13.5.1. Concept Of Accounting Information System

The basic concept of accounting information system can be seen as given in the following diagram:

Concept of Accounting Information System

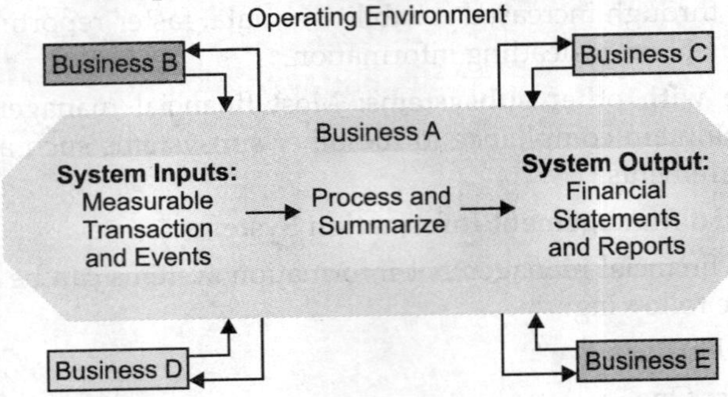

Here, Business A has dealing with the Businesses B, C, D and E. The transactions details are given as inputs and are processed and finally the outputs-financial statements and reports are generated according to the requirements specified by the Firm B.

It involves the following Operations:

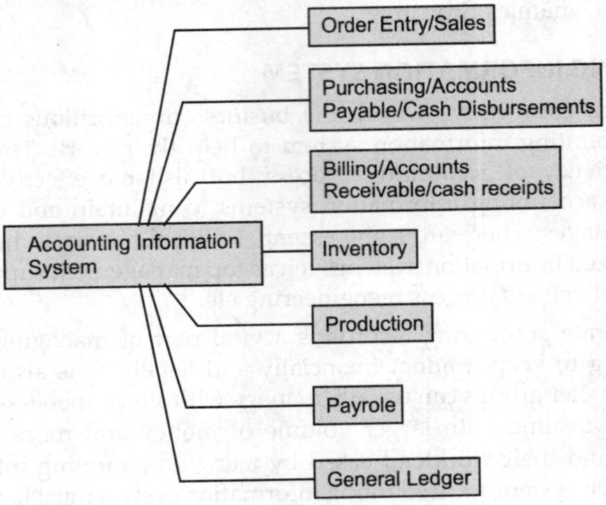

13.5.2. Designing Accounting Information System

The target system for an accounting system has to do with the aspects of business operations that have to do with accountability for the assets/liabilities of the enterprise, the determination of the results of operations that ultimately leads to the computation of comprehensive income, and the financial reporting aspects of business operations. An AIS is a subset of an organization's MIS that provides accounting and financial information other information obtained in the routine processing of accounting transactions. Accounting information system disseminates financial information to interested parties.

Small and medium sized businesses can now buy 'off the shelf' accounting programs at remarkably low cost. Larger businesses will often have customized programs made for their business. The accounting programs carry out functions such as invoicing, dealing with payments, paying wages and providing regular accounting reports such as trading and profit and loss accounts and balance sheets.

If Company plans to design its own information system for accounting the following elements are to be considered:

Designing of Accounting Information Systems

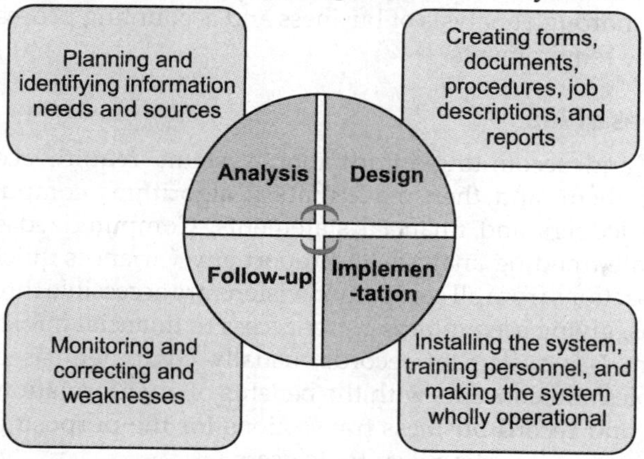

These systems can be customized to meet the needs of a business. For example, information technology professionals responsible for business processes and professionals responsible for the accounting information system can work together to develop and implement such a system so that it automatically gets information from other sources already in use by the business. Also, the systems can be set up to feature certain functions that are important to the business and eliminate functions minor to the business. Information can be automatically fed, or manually fed into a business accounting information system at whatever pace and however often it is necessary.

The accounting system must be cost effective and the benefit of information should overweigh the cost of providing it. The information should be simple to understand, reliable, relevant and timely. The knowledge of different users should also be considered while designing the accounting information. Besides the above, the accounting information system should be flexible enough to accommodate the changing information needs of the organizations.

13.5.3. Role of Accountants In Relation to AIS

The role of Accountants in Relation to AIS can be seen as follows:

(*a*) User

(*b*) Manager

(*c*) Consultant

(*d*) Evaluator

(*e*) Provider of accounting and tax services

Businesses use accounting information systems to make their accounting activities easier, quicker, and more accurate, since accounting records are analyzed and financial statements are prepared within the system, which allows to safe time of employees and avoid mistakes. Since many accounting information systems are equipped with error-reducing mechanisms and gather information regarding transactions electronically and automatically, data entry and computing errors are rare. Also, as mentioned above, since such systems are often automatically populated with transaction information, many accounting processes are less cumbersome and time-consuming when using such system.

Of course implementation of such system requires investment and time to be spent on the implementation, however future benefits are much higher that the expenses incurred.

Also to consider whether business needs accounting information system and what kind of system is required thorough analysis of business and accounting processes has to be made to determine precise requirements.

13.5.4. Advantages of AIS

Spreadsheets and accounting information systems require accountants to enter financial data into them, and then mathematical algorithms compute the information into the necessary ledgers and financial statements. Computerized systems also allow accountants to create trending analysis and report any variances quickly and accurately. Additionally, transactions from all company divisions are accessible through computerized accounting systems, giving accountants better access to financial information. Accounting information system is a system of records, usually computer based, which combines accounting principles and concepts with the benefits of an information system and which is used to analyse and record business transactions for the purpose to prepare financial statements and provide accounting data to its users.

Spreadsheets and accounting information systems require accountants to enter financial data into them, and then mathematical algorithms compute the information into the necessary ledgers and financial statements. Computerized systems also allow accountants to create trending analysis and report any variances quickly and accurately. Additionally, transactions from all company divisions are accessible through computerized accounting systems, giving accountants better access to financial information. With appropriate AIS in the organization, the business enterprises can achieve the following specific advantages:

(*a*) AIS supporting routine activities

(*b*) AIS provides for Decision support

(*c*) AIS supporting planning and control

(*d*) AIS helps in implementing internal control

(*e*) AIS provides for Faster and efficient in processing of information

(*f*) AIS provides for automatic generation of accounting documents like invoices, cheques and statement of account

(*g*) With the larger reductions in the cost of hardware and software and availability of user-friendly accounting software package, AIS is relatively cheaper like maintaining a manual accounting system

(*h*) AIS provides for the production of more timely information

(*i*) No more manual processing of the data- all automatically been posted to the various ledgers/ accounts

(*j*) Many types of useful reports can be generated for management to make decisions

(*k*) AIS helps in producing external reports

(*l*) A typical computerized accounting system will offer a number of different facilities. These include:

- On-screen input and printout of sales invoices
- Automatic updating of customer accounts in the sales ledger
- Recording of suppliers' invoices
- Automatic updating of suppliers' accounts in the purchases ledger
- Recording of bank receipts

- Making payments to suppliers and for expenses
- Automatic updating of the general ledger
- Automatic adjustment of stock records
- Integration of a business database with the accounting program
- Automatic calculation of payroll and associated entries

13.5.5. Limitations of AIS

AIS has certain limitations. They are:

(*a*) Power failure, computer viruses and hackers are the inherent problems of using computerized systems

(*b*) Once data been input into the system, automatically the output are obtained hence the data being input needs to be validated for accuracy and completeness, we should not forget concept of GIGO (Garbage In(Input) Garbage out (Output)

(*c*) Accounting system not properly set up to meet the requirement of the business due to badly programmed or inappropriate software or hardware or personnel problems can cause more destruction

(*d*) Danger of computer fraud-there is chance for computer fraud if proper level of control and security (whether internal and external) are not effectively instituted.

13.5.6. Examples of Accounting Information Systems

The benefits of accounting information systems can be found in popular packages include the following:

- Tally.ERP 9
- Peach Tree Accounting
- MS Accounting-UK and US
- Office Accounting
- There are many generic Accounting packages are available

In general, the computerized accounting offers several more benefits than manual accounting; accountants process more information quicker, formulas verify calculated totals and errors are less common. Accounting systems also are customizable by industry, allowing accountants the opportunity to use preset templates for their general ledger. Accountants also can store several years of financial information with relative ease, giving them the opportunity to review previous year's information without sorting through stacks of paper ledgers. Technological advances (e.g. e-commerce and the Internet) have changed business practices and the process of recording and storing business transactions.

13.6. MARKETING INFORMATION SYSTEM

The marketing of any enterprise is highly challenging and consists of various elements. It is subject to different environmental aspects. It consists of people, equipment, and procedures to gather, sort, analyse, evaluate, and distribute needed, timely, and accurate information to marketing decision makers.

13.6.1. Conceptual Idea of Marketing Information System

The conceptual idea of marketing information system can be seen from the following diagram:

MARKETING INFORMATION SYSTEM-CONCEPTUAL MODEL

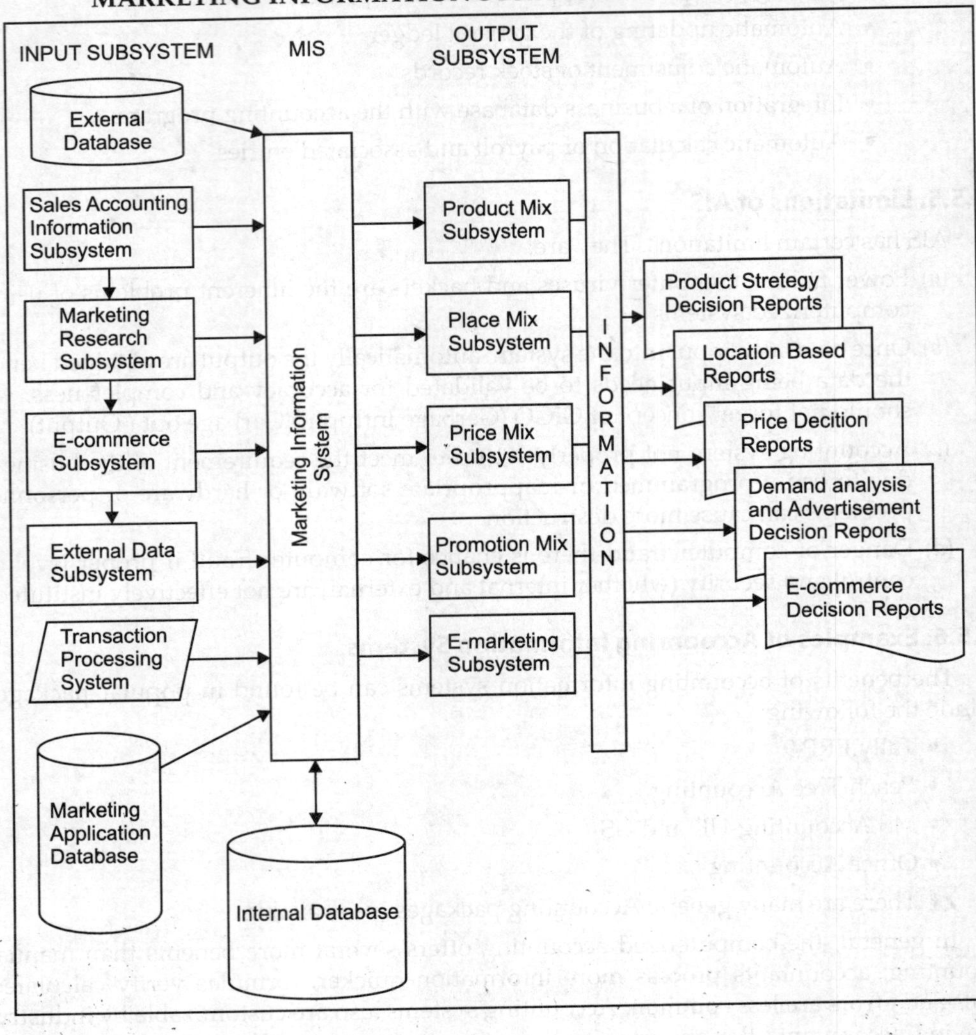

13.6.2. Input Subsystems

The Marketing Information System includes different input subsystems such as sales accounting information subsystem, marketing research subsystem, e-commerce subsystem, and external data subsystem.

It also includes transaction processing system, marketing application database and the like.

13.6.3. Output Subsystems

The Marketing Information System includes different output subsystems such as product mix subsystem, place mix subsystems, price mix subsystems, and promotion mix subsystems, e-marketing subsystem etc.

Importance of Market Information System:

The place of Market information system in the business environment can be seen in the following diagram.

Place of Marketing Information System

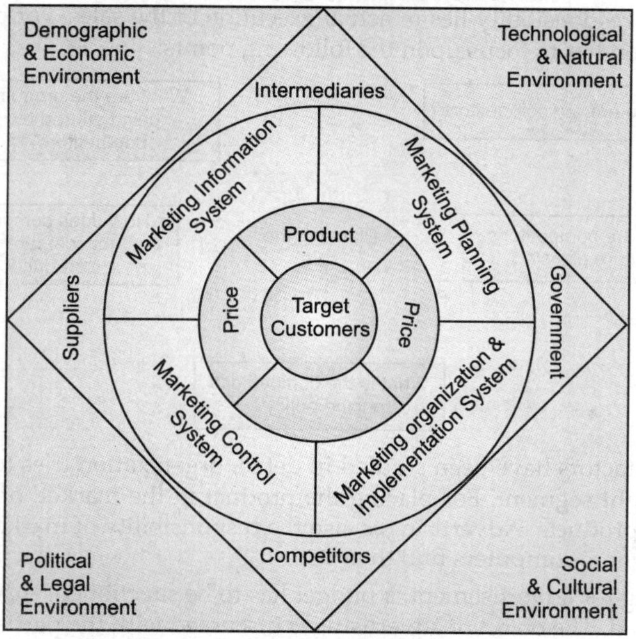

Philip Kotler has developed a model for marketing information system. The basic Schema of marketing information system of the model can be seen as follows:

Kotler's Model of Marketing Information System

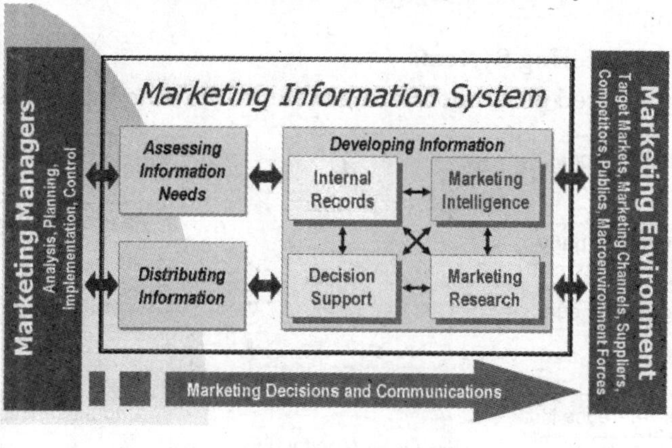

13.6.4. Application of Information Systems in Marketing

There are different types of marketing information systems being applied in the modern business. Let us see the examples of Order Monitoring System and Sales Administration System below:

EXAMPLE-1. ORDER MONITORING SYSTEM

Marketing Department of business organizations are mainly responsible for sales forecasting/sales planning, market research, advertising, pricing, product promotion policies and sales force efforts. Organizations have to sell their products in order to achieve the ultimate objectives. For selling the product, planning has to be done in advance.

Marketing division of a company is basically responsible for planning the sales while sales division's prime responsibility lies in actual execution of the sales. For planning the sale, marketing division has to focus upon the following points:

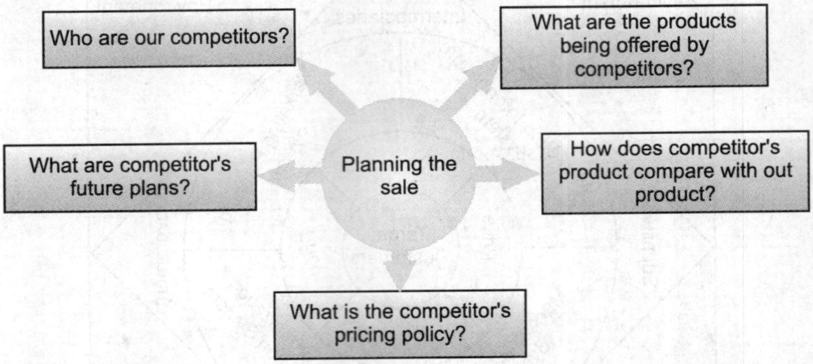

Once these factors have been studied in detail, organization tries to plan for placing its product in right segment. For placing the product in the market, organization has to advertise for its products. Advertising is also the responsibility of marketing division and this is the area where computers find their use.

Before going for advertisement, a budget has to be sanctioned. Advertising agencies are to be identified. The object of advertising is discussed with the parties. Campaigns are finalized. After this, parties place their bills which have to be processed and the payments are made. In this process when number of orders is placed on more than one party, it becomes very difficult to keep track of all the orders and all the parties. For efficient working and effective control over the situation the firms can go for computer order monitoring system.

Inputs for Order Monitoring System:

For the computerized order monitoring system following inputs are given:

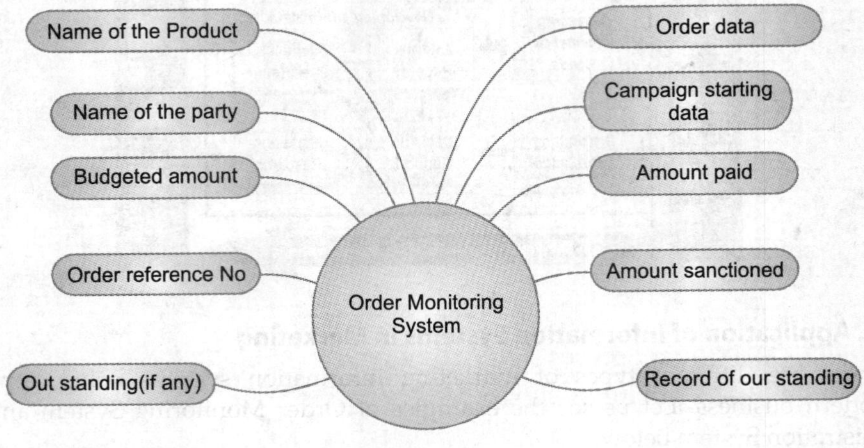

Outputs of Order Monitoring System:

Order Monitoring System processes the inputs given and provides the outputs as below:

(*a*) For a given party how many orders have been placed (product wise).

(*b*) For a given product what are the orders placed (party wise).

(*c*) How much amount has been budgeted on advertisement for different products.

(*d*) How much amount has been spent on advertisement in different products.
(*e*) List of life span of different advertisements.
(*f*) List of outstanding.
(*g*) List of orders that have exceeded the budget.
(*h*) List of orders, placed.
(*i*) These reports can be produced in any suitable format.

EXAMPLE-2. SALES ADMINISTERING SYSTEM:

The modern trading is a dynamic process. There are various factors which hold the key to selling in the market.

(*a*) Force Competition
(*b*) Refined tasks
(*c*) Rate of change of technology
(*d*) Proliferation of products
(*e*) Government policies

From this, one can see that buying and selling has become a very complicated process depending upon various parameters. The customer has to clearly evaluate all the options and make a choice when he should buy. How much quantity he should buy and what should be the terms of purchasing the goods.

Market planning and publicity planning depends upon the creation of number of profiles with full particulars such as customer profile, product profile and user industry profile. Interaction between the seller and the customer keeps generating information about the specification of product, terms and conditions for transacting. Once the user has made up his mind and placed the order, it is the responsibility of the supplier to provide the goods to the user. On the other hand it is the responsibility of the user to pay to the supplier. Both these transactions have to be as per terms and conditions.

Depending on the type of tradé, selling method of an organization may be different from another. However basic steps in the process of selling remain more or less identical. First of all let us deal with advertising. There are different products, different advertising agencies and different terms and conditions with each agency. Hence keeping track of the inputs becomes manually very difficult, time consuming and inefficient.

A customer who wants to buy something shall float an enquiry tender in the newspaper/trade journals. Basically the purpose of floating an enquiry is to ascertain the availability of goods and the terms on which they are offered. The whole process consists of the following steps:

(*a*) Floating of an enquiry by the customer
(*b*) Quotation given by the supplier
(*c*) An appraisal of the terms/conditions of various quotations by the customer.
(*d*) Decision taken by the user to place a letter of intent/ purchase order for the supply of goods.
(*e*) Supplier who has got the purchase order shall make the supplies as per the terms and conditions and shall raise invoices for the supplied goods.
(*f*) After receipt of goods in sound condition user shall make the payment.
(*g*) The supplier maintains the records of goods shipped and received along with data of purchase order, acknowledgement of order, supply of goods and receipt of payment.

All these steps mentioned above require a lot of manual writing and record keeping and processing. Here the Sales Administering system with the application of information technology will be very much helpful and cost effective.

Sales division of an organization is basically responsible for the actual sale of the products. For selling the product effectively and exercising control over the network, complete market is to be divided into small segments. People of various levels have to be made responsible for carrying out the sale. At regular intervals their performance is to be monitored and new guidelines have to be given, if needed. Computerized sales administering system deals with targets and the achievements related to sale.

Inputs for Sales Administering System:

Following vouchers serve as input to Sales Analysis System.

(*a*) Invoice: This is a voucher which is generated at the time of dispatch of the material. This contais all the details related to sale such as, amount, excise tax, VAT, discount, insurance, fright, forwarding charges, etc.

(*b*) Debit and Credit Note: These are the documents that get generated when ever sales adjustments are to be done. Sales adjustments are required in case excess or short payments were made at the time of actual sale.

Outputs for Sales Administering System:

The following are the outputs of the Sales Administration System

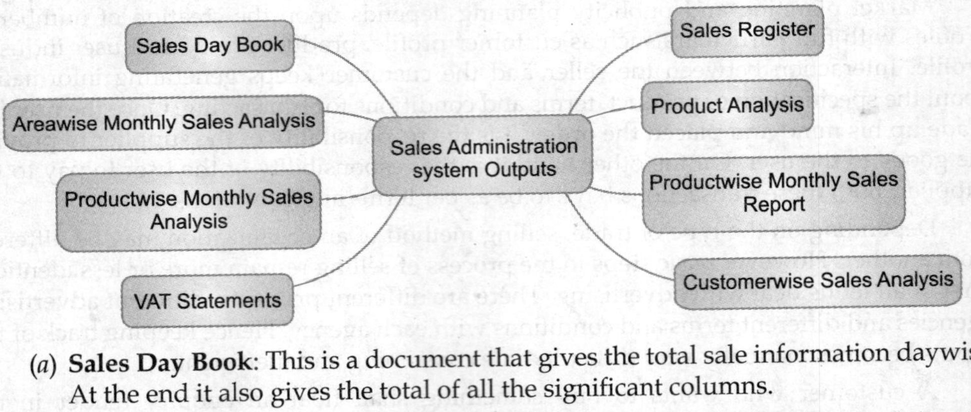

(*a*) **Sales Day Book**: This is a document that gives the total sale information daywise. At the end it also gives the total of all the significant columns.

(*b*) **Sales Register**: This is a document which is printed customer wise, giving the total sale information for a particular period. It also contains control totals for all the relevant columns.

(*c*) **Areawise Monthly Sales Analysis**: this is document which gives areawise monthly sales analysis. It contains the details of the product sold, quantity, value, product returned quantity, returned value and various product category totals.

(*d*) **Product Analysis**: It gives productwise analysis of different products giving the target quantity, monthly sales quantity, percentage achievement, total sale quantity and total sale value.

(*e*) **Productwise Monthly Sales Analysis**: It gives and compares sales in different regions providing the quantities and values of the current year and that of the last year.

(*f*) **VAT Statements**: It gives VAT statements for the sales made with input credit, zero rating if any and final tax to be paid, giving the invoice number, date, customer details, etc.

(g) **Productwise Monthly Sales Report:** It gives productwise sales performance and compares it with the values of previous year also so as to provide the relative performance.

(h) **Customerwise Sales Analysis:** It prints the results of customerwise sales and compares it with last year figures also.

Thus, marketing information system helps the firms to sustain and grow in the modern dynamic, highly challenging and intensively competitive environment. We can not imagine the success of any enterprise with out effective marketing information system.

13.7. PRODUCTION MANAGEMENT INFORMATION SYSTEM

The competition in market becomes very severe in all dimensions for all products. Hence, monitoring the production activities at the edge of competition warrants information to manage, control the entire process of production so as to control the cost of production as well. Many factors are influencing this aspect more specifically, the information i.e., and production information. Information systems play a critical role in today's manufacturing business, and the need for enterprise-wide integrated information system has grown rapidly. Today computers are being used in almost all areas of production system.

Production Information system can be defined as "A computer-based information system that works in combination with other functional information systems to support the management in solving production related problems in the organization". And it the application of computer resources in soliciting information that support the managerial decisions relating to production operations.

The general view of such application can be seen under:

Applications of Computers in Production Management

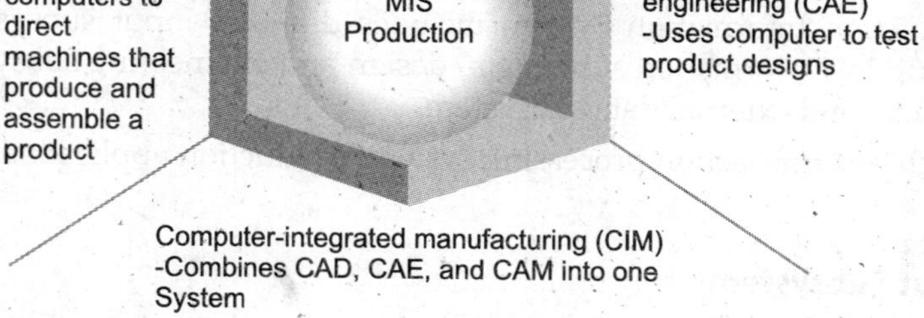

Industrial Robots - Computer-controlled robots perform work that might be hazardous to people.

13.7.1. Concept of Production Information System

Since computers lie behind almost all aspects of new technology, industry now has the chance to develop effective Production Information Systems. The concept of such design can be seen as follows:

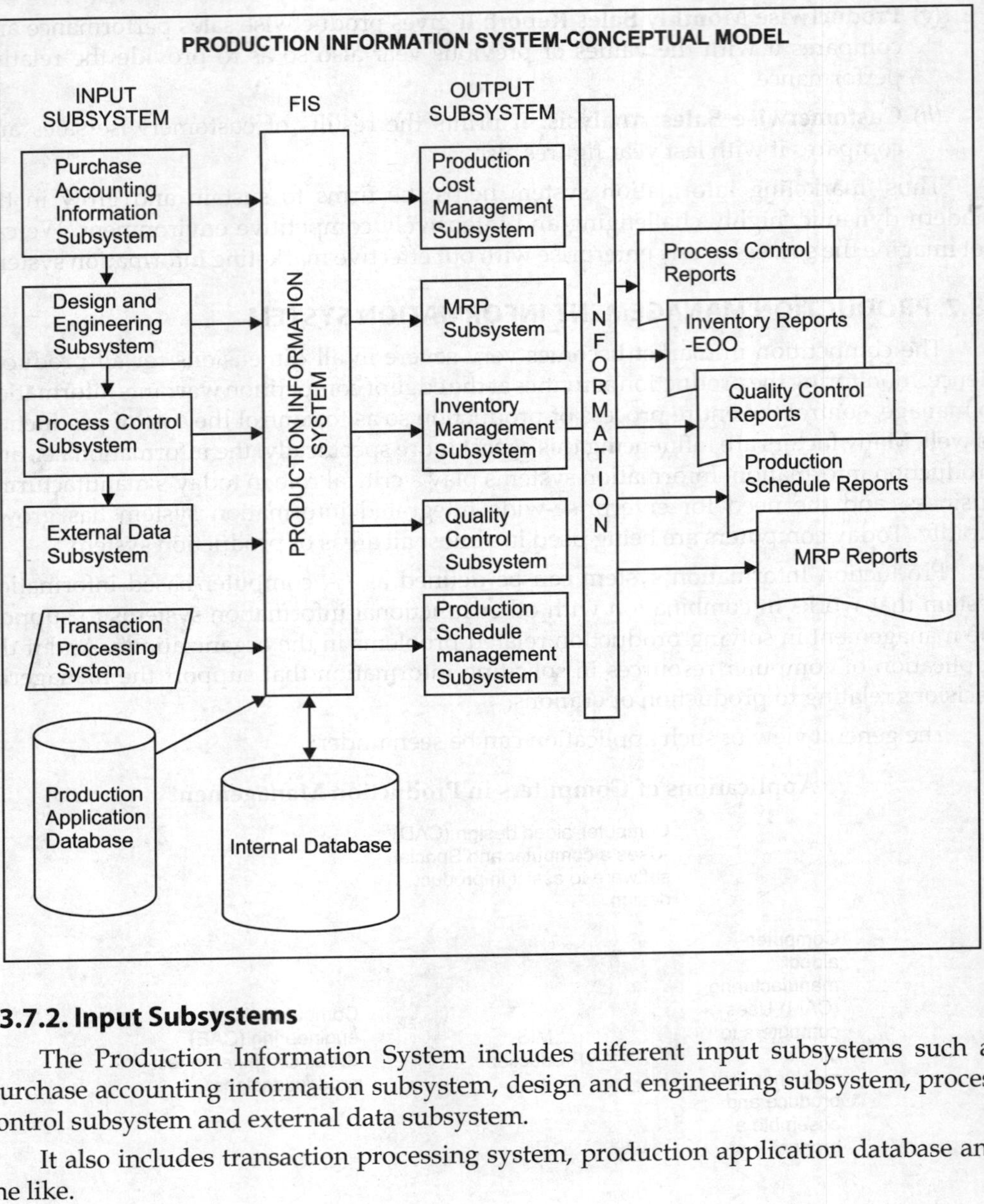

13.7.2. Input Subsystems

The Production Information System includes different input subsystems such as purchase accounting information subsystem, design and engineering subsystem, process control subsystem and external data subsystem.

It also includes transaction processing system, production application database and the like.

13.7.3. Output Subsystems

The Production Information System includes different output subsystems such as cost management subsystem, MRP subsystem, Quality control subsystem and production schedule subsystem etc.

13.7.4. Benefits of Production Information System

The Manufacturing Information Systems/Production Management Information System can provide many benefits to the manufacturing organizations. They include the following:

1. Effective material requirements planning: The Manufacturing Information Systems/Production Management Information System helps in achieving effective material requirements planning by determining when finished products are needed and meet out the production deadlines.

2. Ensures Effective Inventory Control Systems: The Manufacturing Information Systems/Production Management Information System helps in achieving inventory and materials delivered right before usage. It Obtains information directly from POS and it:

(*a*) Provides a real-time look at the availability of products

(*b*) Alerts warehouse when reorder points are reached -Hand scanners update inventory when items are stocked

(*c*) Inventory database can often be accessed by customers over the Web- Inventory is updated when customer reserves a product for pickup

3. Helps in Manufacturing Resource Planning: The Manufacturing Information Systems/Production Management Information System helps in network scheduling and improves customer service and productivity. It includes the following specific benefits:

(*a*) Job-scheduling system - Helps decide when to initiate production based on supplies and customer demand

(*b*) Inventory control system - Tracks and matches current inventory supplies against anticipated future orders to ensure component availability

(*c*) Just-in-time manufacturing - Lets manufacturers acquire components just before they are needed on the assembly line

(*d*) Warehouse management system - Tracks items received, generates pick lists, labels packages, tracks customer receipt.

4. Generation of Reports: The Production Management Information System generates all types of reports and it can be customized according to users' requirements. The reports generated includes, Inventory reports, production control reports, quality control reports, manufacturing resource planning reports, production schedule reports etc.

5. Other benefits: The Production Management Information System provides many other benefits including determination of economic ordering quantity, facilitating reorder point for inventory based on issue of materials, performing ABC analysis for material handling and the like.

13.8. HUMAN RESOURCE INFORMATION SYSTEM

In today's corporate world human resources has come to play a very critical role in a business. Whether it concerns the hiring and firing of employees or whether it concerns employee motivation, the Human Resources department of any organization now enjoys a very central role in not only formulating company policies, but also in streamlining the business process.

To make a human resource department more effective and efficient new technologies are now being introduced on a regular basis so make things much simpler and more modernized. One of the latest human resource technologies is the introduction of a Human Resources Information System. This integrated system is designed to help by providing information used in HR decision making such as administration, payroll, recruiting, training, and performance analysis.

Technology is transforming the work of the human resources professional. Human Resource Information Systems are making tracking employee information easier than ever before. The human resource Information system is a Computer based system for maintenance of the Service Registers of individuals in an organization. The details pertaining to personnel, postings, qualifications, departmental tests passed, training attended, family details etc. are stored in this system. Retrieval of information is possible based on any individuals or on collective information grouped by certain categories namely designation, retirement, length of service, place of working etc. Every company has to develop a personnel information system to meet its own requirements.

In an organization the data of the employees should be maintained in such a way to access the data with out any difficulty and immediately when it is needed. Once the data base is created with out any redundancy, the HR Information system enables the administrators to have reports on their needs and level of management. Generally the organizations need to keep the following data of employees for their decisions and reports.

Employee Information

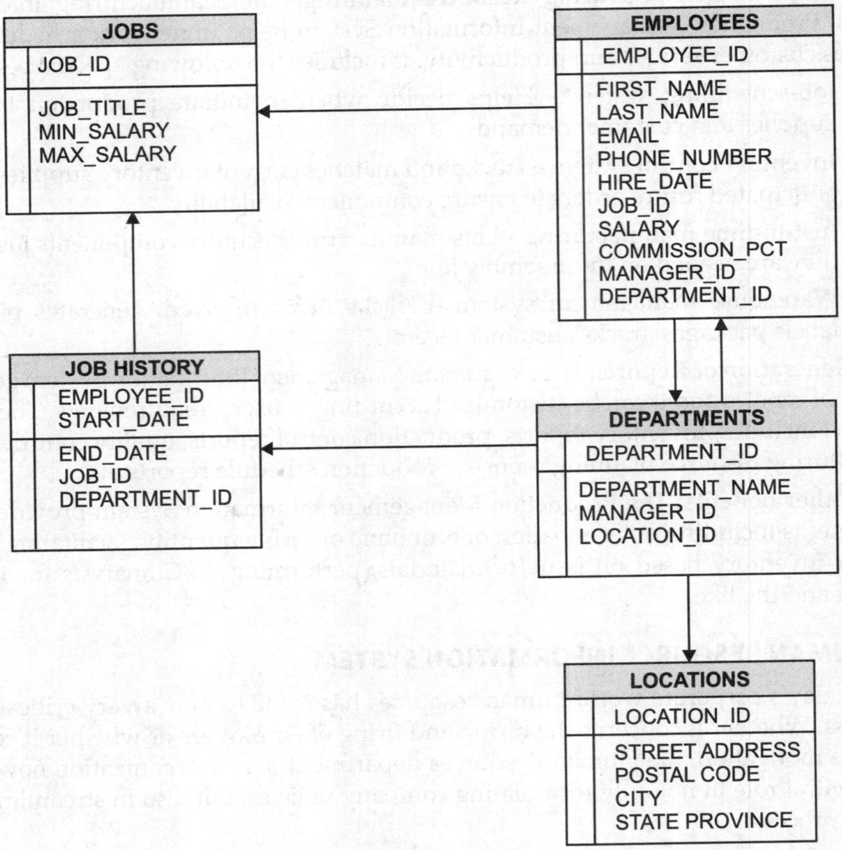

The HR Information system maintains complete Personal Information of the human resources of any organization. Information retrieval on any particular topic becomes very easy with the help of nice graphical interface. Printed Report generation can be done by any criterion. The Human Resources Information System provides with a broad range of functions that enable the organizations to perform standard reporting from all human resource areas. It will help in better administration and management in any organization. Quick decision regarding any particular matter can be possible because of arranged and accurate Information. It lets us define our own reports quickly and efficiently. We can customize our reports according to our requirements.

13.8.1. Objectives of HR Information System

The objectives of HR Information systems could be any of the following:

(*a*) To support wage and salary administration.

(*b*) To facilitate selection and appointments.

(*c*) To help in identifying high potential people.

(*d*) To determine in-company promotions that have to take place

(*e*) To help in administration of management development and training.

(*f*) To help and develop full potential of employees and department.

The HR Information systems deal with the flow of information about people working in the organization as well as future personnel needs. In most organizations, the system is concerned primarily with five basic subsystems of the personnel functions:

(*a*) Recruitment

(*b*) Placement

(*c*) Training and development.

(*d*) Compensation.

(*e*) Maintenance and appraisal.

For efficient working of the department, a human resource management information system is necessary. Like any system it consists of a number of inputs and outputs and a number of related subsystems, processes, activities, all operating through the medium of information.

13.8.2. Primary Areas of Human Resource Information System

The four primary areas of HR that are affected by the Human Resource Information System include; payroll, time and labor management, employee benefits and HR management.

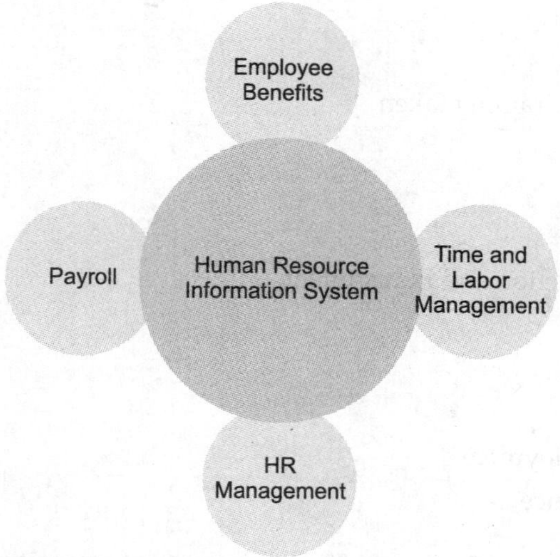

These four basic HR functionalities are not only made less problematic, but they are ensured a smooth running, without any problem. A Human Resources Information System, thus permits a user to see online a chronological history of an employee from his/her position data, to personal details, payroll records, and benefits information.

Human Resource Management Information System is concerned with all of the activities related to employees and potential employees of the organization. A system oriented approach to human resource management interrelates and integrates the functions of the personnel manager who is most benefited from an information system.

13.8.3. General Modules of Human Resource Management Information System

The General Modules included in the personnel System include the following:

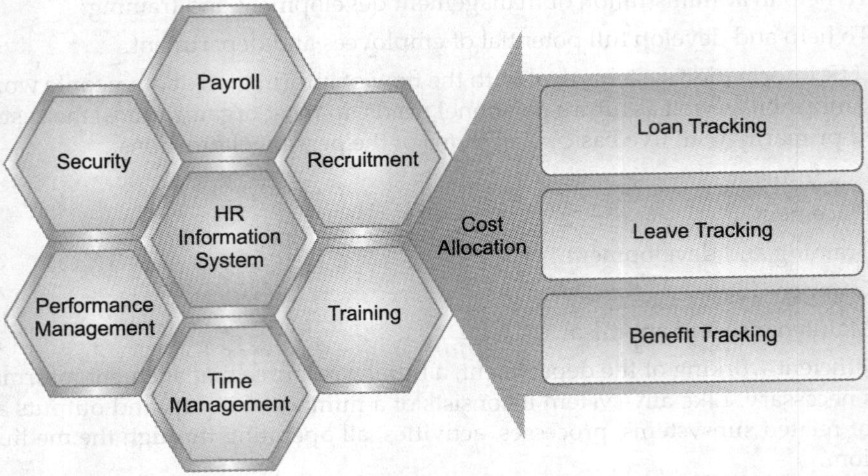

In detail, the human resource management information system includes the following:

- Personal
- Address
- Postings
- Qualification
- Departmental Training taken
- Family
- Nominations
- Loans
- Disciplinary Action and Punishment
- Properties
- Leave
- LTC
- Previous Employment
- Daily Attendance

13.8.4. Concept of Human Resource Management Information System

Human Resource Management Information System receives input data from transaction processing of input subsystems and provides outputs to different output subsystems and in the form of reports. It can be seen in the following figure.

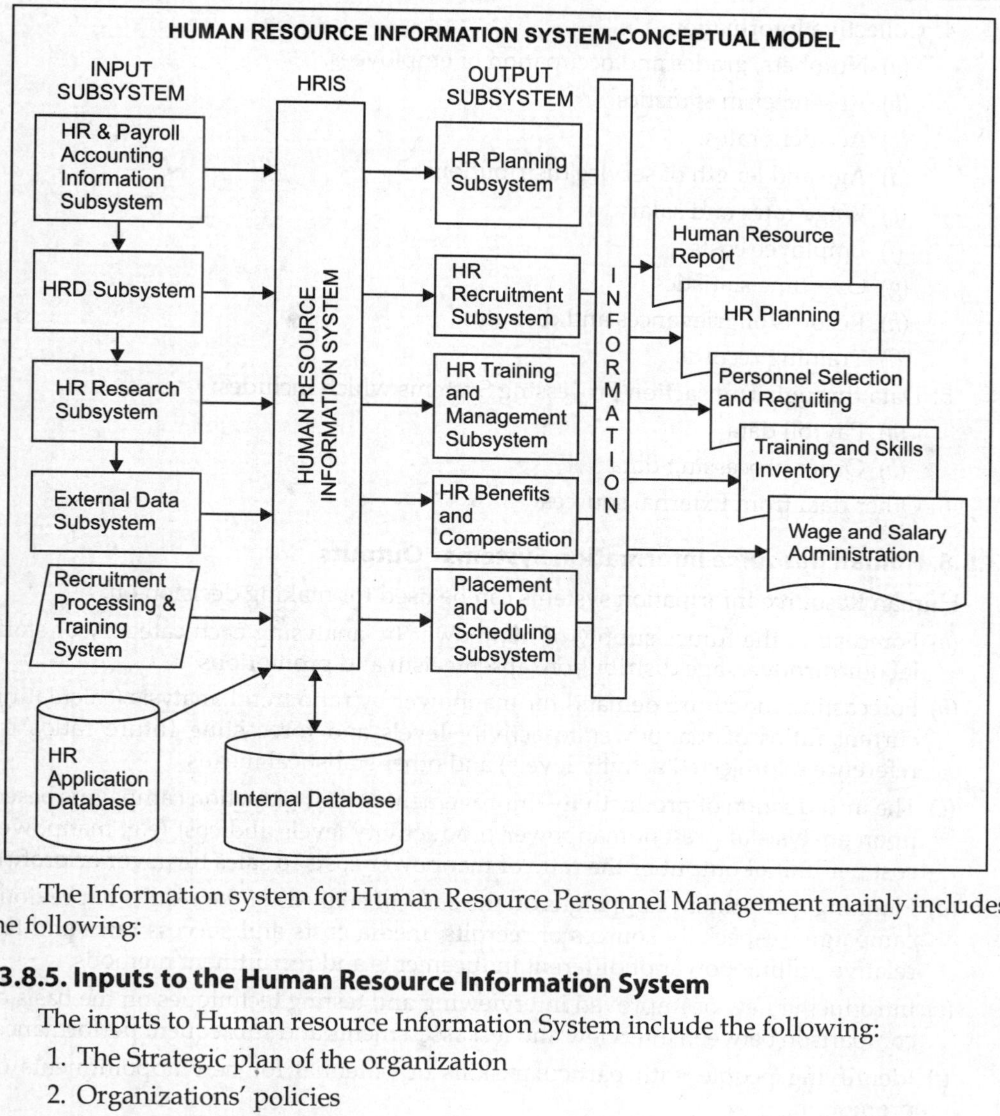

The Information system for Human Resource Personnel Management mainly includes the following:

13.8.5. Inputs to the Human Resource Information System

The inputs to Human resource Information System include the following:

1. The Strategic plan of the organization
2. Organizations' policies
3. Individual Information
   (*a*) The application form giving personal particulars.
   (*b*) Interview and test record.
   (*c*) Job history after joining the firm including details of transfers, promotions and changes in occupation.
   (*d*) Details about the pay and current pay.
   (*e*) Details of self appraisals/counseling session.
   (*f*) Absence, delay, accident, medical and disciplinary records with details of formal warnings and suspensions.
   (*g*) Leave entitlement.
   (*h*) Pension data.
   (*i*) Termination record with details of exit interview.

4. Collective Information
   (*a*) Numbers, grades and occupation of employees.
   (*b*) Absenteeism statistics.
   (*c*) Accident rates.
   (*d*) Age and length of service distributions.
   (*e*) Wage rates and salary
   (*f*) Employee costs
   (*g*) Overtime statistics
   (*h*) Records of grievances and disputes.
   (*i*) Training records
5. Data through Transaction Processing Systems which includes:
   (*a*) Payroll data
   (*b*) Order processing data
6. Other data from External sources

13.8.6. Human Resource Information Systems - Outputs

Human Resource Information systems can be used for making decision on:

(*a*) Forecasting the future supply of manpower by analysing each category of staff, labour turnover, age distribution, absenteeism and promotions.

(*b*) Forecasting the future demand for manpower by ratio trend analysis (calculating current ratios of manpower to activity levels and forecasting future ratios by reference to projected activity levels) and other statistical means.

(*c*) The introduction of productivity improvement or cost reduction campaigns based upon analysis of present manpower productivity levels and cost (e.g. manpower cost per unit of output or the ratio of manpower costs to sales turnover or profit).

(*d*) Planning recruitment campaigns on the basis of analysis of the results of previous campaigns, especially sources of recruits, media costs and success rates and the relative pulling power of different inducements and recruitment methods.

(*e*) Introducing new or improved interviewing and testing techniques on the basis of comparison between interview and test assessments and subsequent performance.

(*f*) Identifying people with particular skills or potential for new appointments or promotion.

(*g*) Improving disciplinary procedures or amending work rules by analyzing disciplinary cases.

(*h*) Planning redundancies - counseling unions, transferring or retaining employees, selecting employees for redundancy, helping to place redundant employees.

(*i*) Planning training programs - subjects to be covered, types of courses and number of courses with reference to analysis of future changes in manpower (numbers and skills), performance review records and job and training specification.

(*j*) Taking steps to improve job satisfaction with reference to statistics on labour turnover, absenteeism, sickness, accidents, discipline cases and grievances.

(*k*) Changing pay systems on the basis of statistics of price index fluctuations in earnings, the proportion of employees on coverage earnings rather than payment by results, cost per unit of output, fluctuations in earnings, the number and consequences of arguments over job rates.

(*l*) Improving health, safety and define precautions by analysing reports on industrial diseases, accidents and dangerous occurrences, monitoring returns on exposure to health hazards in relation to predetermined threshold limits and studying reports on health, safety and fire inspection, spot check and its data banks on individual and collective basis are prepared.

13.8.7. Reports Generation in HR Information System

The Human resource Information System provides different reports as outputs. They include:

1. Human resource report
2. Human resource planning
3. Personnel selection and recruiting
4. Training and skills inventory
5. Scheduling and job placement
6. Wage and salary administration

Restrictions at User Levels:

The system restricts the access to data on security reasons. The users are allowed to view the data with in the authorized levels. Generally three Levels of users are defined in this system. An individual user is able to view his information. The administrative user has access to all the users of that department. The Higher officials at senior managerial cadres will have access to information of all the users of all the departments. Individual user can login and access their data only.

13.8.8. Advantages of A Human Resource Information System

Human Resource Information System merges human resource management with information technology to not only simplify the decision making process, but also aid in complex negotiations that fall under the human resource umbrella. The basic advantages of a Human Resource Information System include the following:

1. Maintaining up to date information: Human Resource Information System not only helps in computerizing the employee records and databases but also in maintaining an up to date account of the decisions that have been made or that need to be made as part of a human resource management plan.

2. Automates the entire payroll process: The advantage of a Human Resource Information System in payroll is that it automates the entire payroll process by gathering and updating employee payroll data on a regular basis. It also gathers information such as employee attendance, calculating various deductions and taxes on salaries, generating automatic periodic paychecks and handling employee tax reports. With updated information this system makes the job of the human resource department very easy and simple as everything is available on a 24x7 basis, and all the information is just a click away.

3. Helps in time and labor management: In time and labor management a Human Resource Information System is advantageous because it lets human resource personnel apply new technologies to effectively gather and appraise employee time and work information. It lets an employee's information be easily tracked so that it can be assessed on a more scientific level whether an employee is performing to their full potential or not, and if there are any improvements that can be made to make an employee feel more secure.

4. Helps in motivating the employees: Employee benefits are very crucial because they help to motivate an employee to work harder. By using a Human Resource Information System (HRIS) in employee benefits, the human resource department is able to keep better track of which benefits are being availed by which employee and how each employee is profiting from the benefits provided.

5. Curtails time and cost consuming activities: A Human Resource Information System also has advantages in HR management because it curtails time and cost consuming activities leading to a more efficient HR department. This system reduces the long HR paper trail that is often found in most HR divisions of companies and leads to more productive and conducive department on the whole.

6. Supports Human Resources processes: The Human Resource Information System helps in the decision support for the (pre-) selection of candidates and their matching with future team members as part of the desire to optimise the allocation of human resources within a company. This system supports in recruiting and recommending the employees on the basis of predefined requirements by matching the skills and experience of the applicants.

13.9. CROSS FUNCTIONAL AND ENTERPRISE INFORMATION SYSTEMS

Generally, the major functional information systems are organized around the traditional functional departments of the business firms including accounting, finance, marketing, production and human resource and Information technology service department. But today, the trend has been changed and the firms shift from function-centered information systems to enterprise information systems or to the cross-functional information systems

Cross functional information system means combining two or more functional information systems together as one information system and widens the coverage and functionality. When all functional information systems of the organization are integrated in to a single system and serve the entire organization or enterprise, it is called Enterprise Information System. ERP-Enterprise Resources Planning is the most popular system in this context.

Enterprise Information System provides the technology base and enables the organizations to incorporate all of their business processes in to one system and facilitates coordination among them. And it establishes a single system that is central to the organization as a whole and makes sure that information is shared across all functional levels and at all managerial hierarchies.

REVIEW QUESTIONS

Short Answer Questions:

1. What is Organization?
2. What are the different functional areas of management?
3. What is strategic information?
4. What is Operational information?
5. What is High potential information?
6. What is support information?
7. Write a brief note on the different functional information system under MIS.
8. What is Business finance?
9. What is Financial Information System?

10. What is accounting information system?
11. Write a brief note on the role of accountants in relation to AIS.
12. What are the limitations of AIS?
13. Give examples of AIS.
14. What is Marketing Information System?
15. Write a note on the application of information systems in marketing.
16. Give a note on inputs for order monitoring system.
17. Write briefly on outputs of order monitoring system.
18. Give a short note on the inputs and outputs of Sales Administering System.
19. What is production management information system?
20. What are the applications of computers in production management?
21. What are the Subsystems of Production Information System?
22. What are the output-Subsystems of Production Information System?
23. What is Human Resource management information system?
24. What are the objectives of HR Information systems?
25. What are the applications of computers in Human Resource management?
26. What are the primary areas of Human Resource Information System?
27. What are the Subsystems of Human Resource Information System?
28. What are the output-Subsystems of Human Resource Information System?
29. Why is it necessary to restrict the access to data under Human Resource Information System?

Essay Type Questions:

1. Explain the different categories of Information.
2. Give a detailed note on the concept of Financial Information System?
3. What are the Inputs to the Financial Information System?
4. Explain the Financial MIS Subsystems.
5. Explain the benefits of financial management information systems.
6. Explain the concept of AIS.
7. Describe the procedure of designing AIS.
8. What are the advantages of AIS?
9. Explain the concept of Marketing Information System?
10. What are the sub systems of Marketing Information System?
11. Explain the necessity of information system in sales administration.
12. Explain the concept of Production Information System.
13. Explain in detail about materials management and the necessity of Information System in its management.
14. What are the inputs for the Production Information System?
15. What are the benefits of Production Information System?
16. Explain the concept of Human Resource Management Information System.
17. What are the general modules of Human Resource Management Information System?
18. Explain the benefits of Human Resource Information System in detail.

CHAPTER

14

Business Process Outsourcing

14.1. INTRODUCTION TO BPO

BPO stands for Business Process Outsourcing. It is basically the process by which a company can delegate certain functions of their business to a specialized organization that can get it done more cheaply, quickly, and efficiently. Outsourcing is a process that a firm or an organization entering into a contract with another firm or an organization to operate and manage one or more of its business processes. Generally the outsourcing processes are the supporting activities and not of extremely high strategic importance, but necessary for doing business or improving business. The key and the strategic benefit of outsourcing is the outsourcing company can focus on core competency of their business by giving the supporting activities to experienced professionals (Outsourcing Service Providers) in relevant area.

Thus, a business process can be viewed as follows:

Business process is viewed as a collection of activities that take one or more kinds of inputs and create an output that is of value to the customer. But, it is not a complete view. Hence a business process can be considered as the following:

Routine: An organizational routine has clearly identified tasks and responsibilities.

Replicable: The process can be transferred to multiple contexts and is not unique to a single company.

Recurrent: Recurrence simply means that people carry this out often and in large numbers.

Consequential: How well the process is carried out have impacts on some aspect of company performance, customer service, revenues, costs, staff productivity, internal efficiency, etc.

Leveragable : Improving the process can used as the base for further improvements in company performance through linkages to other processes, rollout across the firm or releasing constraints and resources.

Well-coordinated: The fundamental element of a process is coordination – coordination of tasks, people, information and procedures. Miscoordination underlies most process mishaps that lead to errors, delays in efficiencies, high costs and customer dissatisfaction.

14.2. CONCEPT OF BUSINESS PROCESS OUTSOURCING

The Harvard Business Review Journal identified the outsourcing as one of the most important management ideas and practices of the last 75 years. Outsourcing was originally defined as hiring an outside firm to supply services that were performed in-house. The main objective of outsourcing is that some one-else can do parts of a business [non-core] both more efficiently and effectively, than the owner can. It is a technique to realign corporations around core competencies and long-term outside relationship and is best driven by clear tactical and strategic goals. Gartner defines BPO as delegating an Information Technology-enabled business process to a third party that owns, administers, and runs the process according to a defined set of metrics.

BPO involves the full transfer of responsibility for functions such as transaction processing, policy servicing, claims management, human resource, finance, and compliance to the outsourcing company. The outsourcing provider then administers these functions on their own systems to agreed service standards and at a guaranteed cost. Some of the BPO contracts call for performance - based payouts, tying vendor payments to business performance, which results in overall cost savings.

Business Process Outsourcing is a business discipline built on a long-term commercial relationship between a process supplier and a process consumer that is enabled by a process infrastructure and maintained at a high level of mutual commitment and collaboration.

14.3. OBJECTIVES OF BPO

Under BPO an external agency or a third-party vendor is engaged or contracted to complete a job assigned or outsourced. BPO involves the full transfer of responsibility for functions such as transaction processing, policy servicing, claims management, human resource, finance, and compliance to the outsourcing company. The outsourcing provider then administers these functions on their own systems to agreed service standards and at a guaranteed cost. The basic objectives of BPO include the following:

1. To attain maximum accuracy
2. To get the work done at comparatively lesser cost
3. To get best quality services
4. To reduce costs through simplification and standardization
5. To increase productivity and service excellence to customers
6. To enhance focus on business unit operations
7. To get support for new business process capabilities
8. To reduce costs through wage and labour arbitrage
9. To improve capability to integrate new business
10. To obtain quality services with timeliness and with alternatives.

14.4. DIMENSIONS OF BPO

BPO is often considered in to the following categories:

1. **Back office outsourcing -** includes internal business functions such as billing or purchasing.
2. **Front office outsourcing -** includes customer-related services such as marketing or technology support.
3. **Offshore outsourcing -** BPO that is contracted outside a company's own country is called offshore outsourcing.
4. **Nearshore outsourcing -** BPO that is contracted to a neighbouring country is sometimes called nearshore outsourcing.
5. **Onshore outsourcing -** BPO that is contracted within the company's own country is sometimes called onshore outsourcing.

14.5. ELEMENTS OF BPO

The business transactions being out sourced could range from customer service, sales, collections, and data processing to high-end technical support, maintaining HR payrolls, predicting market trends and so on. There are different types of services rendered by BPOs. These can be either voice-based or data based. The basic elements of BPO can be seen as follows:

Elements of Businesses Outsourcing

↓

AREAS

Back-office Transaction processing	Customer Interaction Services	IT/ Software Operations	Finance & Accounting Services	Human Resource Services	Administration
Activities	Activities	Activities	Activities	Activities	Activities
↓	↓	↓	↓	↓	↓
Collections & receivables Check, credit/debit Card processing Procurement - direct & indirect Transport management Logistics & dispatch Warehouse Management	Customers service E-mail Marketing Services Telesales Order Processing Customer Support Warranty Services Customer feedback	Engineering requirement Application development Application Testing Packaged Application Outsourcing Services IT Help desk	Billing Services Account Receivable Account payable General Accounting Financial Reporting Auditing Compliance Shareholder Services	Payroll Healthcare Recruitment & staffing Education & Training Retirement benefits	Tax processing Claims processing Asset Management Document Management

14.6. FACTORS INFLUENCING BPO

The Key drivers of the Indian BPO industry include:

1. Competitive pressures on client organizations
2. Ability of Indian vendors to complete operations rapidly
3. Widening breadth of services
4. Shift towards high-value services
5. Sustained cost advantage - In spite of the rising elements of cost, Indian offshore operations provide cost savings of 40-50 percent
6. Delivery process enhancement and improvement
7. Access to an abundant skill pool - India has the largest English speaking IT talent pool in the world

8. Focus on margins and cost pressures: Outsourcing to India has helped companies achieve 40-50% cost savings. Companies are also able to generate higher free cash flows due to reduced investments in physical infrastructures, telecom and equipment. Wage arbitrage has also led to increased cost savings.
9. Growing demand for high quality, skilled workforce: India has a large pool of educated, highly skilled, English speaking manpower. This has placed India favourably over other offshore locations, since other than wage arbitrage, companies benefit from improved quality and higher productivity rates.
10. Global quality accreditations: In an increasingly competitive economy, customers demand and expect highest levels of quality. Indian vendors are quality centric and have adopted several industry standards

14.7. ADVANTAGES OF BPO

In the process, an increasing number of organizations worldwide have turned to BPO, which has significantly lower overhead costs without sacrificing quality and productivity levels. Today, BPO is considered not only as a simple cost-cutting mechanism but also as a strategic initiative, which is expected to shape and ready the organization for future business dynamics. Apart from cost-cutting, BPO saves precious management time and resources by allowing companies to concentrate on core competencies. BPO providers always have a process expertise and enjoy significant economies of scale and scope by offering the same services to different clients.

The benefits of BPO can be explained with the following diagram:

1. Cost Reductions: Cost reduction is done through process improvements, reengineering and use of technologies that reduce and bring administrative and other costs under control.

2. Concentration on Core Business: With the day-to-day back office operations taken care of, the management is free to concentrate more on the core business of the company.

3. Outside Expertise: Company is saved from the hassles of recruiting and training personnel. BPOs ensure that experts from another company provide the needed guidance and skills.

4. Cater to Changing Customer Demands: It is another great advantage of outsourcing the business processes. Many BPOs provide the management with flexible and scalable services to meet the customers' changing requirements, and to support company acquisitions, consolidations, and joint ventures.

5. Revenue Increase: As stated above, by outsourcing non-core processes, companies can concentrate on increasing their sales and market share, develop new products; spread out into new markets and increase customer service and satisfaction. This rebuilts in to increased revenue.

6. Improved Performance and Profitability: Real business value is derived from actual business results. By business process outsourcing the firms can enjoy improved performance and profitability to:

(*a*) Achieve operational excellence, leveraging proven methods and innovative technologies

(*b*) Beat competitors to market, with creative new products supported by full-functioning systems (*c*) Respond quickly to market demands, without the headache of cultural barriers

(*d*) Tap an experienced pool of global resources to achieve cost savings without compromising superior service

(*e*) Realign core talent to focus on market distinction strategies.

7. Other Benefits: In addition to the above, BPO provides some other benefits as well. And they include :

(*a*) Improve service quality

(*b*) Greater business flexibility

(*c*) Lower capital investments

(*d*) Fewer people in function

(*e*) Predictable outcome

(*f*) Increased accountability

14.8. LIMITATIONS OF OUTSOURCING

Even though outsourcing has become popular and is considered beneficial in developed as well as developing countries, it is not free from criticisms. The limitations of BPO include the following:

1. Failed to Create Business value: A common factor was that the objective of the BPO is merely to try and cut costs rather than to use it as means for creating business value. According to University of Missouri and Oxford University Joint study, lack of wholehearted involvement is one of the reasons for unsuccessful implementation of BPO. The study also revealed that the organizations has incurred huge hidden costs and fall in service standards.

2. Failed to Upgrade Technology: Apart from obvious risk of total and sudden collapse in the Service Provider, there is also an additional risk from a `fixed term contractual arrangement' with a service provider if he that fails to upgrade its technology or activities, including training. A service provider which is in financial trouble, and unable to invest properly in technological advances, will limit the competitiveness of the customer.

3. Commercial Sensitivities: When the supplier provider working for competitors also, there may be commercial sensitivities, and it could threaten competitiveness for different levels and priorities of service apportionment between the Customers. In turn, this may cause the customer to be insufficiently open with the service provider about strategic plans to allow the planning and change process to incorporate properly the support for that change.

4. Poor set of Service Level Agreements and Lower Service Quality: Where a poor set of service level agreements has been agreed, it may happen that the expectations of the service provision and the actual service provided will be different. And if the penalties for under provision are unclear or lenient, the service provider may prefer to under provide.

5. Losing Skills and Ability: If the organization out sources everything, then it will lose its ability to use leverage on and control the out sourcer.

6. Employment Problems: Outsourcing creates legal issues of employment regulations and lay off notifications as well as compensation and benefits on continuous basis.

7. Political Risk: Buyers of BPO have to measure the political risk of outsourcing to a foreign company, which is far away instead of closer providers in the country. Offshore outsourcing is highly emotional issue, especially in unionized work forces.

In brief, Business Process Outsourcing provides opportunities in many instances. Companies are already moving towards it, through supply chain relationships, existing outsourcing arrangements and partnerships. Thus, business process outsourcing is the inevitable source of innovation. For the competitive advantage and the possibility to grow with new opportunities attached with BPO, the companies cannot miss it.

REVIEW QUESTIONS

Short Answer Questions:

1. What is BPO?
2. What are the opportunities of BPO?
3. Write a brief note on the limitations of BPO.
4. What are the types of BPO?
5. Explain the objectives of BPO.

Essay Type Questions:

1. Explain the concept of BPO in Detail.
2. Explain the factors influencing BPO.
3. What are the elements of BPO? Explain in detail.
4. Explain the benefits of BPO
5. Write a detailed note on the limitations of BPO.

APPENDIX

MODEL QUESTION PAPER - 1

Time : Three Hours | Maximum : 100 marks

SECTION–A **(20×1 = 20 marks)**

Fill in the blanks :

1. Total turnover of a business of 2004 is an example of .... (data/information)
2. .... computer gives result in the form of graph.
3. Man-Machine interface is called as ....
4. Operating system is an example of .... software.
5. .... is a diagrammatic representation of sequence of instruction for solving a particular program.

State True or False

6. Network of networks is called internet.
7. 0 and 1 are the decimal numbers.
8. MIS provides only quantitative information.
9. Through E-mail, files can be sent.
10. Operating system is an interface between user and computer. Match the following:

11. Internet	(*a*) Processed data
12. Steps to solve a problem	(*b*) Hardware
13. Information	(*c*) Software
14. Group of instructions	(*d*) E-mail
15. Memory	(*e*) Algorithm

Choose the best answer:

16. The unit, which monitors overall operation of the computer system, is
    (*a*) Control unit (*b*) ALU (*c*) Monitor (*d*) None of these
17. E-Business uses
    (*a*) Internet (*b*) Intranet
    (*c*) Electronic Data Exchange (*d*) All of the above
18. A flowchart is
    (*a*) Data diagram (*b*) Data flow diagram
    (*c*) Flow of data (*d*) None of the above
19. Binary number has a base of
    (*a*) 2 (*b*) 8 (*c*) 0 (*d*) 0 and 1
20. Windows NT stands for
    (*a*) Windows Network Technology (*b*) Windows New Technology
    (*c*) Windows Net Technology (*d*) None of the above.

SECTION–B

(5×6 = 30 marks)

Answer All questions.

Each answer not to exceed 2 pages.

21. (*a*) What are the features of a digital computer?

OR

(*b*) Explain RAM and ROM,

22. (*a*) What are the objectives of data processing?

OR

(*b*) What should be the contents and design of a report?

23. (*a*) What do you mean by System software and Application software?

OR

(*b*) What is flowchart? Explain different types of flowchart.

24. (*a*) What are the advantages of using E-mail.

OR

(*b*) Write short notes on : Internet and Extranet.

25. (*a*) What is Transaction processing?

OR

(*b*) Write a short note on WWW.

SECTION–C

(5×10 = 50 marks)

Answer all questions.

Each answer not to exceed 4 pages.

26. (*a*) Explain how computer works with the help of a diagram.

OR

(*b*) How are computers classified on the basis of generation?

27. (*a*) Explain Batch processing, Time sharing and Distributed processing.

OR

(*b*) What are the advantages and disadvantages of sequential file organisation?

28. (*a*) Discuss any three types of input devices used in computers.

OR

(*b*) What are the features of high level languages?

29. (*a*) Define operating system. Explain different types of OS.

OR

(*b*) What are the uses of Internet?

30. (*a*) Define decision support system. State its characteristics.

OR

(*b*) Write short notes on:

(*i*) MIS (*ii*) E-Commerce (*iii*) Expert system.

MODEL QUESTION PAPER - 2

Time : Three Hours | Maximum : 100 marks

SECTION–A **(10×1 = 10 marks)**

Answer all questions.

Choose the best answer.

1. Computer in general is
   (*a*) a digital computer (*b*) an analog computer
   (*c*) a hybrid computer (*c*) None of the above.
2. RAM is a
   (*a*) Primary memory (*b*) Secondary memory
   (*c*) Hard disk (*d*) None of the above.
3. Operating system is a
   (*a*) System software (*b*) Application software
   (*c*) Hardware (*d*) None of the above.
4. E-mail is
   (*a*) an electronic mail (*b*) an electric mail
   (*c*) an electro mail (*d*) None of the above.
5. HTTP is
   (*a*) an Internet protocol (*b*) a file transfer protocol
   (*c*) a transmission control protocol (*d*) None of the above.
6. Network is an interconnection of
   (*a*) Computers (*b*) Printers
   (*c*) Modems (*d*) None of the above.
7. MIS is
   (*a*) Management oriented (*b*) Decision oriented
   (*c*) Policy oriented (*d*) None of the above.
8. Financial information system deals with
   (*a*) Transaction processing data (*b*) Funding data
   (*c*) External data (*d*) All of the above.
9. BPO refers to
   (*a*) Outsourcing (*b*) Assignment
   (*b*) Contract (*d*) None of the above.
10. Data means
    (*a*) Fact (*b*) Details
    (*c*) Statement (*d*) None of the above.

SECTION–B (5×6 = 30 marks)

Answer all questions.

11. (*a*) Explain the characteristics of a computer.

Or

(*b*) Differentiate between Primary Memory and Secondary Memory.

12. (*a*) What are the functions of an Operating System ?

Or

(*b*) Write a note on Programming language.

13. (*a*) What are objectives of Data Processing ?

Or

(*b*) Write a note on Programming Language.

14. (*a*) What is BPO ?

Or

(*b*) What are the elements of MIS ?

15. (*a*) What is Network ?

Or

(*b*) What are the benefits of E-mail ?

SECTION–C (5×12 = 60 marks)

Answer all questions.

16. (*a*) Compare the features of Digital and Analog Computers.

Or

(*b*) Explain the working of a computer with the help of block diagram.

17. (*a*) Explain different types of software.

Or

(*b*) Explain the features of High Level Language.

18. (*a*) What are the characteristics of MIS ?

Or

(*b*) Explain Marketing Information System.

19. (*a*) What are the uses of DBMS ?

Or

(*b*) Explain any one method of DBMS in detail.

20. (*a*) What are the uses of Internet ?

Or

(*b*) Explain the architecture of WWW.